The International Legality of Self-Defense Against Non-State Actors

European University Studies

Europäische Hochschulschriften
Publications Universitaires Européennes

Series II
Law

Reihe II Série II
Rechtswissenschaft
Law

Vol./Bd. 4623

PETER LANG
Frankfurt am Main · Berlin · Bern · Bruxelles · New York · Oxford · Wien

Gregor Wettberg

The International Legality of Self-Defense Against Non-State Actors

State Practice from the U.N. Charter to the Present

PETER LANG
Internationaler Verlag der Wissenschaften

Bibliographic Information published by the Deutsche Nationalbibliothek
The Deutsche Nationalbibliothek lists this publication in the Deutsche Nationalbibliografie; detailed bibliographic data is available in the internet at <http://www.d-nb.de>.

Zugl.: Frankfurt (Main), Univ., Diss., 2007

Printed with financial support of the
Gerhard C. Starck Foundation.

D 30
ISSN 0531-7312
ISBN 978-3-631-57098-2

Printed in Germany 1 2 3 4 5 7

www.peterlang.de

Meinen Eltern, Ingrid und Peter

PREFACE

This work was submitted as a doctoral thesis to Johann Wolfgang Goethe University Frankfurt/Main in the spring term of 2007. I would like to express my sincere thanks to my *Doktorvater*, Prof. Dr. Stefan Kadelbach, LL.M. Not only did he encourage me to pursue my topic, but he also reviewed all of my submissions quickly and thoroughly, and provided me with valuable comments. Primarily, however, he is responsible for my initial interest in international law, an admiration which he had already sparked at Westfälische Wilhelms Universität, Münster.

I also owe great thanks to Prof. Dr. Dr. Rainer Hofmann for so quickly reviewing my dissertation.

My dissertation rests partly on a Master's thesis submitted in 2006 to the George Washington University Law School. Prof. Sean D. Murphy reviewed this work very speedily and ensured that I could always count on his much appreciated advice. Prof. Michael J. Matheson enabled me to get a first hand view of real life international law and international criminal law. I thank both of them for an inspiring year. My stay was made possible through the generous Thomas Buergenthal Scholarship, for which I owe great thanks to the law school.

The Gerhard C. Starck Foundation supported me most generously upon my return to Germany and enabled me to conclude my research.

My friend David Raphael Hildebrand ensured that both my LL.M. thesis as well as my dissertation would not entirely disregard the essential rules of English grammar and syntax.

To my beloved parents, Ingrid and Peter, I owe so much more than merely thanks for their continuous support of my work.

Gregor Wettberg
Berlin, July 20, 2007

Table of Contents

DETAILED CONTENTS

ABBREVIATIONS

Am. J. Int'l L.	American Journal of International Law
Annals Am. Acad. Pol. Soc. Sci.	Annals of the American Academy of Political and Social Science
Ariz. J. Int'l & Comp. L.	Arizona Journal of International and Comparative Law
Asian Aff.	Asian Affairs
Brit. Y.B. Int'l L.	British Yearbook of International Law
Can. Y.B. Int'l L.	The Canadian Yearbook of International Law
Chi. J. Int'l L.	Chicago Journal of International Law
Christian Sci. Monitor	Christian Science Monitor
Colum. J. Transnat'l L.	Columbia Journal of Transnational Law
Cong. Rep. Service	Congressional Report Service
Dep't St.	Department of State (U.S.)
ed., eds.	editor, editors
et al.	et alia; and others
et seq.	et sequentes; and the following
Eur. J. Int'l L.	European Journal of International Law
Fin. Times (London)	The Financial Times (London)
Fla. L. Rev.	Florida Law Review
Fletcher F. World Aff.	Fletcher Forum of World Affairs
Fordham Int'l L.J.	Fordham International Law Journal

G.A. Res.	General Assembly Resolution
Geo. L.J.	Georgetown Law Journal
German Y.B. Int'l L.	German Yearbook of International Law
Gov't	Government
Harv. Int'l L.J.	Harvard International Law Journal
Harv. J. L. & Pub. Pol'y	Harvard Journal of Law and Public Policy
HCJ	High Court of Justice (Israel)
Hous. J. Int'l L.	Houston Journal of International Law
I.C.J.	International Court of Justice
I.L.M.	International Legal Materials
id.	ibidem; in the same place
Int'l & Comp. L. Q.	International and Comparative Law Quarterly
Int'l Inst. for Strategic Stud.	International Institute for Strategic Studies
Int'l J. Refugee L.	International Journal of Refugee Law
Isr.	Israel
Isr. L. Rev.	Israel Law Review
J. Conflict & Security L.	Journal of Conflict and Security Law
J. Legis.	Journal of Legislation
Max Planck Y.B.U.N.L.	Max Planck Yearbook of United Nations Law
Mich. L. Rev.	Michigan Law Review

Mich. St. J. Int'l L.	Michigan State Journal of International Law
mtg.	meeting
Neth. Y.B. Int'l L.	Netherlands Yearbook of International Law
N.Y. Times	The New York Times
p., pp.	page, pages
P.C.I.J.	Permanent Court of International Justice
para., paras.	paragraph, paragraphs
Pol. Sci. Q.	Political Science Quarterly
Rec.	record
S. Afr. Y.B. Int'l L.	South African Yearbook of International Law
S.C. Res.	Security Council Resolution
San Diego Int'l L.J.	San Diego International Law Journal
Sess.	session
Supp.	supplement
T.S.	Treaty Series
Terrorism and Pol. Violence	Terrorism and Political Violence
Tulsa J. Comp. & Int'l L.	Tulsa Journal of Comparative and International Law
U. Chi. L. Rev.	University of Chicago Law Review
UCLA J. Int'l L. & Foreign Aff.	University of California, Los Angeles, International Law and Foreign Affairs

U. Pitt. L. Rev.	University of Pittsburgh Law Review
U.N. Doc.	United Nations Document
U.N. GAOR	United Nations General Assembly Official Records
U.N. SCOR	United Nations Security Council Official Records
U.N.T.S.	United Nations Treaty Series
U.N.Y.B.	United Nations Yearbook
U.S.C.	United States Code
Va. J. Int'l L.	Virginia Journal of International Law
Val. U. L. Rev.	Valparaiso University Law Review
Vand. J. Transnat'l L.	Vanderbilt Journal of Transnational Law
Vill.	village
Wash. Post	The Washington Post
Wis. Int'l L.J.	Wisconsin International Law Journal
Y.B. Int'l L. Commission	Yearbook of the International Law Commission
Yale J. Int'l L.	Yale Journal of International Law

'Sometimes it is not enough to do our best; we must do what is required.'
Sir Winston Churchill (1874-1965)

PART 1 – INTRODUCTION

Article 51 of the Charter of the United Nations lays out one of the fundamental, and yet surprisingly controversial rights of states – the inherent right to self-defense.[1] Despite the necessity of self-defense as a general legal concept, there are neither sufficiently distinct conditions under which states may exercise such a right, nor a precise understanding of the scope of the right as such. One of these obscurities will be discussed in this paper: whether states may resort to force based upon Article 51 of the Charter against non-state actors, even if the latter are not effectively controlled by a state. It will be argued that state practice strongly indicates that states may respond to any armed attack, irrespective of the aggressor's nature as a non-state actor.

Non-state actors are entities that do not meet all the requirements of statehood.[2] They can develop activities together with, or directed against, regular state actors. Therefore, non-state actors can have an effect on the territory of the nation state in which they are present (host state), or on the territory of the nation state against which their activities are directed (victim state). Other state actors may render assistance to non-state entities (third states). Additionally, non-state actors may effectively exercise a state's prerogatives, such as a monopoly on the use of armed force. Non-state entities are able to assume such internal and external roles when neither states nor others ban their actions. Primary responsibility to monitor these activities arguably lies with the state which has the closest connection to the non-state actor – the host state. Unfortunately, host states are often either incapable or unwilling to respond to the activities emanating from within their territories. "Unwillingness" ranges from toleration to active support. "Incapability" comprehends failing as well as already failed states. Failed states can be described as state actors absent of an effective gov-

---

[1] Charter of the United Nations, Article 51, June 26, 1945, 59 Stat. 1031, T.S. 993; Article 51 provides in part: "Nothing in the present Charter shall impair the inherent right of individual or collective self-defense if an armed attack occurs against a Member of the United Nations, until the Security Council has taken measures necessary to maintain international peace and security".

[2] *See* Montevideo Convention on the Rights and Duties of States, Article 1, Dec. 26, 1933, 165 U.N.T.S. 19; Article 1 provides: "The state as a person of international law should possess the following qualifications: a) a permanent population; b) a defined territory; c) government; and d) capacity to enter into relations with the other states".

ernment in combination with a severe inability of a people to rebuild the government in exercise of its right to self-determination.[3]

Political reality provides infinite alternatives to this basic scenario: the degree of involvement of the host state can range from ignorance to active support; the application of self-defense sometimes precedes an imminent attack, sometimes occurs while the attack is still underway, or when the attack is not clearly ongoing anymore. The diversity of actual conflicts provides countless further scenarios.

I. A LEGAL GAP

The basic dilemma victim states face with regard to the legal application of self-defense vis-à-vis non-state entities is a legal gap.[4] Generally, all use of force is prohibited under Article 2 (4) of the Charter. Any recourse to force will, unless specifically authorized, violate international law. In the case of a severe enough aggression – an armed attack – states do not have to wait for further authorization by the Security Council, but are entitled to defend themselves under Article 51 of the Charter. The critical threshold is the "armed attack".[5] If the aggressor does not cross this barrier, states are required to find other means to protect themselves.[6] The use of force is evidently not available. Other countermeasures, short of the use of force, can be policing efforts or non-forceful reprisals. Non-state actors, acting from within a host state, are not provided for in this scenario, thus creating the legal gap: by the time the United Nations Charter was drafted only states were envisioned to be able to use significant force. For any forceful action to become relevant for the purpose of the Charter, it had to be attributable to a state.[7] When the origin of an armed attack is a non-state actor the degree of the attack is suddenly of no relevance. Even if it amounts to an armed attack within the meaning of Article 51 of the Charter,[8] it needs to be attributed to a traditional state actor. Otherwise, there is no armed attack and the victim state cannot invoke its right to self-defense. Any further recourse to force

---

[3] Robin Geiss, *Failed States – Legal Aspects and Security Implications*, 47 GERM. Y.B. INT'L L. 457, 465 (2004).

[4] This "gap" is not be confused with the qualitative discrepancy between the Charter's Article 39 ("aggression") and Article 51 ("armed attack") which is often the starting point for interpretative evaluations of the content of the self-defense regime embedded in the Charter; for an overview over such attempts *see* Jörg Kammerhofer, *Uncertainties on the Law of Self-Defence in the United Nations Charter*, 35 NETH. Y.B. INT'L L. 143, 164-67 (2004).

[5] *See infra* pp. 30-32.

[6] Albrecht Randelzhofer, *Article 51*, *in* THE CHARTER OF THE UNITED NATIONS 790 (Bruno Simma ed., 2nd ed. 2002).

[7] *See infra* pp. 30-48.

[8] *See infra* pp. 64 et seq.

is illegal, unless authorized by the Security Council.[9] Occasionally, the host state may consent to the application of force on its territory by another state out of its own interest in restraining the responsible non-state actor.[10] The consequences of the legal gap are readily apparent ever since the events of September 11, 2001 demonstrated that a capable non-state actor may cause the same or even greater harm than a state actor.

This thesis will argue that state practice indicates a disregard for the formal nature of the attacking entity and thus never accepted this legal gap. A number of states resorted to self-defense against non-state actors operating from the territory of states unwilling or unable to exercise control over them. There is a more or less consistent state practice with regard to the interpretation of Article 51 of the Charter that includes a state's right to resort to force immediately before, during, or in the wake of an attack by a non-state actor emanating from the territory of a host state. This state practice can be inferred from the fact that states almost never explicitly contended that state actors were barred from self-defense against non-state actors based upon the lack of statehood of the attacker. In fact, the – mostly harsh – criticism directed against states acting in self-defense allows one to infer that the methods employed in doing so (the *ius in bello*) rather than the permission to resort to force (the *ius ad bellum*) were at stake.

This consistent practice results in customary law, defining the scope of Article 51 of the Charter and the customary self-defense regime. As a consequence, the concept of self-defense as laid out in the U.N. Charter and as embedded in customary international law can be invoked to respond to armed attacks by terrorist groups and other alliances falling short of either of the 'state' requirements. Such recourse to defensive counter-force may be directed exclusively against the non-state actor. If the victim seeks to expand the use of force to the host or any of the third states such can be achieved only if a) these states

---

[9] *See* Articles 39-42 of the Charter.

[10] *See, e.g., Report of the Special Rapporteur, on extrajudicial, summary or arbitrary executions*, U.N. Doc. E/CN.4/2004/7/Add.1 (March 24, 2004) (reporting the killing of Al Qaeda members through an unmanned U.S. aircraft in Yemen, to which the Yemenite government had consented); John R. Crook, *Contemporary Practice of the United States Relating to International Law*, 100 AM. J. INT'L L. 455, 488 (2006) (referring to unconfirmed reports about targeted killings of Al Qaeda operatives by U.S. missile strikes in Pakistan); for a recent incident involving consent to the use of extraterritorial force against Al Qaeda *see* Karen DeYoung, *U.S. Strike in Somalia Targets Al-Qaeda Figure*, WASH. POST, Jan. 9, 2007, at A1 ("A U.S. Air Force AC-130 gunship attacked suspected al-Qaeda members in southern Somalia on Sunday [Jan. 7, 2007] . . . . Abdirizak Hassan, chief of staff for [Somali] Prime Minister Ali Mohamed Gedi, confirmed the strike. . . . Hassan also said Somali officials authorized the strike. "We gave permission for actions that are more than airstrikes," Hassan said.).

undertook an additional armed attack against the victim state, or b) the non-state actor's actions can be attributed by virtue of the traditional rules of state responsibility to the host or third state. The defense regime based upon Article 51 of the Charter directly against the non-state actor, as suggested in this work, does not cover defensive actions against any other international actor. Particularly the host state will suffer automatic, albeit non-intentional infringements of its sovereign rights as a side-effect of self-defense against the non-state actor present on and operating from the host state's territory. These violations can only be legitimate under Article 51 of the Charter if they are proportionate.[11]

II. THE WALL DECISION AND THE CONGO CASE

While some saw the self-defense regime already clearly shifting towards an allowance to defend oneself against hosts of non-state terrorist actors,[12] the scholarly debate about the role of non-state actors has been fueled by recent decisions of the International Court of Justice (ICJ), namely the Advisory Opinion on the Legal Consequences of the Construction of a Wall in the Occupied Palestinian Territory,[13] and the Case Concerning Armed Activities on the Territory of the Congo.[14]

The *Advisory Opinion* contained a, surprisingly brief,[15] statement which denied the State of Israel the right to invoke Article 51 of the Charter in order to justify the construction of a defensive barrier[16] in the West Bank.[17] The Court found the right to self-defense "irrelevan[t]" for two reasons: first, that Israel did not claim that any of the attacks it had been facing were imputable to a state; and

---

[11] *See infra* pp. 220 et seq.

[12] *See, e.g.*, Thomas Bruha, *Gewaltverbot und humanitäres Völkerrecht nach dem 11. September 2001*, 40 ARCHIV DES VÖLKERRECHTS 383, 393-95 (2002); THOMAS M. FRANCK, RECOURSE TO FORCE 54, 67 (2002); Markus Krajewski, *Selbstverteidigung gegen bewaffnete Angriffe nicht-staatlicher Organisationen – Der 11. September 2001 und seine Folgen*, 40 ARCHIV DES VÖLKERRECHTS 183, 198 (2002).

[13] Legal Consequences of the Construction of a Wall in the Occupied Palestinian Territory, Advisory Opinion (Int'l Ct. Justice July 9, 2004), 43 I.L.M. 1009 (2004) (hereinafter *Advisory Opinion*).

[14] Case Concerning Armed Activities on the Territory of the Congo (Dem. Rep. Congo v. Uganda) Dec. 19, 2005 at para. 65, *available at* http://www.icj-cij.org (last visited July 16, 2007) (hereinafter *Congo* case); *see infra* pp. 42 et. seq.

[15] *See* Sean D. Murphy, *Self-Defense and the Israeli Wall Advisory Opinion: An Ipse Dixit from the ICJ?*, 99 AM. J. INT'L L. 62 (2005) (considering the opinion "startling in its brevity and . . . unsatisfactory").

[16] The correct description of the Israeli construction is subject to disagreement; beside "barrier", suggested terms are "wall" and "fence"; *cf.* Geoffrey R. Watson, *The "Wall" Decision in Legal and Political Context*, 99 AM. J. INT'L. L. 6, 7 at n.3 (2005).

[17] *Advisory Opinion*, at para. 139.

second, that neither United Nations Security Council resolution 1368 (2001)[18] nor 1373 (2001)[19] could be invoked in favor of the Israeli position as the threats had originated from inside a territory that was under the control of the State of Israel.[20] The *Advisory Opinion* did not specify the meaning of "control", neither did it explain why that would be a relevant issue with regard to Article 51 of the Charter.[21] It appears, however, that the ICJ regarded only states and not non-states as capable of launching an armed attack as required by Article 51 of the Charter.[22] The ICJ confirmed this notion in the *Congo* case.[23] The Israeli Supreme Court in the *Mara'abe* case, without deciding whether Article 51 of the Charter could be invoked to erect the separation fence, found the ICJ's approach

> hard to come to terms with . . . . It is not called for by the language of §51 of the Charter of the United Nations . . . . From the point of view of a state's right to self-defense, what difference does it make if a terrorist attack against it comes from another country of from territory external to it which is under belligerent occupation?[24]

Similarly, the statements submitted to the ICJ regarding the Israeli wall prior to the *Advisory Opinion* already seem to reflect a completely different approach. 44 states, three international organizations, and the Palestinian Authority expressed their legal understanding of the situation at stake.[25] None of these statements shares the ICJ's conclusion that self-defense is unavailable towards non-state actors merely based upon the legal nature of the attacker. Rather, states that decided to render substantive statements indicate that Israel may not rely on self-defense due to a lack of proportionality or necessity,[26] violation of the im-

---

[18] S.C. Res. 1368, U.N. Doc. S/RES/1368 (Sept. 12, 2001).
[19] S.C. Res. 1373, U.N. Doc. S/RES/1373 (Sept. 28, 2001).
[20] *Advisory Opinion*, at para. 139.
[21] *Cf. Advisory Opinion* (dissenting opinion of Judge Buergenthal), at para. 6.
[22] *But see Advisory Opinion* (separate opinion of Judge Higgins), at para. 33 (disagreeing with the majority on this issue she states that "[t]here is, with respect, nothing in the text of Article 51 that thus stipulates that self-defence is available only when an armed attack is made by a State").
[23] *See infra* pp. 42 et seq.
[24] HCJ 7957/04 (High Ct. Justice Sept. 15, 2005) Mara'abe v. Prime Minister of Isr. at para. 23, *available at* http://elyon1.court.gov.il/eng/home/index.html (last visited Feb. 2, 2007).
[25] Written Statements, *available at* http://www.icj-cij.org (last visited July 16, 2007).
[26] *See, e.g.*, statements by the following states, all *available at* http://www.icj-cij.org (last visited July 16, 2007); France: Written Statement of the French Republic (Jan. 30, 2004) at para. 58; Indonesia: Written Statement Submitted by the Government of the Republic of Indonesia to the International Court of Justice (Jan. 29, 2004) at paras. 5-7; Jordan: Written Statement of the Hashemite Kingdom of Jordan (Jan. 30, 2004), at para. 5.275 (hereinafter Jordanian

mediacy requirement of Article 51 of the Charter,[27] or the absence of an armed attack for reasons not specified but without reference to the legal status of the attacker.[28] Some states, while criticizing Israel, did not comment on self-defense issues at all,[29] as did the Organization of the Islamic Conference.[30] Several states also explicitly acknowledged a situation in which Israel has a right to respond to the ongoing violence, irrespective of a legal basis for such counterforce.[31] South

---

Statement); Saudi-Arabia: Written Statement of the Kingdom of Saudi-Arabia (Jan. 30, 2004) at paras. 32, 34, (hereinafter Saudi Arabian Statement); Sudan: Statement of the Government of the Sudan to the ICJ on the Construction of a Wall by Israel in the Occupied Palestinian Territory (Jan. 30, 2004) at 1.

[27] *See, e.g.,* statements by the following states, all *available at* http://www.icj-cij.org (last visited July 16, 2007); Lebanon: Written Statement of Lebanon (Jan. 30, 2004) at para. 44 (indicating, however, that "the actions that the construction of the wall is intended to prevent are not consonant with the definition of aggression as given in resolution 3314, adopted by the General Assembly on 14 December 1974 . . . ."); Malaysia: Written Statement by Malaysia (Jan. 30, 2004) at para. 148; Senegal: Written Statement by the Government the (sic) Republic of Senegal (Jan. 2004) at 2.

[28] Jordanian Statement, at para. 5.270.

[29] *See, e.g.,* statements by the following states, all *available at* http://www.icj-cij.org (last visited July 16, 2007); Guinea: Letter to the President of the Court from the Permanent Representative of the Republic of Guinea to the United Nations (Jan. 15, 2004); Malta: Statement of Malta on the Question of the Legal Consequences of the Construction of a Wall in the Occupied Palestinian Territories (Jan. 30, 2004); Morocco: Participation of the Kingdom of Morocco to the procedure (written proceedings) before the International Court of Justice in the case: Legal consequences of the construction of a wall in the occupied Palestinian Territory – Request for an Advisory Opinion (Jan. 2004); Namibia: Written Statement Submitted by Namibia (Jan. 30, 2004); Pakistan: Written Statement Submitted by Pakistan (Jan. 29, 2004); Sweden: Written Statement of the Republic of Cuba (Jan. 2004); Written Statement of Sweden (Jan. 30, 2004); Syria: A memorandum presented by the Syrian Arab Republic in implementation of Section (2) of Article (66) of the International Court of Justice statute and the Court decision of 19 December, 2003 (Jan. 30, 2004);Yemen: Statement from the Republic of Yemen (Jan. 29, 2004).

[30] Written Statement of the Organization of the Islamic Conference (Jan. 2004), *available at* http://www.icj-cij.org (last visited July 16, 2007).

[31] *See, e.g.,* the following statements by different states, all *available at* http://www.icj-cij.org (last visited July 16, 2007); Belgium: Written Statement of the Kingdom of Belgium (Jan. 30, 2004) at para. 4; Senegal: Written Statement by the Government the (sic) Republic of Senegal (Jan. 2004) at 2; Brazil: Commentaries du Gouvernment brésilien sur la question des Conseguénces juridiques de l'édification d'un mur dans la territoire palestinian occupé (Jan. 30, 2004) at 2; Canada: Written Statement by the Government of Canada (Jan. 29, 2004) at 1; Cyprus: Statement of the Government of the Republic of Cyprus (Jan. 30, 2004) at para. 6; France: Written Statement of the French Republic (Jan. 30, 2004) at para 50; Germany: Statement of the Government of the Federal Republic of Germany (January 2004) at 12; Ireland on behalf of the European Union: Letter submitted to the ICJ by Ireland on behalf of the

Africa rejected the existence of an armed attack since the Palestinian irregulars had not been sent on behalf of a state.[32] This statement probably comes closest to the view finally adopted by the ICJ. Not even the statement by the Palestinian Authority goes that far. It outlines, among other reasons for the illegality of Israel's barrier, as to why self-defense was inapplicable as a justification:

> The violence in the Occupied Palestinian Territories is not on a scale or of a nature equivalent to an 'armed attack' against Israel in the sense required for the exercise of a right of self-defense. Self-defense in international law cannot be triggered by individual criminal acts which call for police and prosecutorial action, and not military action.[33]

This statement primarily refers to a lack of significantly grave armed incidents ("scale") and considers them to be merely criminal in "nature", hence not military. The word "nature" may be seen as an implicit reference to a certain understanding as to who is considered as capable of launching the – qualitatively absent – armed attack but it does not reflect an unambiguous rejection of Israel's claim of self-defense due to the lack of statehood of the attacker.[34]

Summarizing the states' submissions in this case, one already gets a good impression as to where the states stand nowadays. Similarly, this thesis will argue that state practice since 1945 indicates a different legal understanding of the requirements of Article 51 of the Charter than developed by the ICJ. States that met threats by non-state actors responded by military force based upon self-defense. That happened on numerous occasions. Whenever states criticized other states for taking recourse to force in such situations they rarely ever based their criticism upon the lack of statehood of the aggressor. Rather, a lot of the legal reasoning put forward often even presupposes the general capability of a non-state actor to exercise an armed attack. The right to self-defense for states against non-state actors is indispensable if the role of the United Nations shall not be jeopardized. Article 51 of the Charter may not have been construed to

---

European Union (Jan. 30, 2004) at 8; Spain: Letter from the Spanish Ambassador to the President of the International Court of Justice (Jan. 30, 2004) at 5.

32 Written Statement Submitted by the Government of the Republic of South Africa (Jan. 30, 2004) at para. 33, *available at* http://www.icj-cij.org (last visited July 16, 2007); Switzerland: Written statement addressed to the International Court of Justice by the Swiss Confederation pursuant to the Order of the Court of 19 December 2003 (Jan. 2004), at par. 27.

33 Written Statement Submitted by Palestine (Jan. 30, 2004) at para. 531, *available at* http://www.icj-cij.org (last visited July 16, 2007); the government of Saudi Arabia uses a similar formulation, *see* Saudi Arabian Statement, at para. 31.

34 *But see* MICHAEL SCHOLZ, STAATLICHES SELBSTVERTEIDIGUNGSRECHT GEGEN TERRORISTISCHE GEWALT 163 (2006).

serve as an exception to Article 2 (4) of the Charter for attacks by non-state actors. Failing to do so now, however, would not serve the interest of international law. Rather, it would play into the hands of those who reject any legal confinements for states whenever crucial issues are at stake.[35]

Numerous monographs[36] and articles[37] mention state practice regarding asymmetric warfare and draw conclusions based upon this practice. None of these works actually covers state practice comprehensively since 1945. This work seeks to contribute to the ongoing debate about a contemporary use of force regime against non-state actors by filling this void.

For the purpose of this introduction, three issues need to be clarified: first, the scope of this work; second, the legal impact of state practice on international law; and third, the origins, relevance, and credibility of a state's legal convictions.

III. Scope of this Work

This work will focus on different conflicts involving states and non-state actors (asymmetric conflicts). These conflicts will show that states invoked self-defense based upon the degree of the threat (the armed attack), not its formal origin (state or non-state actor). More importantly, the evaluation of the statements or comments of third states will show that even the harshest criticism of a

---

[35] For an overview of recent "realist" reasoning *see* John C. Yoo, *Using Force*, 71 U. Chi. L. Rev. 729, 731 at n.6 (2004).

[36] Stanimir A. Alexandrov, Self-Defense Against the Use of Force in International Law 121-188 (1996); Avra Constantinou, The Right of Self-Defense Under Customary Law and Article 51 of the U.N. Charter 136-145 (2000); Franck, *supra* note 12 at 54-68; Manuel R. Garcia-Mora, International Responsibility for Hostile Acts of Private Persons Against Foreign States 53-61 (1962); Christine D. Gray, International Law and the Use of Force (2nd ed. 2004); Richard J. Erickson, Legitimate Use of Military Force Against State-Sponsored International Terrorism (1989); Timothey MacCormack, Self-Defense in International Law (1996), Scholz, *supra note* 34 *at* 134-66; Christiane Wandscher, Internationaler Terrorismus und Selbstverteidigungsrecht 140-48, 179-97 (2006).

[37] *See, e.g.*, Mark B. Baker, *Terrorism and the Inherent Right of Self-Defense (A Call to Amend Art. 51 of the UN Charter)* 10 Hous. J. Int'l L. 25 (1987); Derek Bowett, *Reprisals Involving Recourse to Armed Force*, 66 Am. J. Int'l L. 1 (1972); William O'Brien, *Reprisals, Deterrence and Self-Defense in Counterterror Operations*, 30 Va. J. Int'l L. 421 (1990); Carsten Stahn, *"Nicaragua is dead, long live Nicaragua" - the Right of Self-defence Under Art. 51 UN Charter and International Terrorism, in* Terrorism as Challenge for National and International Law - Security versus Liberty 827 (Christian Walter ed. 2004); Tom Ruys, Sten Verhoeven, *Attacks by Private Actors and the Right of Self-Defense*, 10 J. Conflict & Security L. 289 (2005).

state's resort of force was hardly ever founded on the absence of statehood of the target group.

This approach becomes most clear in the conflicts between Israel and the Palestine Liberation Organization (PLO) or Hezbollah in Lebanon; between South Africa and the African National Congress (ANC) as well as the South West African People's Organization (SWAPO); between Turkey, Iran, and Kurdish groups; and between the United States and Al Qaeda. In all of these, the non-state actor was more or less undisputedly the immediate target for a state's recourse to force in absence of a state actor that could have been blamed instead. Another group of partly interrelated conflicts were also evaluated, although the asymmetric set-up is influenced and slightly altered, mainly by virtue of direct involvement of host states and their own political agendas.

Third states are sometimes the actual motor behind an action and simply seek to disguise their actions behind someone else's work in an agonized state (e.g. Iran and Syria, both heavily supporting Hezbollah which on the other hand mainly operates from and within Lebanon).[38] At other times, it is rather the non-state actor which controls the actions, meanwhile also abusing a paralyzed, perhaps even failing or failed host state (e.g. activities of the PLO in Lebanon).[39] Between both ends the host states behind those non-state actors contribute in varying degrees. Four categories of state involvement may be seen: (1) sponsorship or direction, (2) support, (3) toleration, and (4) inaction.[40] This thesis will show that attacked states applied defensive force in all of these four categories, relying on Article 51 of the Charter. For them, the degree of "effective control"[41] by a state over the violent non-state actor was largely irrelevant. States sought to apply self-defense i.e. to stop ongoing attacks and to prevent further ones. Consequently, self-defense was most often not considered to depend on the responsibility of a host or third state. A non-state actor's sole responsibility (even though often enough supported by varying state parties) was sufficient. Hence, the non-state actor became the target of recourse to defensive force. Attribution issues were not at stake.

---

[38] JUDITH P. HARIK, HEZBOLLAH 39 (2004) (arguing that both states' foreign policy goals were advanced by Hezbollah's fight against Israel which explains their heavy support); Louis Rene Beres, *Israel, Lebanon, and Hizbullah: A Jurisprudential Assessment*, 14 ARIZ. J. INT'L & COMP. L. 141, 148 (1997).

[39] *Cf.* Mary-Ellen O'Connell, *Enhancing the Status of Non-State Actors Through a Global War on Terror?*, 43 COLUM. J. TRANSNAT'L L. 435, 450 (2005) (stating that the U.S. supported Israel's actions against Lebanon because of the absence of any Lebanese ability to control the PLO).

[40] ERICKSON, *supra* note 36 at 98-103; Gregory M. Travalio, *Terrorism, International Law, and the Use of Military Force,* 18 WIS. INT'L L.J. 145, 150 (2000).

[41] *See infra* p. 36 .

Victim states acted accordingly over a period of at least 40 to 50 years, during which neither international organizations nor third states rarely ever complained about the lack of statehood of the aggressor as such. Therefore, it will be argued that Article 51 of the Charter is in no way limited to armed attacks launched by states. Rather, even – and perhaps especially – the complete inability of a state to prevent and fight a non-state actor's military actions emanating from the state's territory does not prevent an "armed attack" by the responsible non-state actor. Additionally, all other conditions must be met for victim states to successfully invoke Article 51 of the Charter.

IV. States and Non-State Actors

First, it is crucial to explore the legal relations between non-state actors, host states, and other states based upon the current jurisprudence in order to show what problems arise from the traditional self-defense regime. Second, it will be outlined which categories of potential violent non-state actors exist and how far their treatment by the international community and by international legal regimes reveal their current status. Finally, an attempt will be made to shed some light on the term "non-state actor", an international entity with numerous faces.[42] It will be evaluated which factors are necessary to incorporate a non-state actor into the international regime on the use of armed force.

1. Article 51, Non-State Actors and State Involvement

The relation between states, self-defense and further internationally relevant actors is defined by the jurisprudence of the ICJ and other sources of international law, sometimes dating back before the foundation of the United Nations and the ratification of the United Nations Charter. It will be evaluated how the current self-defense regime is structured and in how far other groups but states have been considered.

a) From the Caroline to Article 51 of the United Nations Charter

Surprisingly, perhaps trend-setting,[43] the origins of the modern right to self-defense seem to be rooted in an exhaustively debated incident involving not two states, but rather a state and a group of foreign nationals supporting an uprising against the allegedly self-defending state – the famous *Caroline* incident.

---

[42] For a overview over legal and political theories regarding the nature and rights of non-state actors *see, e.g.*, Math Noortmann, *Non-State Actors in International Law,* in NON-STATE ACTORS IN INTERNATIONAL RELATIONS 59-76 (Bas Arts, Math Noortmann, Bob Reinalda eds., 2003).

[43] Sean D. Murphy, *Terrorism and the Concept of "Armed Attack" in Article 51 of the U.N. Charter*, 43 HARV. INT'L L.J. 41, 50 (2002) (arguing that already the *Caroline* incident proposes the legality of self-defense against non-state actors).

Traditionally, it was regarded as the starting point for any customary law of anticipatory self-defense.[44] Lately, its influence on the legality of self-defense is sometimes newly discovered,[45] then again rejected as far as the general content of self-defense as part of customary international law.[46] However, it stands at the beginning of every historical review of the modern concept of self-defense.

The well-known facts,[47] broadly outlined, are as follows: During an uprising in Canada in 1837, a group of U.S. nationals sought to support Canadian insurgents in their fight against the British rulers. Despite U.S. governmental attempts to prevent their citizens from aiding the neighbor's uproar, some Americans managed to provide the rebels with weapons and men. For doing so, they chartered a small steamboat named "Caroline". Upon the boat's return, after having left Canadian territory, the "Caroline" was in December 1837 seized and set on fire by British-Canadian forces upon which it fell over the Niagara Falls. Later, in 1840, a British-Canadian national was arrested in New York and charged with murder of the American citizen Amos Durfee who had been killed in the Caroline raid. The British government requested his release from custody, not wanting him to be tried before a New York District Court. Then-U.S. Secretary of State Daniel Webster, as had his predecessor, exchanged a series of letters with his British counterpart Lord Ashburton, expressing concern about the infringement of American sovereignty by the British raid. Regardless of whether the conduct of those aboard the "Caroline" had been lawful or not, he regarded some precise conditions as crucial, under which the British may have launched their attack legally: "[I]t will be for [a] government to show a necessity of self-defense, instant, overwhelming, leaving no choice of means, and no moment for deliberation. . . [T]he act [in self-defense] . . . must be limited by necessity, and kept clearly within it" as Webster wrote in 1842.[48] With this, he had formulated the conditions of self-defense as they were perceived for the coming decades: (1) an actual violation of the victim state's rights; (2) the failure to prevent these violations by the state of origin; and (3) the limitation of self-defense to the

---

[44] Oscar Schachter, *The Right of States to use Armed Force*, 82 MICH. L. REV. 1620, 1634 (1984).

[45] Timothey Kearly, *Raising the Caroline*, 17 WIS. INT'L L.J. 325 (1999).

[46] Maria Benvenuta Occelli, *"Sinking" the Caroline: Why the Caroline Doctrine's Restrictions on Self-Defense should not be regarded as Customary International Law*, 4 SAN DIEGO INT'L L.J. 467 (2003).

[47] For an overview *see also* Kearly, *supra* note 45 at 328-30; Occelli, *supra* note 46 at 470-75; Abraham D. Sofaer, *On the Necessity of Pre-emption*, 15 EUR. J. INT'L L. 209, 214-20 (2003).

[48] Letter from Daniel Webster to Lord Ashburton (July 27, 1842), in DIPLOMATIC AND OFFICIAL PAPERS OF DANIEL WEBSTER WHILE SECRETARY OF STATE 110 (1848).

stopping of the prior violations by reasonably proportionate means that are limited to what is required to achieve that goal.[49]

The underlying principle in international law was, however, that a war was by itself permitted. Taking recourse to self-defense had rather explanatory or political reasons and was not necessary to render the application of force legal.[50] Once the application of force became more restricted, the concept of self-defense consequently gained wider importance. The Covenant of the League of Nations qualified the right to go to war,[51] but it did not prohibit war as such. After failed consultations among the member states, it was legitimate to resort to force according to Article 15 (7) of the Covenant of the League of Nations.[52]

A subsequent international agreement was more restrictive: the Briand-Kellogg Pact of 1928[53] condemned the use of war in its Article 1.[54] Consequently, self-defense was left as only legitimate recourse to force,[55] whereas a state was not the only subject giving rise thereto: state actors were not included as exclusive origin of an attack by virtue of Article 2 of the Briand-Kellogg Pact in which the parties agreed to settle "all disputes or conflicts of whatever nature or of whatever origin they may be . . . by pacific means."[56] However, history proved this legal framework to be largely hollow and it was on the San Francisco negotiations prior to the foundation of the United Nations to provide for a stringent and respected rule of law restricting the *ius ad bellum*.

b) FROM THE UNITED NATIONS CHARTER TO THE PRESENT

The Charter of the United Nations lays out in its Articles 2 (4) and 51 that the use of force is prohibited and that recourse to force may only be taken in exceptional circumstances, namely if the Security Council says so or if self-defense can be invoked.[57] The right to exercise self-defense is "inherent", a term

---

[49] ALEXANDROV, *supra* note 36 at 20.
[50] Randelzhofer, *supra* note 6 at 789.
[51] ALEXANDROV, *supra* note 36 at 29-34.
[52] *See* FRANCK, *supra* note 12 at 10.
[53] Treaty Providing for the Renunciation of War as an instrument of National Policy (Pact of Paris), Aug. 27, 1928, 94 L.N.T.S. 57, 46 Stat. 2434 (hereinafter Briand-Kellogg Pact).
[54] Article 1 of the Briand-Kellog Pact provides: "The High Contracting Parties solemnly declare in the names of their respective peoples that they condemn the recourse to war for the solution of international controversies, and renounce it as an instrument of national policy in their relations with one another."
[55] Randelzhofer, *supra* note 6 at 789.
[56] Briand-Kellogg Pact, art. 2.
[57] Article 2 (4) of the Charter provides in part: "All Members shall refrain in their international relations from the threat or use of force against the territorial integrity or political inde-

which is not defined in the Charter. The ICJ deemed Article 51 of the Charter "only meaningful on the basis that there is a 'natural' or 'inherent' right of self-defense . . . of a customary nature . . . confirmed and influenced by the Charter".[58] It seems therefore as if states might be able to claim rights beyond those laid down in Article 51 of the Charter, namely from customary international law.[59] This leads back to the conditions for which the *Caroline* incident provided.[60] As was mentioned, this early application of self-defense was triggered by a non-state actor – a group of Canadian insurgents and their American supporters – rather than by a state.[61] However, the Charter does not seem to envision such a rule. Terrorist attacks are considered capable of leading to a victim state's right to self-defense if, and only if, another state can be considered responsible.[62] If not, no recourse to force under Article 51 of the Charter can be taken.

The Charter's wording does not *a priori* warrant such an interpretation. In fact, it does not exclude at all a broader interpretation including more than merely states as potential attackers.[63] The crucial threshold to be met in order to exercise legitimate counter-force under Article 51 of the Charter is the "armed attack" – not an "armed attack by a (member) state", for instance. Additionally, any military response must be proportionate, the state has to report all applied measures to the Security Council without delay, and may continue only until the Security Council takes its own measures.[64]

What exactly is meant by the notion of an "armed attack" is not clear. There is no definition of the precise content and of the boundaries of an "armed attack", primarily due to disagreements between the members of the United Nations.[65] For this reason, it is usually a case by case analysis that is invoked to clarify the term. This analysis becomes more difficult if the origin of an attack is

---

pendence of any state, or in any other manner inconsistent with the Purposes of the United Nations"; for Article 51 of the Charter *see supra* note 1.

[58] Case concerning Military and Paramilitary Activities in and against Nicaragua (Nicar. v. U.S.), 1986 I.C.J Reports 14, para. 176 (27 June 1986) (hereinafter *Nicaragua* case).

[59] *See* Baker, *supra* note 37 at 31, 32.

[60] *See, e.g.*, IAN BROWNLIE, PRINCIPLES OF PUBLIC INTERNATIONAL LAW 701 (6th ed. 2003); *see* also *supra* pp. 28 et seq.

[61] *See* Murphy, *supra* note 43 at 50.

[62] *See, e.g.*, BROWNLIE, *supra* note 60 at 713.

[63] SCHOLZ, *supra* note 34 at 79.

[64] *Nicaragua* case, at para. 194 ("whether the response to the attack is lawful depends on observance of the criteria of the necessity and the proportionality of the measures taken in self-defence"); *see also* Randelzhofer, *supra* note 6 at 790; ROBERT JENNINGS, ARTHUR WATTS (eds.) 1 OPPENHEIM'S INTERNATIONAL LAW 420-421 (9th ed. 1992).

[65] *See* Randelzhofer, *supra* note 6 at 795-96, 800-02.

not a state, but merely a non-state actor. The ICJ case law contains several situations in which the rules surrounding self-defense were shaped or in which recourse to force was triggered by actions of non-state entities. An analysis of the ICJ jurisprudence shows that an armed attack requires some form of state control by which a non-state actor's actions can be attributed to the state. Neither the ICJ, nor existing conventions or resolutions, provide for non-state actor responsibility if a host state is incapable or unwilling to control non-state entities.

i) THE CORFU CHANNEL CASE

The first time the ICJ ruled on self-defense as such was 1949 in the *Corfu Channel* Case.[66] The United Kingdom had complained to the Security Council about the mining of the Straight of Corfu by Albania, thereby depriving British ships of their right of free passage. The Court, without mentioning Article 51 of the Charter, ruled that Albania was in breach of Article 2 (4) of the Charter and the U.K. was consequently allowed to cure Albania's failures by invoking proportional self-defense.[67] Moreover, the Court also decided that every state is under an obligation "not to allow knowingly its territory to be used for acts contrary to the rights of other States."[68] The court also held that states have an obligation to employ all "means of information and inquiry at its disposal" and may not simply refer to their lack of knowledge about activities on their territory.[69] Previously, Albania had argued that it was not proven that it had laid the mines by itself or through a third party,[70] and, among other reasons, since it did not even possess a navy at the time.[71]

It seems therefore that state actors cannot escape responsibility vis-à-vis other states only because it was not their immediate organs which used force, but perhaps a third party, e.g. a non-state actor on the host state's territory. Tolerating terror emanating from a state's territory against third states is unlawful.[72] However, crucial was the state's own responsibility which was extended to acts emanating from its territory, not a hypothetical third party's very own legal accountability. Failed or failing states were not discussed.

---

[66] The Corfu Channel Case (Merits) (U.K. v. Alb.), 1949 I.C.J Reports 4 (19 Apr. 1949) (hereinafter *Corfu Channel* case)

[67] *See* Eugene V. Rostov, *Disputes Involving the Inherent Right of Self-Defense*, in THE INTERNATIONAL COURT OF JUSTICE AT A CROSSROADS (Lori F. Damrosch ed.,1987), at 264, 274.

[68] *Corfu Channel* case, at 22.

[69] *Id.* at 18.

[70] *Id.* at 11.

[71] *Id.* at 15.

[72] YORAM DINSTEIN, WAR, AGGRESSION AND SELF-DEFENCE 206 (4th ed. 2005).

ii) THE FRIENDLY RELATIONS DECLARATION

In 1970, the United Nations General Assembly issued the Declaration on Principles of International Law Concerning Friendly Relations and Co-Operation Among States in Accordance with the Charter of the United Nations. It stipulates that states violate their international obligations merely by acquiescing in terrorist activities emanating from the state's territory.[73] This notion was confirmed by both the United Nations General Assembly[74] as well as by the United Nations Security Council,[75] long before September 11. The Security Council re-confirmed this approach immediately after the attacks on the World Trade Center and the Pentagon and issued resolution 1373 (2001).[76] Its operative part requests that all States shall "[r]efrain from providing any form of support, active or passive, to entities or persons involved in terrorist acts, including by suppressing recruitment of members of terrorist groups and eliminating the supply of weapons to terrorists. . . " and even "[d]eny safe haven to those who finance, plan, support, or commit terrorist acts, or provide safe havens . . . ."[77]

However, neither of these stipulations mean that any such violation of international law, even if it incorporates the use of force, will allow for defensive recourse to force based upon the actions of a non-state terrorist group. The according requirements are to be found exclusively in Article 51 of the Charter and customary law.

iii) THE IRAN HOSTAGES CASE

The ICJ contributed to the question of whether a state is responsible for criminal or terrorist activity on its territory following the Iranian revolution in 1979. The Case Concerning United States Diplomatic and Consular Staff in Teheran was brought before the court by the United States, mainly for violations of international diplomatic and consular agreements.[78]

In the course of the revolutionary overthrow, a demonstration of "approximately 3,000 persons" on November 4, 1979, protested against the Persian Shah's admission to the United States for treatment. Out of their midst, a group

---

[73] Declaration on Principles of International Law Concerning Friendly Relations and Co-Operation Among States in Accordance with the Charter of the United Nations, G.A. Res. 2625, U.N. Doc. A/RES/2625 (XXV) (Oct. 24, 1970) (hereinafter Friendly Relations Declaration).

[74] *See, e.g.*, G.A. Res. 40/61, U.N. Doc. A/RES/40/61 (Dec. 9, 1985).

[75] *See infra* note 102.

[76] S.C. Res. 1373, U.N. Doc. S/RES/1373 (Sept. 28, 2001).

[77] *Id.* at 2.

[78] United States Diplomatic and Consular Staff in Teheran (U.S. v. Iran), 1980 I.C.J. 3, 6-7 (May 24) (hereinafter *Iran Hostage* case).

of "several hundred people" referring to themselves as "Muslim Student Followers" seized the United States' embassy compound and took everybody inside hostage.[79] Responsible Iranian security personnel left without making an attempt to stop the intruders.[80] The religious leader of Iran, the Ayatollah Khomeini, announced that the hostages should not be released and the "policy thus announced . . . of maintaining the occupation of the Embassy and the detention of its inmates as hostages . . . was complied with by other Iranian authorities and endorsed by them repeatedly . . . ."[81] And while the ICJ did not consider the militant students as Iranian agents or organs and their actions hence not attributable to the state of Iran as they were "not charged by some competent organ of the Iranian state to carry out a specific operation",[82] the ICJ held that Iran could be held responsible nonetheless: "The approval given to [the taking of hostages etc.] by the Ayatollah Khomeini and other organs of the Iranian State, and the decision to perpetuate them, translated continuing occupation of the Embassy and detention of the hostages into acts of that State."[83] As a result, the state of Iran was in breach of several international agreements.[84]

As to the relation between state actors and non-state groups, such as student militants, the decision thus simply says that an attack by non-state groups becomes only relevant with regard to international legal provisions if the attack can be attributed successfully to a state, albeit retroactively. This attribution as stipulated in *Iran Hostages* requires that militants acted "on behalf of the State".[85] A breach of international law, much less committing an armed attack merely by allowing militants to train on a state's territory is thus hardly possible.[86] The state is the insofar only internationally relevant actor. If no state can be held responsible, any breaches committed by non-state actors will not be considered, disregarding of their magnitude and severity.

iv) THE NICARAGUA CASE

This approach was confirmed and explained in greater detail with regard to cross-border attacks by armed bands in the next landmark decision, the 1986 *Nicaragua* Case.[87] Nicaragua had complained to the ICJ that the United States

[79] *Id.* at para. 17.
[80] *Id.* at para. 18.
[81] *Id.* at para. 74.
[82] *Id.* at para. 58.
[83] *Id.* at para. 74.
[84] *Id.* at paras. 76-79.
[85] *Id.* at para. 58.
[86] *Cf.* Greg Travalio, John Altenburg, *Terrorism, State Responsibility, and the Use of Military Force*, 4 CHI. J. INT'L L. 97, 104 (2003).
[87] *See supra* note 58.

was supporting the "contras", a group of Nicaraguan rebels, among other things by mining and attacking harbors and other facilities, by which the U.S. allegedly had violated Article 2 (4) of the Charter.[88] The United States invoked collective self-defense on behalf of its allies El Salvador, Honduras, and Costa Rica. It regarded those states under armed attacks, imputable to the government of Nicaragua, as the latter had provided weapons and other assistance to the armed opposition in El Salvador and engaged in cross-border incursions into the other two states.[89] It was therefore crucial for the Court to determine if an "armed attack" had indeed occurred to which the United States could respond in self-defense.

The Court stated that "it will be necessary to distinguish the most grave forms of the use of force (those constituting an armed attack) from other less grave forms."[90] The border incursions did not meet that threshold. More importantly though, with regard to the case of El Salvador, an armed attack could not only originate from a state actor itself but must rather be viewed in accordance with Article 3 (g) of the Definition of Aggression:[91]

> In particular, it may be considered to be agreed that an armed attack must be understood as including not merely action by regular armed forces across an international border, but also 'the sending by or on behalf of a State of armed bands, groups, irregulars or mercenaries, which carry out acts of armed force against another State of such gravity as to amount to' (inter alia) an actual armed attack conducted by regular forces, 'or its substantial involvement therein'.[92]

The limitations of the armed attacks with regard to its degree of gravity nonetheless apply also for the sending of armed bands. The Court therefore emphasized that the "assistance to rebels in the form of the provision of weapons or logistical or other support"[93] does not by itself amount to the use of force as required for an armed attack through armed bands etc. It further laid out that even

> the financing, organizing, training, supplying and equipping of the contras, the selection of its military or paramilitary targets, and the planning of the whole of its operation, is still insufficient in itself, . . . for the purpose of at-

[88] *Nicaragua* case, at para. 227.
[89] *Id.* at paras. 230, 231.
[90] *Id.* at para.191.
[91] Definition of Aggression, G.A. Res. 3314 (XXIX), U.N. Doc. A/9631 (Dec. 14, 1974).
[92] *Nicaragua* case, at para. 195.
[93] *Id.* at para. 195.

> tributing to the United States the acts committed by the contras in the course of their military or paramilitary operations in Nicaragua.[94]

Rather, "[f]or this conduct to give rise to legal responsibility of the United States, it would in principle have to be proved that that State had effective control of the military or paramilitary operations in the course of which the alleged violations were committed."[95] The Court did not explain any further what could constitute such "effective control". On the other hand, the Court held that the United States had violated Article 2 (4) of the Charter by mining and attacking the ports etc, as well as by its assistance to the contras to the extent that this assistance involves a threat or use of force.[96]

The "effective control" standard stirred debates ever since it was proclaimed by the ICJ. In particular, the events after September 11, 2001[97] seem to imply that the test as it was applied in 1986 will be difficult to uphold.[98] Already some of the judges concerned with the *Nicaragua* case seemed to have foreseen that a state's responsibility should start a lot earlier. In his dissenting opinion, Judge Sir Jennings agreed that the mere provision of weapons will not qualify as an armed attack. But, as he went on to say that "the provision of arms, coupled with 'logistical or other support' is no armed attack is going much too far. Logistical support may itself be crucial."[99] Also others agreed that further differentiation was required to effectively protect states under Article 51 of the Charter.[100] Justice Schwebel agreed in his dissenting opinion and considered it to be sufficient for an armed attack to be attributed to a state if it provided logistic support to an armed band.[101]

---

[94] *Id.* at para. 115.
[95] *Id.* at para. 115.
[96] *Id.* at para. 238.
[97] *See infra* p. 153.
[98] *See, e.g.*, Sean D. Murphy, *Terrorism and the Concept of "Armed Attack" in Article 51 of the UN Charter*, 43 HARV. INT'L L.J. 41, 51 (2002) (requesting adaptation and judicial review of the standard "embodied in the Nicaragua Court's scale" in the light of 9/11); Stahn, *supra* note 37 at 838 (stating that 9/11 turned over the ICJ's 'effective control test' in *Nicaragua* as the use of force against the Taliban cannot be explained by it).
[99] *Nicaragua* case, at 528, 543 (dissenting opinion of Judge Sir Robert Jennings).
[100] *See* Randelzhofer, *supra* note 6 at 801.
[101] *Nicaragua* case, at 346 (dissenting opinion of Judge Steven Schwebel); *but see* earlier somewhat broader comments: Steven Schwebel, *Eight Report on State Responsibility*, 1980/I Y.B. INT'L L. COMMISSION 192 (. . .Mr. Ago has said that a State could act in self-defence only in response to the action of another State . . . . [I]f it meant that a State was not entitled to act in self-defence to attacks . . . by other entities, [Schwebel] could not agree).

Nonetheless, it is the state actor that will be considered responsible for actions attributed to it. The non-state actor itself cannot trigger self-defense unless it is "effectively controlled" by a state. States that are unable or unwilling to control seem to escape this rule.

In 1992, the United Nations Security Council declared in an unrelated resolution concerning Libya that the prohibition of the use of force by virtue of Article 2 (4) of the Charter obligated states to "refrain from organizing, instigating, assisting or participating in terrorist acts in another State or acquiescing in organized activities within its territory directed toward the commission of such acts, when such acts involve a threat or use of force."[102] While this does not automatically mean that such use of force and breach of Article 2 (4) of the Charter amounts to an armed attack, it does seem to represent a loosened standard of attribution. This approach was considered to have been confirmed by the next relevant decision of an international tribunal.

v) The Tadic Case

In 1994, the International Tribunal for the Former Yugoslavia (ICTY) contributed the *Tadic* Case, which elaborates on the necessary degree of control.[103] The Court had to determine whether there had been "grave breaches of the Geneva Convention" according to Article 2 of the Statute of the ICTY.[104] While the Court rejected the existence of an international conflict, the Appeals chamber disagreed by reevaluating the conditions of attribution between a paramilitary group and a state actor.[105] The decision seems to loosen the "effective control" requirement by denying a predetermined standard to evaluate whether an individual or a group acted as a *de facto* state organ. Generally, state control is deemed to exist according to *Tadic* "when a State has a role in organizing, coordinating or planning the military actions of the military group, in addition to financing, training and equipping and providing operational support to that group."[106] This threshold is arguably lower, however, it does not provide for practical guidelines for failing and ignorant states. And, as later decisions by the ICJ seem to indicate, it is anything but certain that *Tadic* will actually lead to a broader i.e. less control oriented standard.[107]

---

102 S.C. Res. 748, U.N. Doc. S/RES/748 (March 31, 1992).
103 Prosecutor v. Tadic, *The Appeals* (Int'l Tribunal for the Former Yugoslavia), Case No. IT-94-1-A, 38 I.L.M. 1518 (July 15, 1999) (hereinafter *Tadic* case).
104 Statute of the International Criminal Tribunal for the Former Yugoslavia, http://www.un.org/icty/legaldoc-e/index.htm (last visited Dec. 21, 2006); the statute is based upon S.C. Res. 827, U.N. Doc. S/RES/827 (May 25, 1993) and was amended several times.
105 *Tadic* case, at paras. 80 et seq.; *see also* para. 112.
106 *Id.* at para. 137.
107 *See infra* pp. 42, 44; also *see infra* pp. 44 et seq.

vi) THE OIL PLATFORMS CASE

In 2003, the ICJ was concerned with the notion of an armed attack again, as Iran had complained against the United States' destruction of oil platforms off the Iranian shore.[108] The United States had again invoked Article 51 of the Charter in response to the alleged firing of a missile from Iranian territory in 1987 which destroyed a U.S. vessel in Kuwaiti waters, as well as the laying of mines in international waters by Iran.[109] The Court held that the evidence was not sufficient to attribute the firing of the missile to Iran.[110] More importantly, even if the firing and the mine laying were attributable to Iran, an armed attack by Iran would have been rejected: the missile is unlikely to have been programmed at a specific U.S. target; one of the mined ships was not flying U.S. flags; in case of the other one it could not be established that the mines were laid specifically to attack U.S. ships (Iran was at war with Iraq at this time); and finally an alleged shooting from one of the oil platforms was not proved.

The case does not involve non-state actor issues. What it does stipulate relevant to questions surrounding what constitutes an armed attack is the degree of use of force necessary. None of the alleged applications of force amounted to the "most grave" form as required in the *Nicaragua* case.[111] The case does not elaborate a possible accumulation of a series of minor attacks which can in fact be most relevant to states that face a large number of minor terrorist attacks all of which, by themselves, may not be "most grave". Added up, they may very well constitute a significant threat to a state, particularly to a small state.

It was suggested, among other criticism concerning this case,[112] that the ICJ's findings in *Oil Platforms* with regard to the law of self-defense must be considered as *obiter dictum* since they were not necessary to reach the court's decision.[113]

vii) THE ARTICLES ON STATE RESPONSIBILITY

The International Law Commission (ILC) contributed in 2001 the non-binding Articles on State Responsibility for Internationally Wrongful Acts,

---

[108] Case Concerning Oil Platforms (Iran v. U.S.), 2003 I.C.J. 1334 (Nov. 6, 2003) (hereinafter *Oil Platforms* case).
[109] *Id.* at para. 48.
[110] *Id.* at para. 61.
[111] *Id.* at para. 64.
[112] *See, e.g. Oil Platforms* case, separate opinion of Judge Higgins, paras. 8-28; Judge Parra Aranguen, paras. 1-14; Judge Kooijmans, paras. 17-35; Judge Al-Khasawneh, paras. 1-2; Judge Buergenthal, paras. 4-19; Judge Owada, paras. 2-16.
[113] Leopold von Carlowitz, *Interpreting Self-Defense Restrictively: The World Court in the Oil Platforms Case*, 23 SICHERHEIT UND FRIEDEN 79, 82 (2005).

which were eventually "appreciated" by the General Assembly.[114] These propositions are the first attempt to codify state responsibility and, unlike in classic public international legal theory, attribute the conduct of private persons to a state entity, thereby rendering the state responsible.

Beyond a state's responsibility for the acts or omission of its organs (Article 4 Articles on State Responsibility) or its agents (Article 5), it is Article 8 that deals with two further situations: Either, a private individual is instructed by a state, or it carries out conduct under the "direction or control" of a state.[115] Both cases will lead to state responsibility for wrongful acts of that individual. The ILC comments that the latter "principle does not extend to conduct which was only incidentally or peripherally associated with an operation and which escaped from the State's direction or control."[116] Article 8 is insofar the product of the amalgamated *Nicaragua* and *Tadic* cases.[117] It will not help in solving issues arising from failing states, unable to exercise any control, or with state actors that prefer not to interfere with a non-state actor's actions emanating from its territory for whatever reason. Furthermore, as can been seen in the latest decision by the ICJ,[118] also in cases of perfectly functioning state entities, Article 8 is to be interpreted narrowly along the lines of *Nicaragua*, leaving not much of a leeway for state responsibility prior to "effective control".

Article 9 of the Articles on State Responsibility [119] seeks to provide with rules for revolutions or when a government is overthrown. The Iranian Revolutionary Guards during the 1979 revolution are mentioned as one example the drafters envisioned.[120] The rule stipulates three cumulative conditions: the act was in exercise of governmental authority; while the latter is default or absent; and the situation calls for such action.

---

[114] G.A. Res. 56/83, U.N. Doc. A/RES/56/83 (Jan. 28, 2002).

[115] INTERNATIONAL LAW COMMISSION, DRAFT ARTICLES ON RESPONSIBILITY OF STATES FOR INTERNATIONALLY WRONGFUL ACTS WITH COMMENTARIES 103, 104 (2001), *available at* http://untreaty.un.org/ilc/texts/instruments/english/commentaries/9_6_2001.pdf (last visited March 10, 2006) (hereinafter *Articles on State Responsibility*); Article 8 provides: "The conduct of a person or group of persons shall be considered an act of a State under international law if the person or group of persons is in fact acting on the instructions of, or under the direction or control of, that State in carrying out the conduct."

[116] *Articles on State Responsibility*, at 104.

[117] *Id.* at 105-07.

[118] *See infra* pp. 44 et seq.

[119] Article 9 provides: "The conduct of a person or group of persons shall be considered an act of a State under international law if the person or group of persons is in fact exercising elements of the governmental authority in the absence or default of the official authorities and in circumstances such as to call for the exercise of those elements of authority."

[120] *Articles on State Responsibility*, at 109-10.

Again, given the frequent scenarios in which there is either a weak or ignorant government (but there is one) this provision will not necessarily have any effect. It seems problematic to apply Article 9 in cases of non-state actors waging terrorist war from the territory of a defunct home state, primarily because of the final requirement i.e. that actions by other than governmental authorities are called for.[121] It means that some "exercise of governmental functions was called for, though not necessarily the conduct in question."[122]

Firstly, the rule does not apply in cases of ignorant, but basically functioning, governments. Secondly, terrorist acts are hardly ever "called for" as they will not be an "attempt to exercise police or other functions" in absence of a regular government.[123] Thirdly, it is hard to imagine that the rule means that *any* act is to be attributed to the defunct state actor only because the private non-state actor assumed a task that would otherwise have fallen into a government's responsibility. For instance, if Hezbollah finances a kindergarten in absence of a functioning Lebanese child care program, does that mean that its cross-border rocket launchings are to be attributed to the state of Lebanon? If that was correct, the rule would collide with the limits of the *ultra vires* provision in Article 7.[124] Quite obviously, waging a terrorist attack would exceed a government's legal capabilities. Whatever organ, e.g. a regular army commander, commits terror against others states would hence be acting beyond its authority. Such *ultra vires* acts cannot be attributed to the state if its actions are "so removed from the scope of" an organ's official functions "that it should be assimilated to that of private individuals."[125] While terrorist conduct would probably not be too remote from the usual responsibilities of an army commander, it would be very different from the ordinary responsibility of a teacher, for instance. Returning to the Hezbollah-kindergarten: assuming that by acquiring the state's duty in the child care sector, Hezbollah has now voluntarily taken over governmental authority that was called for. However, it would be quite adventurous to argue that the terrorist entity has now assumed a position in which it is clearly acting on behalf of Lebanon when it fires rockets into other countries. Such an exercise of – *ultra vires* – authority would be extremely removed from child care issues and can thus hardly be covered.

---

[121] *But see* Ruys, Verhoeven, *supra* note 37 at 318, 319.
[122] *Articles on State Responsibility*, at 111.
[123] *Id.* at 111.
[124] Article 7 provides: "The conduct of an organ of a State or of a person or entity empowered to exercise elements of the governmental authority shall be considered an act of the State under international law if the organ, person or entity acts in that capacity, even if it exceeds its authority or contravenes instructions."
[125] *Articles on State Responsibility*, at 102.

Of further interest is Article 10 (1), (2) of the Articles on State Responsibility:[126] It warrants that "insurrectional movements" will render a state responsible if they indeed form the new government, or if they establish a new state on parts of a previous one. With regard to terrorist movements, two major problems prevent the application of this article: one is, (international) terrorists aiming to fight third (victim) states are not insurrectional movements with regard to their host state – they can be, but must not. More importantly, as the ILC notes, the movement must be successful. Acts prior to their success are merely private unless further circumstances kick in, such as Article 9 of the Articles on State Responsibility.[127]

Article 11 of the Articles on State Responsibility also does not lead too far:[128] private conduct can become state conduct if the state endorses it at a later point in time. Failing regimes cannot act at all or endorse anything, while ignorant or silently supportive regimes are very unlikely to admit their support. That is, after all, the reason why they often chose to use a non-state actor rather than sending its army or secret service directly – it is easier to deny.

By and large, the effect of the ILC Articles on State Responsibility on situations involving terrorist non-state actors will be very limited. The Articles on State Responsibility provide for high thresholds and seem not to have been envisioned to render state actors responsible for non-state actors such as Al Qaeda or Hezbollah. Additionally, the concept of state responsibility as laid out in the ILC Articles on State Responsibility does not provide adequately for failed states.[129] The absence of governmental authority as primary characteristic of failed states[130] entails a lack of responsibility for misconduct which ultimately means that "international responsibility, a cornerstone of stability of the international system as whole is nonexistent in a failed State situation."[131]

---

[126] Article 10 (1) provides: "The conduct of an insurrectional movement which becomes the new government of a State shall be considered an act of that State under international law"; Article 10 (2) provides: "The conduct of a movement, insurrectional or other, which succeeds in establishing a new State in part of the territory of a pre-existing State or in a territory under its administration shall be considered an act of the new State under international."

[127] *Articles on State Responsibility*, at 112.

[128] Article 11 provides: "Conduct which is not attributable to a State under the preceding articles shall nevertheless be considered an act of that State under international law if and to the extent that the State acknowledges and adopts the conduct in question as its own."

[129] SCHOLZ, *supra* note 34 at 52-55.

[130] *See* Geiss *supra* note 3 at 461.

[131] *Id.* at 484.

viii) The Congo Case

The Articles on State Responsibility were applied in the *Congo* case. This case is the first contentious case involving non-state actor issues after the events of September 11, 2001, and the subsequent military actions against the Taliban and Al Qaeda.[132]

The Democratic Republic of the Congo (DRC) accused the Republic of Uganda (Uganda) of various flagrant human rights violations. One of its three claims blamed Uganda for "actively extending military, logistic, economic and financial support to irregular forces operating" in the DRC, violating, among other provisions, Article 2 (4) of the Charter.[133] In return, Uganda accused the DRC of having breached Article 2 (4) by supporting irregular forces operating from the territory of the DRC and invoked self-defense to justify interventions on Congolese territory to fight such groups.[134]

The history underlying this conflict is complex and involves more parties than just the DRC and Uganda.[135] Crucial is the initially very close relationship between the Congolese President Kabila with the government of Uganda. As a consequence thereof, Ugandan forces had operated on Congolese territory with the consent of the DRC's government to fight anti-Ugandan militias.[136] The relations between the DRC and Uganda deteriorated, and at least after August 1998 the presence of Ugandan forces on Congolese territory was no longer warranted by consent of the DRC,[137] particularly because Ugandan actions went beyond what both states had initially agreed upon.[138]

Initially, the Court had to determine whether the cross-border actions of a Congolese anti-Ugandan militia, the Allied Democratic Forces (ADF), allowed for the invocation of self-defense by Uganda to justify its continued presence on

---

[132] *See infra* pp. 152 et seq.

[133] *Congo* case, at 16.

[134] *Id.* at para. 43.

[135] In fact, the DRC had also filed claims against Burundi (but withdrew it) and Rwanda. The latter was eventually dismissed by the ICJ on the grounds of lacking jurisdiction; *see* Case Concerning Armed Activities on the Territory of the Congo (New Application 2002) (Dem. Rep. Congo v. Rwanda), para. 126, February 3, 2006, *available at* http://www.icj-cij.org (last visited July 16, 2007).

[136] *Congo* case, at para. 45.

[137] *Id.* at paras. 53, 105-06.

[138] *Id.* at paras. 110, 111 ("Uganda was not in August 1998 engaging in military operations against rebels who carried out cross-border raids. Rather, it was engaged in military assaults that resulted in the taking of the town of Beni and its airfield between 7 and 8 August, followed by the taking of the town of Bunia and its airport on 13 August, and the town of Watsa and its airport at a date between 24 and 29 August").

DRC territory. The DRC asserted that such cross-border attacks took place but regarded the ADF as solely responsible.[139] The Court stated:

> It is further to be noted that, while Uganda claimed to have acted in self-defence, it did not ever claim that it had been subjected to an armed attack by the armed forces of the DRC. The "armed attacks" to which reference was made came rather from the ADF. [T]here is no satisfactory proof of the involvement in these attacks, direct or indirect, of the Government of the DRC. The attacks did not emanate from armed bands or irregulars sent by the DRC or on behalf of the DRC, within the sense of Article 3 (g) of General Assembly resolution 3314 (XXIX) on the definition of aggression . . . [of] 1974.
>
> The Court is of the view that . . . even if this series of deplorable attacks could be regarded as cumulative in character, they still remained non-attributable to the DRC.[140]

With this, the Court "implicitly rejects Uganda's argument that mere tolerance of irregulars 'creates a susceptibility to action in self-defence by neighbouring States'" as Judge Kooijmans noted in his separate opinion.[141]

The DRC claimed in return that Uganda would be violating Congolese sovereignty through another militia, the Congo Liberation Movement (Mouvement de libération du Congo, MLC). The Court held that Uganda did not have sufficient control over the direct actions of the MLC: they do not amount to actions of "an organ" of Uganda (Article 4 Articles on State Responsibility), the MLC was not acting on behalf of the Ugandan government (Article 5), and did not act "on the instructions of, or under the direction or control of" Uganda (Article 8).[142] Furthermore, the Court held that "even if the evidence does not suggest that the MLC's conduct is attributable to Uganda, the training and military support given by Uganda to the ALC, the military wing of the MLC, violates certain obligations of international law."[143] Among them "a grave violation of the prohibition on the use of force expressed in Article 2, paragraph 4, of the Charter."[144] Consequently, the Court held

---

139 *Id.* at para. 133.
140 *Id.* at para. 146.
141 *Congo* case, separate opinion of Judge Kooijmans, at para. 22, *available at* http://www.icj-cij.org (last visited July 16, 2007) (hereinafter *Congo case* Kooijmans).
142 *Congo* case, at para. 160.
143 *Id.* at para. 161.
144 *Id.* at para. 165.

> [b]y sixteen votes to one, [f]inds that [Uganda], by engaging in military activities against the [DRC] on the latter's territory, by occupying [the] Ituri [district] and by actively extending military, logistic, economic and financial support to irregular forces having operated on the territory of the DRC, violated the principle of non-use of force in international relations and the principle of non-intervention.[145]

Once again, the Court did not depart from the scheme of only state actors being capable of launching an armed attack. Non-state actors will only be considered if their actions can be attributed to a state actor successfully. And once again the standard of attribution seems to be nothing less than the "effective control" threshold as announced in *Nicaragua*, and not even a slightly broader version thereof as one might have expected in the light of the ICTY's *Tadic* decision. However, the Court did not elaborate any further on the details of the necessary degree of control over "armed bands" explicitly. It appears as if only Uganda's and the DRC's conduct was regarded to be relevant, but not the conduct of perhaps equally responsible non-state actors different from the parties to the conflict.[146] The Court missed a good opportunity to clarify and update issues such as attribution and non-state actor's responsibility, as Judge Kooijmans observed.[147] Judge Simma, in his separate opinion, noted that the question if the actions by the anti-Ugandan militias could have been responded to in self-defense, regardless of whether they are attributable to the DRC or not, was not answered.[148] He went on, referring to the Court's "succinct" decision in the *Advisory Opinion*, that such a narrow interpretation of Article 51 of the Charter may have been warranted a long time ago, but given the changes in state practice and *opinio iuris* "ought urgently to be reconsidered."[149]

ix) THE BOSNIA CASE

In February 2007, the ICJ decided the Case Concerning the Application of the Convention on the Prevention and Punishment of the Crime of Genocide[150] between Bosnia and Herzegovina as Applicants, and Serbia and Montenegro as

---

[145] *Id.* at 101.
[146] *Id.* at 147.
[147] *Congo case* Kooijmans, at para. 25; *see* also *supra* note 98.
[148] *Congo* case, separate opinion of Judge Simma, at para. 7, *available at* http://www.icj-cij.org (last visited July 16, 2007) (hereinafter *Congo case* Simma).
[149] *Congo case* Simma, at para 11.
[150] Convention on the Prevention and Punishment of the Crime of Genocide, Dec. 9, 1948, 78 U.N.T.S. 277 (hereinafter: Genocide Convention).

Respondents.[151] The case focused on the question if Serbia and Montenegro, in continuity of the Federal Republic of Yugoslavia (FRY), had actively committed genocide or at least failed to prevent acts of genocide – predominately in the course of the Srebrenica massacres of 1995 – and thereby breached its international obligations arising under the Genocide Convention.[152] The Court eventually came to the conclusion that Serbia and Montenegro had in fact violated its international obligations by failing to prevent and punish the acts of genocide that occurred in Srebrenica.[153] Serbia and Montenegro could not be held responsible for having actively committed genocide[154] or having actively engaged in acts of complicity therein.[155]

In order to establish the Respondent's full responsibility for active genocide, the Applicants would have needed to establish that the atrocities could be successfully equated with or attributed to the FRY. However, the Court found that no regular Yugoslav troops or similar immediate organs of the FRY were directly involved in the killings.[156] Accordingly, it needed to be evaluated if the conduct of further entities more loosely associated with the FRY could entail immediate Yugoslav responsibility. Relevant non-state actors were the internationally not recognized "Republica Srpska" and its "Bosnian Serb Army" (VRS) both of which had emerged on the territory of Bosnia and Herzegovina.[157] Furthermore, a number of Serbian militias had been participating in atrocities during the Yugoslav civil war,[158] among them for instance the "Scorpions" which allegedly were controlled directly by Serbian General Ratko Mladić.[159]

First, the Court needed to determine if either of the above entities constituted a *de jure* or, alternatively, at least a *de facto* organ of the FRY hence triggering Respondent's responsibility for the atrocities committed.[160] The Court decided this question based upon the customary international law of state responsibility as "reflected in Article 4 of the ILC Articles on State Responsibility."[161] Formally, domestic Yugoslav law did not indicate that either of the rele-

---

[151] Case Concerning the Application of the Genocide Convention on the Prevention and Punishment of the Crime of Genocide (Bosn. & Herz. v. Serb. & Mont.) Feb. 27, 2007, *available at* http://www.icj-cij.org (last visited July 16, 2007) (hereinafter *Bosnia* case).
[152] *Bosnia* case, at paras. 142 et seq.
[153] *Id.* at para. 450.
[154] *Id.* at para. 415.
[155] *Id.* at para. 424.
[156] *Id.* at para. 386.
[157] *Id.* at para. 233.
[158] *Id.* at para. 289.
[159] *Id.* at para. 395.
[160] *Id.* at paras. 385-95.
[161] *Id.* at para. 385.

vant entities had obtained any regular status as a FRY organ. Although "[t]here is no doubt that the FRY was providing substantial support, inter alia, financial support, to the Republica Srpska . . . this did not automatically make them organs of the FRY"[162] in absence of the "Republica's" *de jure* organ quality. The same applied to the "Scorpions" militia.[163]

The Court therefore turned to the question if either of the relevant entities could have been acting as *de facto* organs of the FRY. This would have been the case if they had acted in "complete dependence" on the state,[164] according to the Court's test as developed in *Nicaragua*.[165] Again, the Court answered the question in the negative for there was no factual indication that either of the relevant groups had previously acted as mere FRY instruments, completely depending on the Yugoslav state.[166]

Consequently, the Court needed to turn to Article 8 of the Articles on State Responsibility to evaluate if perhaps the FRY's responsibility arose from the conduct of "persons who, though not having the status of organs of the Respondent, nevertheless acted on its instructions or under its direction or control."[167] The Court made clear that the relevant standard in order to determine the necessary degree of affiliation between a non-state actor and a state was once again *Nicaragua*'s "effective control" test.[168] Unlike on prior occasions, the Court also continued to comment on a potential alternative standard to determine a state's responsibility for non-state/non-organs, namely the ICTY's "overall control" test developed in the *Tadic* case.[169] In *Tadic*, the ICTY had to determine if the VRS was in fact directed by the Yugoslav army, thereby rendering the conflict an international one. The Appeals Chamber finally answered this question in the affirmative.[170] The Chamber based its evaluations upon the

---

[162] *Id.* at para. 388.
[163] *Id.* at para. 389.
[164] *Id.* at paras. 391-92.
[165] The ICJ refers insofar to para. 109 of the *Nicaragua* case which reads in part: "What the Court has to determine at this point is whether or not the relationship of the contras to the United States Government was so much one of dependence on the one side and control on the other that it would be right to equate the contras, for legal purposes, with an organ of the United States Government, or as acting on behalf of that Government." This is test is not to be confused with the "effective control" standard, *see infra* note 168.
[166] *Bosnia* case, at paras. 394-95.
[167] *Id.* at paras. 396-415.
[168] *Id.* at para. 399; the Court added that the necessary "effective control" by a state over a non-state needs to be present with regard to each singular act of genocide and not merely "in relation to the whole body of operations", *see* id. at para. 401.
[169] *Id.* at paras. 403-07.
[170] *Tadic* case, at para. 147; *see* also *supra* at pp. 37 et seq.

"overall control" standard, rather than the "effective control" test.[171] The ICJ in *Bosnia* clearly rejected the former standard *in casu* as stretching "too far, almost to breaking point, the connection which must exist between the conduct of a State's organs and its international responsibility."[172] However, the ICJ went on to suggest a potentially available field of application for the *Tadic* test: "[i]nsofar as the 'overall control' test is employed to determine whether or not an armed conflict is international, which was the sole question which the [ICTY] Appeals Chamber was called upon to decide, it may well be that the test is applicable and suitable . . . ."[173] The Court continued that

> the degree and nature of a State's involvement in an armed conflict on another State's territory which is required for the conflict to be characterized as international, can very well, and without logical inconsistency, differ from the degree and nature of involvement required to give rise to that State's responsibility for a specific act committed in the course of the conflict.[174]

While for the latter the "overall control" test "has the major drawback of broadening the scope of State responsibility well beyond the fundamental principle governing the law of international responsibility",[175] it appears as if the ICJ would in fact accept an application of either standard to determine if a conflict was international in nature. On the other hand, the Court makes crystal clear that for the entities that are neither *de jure* nor *de facto* organs of a state, such as the non-state entities that will be in the focus of this work, the "effective control" standard remains determinative. Whenever Article 8 of the Articles on State Responsibility is to be interpreted to establish the international responsibility of a state for a non-state actor, *Nicaragua* rules unaltered: "[i]n this regard the 'overall control' test is unsuitable . . . .", as the Court notes.[176]

While the *Tadic* test may be capable to determine if an armed conflict is of an international or non-international character, it will, according to the Court, fail to establish a nexus between a state and a non-state actor. Insofar, also *Bosnia* confirms *Nicaragua*.

---

[171] *Tadic* case, at paras 115-45.
[172] *Bosnia* case, at para. 406.
[173] *Id.* at para. 404.
[174] *Id.* at para. 405.
[175] *Id.* at para. 406.
[176] *Id.*

c) CONCLUSION

As it stands, the *Congo* case is the last immediate example that states are largely left alone vis-à-vis non-state actors operating short of effective control by a state: a state may have been exposed to force that is just grave enough to amount to an armed attack as required by Article 51 of the Charter. However, as the origin of such force is merely an entity that might be equally powerful and militarily equipped as regular state forces but is no state itself, the victim state is deprived of its right to self-defense. In *Bosnia*, the Court paved the way for a slightly alternative and perhaps somewhat broader standard. However, the "overall control" test from *Tadic* will not alter the Court's interpretation of Article 8 of the Articles of State Responsibility. Whenever states act through armed non-state actors, the latter will only render the former responsible if the "effective control" standard can be satisfied. The legal framework as it was interpreted over the past 50 years by international courts does not adequately provide for the increasing importance, and hence danger, that originates from non-state actors. The "effective control" standard as it was developed in *Nicaragua* and upheld most recently in *Congo* and *Bosnia* assumes an outdated relationship between states and non-state actors. It remains to be shown whether state practice condoned such a legal framework.

2. EXISTING CATEGORIES

As this work will show, quite a number of members of the international community of states had to respond to the use of force by non-state actors. These groups fell short of being states themselves as they failed to satisfy one or more of the criteria determining statehood. The common definition of "states" follows the 1933 Montevideo Convention and comprises of four elements, namely a permanent population, a defined territory, a government, and the capacity to enter into relations with other states.[177] Beyond that, further internationally relevant actors are assigned different international legal rights and obligations. Among these are international organizations, non-governmental organizations, liberations movements, and insurgents and others.[178] Inferentially, one can hold that either of the latter is a non-state entity simply by falling short of being a state, for different reasons. These entities become 'actors' for the purposes of international law if they engage in relations vis-à-vis other subjects of international law. Potentially, each of them could, due to their international rele-

---

[177] *See supra* note 2.

[178] For an overview *see, e.g.*, BROWNLIE, *supra* note 60 at 58-67; ANTONIO CASSESE, INTERNATIONAL LAW 71-80, 124-150 (2nd. ed. 2005); PETER MALANCZUK, AKEHURTS'S MODERN INTRODUCTION TO INTERNATIONAL LAW 91-108 (7th ed. 1997).

vance, be one of the terrorist non-state actors as dealt with in this work. Of course, international organizations or non-governmental organizations are hardly entities that would normally be linked to international terror, at least not as immediate perpetrators. Undoubtedly, however, both of them are universally accepted as internationally relevant non-state entities with certain rights and obligations vis-à-vis states. But there are cases in which a categorization in international/non-international and state/non-state entity is not quite as obvious.

For the purposes of this work the primary example of such a problematic distinction is a case in which a particular group is allegedly responsible for terrorist acts but commands limited international relevance. Some will usually argue that this group's actions are of a merely domestic relevance, while others consider international affairs beyond national borders affected. When does a national terror group such as for instance the German Rote Armee Fraktion (RAF) reach the status of an internationally relevant non-state actor and a potential target of armed defensive force? It is relevant to establish conditions that ought to be met in order for a terrorist group or faction to be recognized for the purpose of Article 51 of the Charter. If that is the case, the legal consequences affect both the legal tools available against the non-state actor as well as the treatment of its individual members.

The latter has been subject to cases surrounding some of the detainees in the course of Operation Enduring Freedom.[179] However, individual criminal responsibility in the context of an armed conflict, which in modern times began with the Nuremberg trials,[180] as opposed to domestic criminal law enforcement are issues that differ significantly from the capability of a private group to constitute a legitimate target of responsive military armed force in self-defense. The former concerns issues of international criminal law and hence the individual responsibility of natural persons. The latter is regulated by the laws of armed conflict and addresses the rights and obligations of states and others as subjects of public international law. In order to leave international or merely domestic criminal law enforcement behind, it needs to be evaluated as to what are the re-

---

[179] *See, e.g.*, Hamdan v. Rumsfeld, 548 U.S. 1, 62, 69 (2006) (in this decision, a Yemenite Al Qaeda operative, Hamdan, who was captured in Afghanistan and turned over to U.S. forces, was eventually detained in Guantanamo Bay, Cuba, and charged with conspiracy by a U.S. Military Commission. The U.S. Supreme Court held that "Common Article 3 [of the Geneva Conventions]. . . is applicable here and . . . requires that Hamdan be tried by a 'regularly constituted court affording all the judicial guarantees which are recognized as indispensable by civilized peoples.'" As the U.S. Military Commissions fail to meet that standard, the majority in *Hamdan* decided that "[t]he procedures adopted to try Hamdan . . . violate the Geneva Conventions".

[180] *Cf.* CASSESE, *supra* note 178 at 144, 145.

quirements for armed private groups to rise to the level of a non-state actor, potentially capable of launching armed attacks as required by Article 51 of the Charter.

a) "TERRORISTS"

Looking at non-state actors' primary fields of operation, international terrorism is undoubtedly one of them. Ever since the rise of international political terrorism in the 1960s and 70s, armed groups of varying size, strength, and motivation which operate between two or even more states has continued to evolve. They attacked a number of different targets, most often aiming to fight an individual state or regime. One of the tools that states employed to combat international terrorism has been international law. Accordingly, a vast number of international treaties seek to master at least some of the problems and dangers that are exposed by international terrorist threats. And yet: "terrorists" is by no means a category that would – legally – play a role with regard to the area of international self-defense.

One of the immediate uncertainties each treaty drafting process has to deal with is how "terrorism" and hence "terrorists" ought to be defined, a debate which reveals political rather than legal obstacles. One finds a tremendous array of different general international[181] as well as regional[182] treaties combating ter-

[181] *See, e.g.*, the Convention of Offences and Certain Other Acts Committed on Board Aircraft, Sept. 14, 1963, 704 U.N.T.S. 219; the Convention for the Suppression of Unlawful Seizure of Aircraft, Dec. 16, 1970, 860 U.N.T.S. 105; the Convention for the Suppression of Unlawful Acts against the Safety if Civil Aviation, Sept. 23, 1971, 974 U.N.T.S. 177 (hereinafter Civil Aviation Convention); the Convention on the Prevention and Punishment of Crimes Against Internationally Protected Persons, Dec. 14, 1973, 1035 U.N.T.S. 167; the International Convention against the Taking of Hostages, Dec. 17, 1979, 1316 U.N.T.S. 205 (hereinafter Hostages Convention); the Convention on the Physical Protection of Nuclear Material, March 3, 1980, 1456 U.N.T.S. 101; the Protocol for the Suppression of Unlawful Acts of Violence at Airports Serving International Civil Aviation, supplementary to the Convention for the Suppression of Unlawful Acts against the Safety of Civil Aviation, Feb. 24, 1988, 27 I.L.M. 627; the Convention for the Suppression of Unlawful Acts against the Safety of Maritime Navigation, March 10, 1988, 1678 U.N.T.S. 221 (hereinafter: Maritime Convention); the Protocol for the Suppression of Unlawful Acts Against the Safety of Fixed Platforms Located on the Continental Shelf, March 10, 1988, 1678 U.N.T.S. 304; the Convention on the Marking of Plastic Explosives for the Purpose of Detection, March 1, 1991, 30 I.L.M. 721; the International Convention for the Suppression of Terrorist Bombings, Dec. 15, 1997, U.N. Doc. A/RES/52/164 (Jan 9, 1998); the International Convention for the Suppression of the Financing of Terrorism, Dec. 9, 1999, U.N. Doc. A/RES/54/109 (Feb. 25, 2000); the International Convention for the Suppression of Acts of Nuclear Terrorism, *opened for signature* Sept. 14, 2005, U.N. Doc. A/RES/59/290 (Apr. 15, 2005).

rorism. Among the latter there is, for instance, the European Convention on the Suppression of Terrorism which defines terrorism along the lines of the methods employed, irrespective of a perpetrator's motives.[183] And also the non-regional general conventions follow this neutral, method-based approach.[184] While only few of them do in fact contain a definition of what constitutes "terrorism",[185] none lays out who might be a terrorist non-state actor. Beside treaty law, also the

---

Terrorism/Conv18.pdf (last visited Apr. 11, 2007); Organization of the Islamic Conference, Convention of the Organization of the Islamic Conference on Combating International Terrorism, July 1, 1999, available at http://www.oic-un.org/26icfm/c.html (last visited Apr. 11, 2007) (hereinafter O.I.C. Terror Convention); the Organization of American States, Inter-American Convention Against Terrorism, June 3, 2002, 42 I.L.M. 19 (2003).

183 European Convention on the Suppression of Terrorism, art. I, Nov. 10, 1976, Europ. T.S. No. 90 (Art. I states in part that the Convention covers, *inter alia*, all offences "involving the use of a bomb, grenade, rocket, automatic firearm, or letter or parcel bomb if this use endangers persons").

184 *See, e.g.*, the Civil Aviation Convention (art. I defines that "any person commits an offence if he unlawfully and intentionally: (a) performs an act of violence against a person on board an aircraft in flight if that act is likely to endanger the safety of that aircraft; or" commits similar acts, without further references to motivation or affiliation of the perpetrator; Hostages Convention (art. I (1) similarly plainly states that "[a]ny person who seizes or detains and threatens to kill, to injure or to continue to detain another person . . . in order to compel a third party . . ., to do or abstain from doing any act as an explicit or implicit condition for the release of the hostage commits the offence of taking of hostages . . . ."); Maritime Convention (art. 3 makes it an criminal offence for a person to seize or exercise control over a ship by force, threat, or intimidation; to perform an act of violence against a person on board a ship if that act is likely to endanger the safe navigation of the ship; to place a destructive device or substance aboard a ship; and other acts against the safety of ships.); in each of these convention the offences described ought to be incorporated into a state's domestic criminal law. They do not have any relevance between subjects of international law with regard to the material content of the offences.

185 The O.I.C. Terror Convention provides in its article I (2) with a broad attempt to define terrorist crimes: "'Terrorism' means any act of violence or threat thereof notwithstanding its motives or intentions perpetrated to carry out an individual or collective criminal plan with the aim of terrorizing people or threatening to harm them or imperiling their lives, honour, freedoms, security or rights or exposing the environment or any facility or public or private property to hazards or occupying or seizing them, or endangering a national resource, or international facilities, or threatening the stability, territorial integrity, political unity or sovereignty of independent States"; otherwise the League of Nations attempted to draft a uniform convention against terrorism, the Convention for the Prevention and Punishment of Terrorism which was adopted in Nov. 1937. Although it had been ratified by 21 states in 1938, *see* The League of Nations, *Hundertste Tagung des Völkerbundrates*, 18 MONATSBERICHTE ÜBER DIE TÄTIGKEIT DES VÖLKERBUNDES 23 (1938), it never came into force.

United Nations[186] as well as particularly the United Nations Security Council[187] contributed to the internationally relevant norms fighting international terrorism.

Incoherency and gaps in the law dealing with terrorism is, after all, a phenomenon not limited to international law exclusively.[188] However, for the purposes of combating the effects of terrorism along the lines of its ordinary criminal content, a proper definition is not necessary. Focusing on the actual elements of the *actus reus* is perfectly sufficient to cover all individual aspects usually occurring in the course of terrorist related crimes.[189]

Consequently, all international agreements grappling with terror aim into a direction incongruent with the laws of armed conflicts. The conventions' goal is to make terrorism a punishable offense, be it under domestic or international law. While the addressees of each of the conventions are states – ordering them to amend domestic legislation – none of the treaties addresses a state's rights and obligations vis-à-vis non-individual perpetrators, such as violent non-state

---

[186] *See, e.g.*, Statement by the U.N. Comm. on the Elimination of Racial Discrimination, U.N. Doc. A/57/18 (March 8, 2002) (affirming that all acts of terrorism are violations of the Charter and human rights treaties); also the General Assembly continuously condemned terrorism in all its forms, *see e.g.*, G.A. Res. 48/122, U.N. Doc. A/RES/48/122 (Dec. 20, 1993); G.A. Res. 49/185, U.N. Doc. A/RES/49/185 (March 6, 1995); G.A. Res. 50/186, U.N. Doc. A/RES/50/186 (March 6, 1996); G.A. Res. 52/133, U.N. Doc. A/RES/52/133 (Feb. 27, 1998).

[187] the United Nations Security Council issued S.C. Res. 1566, U.N. Doc. S/RES/1566 (Oct. 8, 2004), which recalled "that criminal acts, including against civilians, committed with the intent to cause death or serious bodily injury, or taking of hostages, with the purpose to provoke a state of terror in the general public or in a group of persons or particular persons, intimidate a population or compel a government or an international organization to do or to abstain from doing any act, which constitute offences within the scope of and as defined in the international conventions and protocols relating to terrorism, are under no circumstances justifiable by considerations of a political, philosophical, ideological, racial, ethnic, religious or other similar nature, and calls upon all States to prevent such acts and, if not prevented, to ensure that such acts are punished by penalties consistent with their grave nature"; this attempt to work towards a general definition of terrorism was endorsed by the United Nations General Assembly, *see* U.N. Doc. A/59/565 (Dec. 2, 2004). The report subsequent to the Millennium Summit noted the "inability of [U.N.] Member States to agree on an anti-terrorism convention including a definition of terrorism" and "welcome[d] the recent passage of Security Council resolution 1566 (2004)"; for an overview over the Security Council's actions against terrorism *see* http://www.un.org/terrorism/securitycouncil.html (last visited Apr. 11, 2007).

[188] While, for instance, the U.S. Criminal Code devotes an entire chapter to specific terrorist offences, *see* 18 U.S.C., pt. I, c. 113B, §§ 2331-2339C, U.S. federal law meanwhile knows in total 22 different definitions of terrorism; *see* Nicholas J. Perry, *The Numerous Federal Definitions of Terrorism: The Problem of Too Many Grails*, 30 J. LEGIS. 249 (2004).

[189] *See, e.g.*, Robert A. Friedlander, *Terrorism*, 4 ENCYCLOPEDIA OF PUBLIC INTERNATIONAL LAW 846 (Rudolf Bernhardt ed., 2000).

entities. These treaties do not contribute to the solution of issues that arise under the laws of armed conflict, at least not regarding aspects in the area of the *ius ad bellum*. The group of subjects of international law relevant to the laws of armed conflict is therefore not extended by virtue of either of the above agreements.

There are few further traditional examples for military responses against attacks by private groups.[190] These include pirates, mercenaries, and insurgents or liberation movements.

b) PIRATES

Traditionally, piracy was defined as and limited to any unauthorized act of violence committed by a private vessel on the high seas against another vessel with the intent to plunder (*animo furendi*).[191] However, also other situations were customarily considered as piracy such as if only one vessel was involved (and the crew plundered it itself) or the perpetrator's intention was not to plunder but to murder.[192] The 1958 Geneva Conventions on the High Seas[193] and the 1982 United Nations Convention on the Law of the Sea[194] define piracy in their Articles 15 and 101 identically as consisting of any of the following acts:

> (a) any illegal acts of violence or detention, or any act of depredation, committed for private ends by the crew or the passengers of a private ship or a private aircraft, and directed: (i) on the high seas, against another ship or aircraft, or against persons or property on board such ship or aircraft; (ii) against a ship, aircraft, persons or property in a place outside the jurisdiction of any State; (b) any act of voluntary participation in the operation of a ship or of an aircraft with knowledge of facts making it a pirate ship or aircraft; (c) any act of inciting or of intentionally facilitating an act described in subparagraph (a) or (b).

This definition, mainly following the Draft Convention on Piracy prepared by the Harvard Research in International Law[195] and the Comment to the Draft,[196] excludes the subjective requirement of an *animo furendi*. Hatred is just as much

---

[190] For the perhaps most famous case, the *Caroline* incident, *see supra* pp. 28 to 30.
[191] JENNINGS, WATTS *supra* note 64 at 746.
[192] Malvina Halberstam, *Terrorism on the High Seas: Achille Lauro, Piracy and the IMO Convention on Maritime Safety*, 82 AM. J. INT'L. L. 269, 273 (1988).
[193] Geneva Convention on the High Seas art. 15, Apr. 29, 1958, 450 U.N.T.S. 82.
[194] United Nations Convention on the Law of the Sea art. 101, Dec. 10, 1982, 1834 U.N.T.S. 1994.
[195] Harvard Research in International Law, *Part 4 Piracy*, 26 AM. J. INT'L L. SUPP. 739-1013 (1932).
[196] Halberstam, *supra* note 192 at 277.

a sufficient motivation for committing piracy as is revenge or lust for gain.[197] The limit is insofar set by the term "private ends". A terrorist is usually motivated by political, religious, or social convictions and motives and does thus not primarily act based upon "private ends" but rather those of a larger group or entity. The Harvard Comment explicitly notes that

> [i]t may be thought advisable to exclude from the common jurisdiction certain doubtful phases of traditional piracy which can now be left satisfactorily to the ordinary jurisdiction of a state . . . . Therefore the draft convention excludes from its definition of piracy all cases of wrongful attacks on persons or property for political ends, whether they are made on behalf of states, or of recognized belligerent organizations, or of unrecognized revolutionary bands.[198]

While that did not exclude terrorists insofar as they still may be motivated less by political conviction but simply by hatred,[199] it was more of an ambiguous definition with regard to terrorist acts than the 1988 International Convention for the Suppression of Unlawful Acts Against the Safety of Maritime Navigation[200] which obliges the signatories to prosecute all forceful or potentially forceful acts endangering maritime safety, regardless of the perpetrators' motivation. And also piracy *iure gentium* as a peremptory norm of public international law creates a duty for each state to prosecute individuals guilty thereof.[201]

As can be seen, however, the legal boundaries of piracy point into a different direction. A legal classification aiming at the creation of state jurisdiction and the possibility of individual prosecution and law enforcement hardly contributes to a state's right to defend itself against a pirate's "armed attack" by the use of armed force. Piracy as a crime was meant to regulate private criminal actions outside the sovereignty and jurisdiction of states.[202] Self-defense as a concept on the other hand is necessary to legitimize the infringement of a state's sovereignty which otherwise is prohibited by virtue of Article 2 of the Charter.

---

[197] JENNINGS, WATTS, *supra* note 64 at 752.
[198] Harvard Research in International Law, *supra* note 195 at 786.
[199] Halberstam, *supra* note 192 at 282.
[200] International Convention for the Suppression of Unlawful Acts Against the Safety of Maritime Navigation art. 3, March 10, 1988, 1678 U.N.T.S. 221; Article 3 provides in part: "(1) Any person commits an offence if that person unlawfully and intentionally: (a) seized or exercises control over a ship by force or threat thereof or any other form of intimidation; or (b) performs any act of violence against a person on board a ship if that act is likely to endanger safe navigation of that ship; . . . ."
[201] STEFAN KADELBACH, ZWINGENDES VÖLKERRECHT 307-308 (1992).
[202] 1 E.D. BROWN, THE INTERNATIONAL LAW OF THE SEA 303 (1994).

Such a justification is obsolete vis-à-vis pirates flying their own flag on the high seas, removed from any state's jurisdiction.

If, however, terrorists use a vessel flying the flag of state A and attack a vessel of state B located on the high seas, then the general rules as provided for by the United Nations Charter kick in, rendering Article 51 of the Charter a legitimate legal response – albeit against state A, not the terrorists as such.[203] The concept of attribution and the self-defense regime work just as they do on a state's soil. If attribution fails, perhaps because of a lack of control of the flag state over the pirates, states have to resort to individual self-defense of the crew as far as their immediate protection is concerned. Subsequent policing efforts followed by an arrest of the perpetrators and their conviction by a court in state B represent an enforcement of criminal law, not a military approach. There are only few examples of states referring to self-defense when they attacked foreign vessels to prevent the transportation of arms or environmental disasters – irrespective of whether this behavior could have constituted an armed attack.[204]

The fight against piracy resembles the fight against a criminal nuisance and an economic threat, albeit sometimes with extended measures. Terrorists and pirates operating on the high seas are subjected to domestic criminal prosecution as proscribed by virtue of *ius cogens* and international agreements. The rules against piracy are inadequate to confront terrorist non-state actors.[205] If pirates act on behalf of a state, their actions may be attributed to that state. Self-defense against pirates themselves – and not a state – is not possible and, in view of the lack of any state's jurisdiction on the high seas, obsolete.

c) Mercenaries

Mercenaries are repudiated by the international community. Even before mercenarism is defined in Article 47 (2) of the Additional Protocol I to the Geneva Convention, section (1) thereof clarifies that mercenaries are not granted the status of prisoners of war.[206] The United Nations Security Council, among

---

[203] Cassese, *supra* note 178 at 476.

[204] Malanczuk, *supra note* 178 at 189-90.

[205] Rüdiger Wolfrum, *Fighting Terrorism at Sea: Options and Limitations under International Law*, in Verhandeln für den Frieden – Negotiating for Peace (Jochen Abr. Frowein, Klaus Scharioth, Ingo Winkelmann, Rüdiger Wolfrum eds., 2003), at 649, 660-661.

[206] Protocol Additional to the Geneva Conventions of 12 August 1949, and Relating to the Protection of Victims of International Armed Conflicts (Protocol I) art. 47, Aug. 12, 1949, 1125 U.N.T.S. 3; Article 47 provides: „1. A mercenary shall not have the right to be a combatant or a prisoner of war. 2. A mercenary is any person who: (a) Is specially recruited locally or abroad in order to fight in an armed conflict; (b) Does, in fact, take a direct part in the hostilities; (c) Is motivated to take part in the hostilities essentially by the desire for private gain and, in fact, is promised, by or on behalf of a Party to the conflict, material compensation

others, repeatedly urged states to refrain from recruiting mercenaries in the course of conflicts these states were engaged in.[207] The General Assembly suggested, aside from several other resolutions,[208] the International Convention against the Recruitment, Use, Financing and Training of Mercenaries in 1989, which asks states to prohibit mercenarism domestically and to refrain from recruiting mercenaries themselves.[209]

However, mercenaries are in any event protected by Common Article 3 of the Geneva Conventions.[210] Additionally, perhaps due to this fundamental recognition, mercenarism as such does not constitute a violation of a peremptory norm of international law.[211] For the purpose of this work it needs to be evaluated if mercenaries conducted armed attacks which in return were responded to by recourse to force in self-defense against the mercenaries, and not their "employer".

In the phase of African decolonization several states and insurgents relied upon mercenaries to fight their respective opponents.[212] Accordingly, the Organization of African Unity responded with a convention clarifying that mercenaries had no POW status and had to be prosecuted.[213] Some examples of state practice regarding mercenaries indicate that states occasionally relied on the consent of the state on the territory of which they attempted to confront merce-

---

substantially in excess of that promised or paid to combatants of similar ranks and functions in the armed forces of that Party; (d) Is neither a national of a Party to the conflict nor a resident of territory controlled by a Party to the conflict; (e) Is not a member of the armed forces of a Party to the conflict; and (f) Has not been sent by a State which is not a Party to the conflict on official duty as a member of its armed forces".

[207] *See, e.g.*, S.C. Res. 239 (July 10, 1967) 1967 U.N.Y.B. 130; S.C. Res. 241 (Nov. 15, 1967) 1967 U.N.Y.B. 130-31; S.C. Res. 405 (Apr. 16, 1977) 1977 U.N.Y.B. 215.

[208] For an overview *see* Antonio Cassese, *Mercenaries*, 3 ENCYCLOPEDIA OF PUBLIC INTERNATIONAL LAW 342, 344 (Rudolf Bernhardt ed., 1997).

[209] International Convention against the Recruitment, Use, Financing and Training of Mercenaries art. 5, G.A. Res. 44/34, U.N. Doc. A/RES/44/34 (Dec. 4, 1989).

[210] Jean de Preux, *Protocol I – Article 47, in* COMMENTARY ON THE ADDITIONAL PROTOCOLS OF 8 JUNE 1977 TO THE GENEVA CONVENTIONS OF 12 AUGUST 1949 577 (Yves Sandoz, Christophe Swinarski, Bruno Zimmermann eds. 1987).

[211] KADELBACH, *supra* note 201 at 313.

[212] For an overview *see* Antonio Cassese, *Mercenaries: Lawful Combatants or War Criminals*, 40 ZEITSCHRIFT FÜR AUSLÄNDISCHES ÖFFENTLICHES RECHT UND VÖLKERRECHT 1, 2-3 (1986).

[213] Organization of African Unity, *OAU Convention for the Elimination of Mercenarism in Africa* art. 3, 6, CM/817 (XXIX) Annex II Rev. 1 (July 3, 1977).

naries which operated against the government of this particular state. Also these situations arose within states formerly governed by colonial powers.[214]

If mercenaries engage in an international armed conflict on behalf of either of the parties, they engage in belligerent actions for a state actor.[215] Inferentially, a mercenary's actions are to be attributed to this state actor assuming the traditional concept of "effective control"[216] is met. For instance, Benin complained to the United Nations in 1977 about "the dastardly act of armed imperialist aggression" by mercenaries, although without explicitly claiming to be entitled to invoke self-defense against such action.[217] The remarks by other representatives appear to employ a vocabulary openly resembling the terms as incorporated in Article 51 of the Charter, such as an "armed attack".[218] However, the Security Council "strongly condemn[ed] the act of armed aggression" and also "any State which persists in permitting or tolerating the recruitment of mercenaries and the provision of facilities to them . . . ."[219] The state behind the mercenaries is the relevant actor, not so much the illegitimate tool the state employs by itself. As the representative from Benin put it: "The question we have to elucidate now is a very simple one: who is it that is hiding behind this vast criminal operation? Who . . . is the master-mind . . . .?"[220]

Non-state actor issues with regard to international self-defense plainly against mercenaries are thus unlikely to arise. In internal armed conflicts national law determines the legality of the use of mercenaries – often directly regulated by virtue of international agreements such as the 1989 International Con-

---

[214] *See, e.g.*, GEORG NOLTE, EINGREIFEN AUF EINLADUNG 342 (1999) (referring to France's dispatch of soldiers to the Comoros in 1995 upon request of Comoros' President based who faced a coup d'état instigated by foreign mercenaries).

[215] Cassese, *supra* note 212 at 5; *see also* Definition of Aggression, G.A. Res. 3314 (XXIX), U.N. Doc. A/9631 (Dec. 14, 1974); Res. 3314 provides in part: "(f) The sending by or on behalf of a State of . . . mercenaries, which carry out acts of armed force against another State" constitutes aggression; an early example for such an approach is S.C. Res. 241 (Nov. 15, 1967), 1967 U.N.Y.B. 130-31, which expresses concern about "the serious situation created in the Democratic Republic of Congo following the armed attacks committed against that country by foreign forces of mercenaries".

[216] *See supra* pp. 34 et seq.

[217] U.N. SCOR, 32nd Sess., 2000th mtg., at 5, U.N. Doc. S/PV.2000 (remarks by Boya (Benin)) (Apr. 6, 1977).

[218] *See, e.g.*, U.N. SCOR, 32nd Sess., 2001st mtg., at 2, U.N. Doc. S/PV.2001 (remarks by Troyanovsky (Soviet Union)) (Apr. 7, 1977); *id.* at 9 (remarks by Ake (Ivory Coast)).

[219] S.C. Res. 405 (Apr. 16, 1977) 1977 U.N.Y.B. 215.

[220] U.N. SCOR, 32nd Sess., 2000th mtg., at 6, U.N. Doc. S/PV.2000 (remarks by Boya (Benin)) (Apr. 6, 1977).

vention. This does not, however, alter issues such as attribution to the state making use of mercenaries.

If not a state, but a terrorist group hires mercenaries[221] one is caught in a circle: the group remains a non-state actor since a mercenary is not bound to any state actor, just as the internationally operating terrorist is often not. The groups' actions will equally not be considered those of a state actor. In the perception of the victim state, the mercenary will be a terrorist like those who hired him to support their cause. Self-defense based upon Article 51 of the Charter meets the same obstacles as if the terrorists acted without further help.

d) Insurgents and Liberation Movements

Insurgents are awarded rights and obligations under international law.[222] As to the international relevance of their conduct, the ILC suggested that the actions of insurgents in the course of a civil war should be disregarded until the insurgents successfully formed a new government. Then, somewhat retroactively, the insurgent's conduct constitutes internationally relevant state action unless the state adopts the insurgents' conduct.[223] Generally, however, insurgents traditionally act within the framework of one state actor in the course of a civil war[224] and are thus largely irrelevant for the international self-defense regime,[225] which is limited to conflicts that are covered by the United Nations Charter and not excluded by Article 2 (7) of the Charter.[226]

---

[221] Occasionally, terrorist groups appear to be seeking assistance from individuals who may only be remotely associated with their immediate cause, but are sent by fellow terrorist groups. However, monetary rewards are not likely to their primary motivation; *see, e.g.*, John Kifner, *A Nation Challenged: Vale of Kashmir; Proxy War Threatens to Unravel U.S. Alliance*, N.Y TIMES, Oct. 29, 2001, at B5 (quoting the Indian governor of the Kashmir region as saying: "Now the foreign mercenaries have taken over [terror against India inside Kashmir], most from Pakistan, a very sizable number of Afghans, quite a few Sudanese, a few from even Chechnya. It's a whole army fighting a proxy war."); Steven Lee Myers, *Russia Recasts Bog in Caucasus as War on Terror*, N.Y. TIMES, Oct. 5, 2001, at A1 (reporting about foreign fighters dispatched by Al Qaeda and the Islamic Jihad to support Chechen armed groups).

[222] For an overview *see* LESLIE C. GREEN, THE CONTEMPORARY LAW OF ARMED CONFLICT 59-61 (2nd ed. 2000).

[223] *See supra* note 126.

[224] MALANCZUK, *supra note* 178 at 318; GREEN, *supra* note 222.

[225] Very rarely, states grant insurgents the recognition of belligerency, thereby rendering an armed conflict involving them and the state against which they rose international in nature, provided that insurgents effectively control at least some territory and reach some organizational solidity. For historical examples *see* CASSESE, *supra* note 178 at 125-26.

[226] *Cf.* France's complaints about the United Nations' alleged violation of French sovereignty in the course of its military actions in Northern Africa, *infra* pp. 168 et seq.

Liberation movements have evolved beyond insurgents.[227] Some of them were explicitly recognized by the General Assembly.[228] The entities recognized as liberation movements have the capacity to conclude international agreements and Protocol I of the Geneva Conventions applies to them, provided Articles 1 (4) and 96 (3) thereof are met.[229] Significantly, liberation movements do not require the control over a territory as basis for their recognition as international legal actor. Rather, they were awarded a designated legal status solely based upon their political motives and their striving for territory.[230] Accordingly, the theory of *bellum justum,* a just war that was pursued by such movements and their supporters, sought to legitimize the status and rights of liberation movements.[231] The General Assembly, based upon a majority of Warsaw Pact and Third World states, confirmed certain alleged rights of liberation movements, most notably a *ius ad bellum*[232] and certain rights under the *ius in bello*[233]. In fact, liberation movements were explicitly excluded from General Assembly resolutions adopted to fight international terrorism, despite their sometimes analogous methods.[234]

This policy has been changing over the years.[235] Beginning with General Assembly resolution 48/122 (1993)[236] none of the subsequent General Assembly resolutions regarding the international fight against terrorism reaffirms the right to self-determination in this context.[237] Accordingly, while many of the relevant

---

[227] MALANCZUK, *supra note* 178 at 104-105; Konrad Ginther, *Liberation Movements, in* 3 ENCYCLOPEDIA OF PUBLIC INTERNATIONAL LAW 211-12 (Rudolf Bernhardt ed., 1997).
[228] *E.g.,* in 1974 the PLO was granted the status of an observer at the United Nations General Assembly, *see* G.A. Res. 3237 (XXIX), U.N. Doc. A/9631 (Nov. 22, 1974).
[229] BROWNLIE, *supra* note 60 at 62.
[230] CASSESE, *supra* note 178 at 140-41.
[231] *See* DINSTEIN, *supra* note 72 at 68-70, 89.
[232] G.A. Res. 2621 (XXV), U.N. Doc. A/8086 (Oct. 12, 1970).
[233] G.A. Res. 3103 (XXVIII), U.N. Doc. A/9030 (Dec. 12, 1973).
[234] *See, e.g.,* G.A. Res. 3034 (XXVII) (Dec. 18, 1972), 1972 U.N.Y.B. 649-50; G.A. Res. 32/147, U.N. Doc. A/RES/32/147 (Dec. 16, 1977); G.A. Res. 34/145, U.N. Doc. A/RES/34/145 (Dec. 17, 1979); G.A. Res. 36/109, U.N. Doc. A/RES/36/109 (Dec. 10, 1981); G.A. Res. 38/130, U.N. Doc. A/RES/38/130 (Dec. 19, 1983).
[235] Malvina Halberstam, *The Evolution of the United Nations Position on Terrorism: From Exempting National Liberation Movements to Criminalizing Terrorism Wherever and by Whomever Committed*, 41 COLUM. J. TRANSNAT'L L. 573 (2003).
[236] G.A. Res. 48/122, U.N. Doc. A/RES/48/122 (Dec. 20, 1993).
[237] G.A. Res. 49/60, U.N. Doc. A/RES/49/60 (Dec. 9, 1994); G.A. Res. 50/53, U.N. Doc. A/RES/50/53 (Dec. 11, 1995); G.A. Res. 51/210, U.N. Doc. A/RES/51/210 (Dec. 17, 1996); G.A. Res. 52/165, U.N. Doc. A/RES/52/165 (Dec. 15, 1997); G.A. Res. 53/108, U.N. Doc. A/RES/53/108 (Dec. 8, 1998); G.A. Res. 55/158, U.N. Doc. A/RES/55/158 (Dec. 12, 2000), G.A. Res. 58/81, U.N. Doc. A/RES/58/81 (Dec, 9, 2003); G.A. Res. 59/46, U.N. Doc.

terrorist non-state actors may have been deemed "national liberation movements" in the past, it is unlikely that such a label will save them from the same treatment that is awarded to today's international terrorist groups. In fact, most of the groups dealt with the in course of this work were classic examples of liberation movements.[238] The term "liberation movement", however, bears no distinct legal difference for the purposes of anti-terror actions and thus self-defense. This is confirmed by Security Council resolutions which condemn terrorism solely based upon the methods employed, not its motives.[239]

Consequently, while domestic insurgents could not be subject to self-defense as embedded in Article 51 of the Charter, "liberation movements" appear to have had that capacity. Inferentially, "liberation movements" belonged to a category of "non-state actors" capable of triggering Article 51 of the Charter, provided they launched an armed attack.

3. Attempt to Define Non-State Actors Relevant Within Article 51

The International Institute for Strategic Studies' annual survey of the world's military forces recently began to include also "non-state armed groups" and lists already over 300 of them for 2006.[240] The list includes all "organized and armed opposition force with a recognised political goal, acting independently from a state or government. . . . if they have an effective command structure." Irrespective of their popular classification also terrorists were included, provided they have "political objectives" and "caused significant damage and casualties over the years." Finally, all groups included needed to pose "a significant threat to states and governments" without being merely criminal in nature.[241] The list incorporates groups such as the American "18th Street Gang", the Khmer Rouge, Al Qaeda, as well as the South African "People Against Gangsterism and Drugs" – hence, a broad array of domestic and international armed bands of manifold ideological backgrounds. Questionable is which of these groups and other non-state armed groups would have the capacity to be recognized as an entity theoretically capable to be responded to in self-defense according to Article 51 of the Charter.

The international legal regime concerning recourse to force has not been accepting non-state actors as equal players. Existing categories of other interna-

---

A/RES/59/46 (Dec. 2, 2004); G.A. Res. 60/43, U.N. Doc. A/RES/60/43 (Dec. 8, 2005); *see also* Halberstam *supra* note 235 at 575-77.

[238] *Cf.* CASSESE, *supra* note 178 at 140.

[239] *See, e.g.*, S.C. Res. 1269, U.N. Doc. S/RES/1269 (Oct. 19, 1999); S.C. Res. 1373, U.N. Doc. S/RES/1373 (Sept. 28, 2001).

[240] INT'L INST. FOR STRATEGIC STUD., THE MILITARY BALANCE 418-34 (2006).

[241] *Id.* at 418.

tionally relevant entities are rare with regard to a possible application of Article 51 of the Charter. Yet, at least since September 11, non-state actors obtained an international relevance that does not exclude the Charter's self-defense regime.[242] Unfortunately, the term "non-state actor" provides merely with a negative definition in dissociation of the legally settled term of the "state" as primary international legal actor. As was seen, some traditional categories of international actors that are not states but have been using force did apparently not have the capacity to trigger Article 51 of the Charter (such as pirates), while some others had (such as liberation movements). It is therefore necessary to define those non-state actors which are relevant for the international use of force regime and separate them from those who are not. Both groups resemble the bifold countermeasures that states have been using to face recent but also traditional methods of international terrorist warfare.

When states unfold anti-terrorist measures to protect themselves, their citizens, and the international community, they can follow two approaches: a law enforcement approach or the use of armed force.[243] Provided that each of the two category's conditions are met, states may also chose to follow both of them parallely as can be seen ever since the Nuremberg trials.[244] Such an approach does not confuse to separate areas of law[245] but it combines the protection of a state and its institutions as a whole against threats from abroad and the determination of individual guilt to deter and punish criminals.

Whenever applied exclusively, the law enforcement approach usually deals with "classic" terrorist acts that occur within the domestic legal framework of a state and was nearly the only approach for many states to respond to terror over the past decades. Policing efforts of varying degrees were undisputed and reasonable tools for counter-measures against most "domestic" terrorists. Hardly anyone would argue that for instance the RAF had to be fought by virtue of Article 51 of the Charter, even during the group's heydays in the late 1970s.

However, only a superficial glimpse at the RAF reveals that the group, that existed for nearly 28 years, combines features that are not too different from

---

[242] *See, e.g.*, S.C. Res. 1368, U.N. Doc. S/RES/1368 (Sept. 12, 2001).
[243] Travalio, Altenburg, *supra* note 86 at 98.
[244] *See* Murphy *supra* note 43 at 49 (arguing that the September 11 incidents represent an occasion on which no "binary choice between . . . a criminal act or . . . a use of force . . . " had to be made as both properly characterize the underlying factual situation).
[245] *Cf.* Carsten Stahn, *Terrorist Acts as "Armed Attacks": The Right of Self-Defense, Article 51 (1/2) of the UN Charter, and International Terrorism*, 27-FALL FLETCHER F. WORLD AFF. 35, 45-6 (2003) (arguing that "[t]he implicit danger of expanding the concept of self-defense lies in the militarization of crime" and that "the boundaries of law enforcement and self-defense can only be defined of the basis of a gravity threshold . . . .").

those of today's internationally operating terror groups. Against these groups, many states chose the second approach, namely the use of armed force exercised by the military. Most notably, the RAF had significant international relations and did not limit its terrorist activities to attacks against German targets. RAF members were trained and supported by several Arab and Muslim states and organizations, such as Palestinian terror groups training in Jordan.[246] Later, some RAF members were hidden by the German Democratic Republic.[247] And while RAF's major actions were limited to German soil,[248] or German targets in other states,[249] it repeatedly attacked U.S. and international installations in Germany.[250] One RAF member also participated in the raid on the headquarters of the "Organization of Petroleum Exporting Countries" (OPEC) in Vienna on December 21, 1975.[251] However, RAF members and structures were fought by means of domestic criminal law[252] – and not by the laws of international armed conflict. Partly, the reason for this approach lies in the German government's immediate and harsh anti-terror responses. But what if Germany had declined to

---

[246] BUTZ PETERS, RAF – TERRORISMUS IN DEUTSCHLAND 84-86 (1993).

[247] *Id.* at 299-334.

[248] *E.g.* killing and attempted killing of several German police officers (Oct. 22, 1971; Dec. 22, 1971; March 3, 1972; May 9, 1975; May 7, 1976; May 3, 1977; Sept. 24, 1978; June 27, 1993); the abductions of Peter Lorentz (Feb. 2, 1975) and Hanns-Martin Schleyer (Sept. 5, 1977), who was eventually killed (Oct., 18 or 19, 1977); murder of several individuals, among them Siegfried Buback (Apr. 7, 1977), Ernst Zimmermann (Feb. 1, 1985), Karl-Heinz Beckurts (July 8, 1986), Alfred Herrhausen (Nov. 30, 1989), Detlev Karsten Rohwedder (Apr. 1, 1991); also, the RAF committed numerous bank robberies and bombings between 1968 and 1993.

[249] Such as the raid on the German embassy in Stockholm, Sweden, on Apr. 24, 1975; *see* KLAUS PFLIEGER, DIE ROTE ARMEE FRAKTION 56-60 (2004).

[250] Such as for instance the attacks against the U.S. Headquarters in Frankfurt on May 11, 1972; the bombing of U.S. Headquarters in Heidelberg on May 24, 1972; the attempted assassination of NATO General Alexander Haig on June 25, 1979; the assassination of U.S. soldier Edward Francis Pimental in Wiesbaden on August 7, 1985, and the subsequent bombing of the Rhein-Main Airbase in on August 8, 1985; for an overview *see* PFLIEGER, *supra* note 249 at 30, 34, 56, 116, 146.

[251] Patricia Clough, *West-Germany holds out its hands to terrorists*, THE TIMES (London), Jan. 12, 1980, at 12 (reporting about members of the "Baader-Meinhof terrorist[s]", among them "Herr Hans-Joachim Klein, who took part in the 1975 attempted kidnapping of the OPEC ministers in Vienna . . . ."); *German Unrest Recalled as a Former Terrorist Gets 9 Years*, N.Y. TIMES, Feb. 16, 2001, at A3 ("A former terrorist [Hans-Joachim Klein] . . . was sentenced to nine years in prison today for killing three people in a 1975 attack on an OPEC meeting ").

[252] Such as through the "Baader-Meinhoff-Prozess", a series of trials held as of May 1975, and the enactment of new anti-terror criminal laws; *see* PFLIEGER, *supra* note 249 at 61-64.

fight the RAF and the latter had expanded its fight against more U.S. targets and installations of the North Atlantic Treaty Organization (NATO)?

In the following, an attempt will be made to evaluate under which circumstances states begin to resort to armed force against a (non state actor) terror group as opposed to law enforcement against a (domestic criminal) terror group.

a) Internationality

Violent action of a non-state actor is only of concern for the international regime on the use of force if there is an international element to it. Otherwise the principle of the sovereign equality of all states and with it Article 2 (7) of the United Nations Charter would not allow for an invocation of principles of international public law. Host state and victim state must hence at least be partly different.

These differences between host and victim state are not limited to a geographical incongruence. Rather, the non-state actor can very well target the victim state without that the impact of its actions leaves the territory of the host state. Foremost, such actions are likely to target foreign located individual representatives (e.g. an ambassador) or institutions (such as an embassy, a consulate, a cultural center etc.) of the victim state. On the other hand, these classic devices of international terrorism are rarely ever likely to amount to the degree of an armed attack and will thus rather concern simple violations of international duties and treaty obligations vis-à-vis the victim state.

Insofar, for the purpose of a distinction among violent non-state entities, one can hold that for instance the RAF or ETA (Euskadi Ta Askatasuna; Basque Homeland and Freedom) mostly operate from within their target states. They kill, extort, and abduct from inside a victim state's territory. They have ties and even goals outside that territory, but most of their activities is unfolded in one state and affects that particular state directly and almost exclusively. Host and victim state are largely identical. Accordingly, they are in immediate reach of domestic law enforcement authorities. Their actions might even raise international legal concerns as to the victim state's duty to protect foreign citizens or compensate them or their host nations.

Terrorist non-state actors as dealt with in the course of this work avoid to be present inside the victim state against which they operate primarily. In fact, hit-and-run tactics involving more than one state is what made them infamously successful. While they may operate through small cells and armed groups on the territory of their victim state, their operative backbones and springboard is somewhere else. They attack from the outside and hide behind the sovereignty of another state actor. This is what differentiates plainly domestic and even internationally connected, but prevailingly domestically operating terrorists from internationally active terrorist non-state actors.

b) MAGNITUDE AND INTENTION OF THE ATTACKS

While the use of force is generally prohibited by virtue of Article 2 (4) of the Charter, the self-defense regime as laid down in the Charter is qualified by the requirement of an armed attack, a term not defined in the Charter.[253] Also the ICJ did not yet clarify the required degree of use of force but merely held that "[t]here appears now to be general agreement on the nature of the acts which can be treated as constituting armed attacks" upon which it referred to "Art. 3 paragraph (g) of the Definition of Aggression annexed to the General Assembly Resolution 3314 (XXIX) . . . ."[254] Accordingly, there can be "measures which do not constitute an armed attack but may nevertheless involve a use of force."[255] The armed attacks are hence a particularly grave form of an aggression. It follows that for the use of force to be relevant within Article 51 of the Charter it must be of a certain magnitude and "it will be necessary to distinguish the most grave forms of the use of force (those constituting an armed attack) from other less grave forms."[256] Among the acts not necessarily grave enough for an armed attack could be, as the ICJ suggested, "mere frontier incident[s]".[257]

What can be drawn from this understanding of an armed attack is that it is measured along objective criteria as to the gravity of the use of armed force. The purpose of an attack i.e. any underlying subjective motivation is completely irrelevant.

The RAF was seeking to attack and overthrow Germany's political system. And although German society was shaken by their ruthless actions, the RAF terrorists were far away from seriously achieving their goals. Between 1970 and 1998 the RAF allegedly committed approx. 20 major crimes including abductions, murder, and armed robberies. They killed 37 people.[258] These figures show that while the RAF must be considered as a threat unknown in its origin and intensity to post-war Germany, it was also clearly limited in its real impact. Beside the fact that host and victim state were largely identical, the RAF's actions never amounted to an armed attack.

Al Qaeda, Hezbollah, the PKK, and the PLO had more "success" and used other methods. They chose not to abduct just one individual, but slaughtered

---

[253] Randelzhofer, *supra* note 6 at 794.
[254] *Nicaragua* case, at para. 195.
[255] *Id.* at para. 210.
[256] *Id.* at para. 191; *see Oil Platforms* case at 1355.
[257] *Nicaragua* case, at para. 195.
[258] PFLIEGER, *supra* note 249 at 183-84.

dozens at once. Even the PLO, for instance, killed almost as many people in a single raid than the RAF in the 28 years of its existence.[259] Equal comparisons are true for almost all other groups dealt with in the course of this work. The dimension of the threats posed by each of the internationally active terror groups is a different one. And while one may argue that the death of just one individual, such as former U.S. President John F. Kennedy, may result in an impact even beyond the scale of above comparisons, it will nonetheless not be able to replace the qualitative requirements of the armed attack threshold. Whoever is sought to be considered as a non-state actor capable of triggering the international regime of self-defense is to be measured by the gravity and magnitude of its application of force.

c) Organizational Structures of the Non-State Actor

According to the International Institute for Strategic Studies, relevant non-state action is based upon "an effective command structure"[260]. However, once a non-state actor operates between at least two states and its actions have a certain degree of magnitude, the non-state group's organizational structure is of no relevance for the exercise of Article 51 of the Charter. For the purpose of *ius in bello* and the treatment of members of a militia as regular prisoners of war, Article 4 of the Third Geneva Convention requires, among other things, a certain command structure and a uniform appearance.[261] These rules are of no further relevance for the *ius ad bellum*. The United Nations Charter does not provide with any further requirements as to who is capable of triggering self-defense. Any insofar detailed regime and hypothetically necessary investigative requirements would divert attention from what it is that an effective self-defense regime seeks to achieve, as does the United Nations Charter as a whole: "to maintain international peace and security", as Article 1 (1) of the Charter lays out. All rights and obligations conferred upon the member states of the United Nations

---

[259] *See, e.g., infra* note 421.
[260] *See supra* note 241.
[261] Geneva Convention (III) relative to the Treatment of Prisoners of War art. 4, Aug. 12, 1949, 75 U.N.T.S. 135 (hereinafter Third Geneva Convention); Article 4 provides in part: "Prisoners of war, in the sense of the present Convention, are persons belonging to one of the following categories, who have fallen into the power of the enemy: . . . Members of other militias and members of other volunteer corps, including those of organized resistance movements, belonging to a Party to the conflict and operating in or outside their own territory, even if this territory is occupied, provided that such militias or volunteer corps, including such organized resistance movements, fulfil the following conditions: (a) that of being commanded by a person responsible for his subordinates; (b) that of having a fixed distinctive sign recognizable at a distance; (c) that of carrying arms openly; (d) that of conducting their operations in accordance with the laws and customs of war."

have to be fulfilled in *bona fide*, Article 2 (2) of the Charter. For the rights vested in Article 51 of the Charter this means that they can only be referred to "restore international peace and security" and only after peaceful means failed. It will hardly be reconcilable with this primary motive – i.e. to achieve peace and return to the negotiation table – if those who disturb the spirit of the Charter and endanger its purposes are disregarded because of formal reasons in complete disregard of an attacker's hostile capabilities.

For instance, Hezbollah has developed into an organization that entails military capacities exceeding those of many state actors.[262] Al Qaeda managed to trigger U.S. and NATO self-defense by virtue of an organizationally largely independent group of students, located in Europe and the United States, armed with box cutters. In both cases, the international community largely consistently supported self-defense as appropriate legal regime to fight either of the groups.[263] Consequently, the organizational structure of the non-state actor is negligible.[264]

d) CONCLUSION

A terrorist group will be considered as a non-state actor against whom recourse to force can be taken in self-defense if the following criteria are met cumulatively:

- The group must operate between at least two states. Host and victim states may not be identical.
- The impact of the entity's attacks against the victim state must be of severe quantitative gravity.

---

[262] *See, e.g.*, Jonathan Finer, *Israeli Soldiers Find a Tenacious Foe in Hezbollah*, WASH. POST, Aug. 8, 2006, at A01 (quoting the former director of analysis for Israeli military intelligence, Brig. Gen. Yossi Kuperwasser, as saying that "[Hezbollah has] some of the most advanced antitank missiles in the world" and summarizing the experiences of several IDF troops who have been fighting Hezbollah and reported about its increasing strength and similarities to regular armed forces).

[263] For Al Qaeda *see infra* pp. 157 to 163; for Hezbollah *see infra* pp. 101 to 123.

[264] *But see* Krajewski, *supra* note 12 at 200 (arguing that a minimum degree of organizational structure is necessary in order to separate individual perpetrators from internationally relevant groups).

PART 2 – SELECTED CONFLICTS AND STATE PRACTICE

In the following, the state practice concerning the right to self-defense against non-state actors will be evaluated along a number of conflicts involving states and non-state entities, covering a period of more than 50 years. Starting point to the analysis is the ratification of the United Nations Charter. Before discussing each conflict individually, it will be outlined as to how the facts and the legal convictions concerning each relevant actor was chosen and weighed.

I. STATE PRACTICE AND A STATE'S LEGAL CONVICTION

One of the sources of international law is international customary law.[265] It consists of a largely uniform state practice of a certain duration with a conception by states that the practice is required by the law (*opinio iuris*).[266] If a treaty is agreed upon by states, it may very well create new rules of treaty law, but existing custom retains a separate identity,[267] even when it is entirely consonant with the treaty norms.[268] Consequently, general principles of international law may be considered to interpret a treaty and subsequent custom may amend or even replace it.[269]

As one of the elements of custom, state practice consists of physical and verbal acts. It is usually referred to as one of the decisive parts of what contributes to the creation of customary international law.[270]

The other element of custom, a state's actual motives and its true *opinio iuris*, are difficult, if ever, to discern. States will often not admit their real beliefs, much less their honest motivation for an act or an omission. Domestic and international political pressure will require the most favorable appearance before the international community, even though what is put forward in public will often not be truthful. However, whatever it is that states hide from the public, or at

---

[265] Statute of the International Court of Justice, Article 38 (1) (b), June 26, 1945, 59, Stat. 1031, T.S. 993.

[266] *Nicaragua* case, at para. 183; for an overview over the foundations of customary international law *see* ANTHONY D'AMATO, THE CONCEPT OF CUSTOM IN INTERNATIONAL LAW (1971); MALANCZUK, *supra* note 178 at 39-48.

[267] BROWNLIE, *supra* note 60 at 14.

[268] *Nicaragua* case, at para. 175.

[269] BROWNLIE, *supra* note 60 at 5; Michael Akehurst, *The Hierarchy of the Sources of International Law*, 47 BRIT. Y.B. INT'L L. 273, 275 (1974-75); *but see* Kammerhofer *supra* note 4 at 147 (arguing that "[s]ubsequent practice can at best be evidence for the meaning(s) of a treaty norm" and is hence negligible for any treaty interpretation. Customary law subsequent to a treaty can only supplant, but never modify a treaty).

[270] INTERNATIONAL COMMITTEE OF THE RED CROSS, 1 CUSTOMARY INTERNATIONAL HUMANITARIAN LAW XXXII (2005), Jean-Marie Henckaerts, Louise Doswald-Beck (ed.) (hereinafter ICRC).

least from relevant legal fora, will hardly ever contribute to the development of any legal authority.[271] Hence, if states never reveal their true beliefs, it does not play a role for the inference of legal rules. This work shall therefore look at official governmental press releases, statements by relevant state officials, submissions to international organizations, and statements before courts to evaluate whether a state considered itself to be exercising self-defense. Such official statements by states can be taken into consideration for assessing state practice as one of the prerequisites of customary international law.[272] Consequently, they evidence a state's legal conviction. This is, inferentially, also the case when the subject matter in question is the interpretation of *lex scripta*, such as Article 51 of the Charter.

Often, these sources are used without any order of preference or weight. However, it must be noted that the ICJ is sometimes reluctant to rely on plain governmental submissions as authoritative source of information. For instance, assertions of fact are regarded more trustworthy if they stem from international, presumably less biased sources, such as the United Nations[273] – although in some conflicts the opposite may be true.[274] Therefore, different sources are used herein for each conflict. It must be assumed that their content is all that is available to infer a state's legal conviction.

1. Automatic Self-Defense?

It has been contended that states will almost inevitably invoke the concept of self-defense whenever they explain why force was applied legitimately.[275] Such automatic reference to self-defense, bare of considerations as to the situa-

---

[271] *Cf.* ICRC, at XXXIV (stating that undisclosed acts cannot contribute to customary law).

[272] Fisheries Jurisdiction case (U.K. v. Ice.), 1974 I.C.J. Reports 47 (July 25, 1974) (separate opinion of Judges Forster, Bengzon, Jiménez de Aréchaga, Singh, and Ruda); 56-58 (separate opinion Judge Dillard); 81-88 (separate opinion of Judge De Castro); 119-20 (separate opinion of Judge Waldock) (all judges referred to claims made by states to infer the existence of a customary rule); Case concerning the Gabčíkovo-Nagymaros Project (Hung. v. Slovk.), 1997 I.C.J. Reports 39-46 (Sept. 25, 1997) (in this case the court relied on official statements used for the drafting of the International Law Commission's Draft Articles on State Responsibility).

[273] *See, e.g.*, *Congo* case, at para. 65 (indicating that evidence directly presented by states involved in litigation before the ICJ will be treated with "great reserve").

[274] *See, e.g.*, Michael J. Jordan, *Unmasking UNRWA*, JEWISH TELEGRAPH AGENCY, March 15, 2006, *available at* http://www.jta.org/unrwa.asp (last visited Apr. 13, 2006) (Report about the yearlong allegations by Israel and the United States regarding the lack of impartiality of the United Nations Relief and Works Agency (UNRWA) in the Occupied Palestinian Territories; for instance, nine supposedly impartial UNRWA staffers quit their jobs to run for Hamas in the January 2006 elections).

[275] *Cf.* GRAY, *supra* note 36 at 96.

tion at hand, makes it difficult to draw legal inferences. Yet, it is important to note that a state is likely to rely on what is available to stop all hazardous armed attacks most effectively. In other words: What other resort can states take? What other equally effective counter-measures are available?

All that is left militarily are actions based upon a Security Council resolution according to Chapter VII of the Charter that may authorize states "to use all necessary means", as did for instance Security Council resolution 678 (1990),[276] as perhaps the most famous example. The Charter of the United Nations deems any other application of force as a violation of Article 2 (4) of the Charter and renders it thereby illegitimate.[277]

Beyond that, a state can only attempt to rely on methods that fall short of a "use of force", Article 2 (4) of the Charter. Conceivable instruments are secret service or policing efforts, as well as coercive, non-forcible countermeasures.[278] It is questionable if these methods prove equally effective vis-à-vis serious military treats from outside a victim state's territory. Additionally, the states which harbor, foster, protect, and support such non-state actors are unlikely, often even unable, to cooperate. That is not to say that military force was a universal remedy. Often enough, recourse to force simply appears to be one of the very few options left. It also is, unfortunately, most often the only device that stands as proof for a nation's strength and determination – a political factor which is often forgotten especially with regard to the 'war against terrorism' – a war that is fought fiercely in the streets of Baghdad, Kabul, or Gaza, as well as on Al Jazeera and CNN.

The notion that states will automatically rely on self-defense is therefore not false, but needs to be put into perspective: the current legal and political circumstances leave little room for alternatives. Consequently, it is even more important to clearly shape, define, and limit Article 51 of the Charter. It needs to be understood in a way that contemporary and future crises require it. Otherwise the danger of a complete disregard of international law will increase. This might lead to a considerable erosion of importance, credibility, and strength of the United Nations given the sensitivity and relevance of the issue.

---

[276] S.C. Res. 678, U.N. Doc S/RES/678 (Nov. 29, 1990) (authorizing the use of force against Iraq).

[277] YOO, *supra* note 35, at 738.

[278] Mary-Ellen O'Connell, *Lawful Self-Defense to Terrorism*, 63 U. PITT. L. REV. 889, 904 (2002).

2. Silence, Omissions as Indication of Legal Conviction?

As was indicated, "hidden legal opinions" cannot contribute to the development of law as far as they cannot alter the actually verbalized or published opinions. That leaves the question if any legal relevance at all can be inferred from what a state did *not* express through its institutions or agents.

The ICJ noted in the *Lotus* case that a state's abstention from *action* (here: from prosecution) can reveal a state's legal conviction only if the state's reason for abstaining is clear. Uncertainties (here: did France abstain from prosecution because it saw itself under a duty to do so or because it lacked interest?) cannot reveal legal belief.[279] To abstain from action, particularly when the use of force is at issue, is different from abstaining from expressing a legal conviction. The threshold before acting as opposed to merely articulating legal belief is arguably higher, particularly when the actor is a state rather than an individual. After all, the conclusion drawn by the ICJ remains applicable by itself: if a state does not express a certain legal conviction and is it unclear why the state did so, uncertainty is the consequence. Such uncertainty will then hardly contribute to the development of legal doctrines.

Often states tend to express a legal conclusion without going into further detail why or why not they regard something as legal or illegal under international law. In those situations, the high degree of uncertainty prevents from drawing a conclusion of what factors led to their view and which factors were regarded as negligible. For instance, if a government announces that one state's actions violated another state's sovereignty, without further specifications on what grounds it reached such a conclusion, it will not be possible to infer that one particular legal aspect was decisive. The violation may have occurred by virtue of the absence of the conditions of self-defense, or because counteractions are regarded as illegitimate forceful reprisal. Perhaps, the applicant of force relied on invalid or totally lacking prior consent of the victim state. Each one of those issues may have been crucial, or of no relevance at all.

On the other hand, there are three exceptions: the first occurs whenever an act or omission was regarded as legal. One can infer from such a finding the absence of circumstances which could have rendered the act or omission illegal. Abidance by the law is, after all, nothing else but the absence of violations thereof. Therefore, this work will assume that if the use of military force was considered to have been legitimate self-defense, despite the fact that it was directed against a non-state actor, a lack of statehood can not have been regarded as decisive in rendering the exercise of self-defense illegitimate *per se*.

---

[279] Lotus case (Fr. v. Turk.), 1927 P.C.I.J. (ser. A) No. 10 at 23, 26, 28-29 (Sept. 7, 1927) (hereinafter *Lotus* case).

Another exception is that states will occasionally offer at least some arguments to support their legal findings. In those cases, it will be assumed that a state took reference to at least some of the most important legal arguments available. The underlying assumption is that all states have an inherent interest in appearing stringent and convincing before the international community. Consequently, non-mentioned factual or legal issues are at least not among the factors which were considered to be decisive. That does not mean that states omitted them because they were of no relevance at all. But it appears to be legitimate to assume that some factors outweigh others by virtue of their decisiveness.

Finally, and perhaps most importantly, some legal findings presuppose the existence or non-existence of other, ground laying legal circumstances. For instance, claiming rights from a sales contract presupposes the claiming party's conviction as to the existence of such a contract. *In casu*, states continuously criticized the exercise of self-defense as disproportionate or unnecessary. If a legal concept is entirely inconceivable simply because it is never available vis-à-vis a non-state entity, recourse to evaluations on proportionality or necessity would be futile (as can be seen in the *Advisory Opinion*). On countless occasions following a state's recourse of force against a non-state actor, states would render a statement such as that "the scale of recent [state] actions and the resulting deaths, particularly the civilian casualties, can in no way be justified."[280] This criticism does not rule out application of counter-force in self-defense *per se*, at least not explicitly. In fact, such remarks merely criticize wrongful application of military force, such as due to a lack of proportionality. Additionally, it would be difficult to infer that such a statement was meant to reserve the speaker's resort to more fundamental criticism, such as that the concerned state was not entitled to apply force at all. Logically, such an argumentative step would already take away the basis, hence the necessity, for remarks regarding proportionality.

A good example for consequences of these antithetic legal approaches is the Israeli Supreme Court's decision in the *Beit Sourik* case, as opposed to the ICJ's findings in the *Advisory Opinion*. The Israeli Supreme Court challenged the fence's proportionality[281] after having deemed it a generally permissible exercise of military necessity during belligerent occupation.[282] The *Advisory Opinion* regarded the fence *per se* as illegitimate, self-defense as a concept was

---

280 U.N.SCOR 36th Sess., 2293rd mtg., at 5, U.N. Doc. S/PV.2293 (remarks by Parsons (United Kingdom)) (July 21, 1981) (these remarks were made in response to the "July-Mini-War" between Israel and the PLO in southern Lebanon in July 1981).

281 HCJ 2056/04 (High Ct. Justice June 20, 2004) Beit Sourik Vill. Council v. Gov't of Isr., I.L.M. 1099, 1113-27 (2004) (hereinafter *Beit Sourik* case).

282 *Beit Sourik* case at 1110.

deemed inapplicable due to the nature of the attacker.[283] A subsequent discussion of proportionality was therefore futile.

The development of firm and solid legal rules based upon the remarks by a state's agents would ideally require even clearer and undeniably certain statements that were made with *opinio iuris*. Until then, the above conclusions are all what is available.

II. Conflicts Between States and Non-States Since the U.N. Charter

The conflicts selected to indicate state practice cover a period of time from the 1950s to the present.[284] Each of the conflicts is between a victim state on the one side, and one or more non-state actors on the other side. The non-state actors operate from within the territory of a host state incapable or unwilling to respond to such actions. In some cases, active support for a non-state actor originates in third states. In all cases, the victim state responded to the non-state actor's force militarily and did so, not always but at least once, relying on self-defense, regardless of the origin of an attack.

In each part, all relevant actors will be introduced briefly, as will the relevant forceful incidents. As some of the conflicts have been or are taking place over several years – sometimes decades – only those incidents were included which by themselves stand out, mostly due to their significance or magnitude. That does not mean, however, that all of the incorporated recourses to force would automatically qualify as armed attacks by themselves.

The Middle East and particularly Israel are mentioned to a relatively high degree. While the concentration in this region of the world is owned to the high number of intertwined, yet different conflicts that arose over the last six decades, it is not intentional. Conflicts were included strictly adhering to the above scheme and not following any regional preference.

Naturally, none of the conflicts could be displayed in full detail and neither does the choice of conflicts claim to represent a complete overview over armed conflicts between states and non-states. It was attempted to concentrate on the major incidents involving self-defense. This work as a whole claims not to constitute a perfect image of reality but rather seeks to indicate tendencies capable of outlining state practice with regard to the conditions of self-defense vis-à-vis non-state actors.

---

[283] *Advisory Opinion*, at para. 139.

[284] Recent developments were included until January 2007.

1. ISRAELI ACTIONS ON LEBANESE TERRITORY TO FIGHT THE PLO AND HEZBOLLAH

The Israeli fight against forces in Lebanon financed and supported through third parties has a long history. Tragically, the almost forty year-long dispute between Israel and different forces in southern Lebanon fell together with a Lebanese state that became an infamous example for a helplessly disrupted and agonized nation, torn apart by a bitter civil war with its never ending clan-feuds. Eventually, several other states and foreign organizations were drawn into the conflict or deliberately chose to exploit the dispute for their purposes. All of them – the PLO, the United States, France, Israel, and Syria – were forced out of the country or decided that withdrawing would be the wiser choice. Syria is likely to retain some control as well as Iran which even quite directly shows its influence through its offspring Hezbollah ("The Party of God"). The United Nations also remains in southern Lebanon with the United Nations Force In Lebanon (UNIFIL) until today.[285] However, neither of them was ever able to improve the situation in Lebanon, but rather, each of them was inevitably made into yet another party in a conflict that followed its very own rules. As Thomas Friedman stated, everyone "who went to Beirut . . . got it the hard way."[286]

This work focuses on Israel's fight with two of the dominant terrorist groups in the Lebanese south, the PLO and Hezbollah. Both groups have various ties to foreign nations, be it financially, logistically, or because their headquarters and administrations are located in different countries. For a period of time, both met in Lebanon.

Interestingly, out of all Arab Muslim countries, the post-Ottoman and post-World War II history of Lebanon began promisingly. Despite an ethnically and religiously diverse society, Lebanon was initially able to arrange for a system in which all of the different groups would find a more or less balanced representation: in 1943 a "National Pact" based upon a 1932 census ordered the political leadership to be allocated by the sizes of all the ethnic and religious groups. All relevant governmental and administrative positions were then filled accordingly.[287] Lebanese society had long been torn between ethnic factions. For

---

[285] *See* S.C. Res. 1697, U.N. Doc S/RES/1697 (July 31, 2006) (extending the old mandate for UNIFIL until August 31, 2006); in the aftermath of the armed conflict between Israel and the Hezbollah in July and August 2006, the Security Council extended the mandate of UNIFIL even until August 31, 2007, and also expanded UNIFIL's competences as to ". . . take all necessary action . . . to ensure that its area of operations is not utilized for hostile activities of any kind . . . .", *see* S.C. Res. 1701, paras. 11-16, U.N. Doc. S/RES/1701 (Aug. 11, 2007).

[286] THOMAS L. FRIEDMAN, FROM BEIRUT TO JERUSALEM 189 (1990).

[287] *See* Stephan Oren, *An Analysis of Lebanese Political Society*, 63 ASIAN AFF. 57-59 (1975) (stating that Lebanon consisted of approx. 29 % Christians, 20 % Sunni and 19 % Shia Mus-

a short period the system worked as laid out by the "National Pact". By the early 1970s, however, the "National Pact" had been outlived by a *de facto* Muslim majority which requested an accordingly adjusted degree of influence.[288] The Christian community feared to lose its privileges and rejected such demands. Over a relatively short period public order degenerated. Countless Lebanese soldiers affiliated with militias of their individual backgrounds and soon Lebanon was caught in a full scale civil war with constantly changing coalitions, invisible front lines, frequent cease-fires, and unpredictable interests in a capricious, surprisingly vibrant country.[289]

Today, the situation within Lebanon is different, although not necessarily less complex. A series of assassinations and covert Syrian influences continue despite attempts to lead Lebanon to an independent and more stable future. Meanwhile, the present government must also deal with Israel's forcible responses following attacks by one of the most ruthless terror organizations in the Middle East – Hezbollah.[290] Despite the Israeli withdrawal under Prime Minister Ehud Barak in May 2000,[291] the conflict is not yet over and for a while was characterized by frequent skirmishes,[292] exchanges of hostages, dead bodies, and prisoners,[293] the official participation of terror groups and militias in Lebanese elections,[294] and Lebanon struggling with its eastern neighbor Syria. The latter officially withdrew its regular armed forces,[295] but is nevertheless blamed for continuing to exert considerable influence on Lebanese politics, notably through

---

lims, and roughly 30 % others, among them Eastern Orthodox and Melkite Christians, as well as Druse and Armenian Gregorians; the President had to be a Maronite, the Prime Minister a Sunni etc).

[288] *See* Oren, *supra* note 287 at 60.

[289] *See* FRIEDMAN, *supra* note 286 at 21 (who assessed the situation just perfectly by the headline of chapter two: "Would You Like to Eat Now or Wait for the Cease-fire?").

[290] As with most transliterations from Arabic or Persian into English it is often not entirely clear, which one suits best. Most of the sources reviews referred to "Hezbollah" instead of *e.g.* "Hizbullah" or "Hizb'allah".

[291] William A. Orme Jr., *Retreat From Lebanon: The Israelis*, N.Y. TIMES, May 24, 2000, at A13.

[292] *See, e.g.*, Greg Myre, *Israel Strikes Northern Gaza And Lebanon With Planes*, N.Y. TIMES, Dec. 28, 2005, at A11.

[293] John Ward Anderson, *Hezbollah Releases Israeli Businessman as Prisoner Swap Begins*, WASH. POST, Jan. 29, 2004, at A 21.

[294] Hussein Dakroub, *Hezbollah Wins Easy Victory In Elections in Southern Lebanon*, WASH. POST, June 6, 2005, at A14.

[295] Colum Lynch, Robin Wright, *Lebanon Free of Syrian Troops; UN Uncertain About Agents*, WASH. POST, May 24, 2005, at A13.

the alleged assassinations of leading personalities through Syrian agents.[296] In mid-2006, the situation exploded once again after Hezbollah intensified its rocket attacks and once again abducted Israeli soldiers. Israel in return launched another invasion of southern Lebanon.[297]

a) PLO IN LEBANON

The PLO was founded by the Arab League of Nations in 1964 to create a platform for Palestinian interests and to work towards an independent state of Palestine. At first, this state was meant to replace the State of Israel; today the PLO accepts a bi-state solution. As of 1969 it was dominated by the Egyptian-born Yasser Arafat and its Fatah group. Fatah ("victory") eventually became the dominant faction within the Palestinian Authority (PA) under PLO chairman Arafat and his successor Mahmud Abbas.

After the expulsion from Jordan by King Hussein during the "Black September" of 1970, Lebanon remained the only accessible country for the PLO having a direct border with Israel. Lebanon became a state bound to serve as a non-state actor's base for extraterritorial violence and terror:[298] the State of Lebanon was failing by the time the PLO decided to turn it into the center of its operations. Basic functions of the Lebanese government were paralyzed due to several religious and ethnic factions struggling over supremacy. The PLO – Sunni Muslim but secular in origin – had its strongholds in the areas dominated by the approximately 300,000 Palestinian refugees, primarily in parts of Beirut and in Southern Lebanon, east of Tyre. It was initially primarily opposed by the Christian militias who spotted yet another rival. They called for a governmental military response to the "state-within-a-state" which the PLO had created.[299] However, an effective executive able to respond to that call, such as the Jordanian government under King Hussein in 1970-71, no longer existed in Lebanon.

Early, the PLO apparently had decided terror against Israel would be best to improve the situation of the Arabs in the West Bank and Gaza. For that purpose, the PLO primarily targeted Israeli nationals, institutions such as embassies, and Israeli airplanes. At no point did the PLO distinguish between combatants and civilians. Rather, it killed Israelis wherever possible: in Greece,[300]

---

[296] John Kifner, Warren Hoge, *Top Syrian Seen a Prime Suspect in Assassination*, N.Y. TIMES, Oct. 21, 2005, at A1.
[297] *See infra* note 589.
[298] For an overview *see* Shlomo Gazit, *Israel in Transition: Israel and the Palestinians: Fifty Years of Wars and Turning Points*, 555 ANNALS AM. ACAD. POL. SOC. SCI. 82, 90-91.
[299] FRIEDMAN, *supra* note 286 at 16-18.
[300] In December 1968, an airplane of the Israeli national airline El Al was attacked in the Athens airport by two PFLP members, *see* Baker, *supra* note 37 at 34, 35.

Germany,[301] France,[302] and other places. First and foremost, the PLO launched terror campaigns inside Israel.[303] In 1975, Israel confronted the U.N. Security Council with "approx. 150 acts of terrorism instigated by the PLO, originating in Lebanon, against Israelis and Jews in Israel and elsewhere: in Athens, Vienna, Paris and London" over a period of not much more than one year.[304] In 1985, the Israeli Foreign Ministry issued figures that state approximately 8,000 minor and major terror attacks, killing more than 650 Israelis since 1969.[305]

Israel reacted by counter-force. As cooperation on a law enforcement basis with the PLO's host and supporter states was not a promising outlook, Israel regarded itself to be limited to the use of military force. The Israeli Defense Forces (IDF) attacked PLO strongholds in southern Lebanon.[306] The IDF pushed the PLO back to Beirut and eventually forced it to leave the Lebanese capital under French supervision in 1982.[307] The PLO leadership was evacuated and the PLO lost its ability to use Lebanon as a safe haven for terror. From its old and new base, Tunis, the PLO continued to engage in terror attacks against Israelis. Among them was the shooting of three Israelis aboard a yacht in Larnaca, Cyprus, in September 1985. In retaliation the Israeli Air Force bombed the PLO headquarters in Borj Cedria, in the vicinity of Tunis.[308] In October, the PLO captured the Italian cruise liner Achille Lauro and killed an American tourist.[309]

Around 1987, the PLO returned to southern Lebanon and continued to attack Israel, but the Palestinian uprising, the first Intifada within the occupied territories, and the impending peace process led to a change of the PLO's role. It

---

[301] In September 1972, a PLO commando murdered eleven Israeli athletes at the Olympic Summer Games in Munich; Israel held Lebanon and Syria responsible for harboring and supporting the killers; *see, e.g.*, *Arab Guerillas Warned By Israel*, N.Y. TIMES, Sept. 7, 1972, at A1.

[302] In April 1982, the Israeli diplomat Yakov Barsimantov was assassinated in Paris by terrorists; Israel held the PLO accountable, *see* O'Brien, *supra* note 37 at 455.

[303] *E.g.* the seizure of a school in the Israeli border town Ma'alot; when Israel rushed the building, 20 students were killed (May 15, 1974); the Fatah attack killing of three civilians in an apartment house in Nahariya (June 24, 1974); the murder of 32 civilians following a bus-hijacking near Haifa by Fatah (March 11, 1978).

[304] *A Debate Flares in Israel Over Air Raids in Lebanon*, N.Y. TIMES, Dec. 5, 1975, at A3.

[305] AMOS GILBOA, *DIE BEDROHUNG DURCH DEN PLO-TERRORISMUS* 5 (1985).

[306] Operation Litani 1978 went as far as the Litani river, south of which the PLO maintained major military bases; *see* O'Brien, *supra* note 37 at 445-50.

[307] The remaining PLO leaders, including Arafat, were evacuated first to Greece and then to Tunis by French peacekeepers in August 1982, *see* FRIEDMAN, *supra* note 286 at 147-155; Gazit, *supra* note 298 at 90, 91.

[308] O'Brien, *supra* note 37 at 460; *see infra* p.186.

[309] *Palestinians hijack an Italian cruise ship*, THE TIMES (London), Oct. 8, 1985, at 1; *see also* Halberstam, *supra* note 191 at 269.

did not regain former strength in southern Lebanon. Rather, the PLO turned its attention to the Occupied Palestinian Territories and established its first internationally accepted government under Yasser Arafat in the mid-90s.

In 2006, the Fatah and the PLO under Arafat's successor Mahmud Abbas lost the first elections for a new Palestinian parliament in ten years to the extreme Islamist terror group Hamas,[310] the Palestinian offshoot of the Egyptian Muslim Brotherhood.[311]

b) HEZBOLLAH IN LEBANON

The other important non-state actor in the Israeli-Lebanese conflict is Hezbollah. It grew out of the Shia minority in Lebanon and was organizationally formed around June 1982.[312] At the same time, the IDF had launched its Lebanese invasion to drive out the PLO.[313] About two months later, Yasser Arafat was evacuated to Tunis.[314] Necessarily, the Israelis interfered during those days also with the Lebanese Shia Muslims – a large portion of the Lebanese population. As in 1978, Israel's major field of military operation was areas inhabited by Sunni Palestinian Arabs on the one hand, and Shia Muslims on the other hand. Both of them, along with the Lebanese Druse, concentrated in southern Lebanon, and were at odds with each other.[315] In fact, the Shi'ites welcomed the Israeli invasion, hoping that it would help them to gain dominance over the Lebanese south from the PLO. Soon, their initial hopes were smashed by the fact that Israel began to arrange for a longer Lebanese occupation, and eventually took sides with the Christian militias. This became most apparent after the murder of the Christian militia leader Bashir Gemayel on September 14, 1982 and the subsequent revenge by Christians who massacred over 1,500 men, women, and children in Sabra and Shatila, two Palestinian refugee camps in Beirut. The Israeli army refused to stop the killings that endured for several days

---

[310] Steven Erlanger, *Hamas Routs Ruling Fraction, Casting Pall on Peace Process*, N.Y. TIMES, Jan. 27, 2006, at A1.

[311] For background information about Hamas and similar groups engaged in terror against Israel *see, e.g.*, HUMAN RIGHTS WATCH, ERASED IN A MOMENT: SUICIDE BOMBING ATTACKS AGAINST ISRAELI CIVILIANS (2002), *available at* http://www.hrw.org/reports/2002/isrl-pa/ (last visited Feb. 2, 2006).

[312] MAGNUS RANSTORP, HIZB'ALLAH IN LEBANON 25 (1997).

[313] John Sharkey, *Israel Launches Invasion of Lebanon,* WASH. POST, June 7, 1982, at A1.

[314] FRIEDMAN, *supra* note 286 at 151-55.

[315] Edward Cody, *Palestinian Guerrillas Begin to Alienate Lebanese Moslem Allies*, WASH. POST, May 27, 1982, at A32.

after September 14, 1982.[316] That which had been known as the Israeli-PLO conflict thus turned into an Israeli-Hezbollah conflict within a very short period of time.

Hezbollah represented the first radically Islamic force of the inner-Lebanese conflict. Iran played an important role here.[317] Like the Amal militias, Hezbollah is a Shi'ite faction but unlike Amal it sought to establish a strictly Islamic Lebanese society. Their concept of "jihad" allowed them to employ measures that had yet been more or less unknown to the inner-Lebanese conflict, such as suicide attacks executed by "martyrs" who considered themselves in accordance with religious duties when they slaughtered "infidels".[318] The Central Intelligence Agency (CIA) noted in an internal memorandum in December 1983 without mentioning Hezbollah explicitly (in the declassified section):

> We are especially concerned about signs of increased cooperation among individual Shia extremist groups . . . . The Shia in particular are prepared – even anxious – to sacrifice themselves as martyrs in terrorist operations . . . . [M]embers of these groups are planning to use . . . human "kamikadze" bombs [to strike again at U.S. and French Multinational Forces targets] . . . . Iran will continue to encourage and provide aide to these groups for the commission of acts of terrorism, particularly against U.S. and French targets . . . . The radical Shias . . . almost certainly have secured at least acquiescence of Syria . . . .[319]

The first years of Hezbollah in Lebanon were characterized by its struggle to dominate the Lebanese factions in the Bekaa region, in Beirut and finally in south of Lebanon. By the active help from Iran and the intentional omissions by Syria, Hezbollah successfully attacked the remainders of the Lebanese army and U.S. marines stationed in Beirut.[320] Despite the uncertainty about the origin of

---

[316] Collin Campbell, *Raids On Camps Started Day After Gemayel Died,* N.Y. TIMES, Sept. 19, 1982, at 14; for an overview over the Sabra and Shatilla killings *see* ZE'EV SCHIFF, EHUD YA'ARI, *Israel's Lebanon War* 250-85 (updated ed. 1986).

[317] RANSTORP, *supra* note 312 at 25-30.

[318] For an overview over Hezbollah's agenda and how they introduced it to the largely secular oriented Lebanese society *see* HARIK, *supra* note 38 at 53-94.

[319] Memorandum for Director of Central Intelligence, William J. Casey, from the Acting Director of Global Issues (Nov. 30, 1983) (declassified CIA document) (on file with author).

[320] Michael Getler, *The Beirut Massacre; Iran-Backed Force Believed Behind Attack on Marines,* WASH. POST, Oct. 24, 1982, at A15.

the suicide bombers that devastated the U.S. marine compound on October 23, 1983, the subsequent U.S. withdrawal was celebrated as a Hezbollah victory.[321]

Hezbollah's support from Iran included direct military help such as the sending of several hundred "Revolutionary Guards" stationed in Baalbeck, 150 of whom had been sent as early as 1982 to fight the Israeli invasion alongside Palestinian forces.[322]

The role that Hezbollah plays in the Middle East and thus its legal relevance for the purpose of this work grew between 2000 and 2006. After Israel's withdrawal the Shi'ite militia was increasingly supported by the Iranian government and supplied with modern rockets and weapon systems.[323] In 2005, Hezbollah gained 14 seats in the newly elected government and dispatched two ministers into Prime Minster Fouad Siniora's government.[324]

---

[321] RANSTORP, *supra* note 312 at 38 (noting that "the alleged complicity of Hizb'allah promoted the movement as the spearhead of the sacred Muslim struggle against foreign occupation).

[322] David B. Ottaway, *Baalbek Seen As Staging Area For Terrorism,* WASH. POST, Jan, 9, 1984, at A1.

[323] *See, e.g.,* James Risen, *A Nation Challenged: A Suspect; U.S. Traces Iran's Ties to Terror Through a Lebanese*, N.Y. TIMES, Jan. 17, 2002, at A17 ("Central Intelligence Agency documents show that Imad Mugniyah, one of the world's most wanted men, has been operating for years with protection and backing of Iranian intelligence services; Mugniyah, Lebanese and leader in Hezbollah guerilla group, is charged with terrorist hijacking of TWA jet in 1985 and implicated in recent shipment of arms from Iran to Palestinians"); Mark Mazettti, Thom Shankner, *Turmoil in Mideast: Weapons; Arming of Hezbollah Reveals U.S. and Israeli Blind Spots*, N.Y. TIMES, July 19, 2006, at A12 ("While Iranian missile supplies to Hezbollah, either by sea or overland via Syria, were well known, [U.S.] officials said the current conflict also indicated that some of the rockets in Hezbollah's arsenal . . . were built in Syria."); Steven Erlanger, Richard A. Oppel Jr., *Hostilities in the Mideast: The Militia; A Disciplined Hezbollah Surprises Israel With Its Training, Tactics, and Weapons,* N.Y TIMES, Aug. 7, 2006, at A8 ("According to Israeli military intelligence, the [Syrian transport] planes [carrying aid supplies after the 2003 Bam earthquake] returned to Syria carrying sophisticated weapons, including long-range Zelzal missiles, which the Syrians passed on to Hezbollah, the Shiite militia group in southern Lebanon that Iran created and sponsors"); Aluf Benn, *IAF wiped out 59 Iranian missile launchers in 34 minutes*, HAARETZ ONLINE, Oct. 24, 2006, available at
http://www.haaretz.com/hasen/spages/778485.html (last visited Oct. 24, 2006) (reporting about a "research recently published by . . . the Washington Institute of Near East Policy" which indicates that an "air attack of 13 July [2006] struck the Zelzal and Fajr missiles in the Hezbollah arsenal, both made in Iran").

[324] Hussein Dakroub, *Hezbollah Wins Easy Victory In Elections in Southern Lebanon*, WASH. POST, June 6, 2005, at A14.

c) SINGULAR INCIDENTS AND STATES' RESPONSES

Not always, though often, Israel relied on self-defense to combat terrorist threats from within the Lebanese borders. The international community and especially the U.N. Security Council almost always rejected Israel's legal reasoning. Some states – most frequently the United States – expressed sympathy for Israel's claim to self-defense. However, criticism almost exclusively focused on the lack of proportionality of Israeli actions. The fact that the PLO and Hezbollah were non-state actors, both of which were also under some degree of "control" by Israel as those terror groups against which the Defense Barrier was erected,[325] was never mentioned in the official complaints and statements reviewed. Israel's chosen methods and their magnitude – not the right to self-defense against non-state actors hiding behind host states – were at stake here.

i) MILITARY RESPONSES AGAINST THE PLO

To fight the PLO, the IDF launched several attacks, most prominent being the Operation Litani between March and June 1978 and Operation Peace for Galilee between June and September 1982. Among the other major operations were the following:[326] an attack on the Beirut airport (December 28, 1968); a raid in south Lebanon (August 26, 1969); the invasion of south Lebanon (May 12, 1970); another invasion of south Lebanon (September 2, 1970); a raid against terror facilities (January 14, 1971); an incursion into Lebanon (February 1972); another Lebanon incursion (June 1972); a strike against Lebanon (September 7, 1972); a raid on Beirut (April 12, 1973); a raid on villages (April 12-13, 1974); attacks on PLO bases (May 16-21, 1974, and May-June, 1975); air raids on various targets (December 2, 1975); commando raids against PLO bases in Lebanon (spring 1980 – spring 1981); the "July Mini-War of 1981" in Lebanon; an air attack on PLO targets in Lebanon (April 21, 1982); an attack on PLO targets in Lebanon (May 9, 1982); an air raid on the Lebanese bases of PLO dissident Abu Musa (September 1985); air raids near Sidon (January 2, 1988); and a small-scale invasion reaching beyond Lebbaya (May 2, 1988).

During the first years of PLO clashes with Israel the pattern of small scale terrorist attacks either directly in Israel, or with an effect on the state, resulted in Israeli counterforce by the IDF. Already in 1968, Israel complained about terrorist attacks emanating from Lebanese territory and responded forcibly in exercise of self-defense.[327] In December, the IDF hit the Beirut airport, a response to prior terrorist attacks on the Israeli civil aviation in Athens emanating from and

---

[325] *Cf. Advisory Opinion*, at para. 139.

[326] Robert J. Beck, *"Don't Treat On Us": International Law and Forcible State Responses to Terrorism*, 12 WIS. INT'L L.J. 153, 184 at n.157 (1994).

[327] 1968 U.N.Y.B. 228.

planned in Beirut. According to the Israeli delegate to the United Nations, any "attack against an Israeli civil aircraft . . . entitles the Israeli Government to exercise its right to self-defense."[328] It is important to note that the target of the counter-attack was an airport under control of the Lebanese government and not the PLO or other groups. Many speakers noted that the state of Lebanon bore no responsibility for the violence that had occurred in Athens.

Accordingly, the Lebanese government announced that this was "the first time in history that a State [i.e. Lebanon] has been held responsible for the acts of persons whom it has in no way assisted . . ., and who [happen] to be on its territory because they cannot return to their Palestinian homeland . . . ."[329]

The United States considered the Israeli response to be clearly disproportionate but also otherwise bare of any justification. Most notably, the United States announced that "[n]othing we have heard has convinced us that the Government of Lebanon is responsible for the occurrence in Athens." In fact, Lebanon "has made efforts to control the actions of fedayeen groups in its territory."[330] Consequently, self-defense against the fedayeen, armed PLO members, appears to be unavailable as such. China announced largely identical comments.[331] The Indian responses could be interpreted similarly, as it described the Israeli response as "unprovoked, unnecessary, and a flagrant violation of the Charter of the United Nations."[332] The attacks by terror groups on an Israeli airplane remained unmentioned and seem not to suffice in order to justify the subsequent military response.

Many other states shared that view or saw the Israeli attacks as illegitimate reprisal.[333] Others condemned it as aggression.[334] Brazil merely considered

---

[328] U.N. SCOR, 23rd Sess., 1460th mtg., at 5, U.N. Doc. S/PV.1460 (remarks by Rosenne (Israel)) (Dec. 29, 1968).

[329] U.N. SCOR, 23rd Sess., 1461st mtg., at 3, U.N. Doc. S/PV.1461 (remarks by Boutros (Lebanon)) (Dec. 30, 1968) (quoting the Lebanese President).

[330] U.N. SCOR, 23rd Sess., 1460th mtg., at 6, U.N. Doc. S/PV.1460 (remarks by Wiggins (United States)) (Dec. 29, 1968).

[331] U.N. SCOR, 23rd Sess., 1461st mtg., at 6, U.N. Doc. S/PV.1461 (remarks by Chang (China)) (Dec. 30, 1968).

[332] U.N. SCOR, 23rd Sess., 1460th mtg., at 9, U.N. Doc. S/PV.1460 (remarks by Parthasarathi (India)) (Dec. 29, 1968).

[333] Paraguay: U.N. SCOR, 23rd Sess., 1461st mtg., at 8, U.N. Doc. S/PV.1461 (remarks by Solano Lopez (Paraguay)) (Dec. 30, 1968); Senegal: U.N. SCOR, 23rd Sess., 1460th mtg., at 12, U.N. Doc. S/PV.1460 (remarks by M'Bengue (Senegal)) (Dec. 29, 1968); Soviet Union: U.N. SCOR, 23rd Sess., 1461st mtg., at 13, U.N. Doc. S/PV.1461 (remarks by Malik (Soviet Union)) (Dec. 30, 1968).

[334] Algeria: U.N. SCOR, 23rd Sess., 1460th mtg., at 11, U.N. Doc. S/PV.1460 (remarks by Ben Kaci (Algeria)) (Dec. 29, 1968); France: U.N. SCOR, 23rd Sess., 1462nd mtg., at 3, U.N. Doc.

Israel's response "unjustified"[335] and added later that the Lebanese government could not be held accountable.[336] The United Kingdom, on the other hand, focused on the disproportionate nature of Israel's counter-measures "against . . . this sombre background."[337] Canada[338] and Denmark[339] joined. However, another British representative later added that "subversive violence . . . is no less aggression than open attack."[340] The Russian delegate eventually explored in greater detail why the use of armed force was not available for Israel: Reprisals may not involve any recourse to force and self-defense required Lebanese responsibility. The latter neither lay in active support of the terrorists nor could be deduced from the fact that the perpetrators had been present in Lebanon.[341] The United Nations Security Council condemned Israel unanimously.[342]

The situation did not improve in 1969. Lebanon once again complained about several armed incidents, among them one assault on villages close to the border in August.[343] Israel invoked self-defense against continuous attacks by "irregular terror forces", namely Fatah and its umbrella organization, the PLO.[344] Again, some states considered the Israeli response an aggression by itself.[345] The United Kingdom, "if it is true, as . . . Israel has stated, . . . that

---

S/PV.1462 (remarks by Chayet (France)) (Dec. 31, 1968); Hungary: U.N. SCOR, 23rd Sess., 1460th mtg., at 10, U.N. Doc. S/PV.1460 (remarks by Csatorady (Hungary)) (Dec. 29, 1968); Pakistan: U.N. SCOR, 23rd Sess., 1461st mtg., at 7, U.N. Doc. S/PV.1461 (remarks by Shahi (Pakistan)) (Dec. 30, 1968); Soviet Union: U.N. SCOR, 23rd Sess., 1460th mtg., at 8, U.N. Doc. S/PV.1460 (remarks by Malik (Soviet Union)) (Dec. 29, 1968).

335 U.N. SCOR, 23rd Sess., 1460th mtg., at 12, U.N. Doc. S/PV.1460 (remarks by De Araujo Castro (Brazil)) (Dec. 29, 1968).

336 U.N. SCOR, 23rd Sess., 1462nd mtg., at 2, U.N. Doc. S/PV.1462 (remarks by De Araujo Castro (Brazil)) (Dec. 31, 1968).

337 U.N. SCOR, 23rd Sess., 1460th mtg., at 7, U.N. Doc. S/PV.1460 (remarks by Glass (United Kingdom)) (Dec. 29, 1968).

338 U.N. SCOR, 23rd Sess., 1461st mtg., at 4, U.N. Doc. S/PV.1461 (remarks by Ignatieff (Canada)) (Dec. 30, 1968).

339 *Id.* at 4 (remarks by Borch (Denmark)).

340 U.N. SCOR, 23rd Sess., 1461st mtg., at 5, U.N. Doc. S/PV.1461 (remarks by Caradon (United Kingdom)) (Dec. 30, 1968).

341 U.N. SCOR, 23rd Sess., 1462nd mtg., at 5, U.N. Doc. S/PV.1462 (remarks by Malik (Soviet Union)) (Dec. 31, 1968).

342 S.C. Res. 268 (Dec. 31, 1968), 1968 U.N.Y.B. 231.

343 1969 U.N.Y.B. 200.

344 1969 U.N.Y.B. 201; U.N. SCOR, 24th Sess., 1501st mtg., at 4, U.N. Doc. S/PV.1501 (remarks by Tekoah (Israel)) (Aug. 15, 1969).

345 Spain: U.N. SCOR, 24th Sess., 1502nd mtg., at 6, U.N. Doc. S/PV.1502 (remarks by De Pinies (Spain)) (Aug. 15, 1969); Soviet Union: U.N. SCOR, 24th Sess., 1504th mtg., at 4, U.N. Doc. S/PV.1504 (remarks by Zakharov (Soviet Union)) (Aug. 26, 1969).

'twenty-one attacks'" have been carried out against Israel, considered the irregular's behavior a "provocation" which, however, could not justify the Israeli response.[346] Finland announced that none of the "essential facts were in dispute."[347] Responsibilities for these facts were disputed. Israel fought Palestinian commandos whose cause, but not whose actions, were supported by Lebanon. Essentially, and regardless of responsibilities, both parties were under an obligation to respect the cease-fire.[348] China stated largely the same.[349] Columbia rejected any kind of reprisals as "indefensible."[350]

Nepal's representative asked whether "a Government [is] justified, in the name of self-defence, in launching air attacks on hostile encampments in a foreign state whose official participation in the hostile activities have been disowned?"[351] The answer given to states that "[v]iolent actions on the part of a Government [i.e. Israel] carried out in an excessive concern for security cannot be justified, as it would seem that the 11 August air attack on foreign territory was far in excess of the strict requirement of self-defence."[352] The nature of the attacker remains unmentioned. It may very well be that the "excess" was meant to include application of counter-force in disregard of the unavailability of the PLO as a legitimate target in absence of their state character – it does not seem the most plausible interpretation yet. Rather, the word "excess" is pointing at the disproportionate use of force. Had the attacks been executed more cautiously self-defense might have been available short of any "excess". The legal nature of the attacker seems to constitute a primary obstacle.

The Spanish delegate also took some time to elaborate on Israel's continuous reliance on self-defense. In his view, self-defense as a concept was "completely unacceptable." Israel's actions were "premeditated" and it was nothing less than a "mockery of the legal principles of self-defence to try to fit preventive war and reprisal into that framework."[353] The absence of an armed attack is apparently what Spain is aiming at. This could be due to the nature of the attacker – who, as a non-state actor, might have been considered as incapa-

---

[346] U.N. SCOR, 24th Sess., 1501st mtg., at 1, U.N. Doc. S/PV.1501 (remarks by Warner (United Kingdom)) (Aug. 15, 1969).
[347] *Id.* at 2 (remarks by Jakobson (Finland)).
[348] *Id.*
[349] U.N. SCOR, 24th Sess., 1502nd mtg., at 3, U.N. Doc. S/PV.1502 (remarks by Liu (China)) (Aug. 18, 1969).
[350] *Id.* at 1 (remarks by Morales Suarez (Columbia)).
[351] U.N. SCOR, 24th Sess., 1501st mtg., at 3, U.N. Doc. S/PV.1501 (remarks by Khatri (Nepal)) (Aug. 15, 1969).
[352] *Id.*
[353] U.N. SCOR, 24th Sess., 1502nd mtg., at 6,7, U.N. Doc. S/PV.1502 (remarks by De Pinies (Spain)) (Aug. 15, 1969).

ble of launching an armed attack – or due to the insignificance of the force applied by the PLO. The legal nature of the attacker is, however, not mentioned as an insuperable *ex ante* obstruction. Israel was condemned unanimously for its "premeditated" attack.[354]

1970 was a year that saw many armed incidents between Israel and armed guerilla forces operating from inside southern Lebanon.[355] In May 1970, Israel invoked self-defense against continuing cross-border raids from Lebanese territory[356] and announced that it consequently destroyed 16 camps and bases used by irregular forces.[357] Lebanon and with it most other states represented at the Security Council condemned Israel's actions as aggression[358] in a lengthy and occasionally peculiar[359] Security Council session. Colombia demanded a resolution that would also deplore guerilla actions emanating from Lebanon. Its representative considered Israel as being compelled to respond to "frontier violations

---

[354] S.C. Res. 270 (Aug. 26, 1969), 1969 U.N.Y.B. 208.

[355] *See, e.g.,* Moshe Brilliant, *Israel aircraft attack Egypt and Lebanon*, THE TIMES (London), Jan. 7, 1970, at 7; Moshe Brilliant, *Raids into Israel from Lebanon increase*, THE TIMES (London), March 3, 1970, at 6; Paul Martin, *Guerillas go back into bases as Israel troops leave*, THE TIMES (London), May 14, 1970, at 5; Moshe Brilliant, *Israelis raid village in Lebanon*, THE TIMES (London), Dec. 29, 1970, at 4.

[356] U.N. SCOR, 25th Sess., 1537th mtg., at 4,5 U.N. Doc. S/PV.1537 (remarks by Tekoah (Israel)) (May 12, 1970).

[357] 1970 U.N.Y.B. 234.

[358] Morocco: U.N. SCOR, 25th Sess., 1538th mtg., at 4, U.N. Doc. S/PV.1538 (remarks by Benhima (Morocco)) (May 12, 1970); Poland: U.N. SCOR, 25th Sess., 1540th mtg., at 3, U.N. Doc. S/PV.1540 (remarks by Kulaga (Poland)) (May 14, 1970); Spain: U.N. SCOR, 25th Sess., 1537th mtg., at 9, U.N. Doc. S/PV.1537 (remarks by De Pinies (Spain)) (May 12, 1970); Soviet Union: *id.* at 6 (remarks by Malik (Soviet Union)); Syria: U.N. SCOR, 25th Sess., 1538th mtg., at 15, U.N. Doc. S/PV.1538 (remarks by Tomeh (Syria)) (May 12, 1970);

[359] The Saudi representative, as on prior occasions, blatantly fostered anti-Semitic prejudices as he elaborated on elusive historical 'explanations' such as that "the United States . . . was railroaded into the First World War to a large extent by the efforts of American Zionists with whom the Zionists in the United Kingdom during the Second World War communicated. . . . Then there was a quarrel [sic] in Europe during the Second World War amongst the Allies and Germans. . . . [T]he Zionists unfortunately succeeded in enlisting [the United States] to enter the Second World War." As to the Middle East he asked "why should we Arabs pay the price just because Zionists have the means to brainwash certain Western peoples?"; *see* U.N. SCOR, 25th Sess., 1538th mtg., at 12,13, U.N. Doc. S/PV.1538 (remarks by Baroody (Saudi Arabia)) (May 12, 1970); later in the discussion, "Ambassador Baroody, with his vast erudition and his great talent" was congratulated by the French delegate for related remarks concerning the fact "that for centuries Jews and Arabs lived and worked side by side"; *see* U.N. SCOR, 25th Sess., 1541st mtg., at 5, U.N. Doc. S/PV.1541 (remarks by Kosciusko-Morizet (France)) (May 15, 1970).

by Palestine commandos" which, however, Columbia could not condone.[360] The United States labeled Israel's actions "reprisals" bur recognized that Israel was "justifiably concerned over its own security . . . ."[361] Otherwise, the U.S. representative considered Israel's actions as disproportionate.[362] Zambia[363] considered the raids as illegitimate reprisals, and Burundi added that these reprisals were also disproportionate.[364] Finland found Israel to have committed an illegitimate act of retaliation and violated the cease-fire.[365] The United Kingdom also spotted a "retaliation" and condemned "the premeditated military action on Lebanese territory."[366] France, while denying Israel the right to annexation, recognized Israel's right to exist and secure borders but considered Israel's raids an "inadmissible" escalation.[367] The Chinese delegate considered it "a well-known fact . . . that . . . Lebanon has tried to use every means at its disposal to restrain the [Palestinian] guerillas." Hence, Israel's actions constituted an illegitimate "military retaliation" against " a country which did not participate in the June 1967 war . . . ."[368]

The subsequent resolution condemned Israel and did not refer to military action from armed bands.[369] Neither did any state respond to Israel's invocation of self-defense, nor reject it based upon the legal nature of the guerilla forces.

Israel either conducted further operations on Lebanese territory or it fired into Lebanese territory to hit PLO forces. The U.N. Security Council responded by continuous condemnations through resolutions.[370] All of them regarded Lebanese sovereignty as having been violated and urged Israel to cease military actions and also to withdraw all forces that were in Lebanon, either permanently

---

[360] U.N. SCOR, 25th Sess., 1541st mtg., at 2, U.N. Doc. S/PV.1541 (remarks by Vallejo-Arbelaez (Columbia)) (May 15, 1970).
[361] U.N. SCOR, 25th Sess., 1540th mtg., at 5, U.N. Doc. S/PV.1540 (remarks by Yost (United States)) (May 14, 1970).
[362] U.N. SCOR, 25th Sess., 1542nd mtg., at 10, U.N. Doc. S/PV.1542 (remarks by Yost (United States)) (May 19, 1970).
[363] U.N. SCOR, 25th Sess., 1540th mtg., at 1, U.N. Doc. S/PV.1540 (remarks by Mwaanga (Zambia)) (May 14, 1970).
[364] *Id.* at 6 (remarks by Magenge (Burundi)).
[365] U.N. SCOR, 25th Sess., 1539th mtg., at 7,8, U.N. Doc. S/PV.1539 (remarks by Jakobson (Finland)) (May 13, 1970).
[366] U.N. SCOR, 25th Sess., 1542nd mtg., at 8, U.N. Doc. S/PV.1542 (remarks by Caradon (United Kingdom)) (May 19, 1970).
[367] U.N. SCOR, 25th Sess., 1541st mtg., at 5, U.N. Doc. S/PV.1541 (remarks by Kosciusko-Morizet (France)) (May 15, 1970).
[368] *Id.* at 4 (remarks by Liu (China)).
[369] S.C. Res. 280 (May 19, 1970), 1970 U.N.Y.B. 243.
[370] *See, e.g.*, S.C. Res. 270 (Aug. 26, 1969), 1969 U.N.Y.B. 208; S.C. Res. 313 (Feb. 28, 1972), 1972 U.N.Y.B. 172; S.C. Res. 347 (Apr. 24, 1974), 1974 U.N.Y.B. 210-11.

or for single missions.[371] Prior to the Lebanese civil war, Israel regarded the still existing and largely functioning Lebanese government as responsible "for the activities of the terrorist groups."[372]

In September 1970, Israel once again pointed at its right to self-defense against armed attacks and counted over 200 acts of aggression from Lebanese territory since May 1970.[373] Before the United Nations Security Council, no state expressed its legal views with regard to Israeli self-defense and the Security Council simply urged Israel to withdraw.[374] Spain considered Israel to have waged an "invasion",[375] the United States recognized "a pattern of guerillas-type raids conducted from Lebanese territory against Israel and Israeli counter-attacks . . . . "[376]

In 1971, Israel again invoked self-defense against armed attacks from Lebanese territory, while Lebanon complained about Israeli aggressions.[377]

In February 1972 the IDF started military incursions into Lebanon after a number of terrorist attacks and Israel's repeated warnings to the Lebanese government.[378] Israel considered itself in exercise of self-defense against armed attacks that were not prevented by the Lebanese government.[379] France, on the other hand, was convinced that Lebanon did all it could to control the armed activities emanating from its territory but did not regard Lebanon responsible for what such groups did abroad. Furthermore, Israel's reprisals were considered as disproportionate.[380] This statement might mean that France did not regard the PLO's actions as attributable to Lebanon and thus denies the possibility of any armed attack against Israel. Accordingly, an armed attack would presuppose the existence of state controlled, rather than "fedayeen" i.e. non-state action. Such legal convictions were, however, not expressed explicitly.

Somalia's delegate also chose to ignore terrorist activities and focused on Lebanese actions which, as he noted, had not occurred: "After all, it is the armed forces of Israel that have violated the territory of Lebanon. Lebanese armed

---

[371] For an overview of the time between 1971 and 1975 *see* O'Brien, *supra* note 37 at 426-43.
[372] *See, e.g.,* 1968 U.N.Y.B. 229.
[373] U.N. SCOR, 25th Sess., 1551st mtg., at 4,5, U.N. Doc. S/PV.1551 (remarks by Rosenne (Israel)) (Sept. 5, 1970).
[374] S.C. Res. 285 (Sept. 5, 1970), 1970 U.N.Y.B. 244.
[375] U.N. SCOR, 25th Sess., 1551st mtg., at 6, U.N. Doc. S/PV.1551 (remarks by De Pinies (Spain)) (Sept. 5, 1970).
[376] *Id.* at 7 (remarks by Buffum (United States)).
[377] 1971 U.N.Y.B. 177-78.
[378] *Israel Warns Lebanon After 2 Die in Border Ambush*, N.Y. TIMES, Feb. 25, 1972, at A1.
[379] U.N. SCOR, 27th Sess., 1643rd mtg., at 5, U.N. Doc. S/PV.1643 (remarks by Doron (Israel)) (Feb. 26, 1972).
[380] *Id.* at 12 (remarks by Kosciusko-Morizet (France)).

forces have not violated the territory of Israel."[381] Again, one could argue that for the purpose of Article 2 (3), (4) of the Charter, also referred to by Somalia in this regard,[382] non-state actions are irrelevant. Beside this very loose interpretation of what it is that was meant to be prohibited by Article 2 (4) of the Charter, such an argument is once again not made explicitly.

The Argentinean representative explained the conditions for the exercise of self-defense in greater detail: "Self-defence and legitimate self-defence are concepts recognized in international law for responding to illegal or aggressive acts committed against States, provided that two indispensable requisites are met: need and proportionality" – neither of which he considered to be present in this case.[383] The fact that the initial attacks stemmed from Palestinian fedayeen, and not regular Lebanese forces, remain unmentioned.

The remarks made by the delegate from the United Kingdom focused on proportionality as "recourse to those measures against Lebanon – measures on that scale – . . . " were considered unjustifiable.[384] Belgium,[385] Japan,[386] Italy,[387] and Sudan[388] also considered Israel's counter-action in excess of the events that had prompted it. Proportionality, rather than the exclusion of non-state action within the Charter's self-defense regime is what dominates their legal views. Many states once again merely saw an Israeli aggression.[389] The United States understood that Israel "is exposed to terrorist attacks and . . . feels compelled to retaliate in self-defence." However, the problem could not be solved by continuous recourse to force.[390] Eventually, United Nations Security Council resolution

---

[381] U.N. SCOR, 27th Sess., 1643rd mtg., at 18, U.N. Doc. S/PV.1643 (remarks by Farah (Somalia)) (Feb. 26, 1972).

[382] *Id.*

[383] U.N. SCOR, 27th Sess., 1644th mtg., at 3, U.N. Doc. S/PV.1644 (remarks by Ortiz de Rozas (Argentina)) (Feb. 27, 28, 1972).

[384] U.N. SCOR, 27th Sess., 1643rd mtg., at 13, U.N. Doc. S/PV.1643 (remarks by Jamieson (United Kingdom)) (Feb. 26, 1972).

[385] *Id.* at 15 (remarks by Longerstaey (Belgium)).

[386] U.N. SCOR, 27th Sess., 1644th mtg., at 21, U.N. Doc. S/PV.1644 (remarks by Ogiso (Japan)) (Feb. 27, 28, 1972).

[387] U.N. SCOR, 27th Sess., 1643rd mtg., at 14, U.N. Doc. S/PV.1643 (remarks by Vinci (Italy)) (Feb. 26, 1972).

[388] U.N. SCOR, 27th Sess., 1644th mtg., at 19, U.N. Doc. S/PV.1644 (remarks by Fakhreddine (Sudan)) (Feb. 27, 28, 1972).

[389] China: U.N. SCOR, 27th Sess., 1643rd mtg., at 17, U.N. Doc. S/PV.1643 (remarks by Huang (China)) (Feb. 26, 1972); Guinea: *id.* at 4 (remarks by Toure (Guinea)); Soviet Union: *id.* at 5 (remarks by Malik (Soviet Union)); Yugoslavia: *id.* at 12 (remarks by Komatina (Yugoslavia)).

[390] U.N. SCOR, 27th Sess., 1644th mtg., at 12, U.N. Doc. S/PV.1644 (remarks by Bush (United States)) (Feb. 27, 28, 1972).

313 (Feb. 28, 1972) called for an end to all military action by Israel against Lebanon.[391]

As the situation did not calm down, resolution 316 (June 26, 1972) condemned the "repeated attacks by Israeli forces on Lebanese territory"[392] after Israel had, according to its representative, responded with artillery and air raids against PLO forces in self-defense to a terrorist attack at Israel's Lod airport and taken Syrian and Lebanese officers prisoner in an unrelated incident.[393] Many states supported the resolution, condemning the repeated Israeli aggression.[394] Belgium[395] saw another Israeli illegitimate military reprisal, which the United Kingdom[396] and France[397] regarded in excess of what would have been justified as legitimate exercise of self-defense. As many comments focusing on proportionality issues, the latter views imply, albeit again not *expressis verbis*, that self-defense against non-state actor attacks is not by itself unthinkable but in the present situation the boundaries of such a legal regime had not been respected by Israel. India did not find that Israel could fall back on "such theories as preemptive or preventive strike[s]" – perhaps would Israel be able to do so if at least its existence was endangered which, however, was not the case ever since the 1967 war.[398]

Argentina, on the other hand, apparently did not consider previous terror attacks as "armed attacks" as it spoke of the Israeli responses as a "preventive war".[399] This comment could also imply that only states could exercise such attacks and hence prohibit self-defense against attacks by non-state actors. Again, such convictions were not expressed explicitly.

---

[391] S.C. Res. 313 (Feb. 28, 1972), 1972 U.N.Y.B. 172.

[392] S.C. Res. 316 (June 26, 1972), 1972 U.N.Y.B. 173.

[393] U.N. SCOR, 27th Sess., 1648th mtg., at 5, U.N. Doc. S/PV.1648 (remarks by Tekoah (Israel)) (June 23, 1972).

[394] China: *id.* at 12 (remarks by Huang (China)); Jordan: *id.* at 5 (remarks by Sharaf (Jordan)); Kuwait: *id.* at 3, (remarks by Bishara (Kuwait)); Soviet Union: *id.* at 8 (remarks by Malik (Soviet Union)); Sudan: *id.* at 11 (remarks by Abdulla (Sudan)); Yugoslavia: U.N. SCOR, 27th Sess., 1649th mtg., at 19, U.N. Doc. S/PV.1649 (remarks by Mojsov (Yugoslavia)) (June 24, 1972).

[395] U.N. SCOR, 27th Sess., 1649th mtg., at 15, U.N. Doc. S/PV.1649 (remarks by Van Ussel (Belgium)) (June 24, 1972).

[396] *Id.* at 19 (remarks by Jamieson (United Kingdom)).

[397] U.N. SCOR, 27th Sess., 1650th mtg., at 2, U.N. Doc. S/PV.1650 (remarks by De Guiringaud (France)) (June 26, 1972).

[398] U.N. SCOR, 27th Sess., 1649th mtg., at 14, U.N. Doc. S/PV.1649 (remarks by Sen (India)) (June 24, 1972).

[399] *Id.* at 18 (remarks by Carasales (Argentina)).

Jordan took a rather unusual stance on self-defense as its representative declared that "Israel cannot justify its aggression by invoking self-defence . . ., for it has by deliberate and stubborn persistence closed itself to any rectification of the situation or any redressing of the enormous human injustice which was brought about by Israel's creation and perpetuated by Israel's conduct."[400] The United States urged both parties to "avoid a repetition of the cycle of attacks and counter-attacks" and called otherwise for a balanced resolution.[401]

Another resolution in September 1972 was accordingly vetoed by the United States which considered it one-sided, failing to mention the cause for Israeli raids into Lebanon and Syria.[402] Israel had not participated in the Security Council deliberations due to the Jewish New Year, but had announced previously that it considered Lebanon, Syria, and Libya as main supporters of recent Palestinian terror attacks, mainly the one on Israeli athletes in Munich.[403] Israel did not specifically refer to its right to self-defense.

The cross-border incursions by PLO terrorists and subsequent Israeli counter-raids continued unabated all through 1972.[404]

In a covert action Israel killed several PLO leaders in Beirut on April 10, 1973. Shortly thereafter, on April 21, 1973 the United Nations Security Council passed resolution 332 (1973) condemning "repeated military attacks" on Lebanon by Israel and urged Israel to stop them immediately.[405]

In 1974, PLO operatives seized an apartment building in Kiryat Shmona and murdered 18 inhabitants. Lebanon asserted that it could not be held responsible for PLO's actions and complained about subsequent Israeli military operations into Lebanon.[406] The Arab countries, the USSR, and China blamed Israel for its "state terrorism" and, without referring to legal implications stemming from the PLO actions, labeled Israel's actions an aggression.[407] The United Kingdom held that even "deplorable" terrorist attacks could not justify Israel's armed retaliation.[408] France and Australia deemed Israel's actions a reprisal.[409] A subsequent resolution condemned Israel and did not include the Kiryat Shmonah

---

[400] *Id.* at 6 (remarks by Sharaf (Jordan)).
[401] *Id.* at 13 (remarks by Bush (United States)).
[402] U.N. SCOR, 27th Sess., 1662nd mtg., at 7, U.N. Doc. S/PV.1662 (remarks by Bush (United States)) (Sept. 10, 1972).
[403] *Israel sees fight against terrorists as main task,* THE TIMES (LONDON), Sept. 9, 1972, at 4 (referring to Israel's Foreign Minister Ebban and U.N. Delegate Tekoah).
[404] 1972 U.N.Y.B. 169-71.
[405] S.C. Res. 332 (Apr. 21, 1973), 1973 U.N.Y.B. 191.
[406] 1974 U.N.Y.B. 206-07.
[407] *Id.* at 207.
[408] *Id.* at 208.
[409] *Id.*

attack, after China, Indonesia, Iraq, Kenya, Mauritania, Peru, and Cameroon voted against an according U.S. proposal.[410]

All through 1975 Israel and Lebanon accused each other of fuelling the cross-border violence. Israel clarified on several occasions that Lebanon fails to control the PLO and other terror groups, ultimately requiring Israel to defend itself.[411] In December 1975, the United Nations Security Council once again convened upon a Lebanese request.

Meanwhile, Israel had begun to act rather than merely to react to prior PLO attacks. In "preventive" attacks Israel attempted to destroy PLO infrastructure in Palestinian camps and headquarters.[412] The Lebanese delegate to the United Nations warned that this might "lead the world back to the law of the jungle."[413] Other members condemned Israel's actions "categorically",[414] "firmly",[415] and deemed them "barbarous [and] unprovoked."[416] As before, military reprisals, much less preventive measures against PLO bases in Lebanon, were not considered legal.[417]

While 1976 was a relatively calm year,[418] 1977 was dominated by internal Lebanese fights between the rivaling militias, one of which was the PLO. Israeli countermeasures only played a smaller role.[419]

During most of the 1970s, Israel was regarded to have been in violation of international law in most cases, if not in all of its actions. With regard to the concept of self-defense Israel's application of force was often deemed a forceful and disproportionate and therefore illegitimate reprisal rather than self-defense. The overall reactions to Israel's invocation of self-defense became more differentiated when Israel began to attack the PLO bases, headquarters, and infrastructure by large scale invasion-type operations, the first of which was Operation Litani in 1978. Launched on March 14, 1978, Israel not only destroyed PLO in-

---

[410] *Id.*; *see* S.C. Res. 347 (Apr. 24, 1974), 1974 U.N.Y.B. 210-11.

[411] 1975 U.N.V.B. 224-26.

[412] *See, e.g.,* 1973 U.N.Y.B. 178, 179; U.N.SCOR, 34th Sess., 2165th mtg., U.N. Doc. S/PV.2165 (Aug. 30, 1979); U.N.SCOR, 36th Sess., 2293rd mtg., U.N. Doc. S/PV.2293 (July 21, 1981).

[413] U.N.SCOR, 30th Sess., 1859th mtg., at 11, U.N. Doc. S/PV.1859 (remarks by Ghorra (Lebanon)) (Dec 4, 1975).

[414] *Id.* at 2 (remarks by Guiringaud (France)).

[415] *Id.* at 2 (remarks by Vinci (Italy)).

[416] *Id.* at 6 (remarks by Malik (USSR)).

[417] U.N.SCOR, 30th Sess., 1861st mtg., at 4, U.N. Doc. S/PV.1861 (remarks by Guiringaud (France)) (Dec 8, 1975).

[418] 1976 U.N.Y.B. 221-22.

[419] 1977 U.N.Y.B. 276-77.

frastructure but also established a ten-kilometer "security zone".[420] It was Israel's response to the killing of approximately 40 Israeli civilians by Fatah, the leading PLO faction. Terrorists had landed by ship south of Haifa, captured a bus, and began killing the occupants. Until Israeli security forces finally killed or captured the terrorists in the vicinity of Herzliya, many women and children had been murdered. Israel considered this to have been the bloodiest attack ever to have occurred inside its territory.[421] The Arab world regarded it as "heroic", "courageous", and "noble".[422] While the subsequent invasion of southern Lebanon through Israel was unilaterally rejected by Arab nations, the U.S. on the other hand at least initially hesitated to condemn it individually.[423] However, the U.N. Security Council called on Israel "immediately to cease its military actions against Lebanese territorial integrity and withdraw forthwith its forces from all Lebanese territory" and eventually also established an "interim force" to monitor the Israeli withdrawal and ensure the subsequent reestablishment of Lebanese power in the area.[424] The Soviet Union and Czechoslovakia chose to abstain from this and the two subsequent resolutions that confirmed U.N. Security Council resolution 425 (1978) and laid out details as to the interim force, the UNIFIL. China did not participate in either voting as it, along with the Soviet Union, disagreed on the terms of the interim force.[425] China,[426] as well as the USSR,[427] however, condemned Israel's military actions in strong terms. The resolutions regard Lebanon as having been violated in its sovereignty and terri-

---

420 O'Brien, *supra* note 37 at 445, 446.

421 H.D.S. Greenway, *Israel Says Raid Reinforces Stand On Palestinians; Begin: Raid Strengthens Israeli Resolve,* WASH. POST, March 13, 1978, at A1 (quoting "Israeli officials" who" said the toll in the attack near Tel Aviv, the worst in Israel's history, was 41 dead and 76 wounded"); *see* also 1978 U.N.Y.B 296 (stating that Israel claimed 37 civilians dead and 76 wounded).

422 *Arab States Praise Attack As 'Noble' and 'Courageous',* WASH. POST, March 13, 1978, at A19 (citing to Saudi Arabia's state radio, the Kuwaiti minister of state Hussein, Jordanian state controlled newspapers, and the official Libyan news agency).

423 Don Oberdorfer, *U.S. Stance Is Cautious On Raid Into Lebanon,* WASH. POST, March 16, 1978, at A17 (mentioning that U.S. Secretary of State Cyrus Vance said he had not "called for a halt yet" and the acceptance of "Israel's rationale for the invasion" by "state department officials." The Egyptian Foreign Ministry and Syria deemed Israel's actions an "aggression").

424 S.C. Res. 425, U.N. Doc S/RES/425 (March 19, 1978); S.C. Res. 426, U.N. Doc. S/RES/426 (March 19, 1978).

425 S.C. Res. 426, U.N. Doc S/RES/426 (March 19, 1978); S.C. Res. 427, U.N. Doc S/RES/427 (May 3, 1978).

426 U.N.SCOR, 33rd Sess., 2074th mtg., at 2, U.N. Doc. S/PV.2074 (remarks by Lai (China)) (March 18, 1978).

427 U.N.SCOR, 33rd Sess., 2073rd mtg., at 4-5, U.N. Doc. S/PV.2073 (remarks by Troyanovsky (USSR)) (March 18, 1978).

torial integrity. Consequently, Israel's use of force was apparently not considered as legitimate under neither Chapter VII nor Article 51 of the U.N. Charter, the only legal options in light of the prohibition of the use of force in Article 2 (4) of the Charter.

Israel invoked its right to self-defense given "the increase in PLO presence and weaponry in the area [and] in the light of the PLO's declared intention to repeat atrocities like the one [on March 14, 1978]." Israel's Ambassador to the U.N., Chaim Herzog, emphasized that "Israel was left with no alternative."[428]

The comments made during the Security Council's meetings reveal few legal arguments that were perceived as decisive: Israel may have acted as if it were responding to a "fedayeen operation carried out a few days before in Palestine [sic]" but the Syrian delegate saw the scale and format of the Israeli operation as indication of Israel's "real objective . . . to expand and to occupy more Arab territory."[429] In other words: merely a military reaction to a "fedayeen operation" is not as entirely inconceivable as the alleged attempt to occupy Lebanese territory.

Most of the speakers focused on the violation of Lebanese sovereignty, not mentioning any attacks emanating from there.[430] Of all Muslim states only Egypt did mention them, calling attention to the "sad and tragic events" that took place in Israel.[431] Other than for the violation of Lebanese territorial integrity, Israel was condemned because it violated previous U.N. Security Council resolutions,[432] caused civilians casualties,[433] and was repeatedly accused of attempting to "exterminate the Palestinian people", as the Sudanese delegate put it.[434] However, nobody claimed that Israel could not resort to military force because their opponent fell short of being a state. In fact, the PLO was not even mentioned by most of the participants.

The tension, particularly inside Lebanon, rose in the coming months: "Incidents involving the Lebanese de facto armed groups" against UNIFIL occurred

---

[428] U.N.SCOR, 33rd Sess., 2071st mtg., at 6-7, U.N. Doc. S/PV.2071 (remarks by Herzog (Israel)) (March 17, 1978).
[429] *Id.* at 10 (remarks by Al-Hussami (Syria)).
[430] *See, e.g., id.* at 14-15 (remarks by Terzi (PLO), Bishara (Kuwait)).
[431] U.N.SCOR, 33rd Sess., 2072nd mtg., at 2, U.N. Doc. S/PV.2072 (remarks by Meguid (Egypt)) (March 18, 1978).
[432] U.N.SCOR, 33rd Sess., 2073rd mtg., at 4, U.N. Doc. S/PV.2073 (remarks by Troyanovsky (USSR)) (March 18, 1978).
[433] *Id.* at 4 (remarks by Troyanovsky (USSR)).
[434] U.N.SCOR, 33rd Sess., 2074th mtg., at 7, U.N. Doc. S/PV.2074 (remarks by Medani (Sudan)) (March 18, 1978).

on a daily basis.[435] This time, pro-Israeli Christian militias under Major Saad Hadad were at stake. As Israel also kept facing ongoing terrorist attacks, it once again invoked Article 51 of the charter specifically against the PLO, not governmental-Lebanese, actions in the course of a Security Council debate mainly about UNIFIL,[436] which had been requested by Lebanon due to the "rapidly deteriorating situation in Southern Lebanon resulting from Israeli escalation of its attacks."[437]

The Kuwaiti representative, without further legal explanation, considered this to be "a bold misinterpretation of the Charter". Accordingly, "Israel . . . has no right to invoke Article 51 of the Charter."[438] The Egyptian representative offered a more detailed evaluation as to why self-defense was inapplicable:

> The scope of self-defence . . . certainly could in no circumstances be stretched and abused to cover the Israeli aggressive acts against Lebanon or to give Israel a free hand to kill innocent civilians. . . . States are required to observe certain limitations which affect the measure and degree of the use of force. . . . Self-defence, according to the former United States Secretary of State [Webster], could be invoked only . . . when an armed attack was 'instant, overwhelming, leaving no choice of means, and no moment for deliberation.'[439]

As Israel also allegedly violated the "1949 Geneva Conventions, as well as the 1977 Additional Protocols to those Conventions [which] clearly prohibit attacks on civilian centers . . . the Israeli actions are beyond any legality and clearly violate the basic norms of international law."[440] The United Kingdom and France once again deplored Israel's "retaliatory actions"[441] and "so-called reprisals".[442] Particularly the Egyptian contribution either seems to ignore the PLO attacks on Israel or disregards them for the purpose of an armed attack. The latter might very well mean that, according to Nabil Elaraby, non-state actors are

---

435 The Secretary General, *Report of the Secretary-General On The United Nations Interim Force in Lebanon,* para. 27, U.N. Doc. S/13026 (Jan. 12, 1979).

436 U.N.SCOR, 34th Sess., 2146th mtg., at 5, U.N. Doc. S/PV.2146 (remarks by Blum (Israel)) (May 31, 1979).

437 U.N. Doc. S/13356 (May 30, 1979).

438 U.N.SCOR, 34th Sess., 2147th mtg., at 5, U.N. Doc. S/PV.2147 (remarks by Bishara (Kuwait)) (June 12, 1979).

439 U.N.SCOR, 34th Sess., 2148th mtg., at 2, U.N. Doc. S/PV.2148 (remarks by Elaraby (Egypt)) (June 14, 1979).

440 *Id.* at 2 (remarks by Elaraby (Egypt)).

441 *Id.* at 4 (remarks by Richard (United Kingdom)).

442 *Id.* at 6 (remarks by Leprette (France)).

incapable of triggering Article 51 of the Charter. On the other hand, a clear statement as to the limitations of the self-defense regime, as envisioned by either Daniel Webster or the United Nations Charter, was not made by either participant to the debate. Most speakers, as on countless further occasion, chose to ignore the actions of non-state armed band operating in and from Lebanon but rather insisted that Israel kept violating the state of Lebanon's sovereignty –[443] a fact, as the Israeli representative added, appears disturbing given the methods that Jordan, for instance, applied towards the PLO itself.[444]

Tensions, cross-border raids, and counter-raids occurred unabated also in the coming year.[445] Eventually, the "July-Mini-War" of 1981 erupted, in the course of which the Israeli Air Force launched a series of attacks on PLO targets,[446] killing an estimated 90 to 175 people.[447] Again, Israel regarded itself entitled to such operations by virtue of its right to self-defense, "a right also preserved under Article 51 of the Charter of the United Nations."[448] This time, just like before the Egyptian delegate,[449] Israeli officials also referred to the *Caroline* incident[450] and U.S. incursions into Mexico in 1916[451] in order to back its legal view.[452] Israel also tried to raise attention to the fact that the PLO had been successfully building an impressive armed force – emphasizing the PLO's role which in fact came quite close to the one of regular armed forces in the region.[453]

---

443 *See, e.g., id.* at 7-8 (remarks by Shamma (Jordan)); *id.* at 8-9 (remarks by Shemirani (Iran)); *id.* at 9-11 (remarks by El-Choufi (Syria)).
444 *Id.* at 11-12 (remarks by Blum (Israel)).
445 1980 U.N.Y.B. 347-58.
446 William Claiborne, *Israel Bombs PLO Sites, Bridges in Lebanon After Rocket Attack,* WASH. POST, July 17, 1981, at A19.
447 O'Brien, *supra* note 37 at 451-54.
448 U.N.SCOR, 36th Sess., 2292nd mtg., at 5, U.N. Doc. S/PV.2292 (remarks by Blum (Israel)) (July 17, 1981).
449 *See supra* at note 439.
450 *See supra* at p. 28.
451 The United States had pursued Mexican armed bands into Mexico; the U.S response had been provoked by Mexican cross-border raids into Columbus, New Mexico, headed by Francisco Villa. The Mexican government had limited influence in the border regions to the United States; for an overview of the incident *see* GEORGE A. FINCH, *Mexico and the United States*, 11 AM. J. INT'L L. 399-406 (1917).
452 William Claiborne, *Begin Widens Targeting To PLO Sites in Cities; Begin Widens PLO Targeting in Lebanon,* WASH. POST, July 18, 1981, at A1 (citing the "Israeli Army command spokesman's office" as referring to the *Caroline* and other similar events).
453 William Claiborne, *Israeli Fear of Guerrilla Bildup Triggered Beirut Strike,* WASH. POST, July 25, 1981, at A18 (referring to Israeli Deputy Defense Minister Mordechai Zippori and Army Chief of Staff Lt. Gen. Raphael Eitan).

The U.N. Security Council apparently disagreed with Israel's point of view, deeming all military operations "armed attacks" by virtue of U.N. Security Council resolution 490 (July 21, 1981).[454] The deliberations reveal, as usual, no legal support for Israel. Muslim countries blamed Israel of "veritable genocide"[455] western countries "vigorously" denied Israel the right to invoke Article 51 of the Charter – not because the PLO was not a state, but this time because Israel was acting preemptively.[456] The United Kingdom emphasized that it was also criticizing "PLO violence" but that the "scale of recent Israeli actions . . . can in no way be justified."[457] In other words: had Israel restrained its actions to less violent behavior, the United Kingdom essentially seems to sympathize with military force as a defensive countermeasure to PLO violence. Their capacity as a state actor did not seem to play a role.

Once again, the Egyptian Elaraby delegate took some time to elaborate on Israel's right to respond forcibly within Article 51 of the Charter. He deemed several conditions thereof not to be fulfilled and that Israel would under no circumstances have the right to "kill innocent civilians at will."[458] Neither had there been a sufficiently grave armed attack given the latest "border incidents." Israel had also failed to report such incidents to UNIFIL and thereby to the United Nations. Apparently in response to Israel's invocation of the *Caroline* incident, the Egyptian representative continued that under this very principle any forcible reaction that "fails to be proportionate . . . must be illegal", such as Israel's "full-scale armed attack launched on innocent civilians".[459] The fact that it was not Lebanon, but the non-state actor PLO which was responsible for the "border incidents," remained completely unmentioned. This seems remarkable especially given the depth to which the Egyptian delegate Nabil Elaraby, in later years a member of the ILC and a judge at the ICJ, discussed the conditions and proper consequences of Article 51 of the Charter. He seemed keen to list everything which bans Israel *per se* from relying on self-defense. The PLO's lack of statehood is missing.

Eventually, the situation was calmed by a cease-fire, effective July 24, 1981. It had been reached by the U.S. special envoy to the Middle East, Phillip Habib, through negotiations with the PLO, Israel, Saudi Arabia, and the United

---

[454] S.C. Res. 490, U.N. Doc S/RES/490 (July 21, 1981).
[455] U.N.SCOR 36th Sess., 2293rd mtg., at 3, U.N. Doc. S/PV.2293 (remarks by Chebaani (Tunisia)); *id.* at 15 (remarks by El-Fattal (Syria)); *id.* at 18 (remarks by Ashtal (Democratic Yemen)) (July 21, 1981).
[456] *Id.* at 4 (remarks by Louet (France)).
[457] *Id.* at 5 (remarks by Parsons (United Kingdom)).
[458] *Id.* at 6 (remarks by Elaraby (Egypt)).
[459] *Id.* at 7 (remarks by Elaraby (Egypt)).

States.[460] This cease-fire was severely disrupted when Israel responded to what it called "32 violations to the truce since . . . July [1981]," as IDF Lt. Gen. Raphael Eitan announced after a number of air strikes on PLO targets and air clashes with Syrian fighter jets on April 21, 1982. PLO Chairman Arafat accused Israel of having endangered the truce one-sidedly by its military actions.[461] The strikes took place during the Israeli withdrawal from the Sinai Peninsula, which is perhaps why most states reacted mildly. The U.S. State Department concluded that there had been a clear violation of the cease-fire and urged Israel to hold back.[462] Despite the tense situation, Israel briefly complied. Soon after, however, "[l]ight arms fire" by guerillas and the explosion of a land mine, wounding an Israeli soldier, triggered new Israeli strikes,[463] and led to the nullification of the ten-month-old cease fire by Prime Minister Menahem Begin four days later.[464] Following a shooting attack on the Israeli ambassador to London the Israeli Air Force was ordered to attack PLO targets in Lebanon on June 4, 1982. Despite a disclaimer by the PLO, Israel regarded it as solely responsible.[465] PLO forces responded with heavy shelling of Israeli towns and Israel extended its air raids the following day.[466] The resulting casualties were significant and most likely disproportionate. A day later, Israel finally invaded Lebanon[467] in exercise of its right to self-defense.[468] Operation Peace for Galilee had begun and would reach as far north into Lebanon as Beirut. The Security Council dealt with the matter upon Lebanon's request. It issued Security Council resolution

---

460 William Claiborne, *Israel and PLO Agree to Cease-Fire; Hostilities Halted in Lebanon As Israel, PLO Accept Truce,* WASH. POST, July 25, 1981, at A1.

461 Edward Cody, *Israeli Jets Strike PLO In Lebanon; Attack Not Meant To End Cease-Fire, Begin's Aide Says,* WASH. POST, Apr. 22, 1982, at A1 (quoting from Arafat's "complaint to U.N. Secretary General Javier Perez de Cuellar, accusing Israel of attacking populated Lebanese areas in violation of the nine-month-old cease-fire").

462 Edward Cody, *PLO Guerillas Forgo Reprisals Against Israel*, WASH. POST, Apr. 23, 1982, at A23 (referring to a meeting between the U.S. Ambassador to Lebanon, Robert Dillon, and the Lebanese Foreign Minister Fuad Butros).

463 William Claiborne, *Israeli Planes Strike Lebanon; PLO Retaliates With Shelling*, WASH. POST, May 10, 1982, at A1.

464 *Begin Said to Call Lebanon Cease-fire 'Null and Void'*, WASH. POST, May 14, 1982, at A32.

465 William Claiborne, *Israel Hits PLO Sites in Beirut, Killing 45; Raid Is in Retaliation for Shooting of Envoy,* WASH. POST, June 5, 1982, at A1.

466 William Claiborne, *130 Said to Die In New Israeli Raids on PLO,* WASH. POST, June 6, 1982, at A1.

467 John Sharkey, *Israel Launches Invasion of Lebanon*, WASH. POST, June 7, 1982, at A1.

468 The Secretary General, *Report of the Secretary-General in Pursuance of Security Council resolution 508 (1982),* at 1, U.N. Doc. S/15174 (June 6, 1982) (referring to a submission by the Permanent Representative of Israel on June 5, 1982).

508 (June 5, 1982) and condemned the Israeli military actions, urging Israel to withdraw immediately.[469]

The Soviet Union as well as the Egyptian Cabinet condemned the Israeli actions, deeming them "aggressions" and a "violation of international laws." They did not specify the grounds upon which Israel had violated international law. The USSR accused Israel of "genocide" and the Egyptian cabinet worried about Lebanon's sovereignty.[470]

Israel in return pointed out that it had no interest in any part of Lebanon's territory: "Our sole aim is to free ourselves from the threat of terrorism. . . . We feel completely justified in defending the lives of our citizens. We are not the aggressors. We are acting in complete and total self-defense of the lives of our citizens", announced Foreign Ministry Director General David Kimche.[471] The Israeli representative at the United Nations, Yehuda Blum, began his remarks by listing all major terrorist incidents that occurred in and against Israel and against Jews in other countries since April 1979. He counted 141 terrorist incidents since the cease-fire agreement in July 1981, 28 of which occurred only since May 1981 in Israel.[472] Blum complained that none of those terrorist actions led to any reaction by the U.N. Security Council.[473] Israel considered the PLO in southern Lebanon responsible where it had "15,000 armed . . . terrorists" and provided training grounds for the "terrorist internationale from all over the world.[474] Consequently, Israel held "Lebanon fully responsible for any atrocity committed against [Israel] when it is conceived and planned in Lebanon, irrespective of whether it is carried out from Lebanon or from any other territory."[475] However, he also noted that "Lebanon lost much of its sovereignty over its own territory to the terrorist PLO [and] also lost its independence to Syria".[476] Nonetheless, Israel saw itself in "exercise of its natural, fundamental and inherent right of self-defense."[477] Furthermore, Israel announced that it did

---

[469] S.C. Res. 508, U.N. Doc S/RES/508 (June 5, 1982).

[470] *Moscow Says Israel Seeks 'Extermination' Of Palestinian People,* WASH. POST, June 7, 1982, at A11 (referring to a report by the official Soviet news agency Tass and a statement by the Egyptian cabinet).

[471] William Claiborne, *Tanks, Troops Seek To Push PLO North*, WASH. POST, June 7, 1982, at A1.

[472] U.N.SCOR 37th Sess., 2375th mtg., at 3, U.N. Doc. S/PV.2375 (remarks by Blum (Israel)) (June 6, 1982).

[473] *Id.* at 4 (remarks by Blum (Israel)).

[474] *Id.* at 5.

[475] *Id.* at 6.

[476] *Id.* at 5.

[477] U.N.SCOR 37th Sess., 2376th mtg., at 3, U.N. Doc. S/PV.2376 (remarks by Blum (Israel)) (June 8, 1982).

not regard captured PLO members as POWs, but recognized them as combatants.[478]

The United States disapproved of Israel's actions and requested a new cease-fire. President Ronald Reagan said that

> there can be no rational excuse [for the murder of the Israeli ambassador to the United Kingdom]. But Israel has lost ground to a great extent among our people as a result of [the invasion]. They cannot believe that this vile attack – not even the accumulation of losses that Israel has suffered from PLO terrorist activity since last summer – justified the death and destruction that the IDF brought to so many innocent people over the past two weeks.[479]

Secretary of State Alexander M. Haig had previously announced that "[w]e certainly do not misunderstand or misappreciate the vulnerability of the Galilee area to terrorist actions, rockets, artillery shelling of the kind that preceded the Israeli invasion."[480] The Reagan administration vetoed a second Security Council Resolution[481] that would have laid the legal basis for sanctions against Israel.[482] Two other permanent members of the Security Council, China and the USSR, condemned the Israeli invasion as "aggression",[483] but neither mentioned self-defense nor the lack of statehood on the side of the PLO.

The European countries had difficulties to combine their points of view, especially once the IDF had surrounded Beirut and demanded a complete evacuation of PLO forces. France called for both an Israeli and PLO withdrawal from Beirut.[484] Germany refrained for quite a while from strong condemnation. Once it did condemn Israel more openly, Chancellor Helmut Schmidt expressed that "he understood Israel's motives and interests, but could also understand the

---

478 William Claiborne, *Israel Does Not Consider Palestinians POWs,* WASH. POST, June 13, 1982, at A25 (referring to an "army command source").

479 Memorandum of conversation between President Reagan and Prime Minister Begin (June 21, 1982) (declassified White House document) (on file with author).

480 John M. Goshko, *U.S. Anger In Check; Tougher Response Still an Option,* WASH. POST, June 8, 1982, at A1.

481 U.N.SCOR 37th Sess., 2377th mtg., at 3, U.N. Doc. S/PV.2377 (June 8, 1982).

482 U.N. Doc. S/15185 (June 8, 1982) ("Demands that within six hours all hostilities must be stopped in compliance with Security Council resolutions 508 (1982) and 509 (1982) and decides, in the event of non-compliance, to meet again to consider practical ways and means in accordance with the Charter of the United Nations").

483 U.N.SCOR 37th Sess., 2375th mtg., at 10, 11, U.N. Doc. S/PV.2375 (remarks by Ling (China), Troyanovsky (USSR), (June 6, 1982).

484 Bradley Graham, *Mubarak, Assailing U.S., Asks Europeans to Help Resolve Crisis,* WASH. POST, June 29, 1982, at A13.

motives and interests of the Palestinians, the Lebanese and other Arabs." His primary concern was that innocent civilians were killed through Israel's indiscriminate attacks.[485] Spain took the view that even if one took into consideration the terror attacks that Israel had pointed to, they could not serve as justification "for an act of armed aggression of such magnitude against the territory of a sovereign state."[486] The Irish representative missed any "sense of proportion" and was sure that "the total of lives lost and casualties suffered in all [attacks on Israel's territory or Israeli citizens elsewhere] over recent years is less than the deaths and injuries caused by the recent major Israeli air attacks on Beirut."[487] For both Spain and Ireland it appeared to have been Israel's "bad luck" that the PLO had not been more successful – then, perhaps, military actions such as ones taken were not as much out of proportion. Israel considered such an argument as "bizarre bookkeeping".[488] Again, however, the PLO itself appeared to have been regarded as perfectly capable of triggering such a forceful response as long as its attacks reached a higher magnitude. Its lack of statehood was at least not a primary obstacle.

In 1983 an "International Commission to Enquire into Reported Violations of International Law by Israel during its Invasion of the Lebanon", chaired by Irish Nobel Peace Prize laureate Seán MacBride, was established. Its report dealt with eight questions, most of which regarded Israeli violations of the *ius in bello.* Regarding the *ius ad bellum* it addressed whether "the Government of Israel committed acts of aggression contrary to international law", or whether it had "valid responses under international law for its invasion of the Lebanon . . . ."[489] Israel chose not to participate in the Commission's work, criticizing its composition as one-sided.[490] The commission's report concluded that Israel "did not have any grounds to rely on self-defense . . . , while the means used to effect the invasion totally lacked proportionality."[491] This decision was rested primarily upon the commission's findings that the 1981 cease-fire had been respected "virtually in total observance", without any "reported serious breaches . . . from the Lebanese side." It also held that Israel's action were "too extensive and

---

[485] Bradley Graham, *West Germans Speaking Out On Beirut Siege,* WASH. POST, Aug. 15, 1982, at A23.
[486] U.N.SCOR 37th Sess., 2377th mtg., at 1,2, U.N. Doc. S/PV.2377 (remarks by Piniés (Spain)) (June 8, 1982).
[487] *Id.* at 4 (remarks by Dorr (Ireland)).
[488] *Id.* at 8 (remarks by Blum (Israel)).
[489] International Commission to Enquire into Reported Violations of International Law By Israel During Its Invasion of the Lebanon, *Israel in Lebanon, The Report of the International Commission*, at Terms of Reference (1983) (hereinafter Commission).
[490] Commission at vii.
[491] *Id.* at 190.

widespread" to be classified as a reprisal following an accumulation of prior events.[492] The possibility of a legitimate preventive measure in absence of an armed attack was equally rejected.[493] Israel had over-reacted, especially as the "PLO military establishments in Lebanon have never represented a serious threat to Israel's security."[494]

In particular this final holding appeared rather surprising, but for the purpose of this work it can be held again that the fact that it was not the Lebanese army or other forces attributable directly to the state of Lebanon, but a private non-state actor that was at stake, did not play any role. If it was regarded as one of the reasons preventing Israel from defending itself against the PLO, it remained unmentioned.

As a result of Israel's Operation Peace for Galilee the PLO leadership was forced to leave Beirut.[495] The PLO did not, however, cease its attacks on Israel and neither did Israel stop reacting by force based upon its right to defend itself against the PLO. Israel accused the PLO of attempting to reestablish itself in southern Lebanon and several states played their part in Lebanon. Lebanon complained to the United Nations Security Council that is sovereignty was being violated by Israel.

An insofar typical situation occurred in 1988, when Israel struck targets near Sidon in response to ongoing rocket attacks from southern Lebanon, among others, by the PLO.[496] Again, it referred to self-defense as legal grounds for such actions.[497] And again, Israel considered the actual Lebanese government crippled and itself accordingly left without any other option than military counterforce against any group that attacks Israel from within Lebanon.[498] Most speakers chose to ignore the Israeli reasoning i.e. the alleged responsibility of other parties to the conflict, and blamed Israel for continuously violating Lebanese sovereignty.[499] If they considered Israel in violation of international self-defense due to the international legal nature of the attacker was never clarified. It was not stated as an individual legal argument, but the reason for this probably lies in a more or less completely different perception – be it because of actual belief or

[492] *Id.* at 16.
[493] *Id.* at 17.
[494] *Id.* at 18.
[495] FRIEDMAN, *supra* note 286 at 151-55.
[496] U.N.SCOR 43rd Sess., 2783rd mtg., at 33 U.N. Doc. S/PV.2783 (remarks by Netanyahu (Israel)) (Jan. 18, 1988).
[497] *Id.* at 34-35 (remarks by Netanyahu (Israel)).
[498] *Id.* at 36 (remarks by Netanyahu (Israel)).
[499] *See, e.g., id.* at 17 (remarks by Shihabi (Saudi Arabia)); U.N.SCOR 43rd Sess., 2784th mtg., at 23-25 U.N. Doc. S/PV.2784 (remarks by Abulhasan (Kuwait)) (Jan. 18, 1988); *id.* at 29-30 (remarks by Sarré (Senegal)); *id.* at 33 (remarks by Ould Boye (Mauritania)).

political tactics and hidden agendas – of what were the causes of sovereignty violations in Lebanon. A resolution was vetoed by the United States, with only the United Kingdom abstaining.[500]

This result occurred once again the same year after in Israeli operation in May 1988. This time the United States made clear why it was that it vetoed another proposed United Nations Security Council resolution – because it ignored the "well-known fact that hostile acts against Israel are originating in Lebanon" from PLO, Hezbollah, and others.[501]

After all of this, the conflict in southern Lebanon continued. Only the primary player in opposition to Israel altered gradually, shifting from secular nationalist movements like the PLO to religious fanatics like Hezbollah.

ii) Military Responses Against Hezbollah

Several militias rushed to fill in the gap that the PLO's initial departure in 1982 had caused. Hezbollah was one of them. Initially, Hezbollah attacked foreign forces within Lebanon.[502] For instance, several Israelis and Palestinians were killed in a suicide attack on Israel's military headquarters in Tyre on November 4, 1983. Israel retaliated with air raids on Hezbollah and Amal militia camp sites.[503] France reacted similarly. French and American troops were also not spared by Hezbollah, which had attacked international military barracks in October 1983.[504]

The United Nations unsuccessfully attempted to reach a cease-fire between Israel and other parties to the conflict and to co-operate with the helplessly overstrained and largely ineffective UNIFIL, while extending the latter's mandate.[505] Israel kept emphasizing that it was acting in self-defense solely

---

[500] *Id.* at 49-50.

[501] U.N.SCOR 43rd Sess., 2814th mtg., at 61 U.N. Doc. S/PV.2814 (remarks by Walters (United States)) (May 10, 1988).

[502] *E.g.* the massive bombings on the U.S. embassy in Beirut and the Marine headquarters in 1982-83, both together killing approx. 300; Philip Taubman, *U.S. Agencies Link a Moslem Group to Beirut Blasts,* N.Y. TIMES, Oct. 5, 1984, at A1.

[503] Glenn Frankel, *Israeli Warplanes Bomb 2 Camps of Moslem Radicals; Raid Into Lebanon Retaliates for Attacks,* WASH. POST, Nov. 17, 1983, at A1.

[504] Glenn Frankel, *French Jets Strike Shiite Position in Eastern Lebanon; 39 Reported Killed, 150 Injured in Raid,* WASH. POST, Nov. 18, 1983, at A1.

[505] *See, e.g.,* S.C. Res. 529 (Jan. 18, 1983), 1983 U.N.Y.B. 295-96; S.C. Res. 536 (July 18, 1983), 1983 U.N.Y.B. 297-98; S.C. Res. 538 (Oct. 18, 1983), 1983 U.N.Y.B. 299; S.C. Res. 542 (Nov. 23, 1983), 1983 U.N.Y.B. 293; S.C. Res. 549 (Apr. 19, 1984), 1984 U.N.Y.B. 299-300; S.C. Res. 555 (Oct. 12, 1984), 1984 U.N.Y.B. 302; S.C. Res. 561 (Apr. 17, 1985), 1985 U.N.Y.B. 307; S.C. Res. 575 (Oct. 17, 1985) 1985 U.N.Y.B. 309; S.C. Res. 583 (Apr. 18, 1986), 1986 U.N.Y.B. 294-95; S.C. Res. 586 (July 18, 1986), 1986 U.N.Y.B. 297; S.C. Res. 594 (Jan. 15, 1987), 1987 U.N.Y.B. 279; S.C. Res. 599 (July 31, 1987), 1987 U.N.Y.B. 282;

against terrorists which were not confined by an unwilling and/or incapable Lebanese government. Israel also repeatedly expressed hope that Lebanon would actively alter this situation and soon restore sovereignty over the entirety of its territory.[506] In Security Council deliberations, usually no state responded to legal issues surrounding self-defense.[507]

Hezbollah eventually expanded its actions significantly beyond Lebanese borders. In 1985 – the year of the Israeli withdrawal to a buffer zone and a time during which Hezbollah began to hit primarily U.S. targets such as by the hijacking of TWA flight 847 – the Reagan administration considered a major military response to face the terrorist threats triggered by the abduction and murder of a navy soldier. It refrained from doing so because "Hezbollah lives in urban areas . . . It is manifestly infeasible, and they know it, to conduct violent raids against them."[508] A military option was likely to result in indiscriminate victims, but had Hezbollah been "on the open field", it appears likely that the U.S. executive would not have hesitated to fight back against the non-state actor with military force. America's concerns regarded the *ius in bello*, not the *ius ad bellum*. And in fact, despite a 1985 report by the Secretary-General that counted "numerous attacks" on the IDF in the security zone occupied by Israel,[509] Israel was repeatedly blamed for violating international humanitarian law by its conduct in southern Lebanon.[510] Israel kept invoking self-defense and referred to its

---

S.C. Res. 609 (Jan. 29, 1988), 1988 U.N.Y.B. 222; S.C. Res. 617 (July 29, 1988), 1988 U.N.Y.B. 223; S.C. Res. 630 (Jan. 30, 1989) 1989 U.N.Y.B. 205-06; S.C. Res. 639 (July 31, 1989) 1989 U.N.Y.B. 206; S.C. Res. 648 (Jan. 31, 1990) 1990 U.N.Y.B. 288; S.C. Res. 659 (July 31, 1990) 1990 U.N.Y:B. 290); *see also supra* note 285, *infra* note 535.

506 *See, e.g.*, U.N. Doc. S/16276 (Jan. 16, 1984); U.N. Doc. S/16671 (July 16, 1984); U.N. SCOR, 39th Sess., 2552nd mtg., at 11, U.N. Doc. S/PV.2552 (remarks by Blum (Israel)) (Aug. 29, 1984); U.N. SCOR, 41st Sess., 2640th mtg., at 58, U.N. Doc. S/PV.2641 (remarks by Netanjahu (Israel)) (Jan. 13, 1986); 1987 U.N.Y.B. 276; U.N. SCOR, 43rd Sess., 2783rd mtg., at 34-35, U.N. Doc. S/PV.2783 (remarks by Netanjahu (Israel)) (Jan. 18, 1988).

507 *See, e.g.*, U.N. SCOR, 39th Sess., 2552nd to 2555th mtg., U.N. Docs. S/PV.2552 to 2555 (Aug. 29, 30; Sept. 4, 1984).

508 George C. Wilson, Lou Cannon, *Military Retaliation Unlikely Option; Reagan Settling for Broad-Based Attack on Terrorism's Roots,* WASH. POST, July 1, 1985, at A21 (referring to a "senior administration official").

509 The Secretary-General, Report of the Secretary-General on the United Nations Interim Force in Lebanon (from the period of 10 October 1984 to 11 Apr. 1985), at 5, *delivered to the Security Council*, U.N. Doc. S/17093 (Apr. 11, 1985).

510 *See, e.g.*, U.N. SCOR, 40th Sess., 2568th mtg., at 6, U.N. Doc. S/PV.2568 (remarks by Shaker (Egypt)) (Feb. 28, 1985); *id.* at 9 (remarks by El-Fattal (Syria)); U.N. SCOR, 40th Sess., 2570th mtg., at 3, U.N. Doc. S/PV.2570 (remarks by Djoudi (Algeria)) (March 7, 1985); *id.* at 5 (remarks by Verma (India)); U.N. SCOR, 40th Sess., 2572nd mtg., at 6, U.N. Doc.

plans about a unilateral withdrawal.[511] A subsequent draft resolution was considered "unbalanced", following a generally "hostile" attitude towards Israel and consequently vetoed by the United States,[512] with Australia, Denmark, and the United Kingdom abstaining.[513] However, despite Israel's partial withdrawal, Hezbollah would ultimately aim for attacks inside Israel,[514] also because Israel kept supporting Christian militias in their inner-Lebanese fights.[515]

Meanwhile, the PLO had reappeared in southern Lebanon – with its leadership located in Tunis – and it seemed likely that Lebanon would remain a major source and basis for terrorists to attack Israel directly.[516] Eventually, it resumed terrorist attacks against Israel from the south of Lebanon.[517] Hezbollah followed suit. They began to attack the IDF not only in the "security zone", but also in northern Israel with Russian-made rockets.[518] Mostly, however, the coming years saw Hezbollah attack the IDF inside Lebanon, and the Israelis responded immediately.[519] In 1987, Israel began to extend border fortifications to prevent Hezbollah from attacking northern Israel.[520]

S/PV.2572 (remarks by Ling Qing (China)) (March 11, 1985); *id.* at 8 (remarks by de Kémoularia (France)).

[511] U.N. SCOR, 40th Sess., 2568th mtg., at 8, U.N. Doc. S/PV.2568 (remarks by Netanjahu (Israel)) (Feb. 28, 1985).

[512] U.N. SCOR, 40th Sess., 2573rd mtg., at 18, U.N. Doc. S/PV.2573 (remarks by Kirkpatrick (United States)) (March 12, 1985).

[513] U.N. SCOR, 40th Sess., 2572rd mtg., at 18-19, U.N. Doc. S/PV.2573 (March 12, 1985).

[514] *See, e.g.*, U.N. Doc. S/17698 (Dec. 26, 1985) at 2 (stating that since June 1985 over 280 rocket attacks hit northern Israel and reporting a number of foiled terrorist attacks).

[515] Glenn Frankel, *Hezbollah Challenges Forces in S. Lebanon,* WASH. POST, Sep. 28, 1986, at A27 (referring to "senior Israeli defense officials, starting with Defense Minister Yitzhak Rabin, [who] repeatedly stated their public support and confidence in the SLA and let leak plans for a troop buildup along the border with Lebanon").

[516] Patrick E. Tyler, *PLO Military Buildup in Lebanon Worries Israel*, WASH. POST, Jan. 7, 1987, at A16 (referring to "Israeli military intelligence" estimating "that 9,500 PLO fighters loyal to PLO Chairman Yasser Arafat are now in Lebanon, about 3,000 of them in southern Lebanon near the security zone").

[517] *See, e.g.,* 1986 U.N.Y.B. 285; Glenn Frankel, *PLO Squad Is Crushed Inside Israel; 2 Soldiers Killed By 3 Infiltrators in Clash Near Border,* WASH. POST, Apr. 20, 1987, at A1.

[518] *Israelis Raid Southern Lebanon,* WASH. POST, Aug. 10, 1987, at A11.

[519] *See, e.g.,* 1986 U.N.Y.B. 283; Nora Boustany, *Raids by Israel, Allied Militia Kill 19 in Southern Lebanon,* WASH. POST, Oct. 27, 1988, at A56.

[520] 1987 U.N.Y.B. 277.

In 1992 Israel counted 52 attacks on Israeli or allied armed forces in Lebanon through Hezbollah.[521] Eventually, the (secular) PLO-Fatah movement, and (radically Islamist) Hezbollah joined forces. Having been bitter rivals over Lebanese supremacy, the First Gulf War turned them into something like allies, as they both supported Iraq against the U.S.-led allied forces.[522]

During all this time once again few legal arguments were announced. Israel thought of itself as acting in self-defense while being caught up in fights on Lebanese soil and beyond.[523] In 1992, Islamic Jihad, a group closely affiliated with Hezbollah, attacked the Israeli embassy in Buenos Aires[524] and in 1994, the Jewish community center AMIA in the Argentine capital was torn apart by a bomb.[525] Initially, Hezbollah denied responsibility for the attack that killed over 80 people, mostly Jews.[526] In 2005, however, an Argentinean court charged Hezbollah member Ibrahim Berro with the attack.[527] A year later, in July 2006, Interpol issued arrest warrants for Hezbollah members suspected of being responsible for the bombing and residing in South America.[528] In October 2006, Argentinean prosecutors requested an arrest warrant for former Iranian president Ali Akbar Hashemi Rafsanjani while contending that the actual attacks on the AMIA center had been executed by Hezbollah but "suspected that Hezbollah undertook activities outside Lebanon only 'under orders directly emanating from the regime in Tehran.'"[529] Among these external activities of Hezbollah forces

---

521 Carlyle Murphy, *Israeli Raid Kills Hezbollah Leader; Attack Called 'Message' to Terrorists,* WASH. POST, Feb 17, 1992, at A1 (stating that "Israel has accused Hezbollah of 52 attacks on Israeli troops and its allied South Lebanon Army militia inside Lebanon.").

522 Jackson Diehl, *Israel Raids PLO Camp After Rockets Hit Lebanon Border Zone,* WASH. POST, Jan 30, 1991, at A23.

523 *See, e.g.,* U.N. Doc. S/24032 (May 29, 1992).

524 Nathaniel C. Nash, *At Least 6 Die as Blast Destroys Israel's Embassy in Buenos Aires,* N.Y. TIMES, March 18, 1992, at A1.

525 *26 Die and 127 Hurt in Blast at Argentine Jewish Center,* N.Y. TIMES, July 19, 1994, at A3.

526 Gabriel Escobar, *Iranian Diplomats Said to Be Suspects in Blast at Argentine Jewish Center,* WASH. POST, July 29, 1994, at A27.

527 *AMIA Bomber Named; Hezbollah militant identifies as being behind Argentina's worst terror attack*, THE BUENOS AIRES HERALD, Nov 10, 2005, *available at* http://www.buenosairesherald.com/argentina/note.jsp?idContent=223825 (last visited Feb. 24, 2006).

528 *Hezbollah names tied to AMIA bombing,* JEWISH TELEGRAPH AGENCY, July 28, 2006, *available at* www.jta.org (last visited July 28, 2006).

529 Oscar Serrat, *Iranian Ex-Leader Sought in Argentina*, WASH. POST, Oct. 26, 2006, at A19.

was allegedly also a bombing attack on the Israeli embassy in London in 1994.[530]

Eventually, at least as of 1992, Israel was back to where it had been with the PLO: cross-border and international attacks by a non-state actor, this time Hezbollah,[531] and a Lebanese government either unable or unwilling to intervene. In 1993 Israel conducted a large-scale military operation as it had last done in 1982 in order to remove Hezbollah and its entire support system from southern Lebanon.[532] Without naming specific attacks, but speaking of "a serious escalation of terrorist attacks by Hezbollah [and others] against Israeli civilians in northern Israel" and IDF personnel, Israel once again referred to self-defense to justify its actions.[533]

As in 1982, Israel's military actions in 1993 did not meet much support from such actions, particularly as the Israeli raids had caused approximately 500,000 Lebanese to leave their homes in southern Lebanon. U.N. Secretary General Boutros-Gali deemed this "deplorable" and U.S. President Clinton urged both sides to cease fighting.[534] The only tangible reaction from the United Nations Security Council remained constant extensions of the UNIFIL mandate and criticism as to the ongoing violence by the parties.[535] The tense situation

---

530 Ewen McAskill, *Israeli Embassy in London Hit by Car Bomb;13 Hurt; Second Blast Injures 5 Outside Jewish Groups' Offices* WASH. POST, July 27, 1994, at A22.

531 *See, e.g.*, John M. Goshko, *Israel Warns Lebanon, Syria As Mideast Talks Resume; Sides Swap Charges in Tense Post-Election Session,* WASH. POST, Nov. 10, 1992, at A27; David Hoffman, *Israel Bombards Guerrilla Targets in Lebanon*, WASH. POST, July 27, 1993, at A11.

532 David Hoffman, *Israeli Offensive Sends Civilians Fleeing From Southern Lebanon,* WASH. POST, July 28, 1993, at A1 (deeming the Israeli offensive "the most ambitious offensive by Israel into Lebanon since 1985" and citing remarks by the Israeli Prime Minister Yitzchak Rabin who said "Israel aims to cause a mass flight of residents" from southern Lebanon "and to cause damage to all those who cooperate with Hezbollah"); *see* also Lebanon's complaints to the United Nations in this matter: U.N. Doc. S/26165 (July 26, 1993); U.N. Doc. S/26192 (July 28, 1993); U.N. Doc. S/26202 (July 30, 1993).

533 U.N. Doc. S/26152 (July 26, 1993).

534 David Hoffman, *Israeli Offensive Draws Criticism; U.S. 'Deeply Disturbed' as Shelling Forces Mass Exodus of Lebanese Civilians From South,* WASH. POST, July 29, 1993, at A15.

535 *See, e.g.,* S.C. Res. 684 (Jan. 30, 1991), 1991 U.N.Y.B. 239; S.C. Res. 701 (July 31, 1991), 1991 U.N.Y.B. 240; S.C. Res. 734 (Jan. 29, 1992), 1992 U.N.Y.B. 411; S.C. Res. 768 (July 30, 1992), 1992 U.N.Y.B. 413; S.C. Res. 803, U.N. Doc. S/RES/803 (Jan 28, 1993); S.C. Res. 852, U.N. Doc. S/RES/852 (July 28, 1993); S.C. Res. 895, U.N. Doc. S/RES/895 (Jan. 28, 1994); S.C. Res. 938, U.N. Doc. S/RES/938 (July 28, 1994); S.C. Res. 974, U.N. Doc. S/RES/974 (Jan. 30, 1995); S.C. Res. 1006, U.N. Doc. S/RES/1006 (July 28, 1995); S.C. Res.

continued with skirmishes by both sides also throughout the coming years.[536] Israel again pointed to its right of defend itself.[537]

In early 1996 the situation escalated entirely once again. Israel counted over 100 rocket attacks, hitting 20 Israeli cities, launched by Hezbollah from southern Lebanon.[538] In large scale military attacks – Operation Grapes of Wrath – Israel sought to crush the terrorist organization once and for all. Again, Israel invoked self-defense.[539] The IDF also hit a U.N. camp in Qana, as Israeli soldiers had come under fire from nearby Hezbollah forces, which were known to fire from nearby civilian targets.[540] As a result, about 100 civilian refugees were killed. A U.N. investigation later discovered that Hezbollah terrorists had actually entered the camp. It remained unclear if Israel had fired deliberately at the camp or if it had been aiming at the origin of the rockets, several hundred meters away.[541] This time the Security Council resolution – from the day of the Qana attacks – did not condemn Israel exclusively, but merely called for an "immediate cessation of hostilities by all parties."[542] Equally mild were the remarks by the individual member states in the according deliberations: France reaffirmed "the right of all States in the region, including Lebanon and Israel, to live in security."[543] The German delegate Eitel even went so far as to announce that "self-defence is clearly legitimate, measures of self-defence can become illegal if they do not abide by the basic rule of law prescribing proportionality."[544] The Russian view was somewhat similar, as ambassador Lavrov asked "to what extent are strikes by the Israeli army in proportion to the actions of extremists? We believe that Israel's military operations are an inappropriate reaction to these ac-

---

1039, U.N. Doc. S/RES/1039 (Jan. 29, 1996); S.C. Res. 1068, U.N. Doc. S/RES/1068 (July 30, 1996); S.C. Res. 1095, U.N. Doc. S/RES/1095 (Jan 28, 1997).

[536] *See* 1994 U.N.Y.B. 628-34; 1995 U.N.Y.B. 672-73.

[537] *See, e.g.*, U.N. Doc. S/1994/915 (Aug. 1,1994).

[538] U.N. SCOR, 51st Sess., 3653rd mtg., at 6, U.N. Doc. S/PV 3653 (remarks by Yaakobi (Israel)) (Apr. 15, 1996).

[539] *Id.*

[540] John Lancaster, *Israeli Shells Kill 90 in Lebanon Camp; U.N. Site Struck; Peres Offers Truce To Guerrilla Group*, WASH. POST, Apr. 19, 1996, at A11 (referring to U.N. officials "acknowledging that Hezbollah guerrillas often fire on Israeli targets from near Lebanese civilian areas").

[541] John M. Goshko, *Guerrillas Entered U.N. Base Before Israeli Shelling, Inquiry Finds; Investigators Debating Whether Refugee Area Deliberately Targeted,* WASH. POST, May 4, 1996, at A01; *Israel Rejects U.N. Findings,* WASH. POST, May 5, 1996, at A29.

[542] S.C. Res. 1052, U.N. Doc. S/RES/1052 (Apr. 18, 1996).

[543] U.N. SCOR, 51st Sess., 3653rd mtg., at 7, U.N. Doc. S/PV 3653 (remarks by Dejammet (France)) (Apr. 15, 1996).

[544] *Id.* at 9 (remarks by Eitel (Germany)).

tions."[545] The United States openly expressed understanding for "self-defence by Israel in response to Hezbollah violence."[546]

It was again on the Egyptian delegate Nabil Elaraby to elaborate on the conditions of Article 51 of the Charter in greater detail:

> First and foremost, under Article 51 of the Charter, there must have been an actual armed attack. Firing Katyusha rockets across borders is indeed a proscribed act which must cease forthwith. This is clear. However, the armistice agreement between Lebanon and Israel continues officially to stand; the mechanisms provided for in the armistice should have been invoked to deal with these events.[547]

He continued that Israel did fail, however, to refer the matter to the Security Council and that, third, proportionality was not met either.[548] He also referred to Daniel Webster and the *Caroline* prerequisites,[549] as he had done 15 years before.[550] Elaraby also reached a similar conclusion as he denied Israel the right to self-defense based upon the above arguments. And, as in 1981, he did not criticize that Israel was fighting a non-state actor while invoking self-defense.

Despite the slightly more favorable tone towards Israel, the international reaction did not differ from the previous ones, as the deliberations of the General Assembly also revealed: Israel's actions were either deemed to be disproportionate;[551] or merely an aggression.[552] Those who contested Israel's right to self-defense did so not because Hezbollah lacked state-capacity – which, like the PLO formerly, remained largely unmentioned – but because Israel could "no longer fall back on the pretext of self-defence" which could not "justify . . . air raids and . . . the shelling of a United Nations post . . . ."[553] Finally, the General Assembly voted for a resolution that condemned Israel,[554] with 68 nations ab-

---

545 *Id.* at 10 (remarks by Lavrov (Russian Federation)).
546 *Id.* at 13 (remarks by Albright (United States)).
547 *Id.* at 14 (remarks by Elaraby (Egypt)).
548 *Id.* at 14, 15.
549 *Id.* at 15.
550 *See supra* note 459.
551 U.N. GAOR, 50th Sess., 114th mtg., at 16 , U.N. Doc. A/50/PV.114 (remarks by Lian (Norway)) (Apr. 24, 1996); U.N. GAOR, 50th Sess., 115th mtg., at 10 , U.N. Doc. A/50/PV.115 (remarks by Park (Republic of Korea)) (Apr. 24, 1996).
552 U.N. GAOR, 50th Sess., 114th mtg., at 19 , U.N. Doc. A/50/PV.114 (remarks by Razali, Malaysia)) (Apr. 24, 1996); *id.* at 16 (remarks by Al-Khussaiby (Oman)).
553 U.N. GAOR, 50th Sess., 115th mtg., at 4 , U.N. Doc. A/50/PV.115 (remarks by Al-Nim'ah (Qatar)) (Apr. 24, 1996).
554 G.A. Res. 50/22, U.N. Doc. A/RES/50/22C (Apr. 25, 1996).

staining and the United States and Israel voting against it.[555] Eventually, the United States was able to broker a cease-fire. Israel and United States agreed upon an understanding on how self-defense with regard to Hezbollah is to be interpreted.[556] The content of this agreement is not available: however, it can be inferred that the understanding was rather about the conditions of self-defense as an available reaction rather than if self-defense could be exercised at all. A non-state actor's involvement as origin of the attacks did not seem to have hindered such an agreement; otherwise there might have been none at all.

The inner-Lebanese fighting between the IDF and its allies on one side, and Hezbollah and associated militias on the other side, continued nevertheless from 1996 through 1999 with sporadic rocket attacks reaching Israeli territory, and Israeli counter-attacks,[557] sometimes explicitly based upon self-defense in response to Hezbollah attacks on Israel.[558] Israel repeatedly emphasized that Hezbollah was ultimately aiming at the destruction of the State of Israel, and not merely the end of the Israeli occupation in southern Lebanon.[559]

In May 2000 Israel withdrew from Lebanon after more than 20 years of military clashes along its northern border and inside southern Lebanon.[560] The United Nations Security Council confirmed the complete withdrawal.[561]

The Israeli government once again emphasized that all its military operations had been "carried out as part of Israel's right to self-defense."[562]

After Israel's withdrawal the situation improved. What nevertheless remained were continuous, but less intense rocket attacks by Hezbollah and lim-

---

[555] *Majority Abstain as U.N. Votes to Condemn Israel,* WASH. POST, Apr. 26, 1996, at A31.

[556] William Drozdiak, *Israel and Lebanon Agree To U.S.-Mediated Cease-Fire,* WASH. POST, Apr. 27, 1996, at A01 (citing to "U.S. officials [who] said an interpretive letter would be exchanged between the United States and Israel outlining the parameters of 'self-defense' and how they would apply to any attacks against Israeli forces by Hezbollah").

[557] *See, e.g.,* 1997 U.N.Y.B. 456-57; William Drozdiak, *Israel Warns Hezbollah After Attack,* WASH. POST, Aug. 20, 1997, at A22; James Rupert, *12 in Israel Wounded by Hezbollah Rocket Salvo; Attack Called Retaliation For Deaths of 7 Lebanese When Jet Bombed House,* WASH. POST, Dec. 24, 1998, at A11; Lee Hockstader, *Israeli Bombs Hit Targets Near Beirut; Raid Follows Hezbollah Border Attack,* WASH. POST, June 25, 1999, at A21; Lee Hockstader, *Lebanese Guerrillas Rocket Israel; Barak Orders Retaliatory Strikes, Raising Fears of New Cycle of Violence,* WASH. POST, May 5, 2000, at A20.

[558] *See, e.g.* U.N. Doc. S/1997/108 (Feb. 3, 1997); U.N. Doc. S/1998/75 (Jan. 27, 1998); U.N. Doc. S/1999/1178 (Nov. 17, 1999)

[559] *See, e.g.* U.N. Doc. S/1999/463 (Apr. 22, 1999).

[560] William A. Orme Jr., Retreat from Lebanon: The Israelis; *Barak Declares End to 'Tragedy' as Last Troops Leave Lebanon,* N.Y. TIMES, May 24, 2000, at A13.

[561] S.C. Res. 1310, U.N. Doc. S/RES/1310 (July 27, 2000).

[562] U.N. Doc. S/2000/99 (Feb. 9, 2000).

ited Israeli counter-force in each year ever since the withdrawal[563] until the outbreak of the full-blown armed conflict in July 2006, as well as unabatedly aggressive propaganda by Hezbollah.[564] Between 2000 and 2006 Israel continuously complained to the United Nations about Hezbollah's ongoing cross-border incursions – ranging from throwing stones at IDF posts to killing and abducting civilians and IDF personnel – and warned from a further deterioration unless Lebanon took full control of the areas.[565] Sometimes, Israel reserved or referred directly to its right to engage in self-defense, or emphasized its right to protect

---

563 *See, e.g.*, Deborah Sontag, *Whose Holy Land? The Overview; Arab-Israeli Conflict Spreads to Border With Lebanon* , N.Y Times, Oct. 8, 2000, at 11 (The Shiite Muslim guerrillas of the Hezbollah movement lobbed Katyusha rockets at an Israeli military post, injuring three soldiers. [They] also sneaked across the border and kidnapped three Israeli soldiers . . . .); Joel Greenberg, *Israeli Killed at Lebanon Frontier; Airstrike Follows*, N.Y. Times, Nov. 27, 2000, at A6; Daniel Williams, *Israeli Jets Attack Southern Lebanon; Airstrikes Follow Strife in Disputed Area,* WASH. POST, Apr. 15, 2001, at A15; Karen DeYoung, *U.S. Fears 2nd Front In Mideast Conflict; Israel, Hezbollah Clash on Northern Border*, WASH. POST, Apr. 10, 2002, at A18; Joel Greenberg, *Mideast Turmoil: The Border: Day by Day, Arab Shells Fray Nerves In the Golan*, N.Y. TIMES, Apr. 12, 2002, at A12; 2002 U.N.Y.B. 473-74; John Ward Anderson, *Hezbollah Shells Kill Israeli Boy, Injure 4; Cross-Border Strikes Are Stepped Up,* WASH. POST, August 11, 2003, at A12; Greg Myre, *The Mideast Turmoil: In the North; Israeli Soldier Shot to Death Near Lebanon*, N.Y. TIMES, Oct. 7, 2003, at A13; Keith B. Richburg, *Israeli Planes Retaliate; Hezbollah Targets Hit in Lebanon*, WASH. POST, Jan 21, 2004, at A24; Greg Myre, *Israelis and Hezbollah Clash at Lebanon Line*, N.Y. TIMES, May 8, 2004, at A6; Hassan M. Fattah, *Israeli Troops and Hezbollah Clash Again Near the Border*, N.Y TIMES, Nov. 24, 2005, at A16; Greg Myre, *Israel Strikes Northern Gaza And Lebanon With Planes,* N.Y. TIMES, Dec. 28, 2005, at A11; Greg Myre, Hassan M. Fattah, *Israel and Militants Trade Fire Across Lebanese Border,* N.Y TIMES, May 29, 2006, at A3.

564 *World Briefing Middle East: TV Channel Designated A Terror Group*, N.Y. TIMES, Dec. 18, 2004, at A9 ("The United States designated [Hezbollah-run] Al Manar television . . . a terrorist organization . . . . The designation came less than a week after France banned broadcasts of Al Manar . . . after accusations that its programs were anti-Semitic . . . ."); Daniel Kilpert, *Hizbollahs al-Manar: Tödliche Sendung*, Jan. 18, 2006, *available at* www.hagalil.com (last visited Jan. 18, 2006) (reporting about the anti-Israeli and anti-Semitic broadcasts on the Hezbollah TV station al-Manar).

565 *See, e.g.*, U.N. Doc. S/2000/661 (July 6, 2000); U.N. Doc. S/2000/689 (July 13, 2000); U.N. Doc. S/2000/769 (Aug. 4, 2000); U.N. Doc. S/2000/805 (Aug. 15, 2000); U.N. Doc. S/2000/969 (Oct. 7, 2000); U.N. Doc. S/2000/1002 (Oct. 19, 2000); U.N. Doc. S/2000/1011 (Oct. 23, 2000); U.N. Doc. S/2000/1121 (Nov. 26, 2000); U.N. Doc. S/2001/55 (Jan. 18, 2001); U.N. Doc. S/2001/142 (Feb. 14, 2001); U.N. Doc. S/2001/367 (Apr. 17, 2001); U.N. Doc. S/2002/79 (Jan. 18; 2002); U.N. Doc. S/2002/345 (Apr. 3, 2002); U.N. Doc. S/2002/348 (Apr. 3, 2002); U.N. Doc. S/2002/743 (July 10, 2002); U.N. Doc. S/2002/1347 (Dec. 11, 2002).

its borders and inhabitants.[566] Sometimes, albeit rarely, groups other than Hezbollah claimed responsibility for cross-border raids.[567] In the course of the Israeli complaints it repeatedly stressed all Lebanese obligations under previous United Nations Security Council resolutions such as to the Lebanese government's responsibility to "ensure the return of its effective authority and presence in the south, and in particular to proceed with a significant deployment of the Lebanese armed forces as soon as possible."[568]

In return, the state of Lebanon usually complained about the violation of its sovereignty by Israeli counter-attacks, reconnaissance missions, overflights by Israeli aircrafts, etc.[569] Sometimes Israel blamed Hezbollah – and not the state of Lebanon for its omissions – of having provoked such reactions and

---

566 *See, e.g.,* U.N. Doc. S/2001/385 (Apr. 19, 2001); U.N. Doc. S/2001/673 (July 6, 2001); U.N. Doc. S/2002/115 (Jan. 24, 2002); U.N. Doc. S/2002/301 (March 22, 2002); U.N. Doc. S/2002/374 (Apr. 11, 2002); U.N. Doc. S/2002/986 (Sept. 5, 2002); U.N. Doc. S/2003/976 (Oct. 9, 2003); U.N. Doc. S/2004/61 (Jan. 21, 2004); U.N. Doc. S/2004/465 (June 8, 2004); U.N. Doc. S/2004/906 (Nov. 17, 2004); U.N. Doc. S/2005/312 (May 12, 2005); U.N. SCOR, 61st Sess., 5404th mtg., at 10 U.N. Doc. S/PV 5404 (remarks by Carmon (Israel)) (March 30, 2006).

567 Such as the P.F.L.P., *see* U.N. Doc. S/2001/111 (Feb. 6, 2001) at 1.

568 *See* S.C. Res. 1310, par. 6, U.N. Doc. S/RES/1310 (July 27, 2000).

569 *See, e.g.,* U.N. Doc. S/2000/1118 (Nov. 26, 2000); U.N. Doc. S/2000/1172 (Dec. 11, 2000); U.N. Doc. S/2000/1223 (Dec. 21, 2000); U.N. Doc. S/2001/; U.N. Doc. S/2001/110 (Feb. 7, 2001); U.N. Doc. S/2001/164 (Feb. 22, 2001); U.N. Doc. S/2001/184 (March 1, 2001); U.N. Doc. S/2001/312 (Apr. 2, 2001); U.N. Doc. S/2001/344 (Apr. 10, 2001); U.N. Doc. S/2001/371 (Apr. 17, 2001); U.N. Doc. S/2001/430 (May 1, 2001); U.N. Doc. S/2001/45 (May 8, 2001); U.N. Doc. S/2001/476 (May 14, 2001); U.N. Doc. S/2001/478 (May 14, 2001); U.N. Doc. S/2001/502 (May 18, 2001); U.N. Doc. S/2001/531 (May 29, 2001); U.N. Doc. S/2001/606 (June 19, 2001); U.N. Doc. S/2001/630 (June 25, 2001); U.N. Doc. S/2001/901 (Sept. 24, 2001); U.N. Doc. S/2001/1004 (Oct. 24, 2001); U.N. Doc. S/2001/1119 (Nov. 28, 2001); U.N. Doc. S/2001/1177 (Dec. 11, 2001); U.N. Doc. S/2001/1206 (Dec. 13, 2001); U.N. Doc. S/2001/1337 (Dec. 31, 2001); U.N. Doc. S/2001/1336 (Dec. 31, 2001); U.N. Doc. S/2003/1220 (Dec. 31, 2003); U.N. Doc. S/2004/15 (Jan. 13, 2004); U.N. Doc. S/2004/55 (Jan. 21, 2004); U.N. Doc. S/2004/64 (Jan. 27, 2004); U.N. Doc. S/2004/83 (Feb. 3, 2004); U.N. Doc. S/2004/217 (March 26, 2004); U.N. Doc. S/2004/278 (Apr. 6, 2004); U.N. Doc. S/2004/357 (May 5, 2004); U.N. Doc. S/2004/457 (June 7, 2004); U.N. Doc. S/2004/574 (July 16, 2004); U.N. Doc. S/2004/631 (Aug. 9, 2004); U.N. Doc. S/2004/705 (Sept. 1, 2004); U.N. Doc. S/2004/818 (Oct. 15, 2004); U.N. Doc. S/2004/911 (Nov. 18, 2004); U.N. Doc. S/2004/954 (Dec. 6, 2004); U.N. Doc. S/2005/23 (Jan. 13, 2005); U.N. Doc. S/2005/105 (Feb. 24, 2005); U.N. Doc. S/2005/242 (Apr. 13, 2005); U.N. Doc. S/2005/304 (May 9, 2005); U.N. Doc. S/2005/369 (June 6, 2005); U.N. Doc. S/2005/435 (July 7, 2005); U.N. Doc. S/2005/526 (Aug. 12, 2005); U.N. Doc. S/2005/568 (Sept. 9, 2005); U.N. Doc. S/2005/641 (Oct. 11, 2005); U.N. Doc. S/2005/715 (Nov. 14, 2005); U.N. Doc. S/2005/747 (Dec. 1, 2005).

noted that Lebanon's territory was not even concerned since most of the incidents occurred at the Syrian Shab'a Farms which are still occupied by Israel as part of the Golan Heights.[570] Lebanon, on the other hand, occasionally openly defended Hezbollah's actions as "legitimate resistance" with regard to the Shab'a Farms.[571]

The Secretary-General's reports state that southern Lebanon remained comparably calm while, for example, "[t]he serious breaches of the ceasefire in the Shab'a farms area remained a significant cause of concern."[572]

UNIFIL noted several violations of the Blue Line in its reports, but otherwise played a largely unfortunate role. On one occasion, UNIFIL soldiers had filmed the abduction of Israeli servicemen and subsequently denied the existence of according tapes. The UNIFIL report for the concerned period expressed UNIFIL's satisfaction that "the general situation in south Lebanon has remained calm and orderly. Most of the violations of the Blue Line were minor and quickly corrected once UNIFIL raised them with the party concerned."[573] Even-

---

[570] *See, e.g.,* U.N. Doc. S/2000/1121 (Nov. 27, 2000) at 1 ("It should further be recalled that . . . the Secretary-General specifically determined that the area known as "Shaaba" is not Lebanese territory. Consequently, subsequent Lebanese claims against Israel regarding that area, justifying aggressive activity by terrorists emanating from Lebanese territory, is in direct contravention of the aforementioned determination of the Secretary-General").

[571] *See, e.g.,* U.N. Doc. S/2002/473 (Apr. 22, 2002) at 1.

[572] *See, e.g.,* The Secretary-General, Report of the Secretary-General on the United Nations Interim Force in Lebanon (from the period of 21 July 2001 to 16 January 2002), at 3, *delivered to the Security Council*, U.N. Doc. S/2002/55 (Jan. 16, 2002); *see* also with similar content, *e.g.*, The Secretary-General, Report of the Secretary-General on the United Nations Interim Force in Lebanon (from the period of 17 January 2002 to 12 July 2002), at 4, *delivered to the Security Council*, U.N. Doc. S/2002/746 (July 12, 2002); The Secretary-General, Report of the Secretary-General on the United Nations Interim Force in Lebanon (from the period of 13 July 2002 to 14 January 2003), at 5, *delivered to the Security Council*, U.N. Doc. S/2002/38 (Jan. 14, 2003); The Secretary-General, Report of the Secretary-General on the United Nations Interim Force in Lebanon (from the period of 15 January 2003 to 23 July 2003), at 4, *delivered to the Security Council*, U.N. Doc. S/2002/728 (July 23, 2003); The Secretary-General, Report of the Secretary-General on the United Nations Interim Force in Lebanon (from the period of 24 July 2003 to 19 January 2004), at 1, *delivered to the Security Council*, U.N. Doc. S/2004/50 (January 20, 2004); The Secretary-General, Report of the Secretary-General on the United Nations Interim Force in Lebanon (from the period of 21 January 2004 to 21 July 2004), at 1, *delivered to the Security Council*, U.N. Doc. S/2004/572 (July 21, 2004); The Secretary-General, Report of the Secretary-General on the United Nations Interim Force in Lebanon (from the period of 21 January 2005 to 20 July 2005), at 1,2, *delivered to the Security Council*, U.N. Doc. S/2005/460 (July 21, 2005).

[573] U.N. Doc. S/2001/66 (Jan. 22, 2001) at 3.

tually, UNIFIL admitted the existence of the tapes and permitted Israel to view them.[574]

Also throughout 2004 and 2005 Israel continued to blame Hezbollah for a number of cross-border raids[575] and emphasized its right to "self-defence" or "defence".[576] In 2004, the United Nations Security Council finally responded to the fact that Hezbollah was still heavily intertwined with southern Lebanon, and that no serious attempts by the Lebanese government to gain control over these areas were in sight. Security Council Resolution 1559 (2004) urged the government of Lebanon to disband and disarm "all Lebanese and non-Lebanese militias" as well as to extend its control "over all Lebanese territory."[577] Shortly afterwards, Secretary General Kofi Annan delivered one of his bi-annual reports pursuant to resolution 1559 (2004). With regard to foreign influence on Lebanon he complained that "[t]he Syrian military and intelligence apparatus in Lebanon had not been withdrawn as of 30 September 2004."[578] Hezbollah, referred to by the Lebanese government as "'national resistance group' that has as its goal the defence of Lebanon from Israel and the removal of Israeli forces from Lebanese soil, namely, the Shab'a farms,"[579] remained the "most significant remaining armed group" among "several armed elements remain[ing] in the South [of Lebanon]."[580] After another negative report in early 2005,[581] the United Nations

[574] *U.N. to Let Israelis See Abduction Tape*, N.Y TIMES, Aug. 8, 2001, at A6; *see* also U.N. Doc. S/2001/714 (July 20, 2001) at 2.

[575] *See, e.g.*, U.N. Doc. S/2004/61 (Jan. 21, 2004); U.N. Doc. S/2004/465 (June 8, 2004); U.N. Doc. S/2004/906 (Nov. 17, 2004); U.N. Doc. S/2005/312 (May 12, 2005).

[576] *See, e.g.*, U.N. Doc. S/2004/890 (Nov. 9, 2004); U.N. Doc. S/2005/14 (Jan. 11, 2005); U.N. Doc. S/2005/546 (Aug. 29, 2005); U.N. Doc. S/2005/731 (Nov. 22, 2005); U.N. Doc. S/2005/837 (Dec. 28, 2005).

[577] S.C. Res. 1559, U.N. Doc. S/RES/1559 (Sept. 2, 2004).

[578] The Secretary-General, Report of the Secretary-General pursuant to Security Council resolution 1559 (2004), para. 15, delivered to the Security Council, U.N. Doc. S/2004/777 (Oct. 1, 2004) (hereinafter referred to as *Report on S.C. Res. 1559*).

[579] *Report on S.C. Res. 1559*, at para. 19; in 2000, the Security Council had concluded that Israel had entirely withdrawn from Lebanon in accordance with S.C. Res. 425 (March 19, 1978); the Shab'a farms were apparently not considered part of Lebanon, but rather of Syria; *see* Press Release, Security Council, Security Council Endorses Secretary-General's Conclusion on Israeli Withdrawal from Lebanon as of 16 June, U.N. Doc. SC/6878 (June 18, 2000).

[580] *Report on S.C. Res. 1559*, at paras. 18, 19.

[581] The Secretary-General, Report of the Secretary-General on the United Nations Interim Force in Lebanon (from the period of 21 July 2004 to 20 January 2005), paras. 16, 17, 28, *delivered to the Security Council,* U.N. Doc. S/2005/36 (Jan. 20, 2005) (stating that "[t]he Government of Lebanon continued to maintain the position that, so long as there was no comprehensive peace with Israel, Lebanese armed forces would not be deployed along the line of withdrawal." Consequently, "Hizbollah maintained its visible presence near the Blue Line

Security Council reaffirmed its intention to force the government of Lebanon to regain control over the southern part of its territory.[582] Despite slight signs of improvement through the Lebanese "National Dialogue", the reports on the implementation of Security Council resolution 1559 (2004) kept noting that

> the provisions of resolution 1559 (2004) calling for the disbanding and disarmament of all Lebanese and non-Lebanese militias, the extension of the control of the Government of Lebanon over all Lebanese territory and strict respect of the sovereignty, territorial integrity, unity and political independence of Lebanon under the sole and exclusive authority of the Government have not yet been fully implemented.[583]

A subsequent United Nations Security Council resolution welcomed "the decision of the Lebanese national dialogue to disarm Palestinian militias outside refugee camps within six months."[584] But the Security Council had to realize that Lebanon had not yet begun a process of disarmament, as it urged the "Government of Lebanon [to undertake] measures against movements of arms into Lebanese territory and calls on the Government of Syria to take similar measures."[585] A month later, Mr. Ibrahim Gambari, Under-Secretary-General for Political Affairs, briefed the Security Council on recent armed incidents in the Middle East and referred to "unidentified armed elements" firing at IDF forces from inside Lebanon.[586] Also UNIFIL used this wording occasionally.[587]

---

through a network of mobile checkpoints, fixed positions and patrols [and] established several new positions and observation points." With regard to Hezbollah's cross-border attacks the report held and that "[t]he resumption of military measures, for which Hizbollah took credit, asserting its claimed prerogative to resist Israeli occupation of Lebanese territory by force, was disturbing").

[582] S.C. Res. 1583, para. 4, U.N. Doc. S/RES/1583 (Jan. 28, 2005) (urging the government of Lebanon once again ". . . to fully extend and exercise its sole and effective authority throughout the south, including through the deployment of sufficient numbers of Lebanese armed and security forces, to ensure a calm environment throughout the area, including along the Blue Line, and to exert control over the use of force on its territory and from it[.]"

[583] The Secretary-General, Third semi-annual report of the Secretary-General to the Security Council on the implementation of Security Council resolution 1559 (2004), para. 14 U.N. Doc. S/2006/248 (Apr. 19, 2006).

[584] S.C. Res. 1680, para. 6, U.N. Doc. S/RES/1680 (May 17, 2006).

[585] *Id.* at para. 5.

[586] U.N. SCOR, 61st Sess., 5472nd mtg., at 4, 5 U.N. Doc. S/PV 5472 (June 21, 2006).

[587] *See, e.g.*, The Secretary-General, Report of the Secretary-General on the United Nations Interim Force in Lebanon (from the period of 22 July 2005 to 20 January 2006), at 2, *delivered to the Security Council*, U.N. Doc. S/2006/26 (January 18, 2006).

Prior to July 2006, Hezbollah, as well as other groups, remained in southern Lebanon and kept attacking Israel. The state of Lebanon did not regain control over the area. The United Nations' attempts to dissolve or simply disarm Hezbollah failed. As was shown, the terrorists remained an active player between Israel, Lebanon, Syria, and Iran. Hezbollah never stopped its actions to an extent that would have been equal to a true peace along Israel's northern border.

In July 2006, the Middle East encountered another full-blown war. Despite the unilateral withdrawal from southern Lebanon by Israel in 2000, Israel had remained under attack from Hezbollah forces.[588] The abduction of two and killing of three other IDF soldiers by Hezbollah fighters sparked an Israeli offensive as of July 12, 2006, including massive air strikes combined with subsequent ground and naval operations.[589] In doing so, Israel referred to Article 51 of the Charter vis-à-vis Hezbollah but also attributed responsibility to the governments of Lebanon, Syria, and Iran.[590] Israel announced before the United Nations Security Council that "[o]ver the last 48 hours, more than 500 Katyushas and mortar shells were fired into the northern part of Israel . . . . Israeli civilians and eight soldiers have been killed, hundreds have been wounded." The Israeli representative continued that

> Israel's actions were in direct response to an act of war from Lebanon. Although Israel holds the Government of Lebanon responsible, it is concentrating its response carefully, mainly on Hizbollah strongholds, positions and infrastructure. . . . The real occupying power in Lebanon is terror, terror instigated by Hizbollah but initiated, funded and perpetrated by Syria and Iran.[591]

These remarks reveal that Israel regarded Hezbollah as its direct enemy, but continued to attribute responsibility to the state of Lebanon, as well as others. This responsibility, according to Israel, is rooted in the Lebanese government's failure to oppose and abandon Hezbollah's influence subsequent to Israel's with-

---

[588] *See supra* notes 563, 566, 572.

[589] Anthony Shadid, Scott Wilson, *Hezbollah Raid Opens 2nd Front for Israel*, WASH. POST, July 13, 2006, at A01 (stating that "The Lebanese Shiite Muslim group Hezbollah infiltrated the Israeli border Wednesday in a brazen raid, capturing two Israeli soldiers, killing three others and prompting Israeli attacks on the airport in Beirut and bridges, roads, power stations and military positions across the hillsides of southern Lebanon.").

[590] UN. Doc. S/2006/515 (July 12, 2006).

[591] U.N. SCOR, 61st Sess., 5489th mtg., at 6, 7 U.N. Doc. S/PV 5489 (remarks by Gillerman (Israel)) (July 14, 2006).

drawal.[592] Later, however, the Israeli representative said: "The international community must finally address the terrorism that occupies Lebanon. The current crisis is not only a danger to Israel and Lebanon, but to the entire region. We should have no illusions: the terrorism at the root of this crisis is a danger everywhere."[593]

These remarks rather point to a direction closer to previous Israeli legal views: that Hezbollah occupies and controls parts of Lebanon, leaving no choice for the Lebanese government but rather subjecting itself to the will of a non-state actor and its third state supporters.

The government of Lebanon acknowledged "that it was not aware of the incident that occurred on the Blue Line on [July 12th], that it did not take responsibility for it and that it did not endorse that act."[594] However, in Lebanon's eyes "Israel is committing . . . an act of aggression."[595] Hezbollah responded with a continuous bombardment of northern Israel, this time also with rockets of improved quality and most likely Iranian origin.[596]

The legal responses by the international community differed significantly from any previous Israeli incursion into Lebanon or from those against any other terrorist group. The initial international reaction resembled the one after September 11, 2001.[597]

United Nations Secretary General Kofi Annan clearly recognized Israel's right to defend itself in accordance with Article 51 of the Charter. He said:

> I have already condemned Hizbollah's attacks on Israel, and acknowledged Israel's right to defend itself under Article 51 of the UN Charter. I do so again today. I also condemn Hizbollah's reckless disregard for the wishes

---

[592] *Id.* at 6 (stating that "[Israel's withdrawal in 2000] was Lebanon's moment of truth. Would its Government look inward and free its people from the stranglehold of terror? Or would it allow its territory to become a base from which Hizbollah terrorists would launch attacks against Israeli civilians? Tragically, the Lebanese Government chose the latter.")

[593] U.N. SCOR, 61st Sess., 5493rd mtg., at 12 U.N. Doc. S/PV 5493 (remarks by Gillerman (Israel)) (July 21, 2006).

[594] U.N. SCOR, 61st Sess., 5489th mtg., at 4 U.N. Doc. S/PV 5489 (remarks by Mahmoud (Lebanon)) (July 14, 2006).

[595] *Id.* at 5.

[596] Markus Becker, *Die Hightech-Waffen der Hisbollah,* SPIEGEL ONLINE, July 17, 2006, *available at* www.spiegel.de (last visited July 17, 2006) ("Inzwischen besitzt die Hisbollah Projektile, die deutlich tiefer in israelisches Gebiet eindringen können . . . Darunter sind etwa iranische Raketen der Typen Fajr-3 und Fajr-5 mit Reichweiten von jeweils 45 Kilometern und Gefechtsköpfen mit 100 bis 200 Kilogramm Sprengstoff").

[597] *See infra* pp. 157-163.

> of the elected Government of Lebanon, and for the interests of the Lebanese people and the wider region.[598]

Annan clearly referred to Hezbollah, not the state of Lebanon, as origin of the attacks and target of Israel's self-defense. In fact, according to Annan, "[i]t is clear that the Lebanese Government had no advance knowledge of this attack."[599] Irrespective of the existence of Israel's right to self-defense Annan urged Israel not to disregard the proportionality of its actions when he said: "[w]hile Hizbollah's actions are deplorable and, as I've said, Israel has a right to defend itself, the excessive use of force is to be condemned."[600]

The Council of the European Union "recognize[d] Israel's legitimate right to self-defence, but . . . urge[d] Israel to exercise utmost restraint and not to resort to disproportionate action." Additionally, the E.U. recalled "the need for the Lebanese state to restore its sovereignty over the whole of its national territory" and to fully implement "UNSCR 1559 and UNSCR 1680, including disbanding and disarming of all Lebanese and non-Lebanese militias. . . ."[601]

The Council of Europe was less precise on its attitude towards Israeli self-defense as it announced support for the "objective of the Israeli government to free captured Israeli soldiers and protect Israeli citizens from terrorist attacks" but considered the chosen methods to be "inappropriate and counterproductive."[602]

The reaction of the Arab League of Nations was unclear. Initially, several countries expressed criticism regarding Hezbollah's "unexpected, inappropriate and irresponsible acts."[603] Particularly Saudi Arabia's foreign Minister was quoted as having said that "[Hezbollah's] acts will pull the whole region back to

---

598 Press Release, Secretary-General, Secretary-General says 'Immediate cessation of hostilities' needed in Lebanon, describes package aimed at lasting solution, in Security Council Briefing, U.N. Doc. SC/8781 (July 20, 2006).

599 *Id.*

600 *Id.*

601 Press Release from the Council of the European Union, *Main Results of the Council* 2, 13 (July 17-18, 2006), 11575/06 (Presse 219), *available at* http://www.consilium.europa.eu/ (last visited July 21, 2006).

602 Press Release from the Council of Europe, *Statement by Council of Europe Secretary General on the situation in the Middle East* (July 13, 2006), *available at* http://www.coe.int/T/DC/Press/WCD/AllPR_en.asp# (last visited July 24, 2006).

603 *Arab League chief Amr Moussa says Middle East peace process is 'dead',* HAARETZ ONLINE, July 16, 2006, *available at* http://www.haaretz.com/hasen/spages/738712.html (last visited July 16, 2006) (quoting the Saudi foreign minister).

years ago, and we cannot simply accept them."[604] Shortly afterwards, however, the allegedly leading critics, Saudi Arabia and Jordan, denounced Israel's military actions as "aggression" rather than self-defense.[605] Syria expressed open hostility towards Israel as President Assad bluntly expressed his hope that ". . . future generations in the Arab world will find a way to defeat Israel . . . ." and blamed Saudi Arabia, Egypt, and Jordan for their initial criticism of Hezbollah's actions.[606]

The G 8, composed of Canada, Germany, France, Italy, Japan, Russia, the United Kingdom, and the United States, on the occasion of its annual summit, also acknowledged that Israel was defending itself against attacks by Hezbollah.[607]

Argentina,[608] Denmark,[609] Germany,[610] Greece,[611] Peru,[612] Slovakia,[613] the United Kingdom,[614] and the United States[615] *expressis verbis* referred to Israel's

---

[604] Hassan M. Fattah, *Militia Rebuked by Some Arab Countries,* N.Y. TIMES ONLINE, July 17, 2006, *available at* http://www.nytimes.com/2006/07/17/world/middleeast/17arab.html?_r=1 (last visited July 18, 2006).

[605] Press Release from the Kingdom of Saudi Arabia, Ministry of Foreign Affairs, *Prince Saud Al-Faisal holds press briefing* (July 2006), *available at* http://www.mofa.gov.sa/Detail.asp?InSectionID=3986&InNewsItemID=52803 (last visited July 28, 2006); Press Release from the Hashemite Kingdom of Jordan, Foreign Ministry, *Khatib condemns Israeli aggression against Lebanon* (July 19, 2006), *available at* http://www.mfa.gov.jo/events_details.php?id=15465 (last visited July 28, 2006); Press Release from the Hashemite Kingdom of Jordan, Foreign Ministry, *King calls for end to Israeli aggression* (July 27, 2006), *available at* http://www.mfa.gov.jo/events_details.php?id=15546 (last visited July 30, 2006).

[606] Eli Ashkenazi, *Assad warns Israel to seek peace or risk defeat in the future,* HAARETZ ONLINE, August 15, 2006, *available at* http://www.haaretz.com/hasen/spages/750834.html (last visited Aug. 16, 2006).

[607] Press Release from the G 8, *Middle East* (July 16, 2006) *available at* http://en.g8russia.ru/docs/21.html (last visited July 25, 2006) ("In Lebanon, Hizbollah, in violation of the Blue Line, attacked Israel from Lebanese territory . . . It is . . . critical that Israel, while exercising the right to defend itself, be mindful of the strategic and humanitarian consequences of its actions").

[608] U.N. SCOR, 61st Sess., 5489th mtg., at 9 U.N. Doc. S/PV 5489 (remarks by Mayoral (Argentina)) (July 14, 2006) (stating that "Argentina does not deny the fact that Israel has the right to defend itself against foreign attack. However, we also believe that it must do so in accordance with international law and in particular with the provisions of international humanitarian law").

[609] *Id.* at 15 (remarks by Løj (Denmark)) (stating that "Denmark is unwavering in its recognition of the right of States to self-defence — in this case Israel's. However, care must be taken to ensure that the exercise of that right is proportional and measured").

[610] *Merkel und Bush einträchtig in Stralsund,* FRANKFURTER ALLGEMEINE ZEITUNG, July 14, 2006, at p. 1 ("[Präsident] Bush und Frau Merkel äußerten mit Blick auf die kriegerischen

right to self-defense against the non-state actor Hezbollah immediately after Israel's initial forcible responses to Hezbollah's attacks, but urged Israel not to disregard the proportionality of its response.

France, previously also in charge of Lebanon by virtue of its mandate over Syria and perhaps its closest European ally, in an individual reaction condemned Israel's military responses as disproportionate but nevertheless acknowledged Israel's right to defend itself.[616] French President Chirac personally regarded Israel's actions as "disproportionate", while considering Hezbollah's guerillas "completely irresponsible" for firing rockets at Israel.[617] Prime Minister De

---

Ereignisse im Libanon, Israel habe das Recht, sich zu verteidigen. Auch sei der neuerliche Konflikt von der terroristischen Hizbullah ausgegangen").

[611] U.N. SCOR, 61st Sess., 5489th mtg., at 17 U.N. Doc. S/PV 5489 (remarks by Papadopoulou (Greece)) (July 14, 2006) ("We continue to believe that, while preserving the right of self-defence, Israel must respect its obligations under international law, including international humanitarian law, as well as the sovereignty and territorial integrity of Lebanon").

[612] U.N. SCOR, 61st Sess., 5488th mtg., at 4 U.N. Doc. S/PV 5488 (remarks by Pereyra (Peru)) (July 13, 2006) (stating that "Peru recognizes Israel's right to defend itself. However, Israel must do so in accordance with international humanitarian law, avoiding causing harm to civilians and damage to the infrastructure of Lebanon and Gaza").

[613] U.N. SCOR, 61st Sess., 5489th mtg., at 16 U.N. Doc. S/PV 5489 (remarks by Mlynár (Slovakia)) (July 14, 2006) (stating that " [Slovakia] recognize[s] and acknowledge[s] the right of each and every State to self-defence. But that right cannot, and should not, be confused with counterattacks or acts of military provocation. Both parties must refrain from the disproportionate use of force. We call upon them to exercise the utmost restraint").

[614] U.N. SCOR, 61st Sess., 5488th mtg., at 5 U.N. Doc. S/PV 5488 (remarks by Sir Emyr Jones Parry (United Kingdom)) (July 13, 2006) (stating that ". . . Israel has every right to act in self-defence, [but] should do so in a way that does not escalate the situation, that is proportionate measured and that conforms to international law and avoids civilian deaths and suffering").

[615] U.N. SCOR, 61st Sess., 5493rd mtg., at 17 U.N. Doc. S/PV 5493 (remarks by Bolton (United States)) (July 21, 2006) (stating that "[t]here is no moral equivalence between acts of terrorism [by Hezbollah and Hamas] and Israel's exercise of its legitimate right to self-defence").

[616] U.N. SCOR, 61st Sess., 5489th mtg., at 17 U.N. Doc. S/PV 5489 (remarks by De La Sablière (France)) (July 14, 2006) (stating that "Israel has the right to defend its territory and its citizens when they are attacked — and they have been attacked. But we condemn the disproportionate nature of the response, which has already claimed many civilian victims and has caused significant material damage").

[617] Peter Baker, Colum Lynch, *Bush Declines to Call for Israeli Cease-Fire; Other World Leaders Denounce Military Strikes Against Lebanon, Which Seeks U.N. Action,* WASH. POST, July 15, 2006, at A16.

Villepain accepted Israel's right to self-defense, but also urged Israel to restrain itself.[618]

Another group of states did not refer to Israel's right to self-defense explicitly or implicitly denied such a right: China considered Israel's actions in southern Lebanon as aggression.[619] The Republic of Congo identified Hezbollah as the root cause of the current crisis, but "equally firmly [condemned] the disproportionate reprisals by the Israeli army . . . ."[620] Japan acknowledged "legitimate security concerns of Israel" but "urge[d] Israel to refrain from excessive use of force."[621] Qatar referred to a right to self-defense in the current situation in somewhat nebulous terms – rather assigning it to Lebanon and referring to Israel's campaign as "aggression", but pointed to a right to self-defense's definite limitation after the Security Council took action – which it did not.[622] Tanzania condemned Hezbollah's actions, but was otherwise only concerned about a "disproportionate use of force" and did not mention self-defense as legitimizing legal concept.[623] The Vatican "deplore[d] right now the attack on Lebanon, a free and sovereign nation."[624]

While the armed conflict between Israel and Hezbollah continued unabated for four weeks, United Nations Security Council resolution 1701 (2006) was issued to end the hostilities.[625] It recognized "Hizbollah's attack on Israel on 12 July 2006" as starting point of the recent conflict.[626] On the other hand, while it mentions the non-state actor Hezbollah and encourages its host state Lebanon to regain complete control over its territory, it does refer to alleged supportive

---

[618] Gerd Krönke, *Ein Franzose in Beirut,* SÜDDEUTSCHE ZEITUNG, July 20, 2006, at p. 5 ("Natürlich habe Israel das ‚Recht sich selbst zu verteidigen', sagte [de Villepain], aber es müsse auch ‚größtmögliche Zurückhaltung' an den Tag legen").

[619] U.N. SCOR, 61st Sess., 5489th mtg., at 11 U.N. Doc. S/PV 5489 (remarks by Liu Zhengmin (China)) (July 14, 2006) (stating that "[w]e denounce the armed aggression by Israel against Lebanon. The Israeli military forces have used disproportionate force and have caused massive destruction of infrastructure in Lebanon").

[620] *Id.* at 13 (remarks by Ikouebe (Congo)).

[621] *Id.* at 12 (remarks by Kitaoka (Japan)).

[622] *Id.* at 10, 11 (remarks by Al-Qahtani (Qatar)) (stating that "[w]hile we recognize the right of all States, including Lebanon, to defend themselves, the waging of a wide-spread military campaign directly targeting civilians and hitting their infrastructure, such as in the current campaign by the Israeli forces, can in no way be consonant with that objective. . . . The alleged right of Israel to self-defense ends when the Security Council takes the necessary measures to maintain international peace and security. Will the Security Council be allowed to stop Israel's aggression against this wounded country?").

[623] *Id.* at 13 (remarks by Mahiga (Tanzania)).

[624] Baker, Lynch, *supra* note 617.

[625] S.C. Res. 1701, U.N. Doc. S/RES/1701 (Aug. 11, 2006).

[626] *Id.* at 1.

third states, most likely Syria and Iran. The resolution takes reference to Security Council resolution 1559 (2004) which explicitly calls for Hezbollah's disarmament[627] – and not merely for a withdrawal from UNIFIL's operational areas. Resolution 1701 (2006) does not explicitly mention Israel's right to self-defense against Hezbollah, but it certainly does not condemn the Israeli military responses, much less exclude Israel's right to defend itself. Finally, the resolution was not enacted under Chapter VII of the Charter.

In the course of debates prior to and after the vote before the Security Council, several states affirmed Israel's right to defend itself against Hezbollah: the United States emphasized that the resolution urged Israel to cease its "offensive military operations in Lebanon, while reserving the right of any sovereign State to defend itself."[628] France merely affirmed "Israel's right to security."[629] The Greek representative emphasized ". . . that, while preserving the right of self-defence, Israel must respect its obligations under international law, including international humanitarian law."[630] The United Kingdom requested that "we must also see an end to Hizbollah's random attacks continually directed against Israeli civilians. No country can accept its citizens having to live under the shadow of rockets fired from across the border."[631] Implicitly, that seems to affirm Israel's right to protect its citizens against attacks from abroad, regardless of the legal nature of the attacker.

Israel itself announced that it, ". . . like any State, has the right and the duty to defend its citizens from Hizbollah's unprovoked attacks . . . ."[632]

Denmark implicitly recognized Israel's right to respond by force to Hezbollah's attack, beside Syria and Iran, the "main cause" for this conflict", as its representative called on Israel "to show the utmost restraint and to avoid disproportionate action, and have warned it against destroying Lebanon in its fight against Hizbollah."[633] As was seen before, it seems logical to infer from such remarks that while Israel is in compliance with the *ius ad bellum*, Denmark expressed concern about Israel's adherence to the *ius in bello*. Such an emphasis would be largely futile if the former, the *ius ad bellum*, would have already proven to constitute a primary legal obstacle – namely that Israel may not exer-

---

627 S.C. Res. 1559, U.N. Doc. S/RES/1559 (Sep. 2, 2004) ("Calls for the disbanding and disarmament of all Lebanese and non-Lebanese militias;").
628 U.N. SCOR, 61st Sess., 5511th mtg., at 5 U.N. Doc. S/PV.5511 (remarks by Rice (United States)) (Aug. 11, 2006).
629 *Id.* at 7 (remarks by Douste-Blazy (France)).
630 *Id.* at 10 (remarks by Bakoyannis (Greece)).
631 *Id.* at 11 (remarks by Beckett (United Kingdom)).
632 *Id.* at 21 (remarks by Gillerman (Israel)).
633 *Id.* at 12 (remarks by Moeller (Denmark)).

cise forceful counter-measure, regardless of issues such as proportionality against a non-state actor. This, however, is of no further concern. In fact, almost all speakers in favor of Israel's military responses – despite their worries about international humanitarian law as interpreted by Israel – took great care to differentiate between the state of Lebanon and the non-state actor Hezbollah. For instance, the Slovakian representative emphasized in his brief statement that it was of great importance for Lebanon to regain complete control over its territory which "also means taking appropriate measures against the illegal movement of arms and people across its borders and against illegal attacks on the territory of neighbouring States."[634] Tanzania referred to its previous statement in which it had already called "for an immediate ceasefire in the hostilities between Israel and Hizbollah . . . ."[635] Others were less clear on this issue as to who was the responsible party on Lebanon's side. Japan, for instance, called "for a full and immediate cessation of hostilities by the parties in conflict and for Israel and Lebanon to support a permanent ceasefire and a long-term solution . . ." Hezbollah is not mentioned. Lebanon itself complained that while "Israel says that this war is against Hezbollah, not against Lebanon . . . the Israeli strategy of terror is inflicted on all Lebanese." As to the legal nature of Israel's response, the Lebanese representative regarded it as an "obscenely disproportionate and unjustifiable Israeli retaliation."[636]

Also some other states do not seem to be in favor of Israel's right to self-defense, neither implicitly nor explicitly: China merely stated that the "conflict broke out", without pointing at who might have carried according responsibility and furthermore condemned "the excessive use of force and attacks on civilians, civilian facilities and United Nations personnel."[637] Qatar complained about Israel's "aggression."[638]

After the resolution was issued, the cease-fire was obeyed initially. However, it became clear soon enough that Hezbollah was anything but willing to withdraw or even be disarmed.[639] In April 2007, the newly elected United Nations Secretary-General, Ban Ki-Moon, announced that he "received information from Israel and other countries" as to continuous arms smuggling from Syria

---

634 *Id.* at 14 (remarks by Burian (Slovakia)).
635 *Id.* at 16 (remarks by Manongi (Tanzania)).
636 *Id.* at 18 (remarks by Mitri (Lebanon)).
637 *Id.* at 13 (remarks by Liu Zhenmin (China)).
638 *Id.* at 8 (remarks by Sheikh Al-Thani (Qatar)).
639 Edward Cody, Doug Struck, *Hezbollah Balks At Withdrawal From the South*, WASH. POST, Aug. 16, 2006, at A01 (referring to Hezbollah leader Hasan Nasrallah who offered merely a pullback and that only in exchange for the Lebanese army's commitment "not to probe too carefully" for Hezbollah installations).

and Iran into Lebanon, and hence into Hezbollah's hands. Meanwhile, Hezbollah Deputy Secretary General Sheikh Naim Kassem openly announced that his organization was "prepared for the possibility of another adventure or the demand of American policy that might push the IDF in that direction", referring to yet another military confrontation in the summer of 2007.[640]

Whatever Israel did to fight terrorism in Lebanon met harsh criticism from countless sides. The frequency of arguments against Israel's invocation of self-defense was consistently high, but yet quite monotone. The unavailability of self-defense as a legal concept because the opponent was a non-state actor rather than a state was not among them. The predominant criticism that Israel has faced, arguably with good reason, has been the lack of proportionality of its military responses. The raid on Beirut in the course of the 1982 invasion is particularly noteworthy here.

What needs to be emphasized is that all military counteraction Israel employed was exclusively directed against armed bands operative in Lebanon and, at least since 1982, never against regular Lebanese troops.[641]

The responses by the international community in the course of the 2006 military responses to cross-border raids by Hezbollah implies a more or less explicit support for the use of Article 51 of the Charter against non-state actors. Few nations or organizations doubted that Israel could defend itself against attacks such as the ones emanating from southern Lebanon in absence of governmental capabilities to confine them. Proportionality and the *ius in bello* became the predominant legal issues for the international community to worry about.[642] The Israeli interpretation of the relevant *ius ad bellum* – partly quite explicitly – based upon Article 51 of the Charter seems on the other hand to be clearly accepted.

While the world appears to have been receptive for the concept of self-defense against a non-state actor, Israel kept emphasizing governmental Lebanese responsibility. Lebanon was considered to be in breach of its obligations arising under Security Council resolution 1559 (2004). Since such a breach can

---

[640] *Report: Hezbollah says rearming, prepared for summer war with Israel*, HAARETZ ONLINE, Apr. 11, 2007, *available at* http://www.haaretz.com/hasen/spages/847389.html (last visited Apr. 11, 2007).

[641] Yoram Dinstein, *The International Legal Dimensions of the Arab-Israeli Conflict*, in ISRAEL AMONG THE NATIONS (Alfred Kellerman, Kurt Siehr, Talia Einhorn eds., 1998) at 137, 145.

[642] However, Hezbollah was only rarely the target for such criticism despite vital reasons to include them into the legitimate rage about civilian casualties; *see, e.g.,* Sabrina Tavernise, *Christians Fleeing Lebanon Denounce Hezbollah,* N.Y. TIMES ONLINE, July 28, 2006, *available at* http://www.nytimes.com (last visited July 28, 2006) (stating that Hezbollah continuously abuses residential areas to fire rockets).

by itself hardly constitute an armed attack it is quite doubtful whether the Israeli point of view would be sufficient to justify attacks against specifically Lebanese targets without immediate connection to Hezbollah.

In this regard it must be noted that the international community's initial unity with regard to Israel's right to justify its use of force based upon Article 51 of the Charter also means that the use of force emanating from Hezbollah was apparently regarded as an armed attack. Otherwise, the repeated references to Article 51 of the Charter would of course be pointless. Consequently, one must ask which of Hezbollah's actions can be regarded as an armed attack. The abduction of two members of the IDF hardly suffices here. It rather is plausible to accumulate the continuous indiscriminate rocket barrages in the time prior to Israel's invocation of self-defense.

2. South Africa's Military Actions In Neighboring Countries

The South African Apartheid regime occasionally relied on self-defense as it attempted to destroy structures by anti-South African guerilla groups, predominately the African National Congress (ANC, founded 1912), and the South West African People's Organization (SWAPO, founded in the 1960s). The South African Defense Forces (SADF) carried out those attacks in all neighboring countries ("front line-States"). While the conflict with ANC, if fought outside South Africa, took largely place on the territory of states quite able – albeit unwilling – to confine ANC's activities, SWAPO took advantage of the Angolan civil war that disallowed the government to exercise complete control over all its territories.

a) History of the Conflicts

Between 1948 and 1990 South Africa was governed based on the strictly racist Apartheid ("Separateness") agenda. The United Nations repeatedly condemned Apartheid.[643] It was deemed a crime against humanity in 1973,[644] and was eventually incorporated as a crime punishable under the Rome Statute of the

[643] The first United Nations General Assembly resolution noting human rights violations in South Africa was G.A. Res. 44 (I) (Dec. 8, 1946), 1946 U.N.Y.B. 148; for an overview over South Africa related actions of the United Nations *see* 2 RÜDIGER WOLFRUM, UNITED NATIONS: LAW, POLICIES AND PRACTICE 317-28 (Engl. ed. 1995); for an overview over general anti-Apartheid actions *see* Ibrahim J. Gassama, *Reaffirming Faith in the Dignity of each Human Being: The United Nations, NGOs, and Apartheid*, 19 FORDHAM INT'L L.J. 1464, 1471-1522 (1996).

[644] International Convention on the Suppression and Punishment of the Crime of Apartheid, G.A. Res. 3068 (XXVIII) (Nov. 30, 1973).

International Criminal Court in 1998.[645] In 1977 a previously voluntary arms embargo[646] against South Africa was rendered mandatory in order to continue isolating the South African Apartheid regime.[647]

Generally, South Africa faced criticism at nearly all times due to its abhorrent Apartheid policy. As understandable as that might be, it seems as if many states, particularly those that may have had an equally questionable human rights record, criticized South Africa regardless of what particular legal issues may have been at stake. Even more than as was the case with Israel, South Africa's legal allegations regarding recourse to force were hardly ever responded to. Therefore, it is quite difficult to separate the states' legal convictions about non-state actor issues and recourse to force from their general rejection of Apartheid. That is especially true since the ANC and SWAPO were largely regarded as legitimate responses to South African racism and occupation. Its methods were therefore rarely ever subject to legal evaluation.

i) THE ANC

The resistance movement against Apartheid within South Africa had grown over the years and was eventually forced to leave South Africa and to operate from within bordering states. Such host states served as bases for ANC members when committing terrorist attacks on South African soil directed against the Apartheid regime. South Africa responded through military attacks on training camps and other ANC facilities abroad.

The ANC's military wing ("Umkhonto we Siwze" or "Spear of the Nation"), founded by Nelson Mandela and others in the early 1960s, never actually had military capabilities comparable to those of Hezbollah, the PLO, or Kurdish militias in Turkey, Iraq, and Iran.[648] It operated on the basis of small cells inside South Africa, trained and supported from ANC bases abroad. More importantly, unlike Hezbollah, the PLO, and others, the ANC never openly chose to fight with mass-murderous methods such as intentional killings of as many civilians as possible. Rather, the ANC sought to attack only the South African regime and all its representatives, and to limit civilian casualties.[649] Such self-given rules

---

[645] Rome Statute of the International Criminal Court, Article 7 (1) (j), 2187 U.N.T.S. 90, U.N. Doc. A/CONF.183/9 (July 17, 1998).

[646] S.C. Res. 181, U.N. Doc. S/5386 (Aug. 7, 1963).

[647] S.C. Res. 418, U.N. Doc. S/RES/418 (Nov. 4, 1977).

[648] Steven Mufson, *The War for South Africa; How the ANC's Black Guerillas Think They Can Defeat the Afrikaners,* WASH. POST, Dec. 14, 1986, at H1 (quoting South African Brigadeer Hermann Stadler of the South African Defense Forces: "The ANC has no military capability, not in the conventional sense").

[649] *See* Mufson, *supra* note 648 (referring to an ANC explosive manual: "The target must always be carefully selected. . . . The target must symbolize the people's hatred for the govern-

were not always obeyed, but often civilian losses consisted of bystanders who were killed when the ANC attacked governmental or military facilities.[650] In 1962 the Umkhonto leaders including Mandela were arrested. The ANC was banned soon after, which put an end to the ANC's forceful resistance for quite a while. Only the bases in bordering countries and financial assistance from the Soviet Union, as well as from other countries, made it possible for the ANC to resume fighting. In the late 1970s and through the 1980s it carried out several bombing attacks inside South Africa. Only between 1976 and 1984 the South African government counted a total of 197 attacks on industry installations, power stations, governmental institutions, as well as attempted assassinations of individuals.[651] The South African counter-raids led the SADF military into Angola,[652] Botswana,[653] Congo,[654] Lesotho,[655] Mozambique,[656] Zambia,[657] and Zimbabwe.[658] In 1990 Nelson Mandela was released from prison and the prohibition of the ANC was rescinded under the South African President de Klerck,[659] one of the major steps on the way to abandon Apartheid.

---

ment and its system. . . . The action can be directed against government personnel, police and soldiers, spies, agents, students, stooges and informers; but not against innocent bystanders of any description"); Glenn Frankel, *S. African Rebels Make Comeback*, WASH. POST, Jan. 1, 1984 (quoting then-ANC spokesman and current South African President Thabo Mbeki: "[I]f we can attack Koeberg [South Africa's first Nuclear facility], there is nothing to stop us from placing a bomb in a cinema of 300 white people. But we don't do it.").

[650] *See, e.g.*, Glenn Frankel, *Rebel Plans More Violence; 'This Is No Time to Talk,' Exiled S. African Says*, WASH. POST, Feb. 1, 1985, at A1 (referring to car bombing attack on the headquarters of the South African Air force on May 20, 1983 that "killed 19 persons and injured 200, many of them civilians").

[651] Glenn Frankel, *Loss of Bases in Mozambique Is Severe Test for S. African Rebels* , WASH. POST, Apr. 16, 1984, at A15 ("The government [of South Africa] has acknowledged 197 attacks during the past eight years, including, by one account, 25 assaults on industrial installations and power stations, 35 assassination attempts and 30 attacks on police stations, government buildings and military centers").

[652] 1981 U.N.Y.B. 217; 1982 U.N.Y.B. 312; 1984 U.N.Y.B. 180; 1985 U.N.Y.B. 180; 1986 U.N.Y.B. 162; 1987 U.N.Y.B. 163, 167.

[653] 1985 U.N.Y.B. 189; 1986 U.N.Y.B. 165.

[654] 1974 U.N.Y.B. 172.

[655] 1981 U.N.Y.B. 221; 1982 U.N.Y.B. 313; 1985 U.N.Y.B. 193.

[656] 1980 U.N.Y.B. 263; 1981 U.N.Y.B. 221; 1982 U.N.Y.B. 318; 1986 U.N.Y.B. 175.

[657] 1971 U.N.Y.B. 113; 1976 U.N.Y.B. 163; 1979 U.N.Y.B 221; 1980 U.N.Y.B. 263; 1986 U.N.Y.B. 165; 1986 U.N.Y.B. 176.

[658] 1986 U.N.Y.B. 165.

[659] 1990 U.N.Y.B. 135.

ii) SWAPO

The other group which was targeted by South Africa was SWAPO. It operated from the territories of Angola and Namibia. The latter was claimed by South Africa even after its mandate from the League of Nations over the former German colony of "South West Africa" had been terminated in 1966 by the U.N. General Assembly.[660] Namibia gained full independence only on March 21, 1990.[661]

The conflict with SWAPO was deemed a proxy conflict of the Cold War due to the involvement of both superpowers in the Angolan civil war. After Angola's independence from Portugal in November 1975, three national movements sought to gain dominance over the state: the Popular Movement for the Liberation of Angola (Movimento Popular de Libertação de Angola, MPLA), the National Liberation Front of Angola (Frente Nacional de Libertação de Angola, FNLA), and the National Union for Total Independence of Angola (União Nacional para a Independência Total de Angola, UNITA).

While the MLPA received support by the USSR and its allies – foremost Cuba – the FNLA and UNITA were mainly supported by the United States and South Africa.[662] Due to the struggle of all of those groups and the resulting civil war, Angola became another example of a state where the government was not at all times able or willing to exercise full control over its territories. Once the MLPA became the dominating faction in Angola, it extended support to the ANC and SWAPO alike.[663] Today, SWAPO is the dominating political party in Namibia. In 2004 it won 55 of the 72 elected seats in the National Assembly.[664]

b) Singular Incidents and States' Responses

The South African regime faced strongest criticism in its fight against non-state actors operating from host states, starting in the early 1970s.[665] Typically, whenever South Africa regarded itself in defense against attacks from abroad, it would not distinctly rely on self-defense as a concept or name Article

---

[660] G.A. Res. 2145 (XXI), U.N. Doc. A/6316 (Oct. 27, 1966).

[661] David B. Ottaway, *Namibia Gains Freedom In Midnight Celebration; Africa's Last Colony Becomes Newest Nation,* WASH. POST, March 21, 1990, at A1.

[662] *Angola's Three Rival Movements,* WASH. POST, Aug. 9, 1977, at A8.

[663] *See, e.g.,* U.N. SCOR, 40th Sess., 2696th mtg., at 4 U.N. Doc. S/PV.2696 (remarks by van Dunem (Angola)) (June 20, 1986) (stating that "Angola will not stop giving its support to SWAPO and the freedom fighters of the people of Namibia and South Africa. We consider ourselves in duty bound to do so, since Angola is part of the United Nations").

[664] *See* U.S. Dep't St., *Country Report on Namibia*, March 2006, *available at* http://www.state.gov/p/af/ci/wa/ (last visited Apr. 13, 2006).

[665] *See* the first of many resolutions condemning South Africa: S.C. Res. 300 (Oct. 12, 1971).

51 of the Charter. Rather, Pretoria would for instance announce taking "whatever steps . . . necessary to protect South African life and property" in response to "sabotage" emanating from host states of alleged terrorism, e.g. Mozambique. South Africa regarded such states as "fully responsible" for harboring terrorists.[666] Other terms used were e.g. "protective action",[667] or "curbing the [terrorist] violence and aggression".[668]

South Africa did not always rely on self-defense in response to an armed attack. Often, the government chose to act anticipatorily and not in immediate response to ANC or SWAPO actions. It would assert to hunt responsible individuals in prevention of further terror. Therefore, self-defense as reaction to prior armed attacks was often not a legal issue. In return, host and other states would deny that they were harboring or supporting terrorists. South African nationals on foreign soil were rather all considered as "refugees" without further distinctions whether they might engage in terror.[669] On some occasions, South Africa unsuccessfully attempted to justify its resort to force by invoking the "hot pursuit" doctrine,[670] or referring to the host state's alleged consent.[671]

Regardless of the legal concepts invoked, the initial legal and factual setting is comparable with the other factual patterns dealt with here: non-state actors operating from the territory of host states which are unwilling or unable to stop such actions against the victim state. The victim state responds by resorting to force.

i) Military Responses Against the ANC

Over a period of nearly 30 years the South African regime consistently fought against the ANC and similar groups with bases abroad. In the beginning, the legal doctrine of "hot pursuit" was invoked to justify incursions into foreign countries to which ANC forces withdrew.[672] Over the time, this legal justifica-

---

[666] U.N. Doc. S/13822 (Feb. 26, 1980) at Annex II (subsequent to violations of Mozambique's airspace).
[667] U.N. Doc. S/13886 (Apr. 10, 1980) at Annex (referring to "protective action against aggression committed from Zambian soil"); *see also* U.N. Doc. S/14937 (March 31, 1982) (referring to "necessary steps to protect the people of the Territory . . . ." against attacks emanating from Angola).
[668] U.N. Doc. S/15303 (July 21, 1982).
[669] *See, e.g.,* 1982 U.N.Y.B. 316.
[670] *See, e.g.,* 1971 U.N.Y.B. 113-14; U.N. SCOR, 31st Sess., 1944th mtg., at 3, 9, U.N. Doc. S/PV.1944 (remarks by Mwale (Zambia), El Hassen (Mauritania)) (July 27, 1976); 1985 U.N.Y.B. 184.
[671] *See* G. Carpenter, *The South African Raid on Terrorist Bases in Lesotho*, 8 S. AFR. Y.B. INT'L L. 154 (1982).
[672] *See, e.g.,* 1971 U.N.Y.B. 113-14.

tion proved to be not convincing and was eventually "[d]enounce[d] and reject[ed]" by the United Nations Security Council.[673]

One major South African military offensives took place on December 9, 1982 against ANC facilities and homes of ANC members in Maseru, the capital of Lesotho.[674] The SADF completely destroyed ANC structures and killed over 30 alleged ANC members in Lesotho as well as a number of civilians, arguing that such conduct was warranted by prior consent of the Lesotho government.[675] Lesotho, however, complained to the Security Council about the "brutal killings, [in which] the victims were eliminated either through indiscriminate bombings of dwellings and in some cases victims were awakened and callously shot in a cold, criminal manner." Lesotho also noted that the attacks were executed by the SADF, but that they were "led and guided by members of the so-called Lesotho Liberation Army."[676]

The Security Council condemned South Africa's regime and expressed grave concern about its behavior and that of its "proxies", affirming Lesotho's "right to receive and give sanctuary to the victims of apartheid."[677] The General Assembly acted accordingly.[678] Later, the United Nations Security Council repeated its "deep concern" over the South African "aggressive acts . . . against the territorial integrity and independence of Lesotho".[679]

South Africa asserted that its military actions were pre-emptive in nature, seeking to prevent an escalation of terror by destroying ANC headquarters and bases, and complained that neither of the resolutions mentioned prior ANC forceful conduct.[680]

All states strongly condemned South Africa, usually without referring to other potential parties to the conflict. Only the United States extended their condemnation to all violence from whatever side it may have come, most likely hinting at the ANC.[681] Kenya, on the other hand, openly announced its very own

---

673 S.C. Res. 568 (June 21, 1985), 1985 U.N.Y.B. 191.

674 Joseph Lelyveld, *South Africa Reports Killing 30 in Attack on Foes in Lesotho*, N.Y. TIMES, Dec. 9, 1982, at A1.

675 *See* Carpenter, *supra* note 671; *see also* U.N. SCOR, 37th Sess., 2406th mtg., at 2, U.N. Doc. S/PV.2406 (remarks by King Moshoeshoe (Lesotho)) (Dec. 14, 1982).

676 U.N. Doc. S/15515, at 2 (Dec. 9, 1982).

677 S.C. Res. 527(Dec. 15, 1982), 1982 U.N.Y.B. 317.

678 G.A. Res. 37/101 (Dec. 14, 1982).

679 S.C. Res. 535, U.N. Doc. S/RES/535 (June 29, 1983).

680 U.N. SCOR, 37th Sess., 2409th mtg., at 15, U.N. Doc. S/PV.2409 (remarks by Steward (South Africa)) (Dec. 16, 1982).

681 U.N. SCOR, 37th Sess., 2408th mtg., at 3, U.N. Doc. S/PV.2408 (remarks by Lichtenstein (United States)) (Dec. 16, 1982).

as well the OAU's continuing support for the ANC,[682] while Botswana denied that the ANC would be harbored by South Africa's neighbors.[683] The ANC itself denied having conducted terrorist operations from Lesotho.[684]

Given the anticipatory/pre-emptive nature of Pretoria's actions, traditional self-defense was not an issue here. The fact that South Africa was not acting in anticipation of non-state actor violence – as opposed to actions attributable to a state such as Lesotho – was not an issue by itself. As on further occasions, the non-state actor's relevance remained largely unmentioned.

Similar "preventive" operations had taken place on the territory of Mozambique on January 30, 1981,[685] August 22,[686] November 11,[687] and December 6, 1982.[688] In response to Mozambique's complaints about the violation of its sovereignty, the South African government asserted as it had done previously – without mentioning self-defense specifically – "that acts of violence by ANC who enjoy facilities in Mocambique" jeopardized peace on the region and that "it is South Africa's policy not to allow [Mozambique's] territory to be used for carrying out violence against others."[689] In March 1983, Lesotho complained about further South African incursions,[690] but South Africa denied any involvement.[691] Two months later, it was again on Mozambique to express outrage about military actions by South Africa, which "regime consistently uses the alleged presence of the [ANC] in Mozambique as merely a strategy of the South African régime to intimidate and terrorize the countries in the region . . . ."[692] South Africa had responded to a prior bombing attack by the ANC on South African air force installations in Pretoria on May 20, for which the group had announced its responsibility.[693] Mozambique did not say that South African military responses against the non-state actor ANC were not permissible, but rather denied even the ANC's presence on its territory. Pakistan[694]

---

682 U.N. SCOR, 37th Sess., 2409th mtg., at 4, U.N. Doc. S/PV.2409 (remarks by Wabuge (Kenya)) (Dec. 16, 1982).
683 *Id.* at 2 (remarks by Legwaila (Botswana)).
684 1982 U.N.Y.B. 317.
685 U.N. Doc. S/14358 (Feb. 2, 1981).
686 U.N. Doc. S/15380, at 1 (Aug. 27, 1982).
687 U.N. Doc. S/15501, at 2 (Nov. 24, 1982).
688 1982 U.N.Y.B. 318.
689 *See, e.g.,* U.N. Doc. S/15506, at 2, 3 (Dec. 2, 1982).
690 U.N. Doc. S/15658 (March 28, 1983).
691 U.N. Doc. S/15664 (March 30, 1983).
692 U.N. Doc. S/15801 (May 27, 1983).
693 Alan Cowell, *Damage in Mozambique Raid Looks Surprisingly Light*, N.Y. TIMES (May 25, 1983) at A12.
694 U.N. Doc. S/15794 (May 26, 1983).

and the German Democratic Republic[695] condemned South Africa for its "aggression", but neither the Security Council, nor the General Assembly, released according statements. Only the Economic and Social Council took action, condemning the "blatant aggression" by South Africa.[696]

South Africa and Mozambique announced in 1984 the Nkomati Accord in which both states agreed not allow their territories to be used for attacks against each other.[697] Soon Mozambique accused South Africa of continuously violating the Accord by providing supplies to another non-state actor, the National Resistance of Mozambique (Resistência Nacional de Mozambique, RENAMO).[698]

1985 was a year in which the United Nations were constantly concerned with South Africa and the "front line-states". No less than ten Security Council resolutions were passed concerning South Africa.[699] Besides Angola, particularly South African actions against Botswana and Lesotho were at stake.[700] The SADF attacked ANC facilities directly but also supplied non-state actors within the countries it sought to destabilize: UNITA in Angola, the National Resistance Movement in Mozambique, and the Lesotho Liberation Army.

In May 1985 South African commandos were caught in Angola in the vicinity of a U.S. owned oil facility, provoking strong American reactions.[701] South Africa asserted that the MPLA was providing massive support to the ANC in Angola and that South Africa "shall take whatever action is necessary and appropriate to defend ourselves." In doing so South Africa regarded itself in accordance with international law: "[A] State may not permit or encourage on its territory activities for the purpose of carrying out acts of violence on the territory of another State, and . . . a State has a right to take appropriate steps to protect [itself] . . . against such acts."[702] All other speakers condemned South Af-

---

[695] U.N. Doc. S/15802 (May 27, 1983).
[696] 1983 U.N.Y.B. 180.
[697] 1984 U.N.Y.B. 178.
[698] 1986 U.N.Y.B. 156.
[699] S.C. Res. 560, U.N. Doc. S/RES/560 (March 12, 1985); S.C. Res. 566, U.N. Doc. S/RES/566 (June 19, 1985); S.C. Res. 567, U.N. Doc. S/RES/567 (June 20, 1985); S.C. Res. 568, U.N. Doc. S/RES/568 (June 21, 1985); S.C. Res. 569, U.N. Doc. S/RES/569 (July 26, 1985); S.C. Res. 571, U.N. Doc. S/RES/571 (Sept. 20, 1985); S.C. Res. 572, U.N. Doc. S/RES/572 (Sept. 30, 1985); S.C. Res. 574, U.N. Doc. S/RES/574 (Oct. 7, 1985); S.C. Res. 577, U.N. Doc. S/RES/577 (Dec. 6, 1985); S.C. Res. 580, U.N. Doc. S/RES/580 (Dec. 30, 1985).
[700] 1985 U.N.Y.B. 189-96.
[701] Don Oberdorfer, *U.S. Reacts Angrily To South Africa's Raid Near Oil Plant; Explanation of Angolan Foray Demanded,* WASH. POST, May 25, 1985, at A1.
[702] U.N. SCOR, 40th Sess., 2597th mtg., at 6, U.N. Doc. S/PV.2597 (remarks by von Schirnding (South Africa)) (June 20, 1985).

rica, deeming its behavior an aggression.[703] Obviously, the absence of any direct prior armed incident left no room for South Africa's legal assessment.

Following a raid into Botswana in June 1985, South Africa asserted that it had urged the government of Botswana repeatedly to prevent the ANC from executing terror attacks inside South Africa, namely "36 acts of terror" since August 1984. As Botswana did not react "[t]he South African security forces had no alternative but to protect South Africa and its people from . . . terrorist attacks emanating from Botswana."[704] The only country which directly responded with a reference to Article 51 of the Charter was Swaziland. It disagreed with South Africa as there was no imminent armed attack to which the SADF could have been responding.[705] The fact that such an armed attack would have been exercised by a non-state actor (ANC) rather than by the state of Botswana – which did not even possess armed forces of its own –[706] was not so much of the delegate's concern.

In late 1985 Lesotho requested that the Security Council convene to deal with an a series of armed attacks against Lesotho by South Africa.[707] It accused South Africa of an "unprovoked armed aggression" against Lesotho, killing nine individuals during a cross-border raid.[708] South Africa rejected this and stated that it had "experienced terrorist violence emanating from Lesotho's territory, where the ANC is given sanctuary under the convenient guise of refugee status."[709] The Security Council did not elaborate further on the actions of the ANC and condemned South Africa's conduct as aggression.[710] The United States made clear that it would not "accept the idea that South Africa may dispatch troops for military actions beyond its borders."[711] This statement does seem to exclude the possibility of South Africa's successfully pointing at non-state actors – or anyone – as triggering South African cross-border raids.

---

[703] 1985 U.N.Y.B. 182.

[704] U.N. Doc. S/17282, at 3, 4 (June 17, 1985).

[705] U.N. SCOR, 40th Sess., 2599th mtg., at 14, U.N. Doc. S/PV.2599 (remarks by Malinga (Swaziland)) (June 21, 1985).

[706] U.N. SCOR, 40th Sess., 2598th mtg., at 7, U.N. Doc. S/PV.2598 (remarks by Khalil (Egypt)) (June 21, 1985).

[707] U.N. Doc. S/17689 (Dec. 23, 1985).

[708] U.N. Doc. S/17692 (Dec. 23, 1985).

[709] U.N. SCOR, 40th Sess., 2639th mtg., at 12, U.N. Doc. S/PV.2639 (remarks by Aldrich (South Africa)) (Dec. 30, 1985).

[710] 1985 U.N.Y.B. 194.

[711] U.N. SCOR, 40th Sess., 2639th mtg., at 53, U.N. Doc. S/PV.2639 (remarks by Okun (United States)) (Dec. 30, 1985).

Another example of South Africa's reference to self-defense is its military actions against Botswana, Zambia, and Zimbabwe in May 1986.[712] The SADF struck several ANC targets in the three states' capitals, killing three foreign nationals. Before the United Nations, South Africa justified these actions "against ANC bases" as "appropriate for the defense . . . of our people and for the elimination of terrorist elements . . . ."[713] South African President Botha drew parallels to American and Israeli counter-terrorism efforts,[714] despite the fact that the latest South African actions were not immediately triggered by a particular terrorist attack.

The rejection of South Africa's actions is quite unisonous, as is the silence to the ANC or non-state actors in general. The United Kingdom and the United States condemned South Africa's resort to force "totally and utterly"[715] and rejected any "connection between the United States action against Libya and the South African raids . . . ."[716] Both governments nonetheless vetoed a Security Council resolution stipulating mandatory economic sanctions against South Africa.[717] Foremost, the United States differentiated between its own actions against Libya under Article 51 of the Charter from South Africa's actions "against the Governments of Botswana, Zambia and Zimbabwe, which were engaged in discussions with South Africa to end cross-border violence."[718] The American representative emphasized that the three governments had not only been engaged in negotiations but had "made efforts to limit cross-border violence directed at South Africa."[719] It was suggested that the American point of view deeming the application of force "particularly inexplicable" given the on-

[712] Alan Cowell, *Pretoria's Forces Raid 3 Neighbors in Move on Rebels*, N.Y. TIMES, May 20, 1986, at A1; for an overview *see* Edward Kwakwa, *South Africa's May 1986 Military Incursions Into Neighboring African States*, 12 YALE J. INT'L L. 421, 425-26 (1987).
[713] U.N. SCOR, 41st Sess., 2684th mtg., at 27, 28, U.N. Doc. S/PV.2684 (remarks by von Schirnding (South Africa)) (May 22, 1986).
[714] *South African President Defends Raids on 3 Neighboring Nations*, N.Y. TIMES, May 21, 1986, at A10 (referring to Botha's comparison with the U.S. raid on Tripoli, Libya, and Israel's strike on PLO headquarters in the vicinity of Tunis, Tunisia, each of which had occurred in response to prior terrorist attacks on U.S. and Israeli targets).
[715] U.N. SCOR, 41st Sess., 2686th mtg., at 13, U.N. Doc. S/PV.2686 (remarks by Thomson (United Kingdom)) (May 23, 1986).
[716] *Id.* at 111 (remarks by Byrne (United States)).
[717] *Id.* at 128-30.
[718] U.N. SCOR, 41st Sess., 2684th mtg., at 49, U.N. Doc. S/PV.2684 (remarks by Okun (United States)) (May 22, 1986).
[719] U.N. SCOR, 41st Sess., 2685th mtg., at 7, U.N. Doc. S/PV.2685 (remarks by Okun (United States)) (May 23, 1986).

going negotiations[720] left room for the assumption that the United States might have "found the raids acceptable if they had been carried out at a more appropriate time".[721] The Organization of the Islamic Conference condemned the actions as South African aggression.[722] Botswana denied harboring any "ANC gangsters",[723] while Zimbabwe rejected South Africa's invocation of Article 51 of the Charter, but admitted openly that it had been supporting "liberation movements of South Africa" politically, materially, and morally.[724]

Finally, South Africa's point of view was rejected unanimously. The absence of an immediately prior attack brushed aside any aspects regarding the involvement of non-state actors even though they had been the sole target of South Africa's resort to force. Given the hostility which the Apartheid regime was facing and the corresponding high degree of tolerance towards national liberation movements[725] such as the ANC, it seems unlikely that most nations would have reacted differently had there been such an immediately prior terrorist attack.

A similar outcome can be seen in mid-1988: Botswana considered South African cross-border raids to constitute "state terrorism",[726] while South Africa accused Botswana once again of allowing a "bulk of terrorists" to infiltrate "South Africa . . . through . . . Botswana." Accordingly, South Africa saw itself "compelled to take effective action" as it would do also in the future "whenever required."[727] The Security Council did not refer to South Africa's arguments, but "strongly condemned there aggressive acts . . . in violation of international law."[728] It did not specify the exact violations of international law and if it was because of the absence of prior attacks by or with help of Botswana or because of the nature of the attacker.

On other occasions it is not entirely clear if and by whom SADF actions were triggered. In July 1988 for instance, an SADF soldier was killed in an incident at the border with Mozambique.[729] Mozambique insisted that the SADF had

---

[720] *Id.* (referring to a statement "issued by the White House").
[721] *Cf.* KWAKWA, *supra* note 712 at n.45.
[722] U.N. SCOR, 41st Sess., 2685th mtg., at 19-20, U.N. Doc. S/PV.2685 (remarks by Pirzada) (May 23, 1986).
[723] U.N. SCOR, 41st Sess., 2686th mtg., at 52, U.N. Doc. S/PV.2686 (remarks by Legwaila (Botswana)) (May 23, 1986).
[724] *Id.* at 83-85, 87 (remarks by Mudenge (Zimbabwe)) (partly citing a statement by Zimbabwe's president Robert Mugabe).
[725] *See* Kwakwa, *supra* note 712 at 431.
[726] U.N. Doc. S/19952 (June 22, 1988).
[727] U.N. Doc. S/19960 (June 24, 1988).
[728] U.N. Doc. S/19959 (June 24, 1988).
[729] U.N. Doc. S/20293 (Nov. 23, 1988).

been hunting down ANC members,[730] while South Africa asserted that its forces were accidentally drawn into an exchange of fire between RENAMO and another armed militia on the territory of Mozambique.[731]

ii) Military Responses Against the SWAPO

South Africa fought the Angolan-based SWAPO for several years until Namibia's independence in March 1990. Only between 1981 and 1984, South Africa launched at least five major military campaigns into Angola, allegedly killing approximately 1,600 SWAPO members.[732] Such actions, emanating from Namibia, seem often to have been unprovoked i.e. in absence of armed attacks immediately prior to SADF military operations. Many states repeatedly condemned South Africa's presence in Namibia as unlawful occupation, confirming prior legal assessments by the Security Council and ICJ.[733] On other occasions South Africa announced that all military responses on Zambian territory could be "directly attributed to the presence of [SWAPO] terrorists." It pointed out, in response to an attack by SWAPO forces on August 23, 1978, that "Zambia had . . . allowed SWAPO practical control of part of its territory . . . ."[734] Rather than mentioning self-defense, South Africa repeatedly announced its "responsibility" for the territory of Namibia.[735] Usually, the Security Council rejected such arguments and "strongly condemned South Africa's aggression against . . . Angola."[736] It usually failed to comment on the distinction that South Africa attempted to draw between the host state and the actual target of the SADF, the non-state actor SWAPO.[737] South Africa also made clear that it did not try to intervene in the Angolan civil war and that it was not attempting to interfere with the MLPA.[738]

---

[730] U.N. Doc. S/20357 (Dec. 28, 1988).
[731] U.N. Doc. S/20326 (Dec. 13, 1988).
[732] Glenn Frankel, *Fighting in Angola Seen Peril to Namibian Talks,* WASH. POST, Dec. 28, 1983, at A15.
[733] S.C. Res. 270, U.N. Doc. S/RES/270 (Jan. 30, 1970) (declaring the continued presence of South Africa in Namibia illegal); *see also* Legal Consequences for States of the Continued Presence of South Africa in Namibia (South West-Africa) Notwithstanding Security Council Resolution 276 (1970), Advisory Opinion, 1971 I.C.J. 16 (July 21, 1971); for states' remarks *see, e.g.,* 1976 U.N.Y.B 165 (referring to statements by the USSR, China, and the United Kingdom, among others, considering South Africa's presence in Namibia as unlawful occupation and the illegality of ifs use as base for military actions against SWAPO in Zambia); *see also* S.C. Res. 393 (July 30, 1976), 1976 U.N.Y.B. 166-67.
[734] U.N. Doc. S/13541 (Sept. 17, 1979).
[735] *Id.*; *see also, e.g.,* U.N. Doc. S/13608 (Nov. 5, 1979) at 2.
[736] S.C. Res. 454 (Nov. 2, 1979), 1979 U.N.Y.B. 233-34.
[737] *See, e.g.,* U.N. Doc. S/13886 (Apr. 10, 1980).
[738] U.N. Doc. S/14028, at 2 (June 27, 1980).

One of South Africa's major operations against SWAPO took place in July 1981. Angola complained to the Security Council about the attacks by the SADF.[739] Several states condemned South Africa's actions as "aggression", among them China,[740] Egypt,[741] Spain,[742] and the USSR.[743] South Africa stated that it was merely reacting to increasing SWAPO cross-border violence against civilians in Namibia, supported by the USSR and Cuba. In particular, the South African Foreign Minister stated that SWAPO's "hit-and-run" tactic "deliberately provokes counter-operations. . . ." [744] South Africa's reasoning was rejected by France, asserting that "[t]he arguments advanced by Pretoria according to which the attacks were allegedly made in self-defence against incursions by SWAPO fighters are not at all valid. The territory of the Republic of South Africa is not in danger."[745] France was referring to South Africa's generally rejected "unjustified maintenance in Namibia"[746] rather than attacks directly on undisputed South African territory. However, there seems to be room for the assumption that France might not have ruled out self-defense against the non-state actor SWAPO had they attacked South Africa directly, rather than South African forces in Namibia.

A subsequent Security Council resolution was voted against by the United States because it once again failed to mention the presence of foreign troops in Angola, prevailingly Cuban soldiers, as well as the consistent provision of arms to the SWAPO by the USSR.[747] The United States was among the only ones to mention the cause of South African resort to force: SWAPO and its foreign supporters.[748] Many other states clearly condemned the South African resort to

---

739 U.N. Doc. S/14623 (July 30, 1981).
740 U.N. Doc. S/14665 (Aug. 28, 1981).
741 U.N. Doc. S/14655 (Aug. 28, 1981).
742 U.N. Doc. S/14650 (Aug. 27, 1981).
743 U.N. Doc. S/14658 (Aug. 28, 1981).
744 U.N. Doc. S/14652, at 2 (Aug. 27, 1981).
745 U.N. SCOR, 36th Sess., 2297th mtg., at 4, U.N. Doc. S/PV.2297 (remarks by Leprette (France)) (Aug. 29, 1981).
746 *Id.* at 5.
747 1981 U.N.Y.B. 218.
748 U.N. SCOR, 36th Sess., 2296th mtg., at 16, U.N. Doc. S/PV.2296 (remarks by Lichtenstein (United States)) (noting ". . . that substantial supplies of foreign arms have been shipped into Angola to supply and resupply elements of SWAPO that have engaged in violence across the Angolan frontier.") (Aug. 28, 1981).

force and demanded immediate withdrawal.[749] Additionally, the General Assembly strongly condemned South Africa's "aggression".[750]

As the conflict continued, South Africa complained that while it aimed solely at SWAPO and not Angola or any other state, Angola failed to address such a distinction. South Africa would cease its actions immediately if only SWAPO was not harbored and assisted by Angola as well as others.[751]

In late 1983 and early 1984 South Africa launched another major campaign.[752] South Africa had asserted that its sole aim was once again to track down SWAPO terrorists operating from Angolan territory but added that Angola bore responsibility for any support it awarded to the non-state actor.[753] The Security Council's reaction was exceptional in its quantity: within three weeks the Security Council responded by three consecutive resolutions all of which condemned South Africa's attacks.[754]

France clearly rejected South Africa's references to self-defense as "unacceptable" due to the absence of any threat to the territory of South Africa – not due to the legal nature of the alleged attacker.[755] All other states condemned the South African actions in varying terms,[756] self-defense was only debated as possible legal grounds for Angolan responses.[757] The United Kingdom and the United States, despite their abstaining and hence not negative votes, announced that they did not regard the propositions suggested by the resolution as "useful"[758] or suitable for a peaceful reconciliation.[759]

Angola and South Africa reached the Lusaka Understanding in February 1984 according to which the SADF had to withdraw from Angolan territory.[760]

---

[749] *See, e.g.,* U.N. SCOR, 36th Sess., 2297th mtg., at 4, U.N. Doc. S/PV.2297 (remarks by Leprette (France)) (Aug. 29, 1981); U.N. SCOR, 36th Sess., 2298th mtg., at 2, U.N. Doc. S/PV.2298 (remarks by van Well (West Germany)), (Aug. 29, 1981).

[750] G.A. Res. 36/172 C, at 41 (Dec. 17, 1981).

[751] U.N. Doc. S/15338 at 1, 2 (Aug. 3, 1982).

[752] *See* Frankel, *supra* note 732.

[753] *See, e.g.,* U.N. SCOR, 39th Sess., 2509th mtg., at 4, U.N. Doc. S/PV.2509 (remarks by von Schirnding (South Africa)) (Jan. 4, 1984).

[754] S.C. Res. 545, U.N. Doc. S/RES/545 (Dec. 20, 1983); S.C. Res. 546 (Jan. 6, 1984) 1984 U.N.Y.B. 182-83; S.C. Res. 547, U.N. Doc. S/RES/547 (Jan. 13, 1984).

[755] U.N. SCOR, 39th Sess., 2511th mtg., at 2,3, U.N. Doc. S/PV.2511 (remarks by Louet (France)) (Jan. 6, 1984).

[756] 1984 U.N.Y.B. 180-82.

[757] *See, e.g.,* U.N. SCOR, 39th Sess., 2510th mtg., at 11, U.N. Doc. S/PV.2510 (remarks by Lusaka (Zambia)) (Jan. 5, 1984).

[758] U.N. SCOR, 39th Sess., 2511th mtg., at 6, U.N. Doc. S/PV.2511 (remarks by Margretson (United Kingdom)) (Jan. 6, 1984).

[759] *Id.* at 8 (remarks by Lichtenstein (United States)).

[760] 1984 U.N.Y.B. 178.

It was never fully implemented until the end of the South African Apartheid regime.

In 1987 the tense situation between Angola and South Africa was about to fully escalate despite intergovernmental negotiations, the Lusaka agreement, and Security Council resolution 601 (1987) which had called for cease-fire between SWAPO and South Africa.[761] South Africa launched another massive military campaign from Namibia into Angola. The Security Council unanimously condemned such actions as South African aggression.[762] Before the United Nations Security Council, Angola complained about numerous South African violations of Angolan territory during all of 1987, culminating in a large scale campaign together with UNITA.[763] Angola's representative referred to a statement by the South African Defense Minister which allegedly revealed that the SADF was acting in prevention of UNITA's destruction rather than in pursuit of "Namibian patriots"[764] i.e. the SWAPO. Other countries shared Angola's view.[765] South Africa contended that it was acting in protection of Namibia's territory from terrorist attacks and accused one of the Angolan factions – the MLPA – of extending support to the SWAPO and the ANC.[766] The permanent representative of South Africa admitted that SDAF forces were supporting UNITA. In fact, South African President Botha had visited the South African forces in Angola.[767] The West German delegate, referring to statements made by German Foreign Minister Genscher, held that both South Africa's abuse of Namibia as a "springboard" for aggression against Angola as well as cross-border violence emanating from Angola were illegal.[768] He did not mention that the latter would give rise to self-defense. The delegate of Ghana addressed the arguments put forward by South Africa and held that there was no justification of South Africa's violation of Article 2 (4) of the Charter. It could not claim to act on behalf of Namibia and the mere presence of foreign troops on Angolan territory did not threaten South Af-

---

[761] S.C. Res. 601, U.N. Doc. S/RES/601 (Oct. 30, 1987).

[762] S.C. Res. 602, U.N. Doc. S/RES/602 (Nov. 25, 1987).

[763] U.N. SCOR, 41st Sess., 2763rd mtg., at 11-16, U.N. Doc. S/PV.2763 (remarks by da Silva de Moura (Angola)) (Nov. 20, 1987).

[764] *Id.* at 16 (remarks by da Silva de Moura (Angola)).

[765] For a summary *see* 1987 U.N.Y.B. 168-72; *see* also 1985 U.N.Y.B. 186 (also on this occasion, many states accused South Africa of merely assisting foreign rebel groups in Angola, such as UNITA).

[766] U.N. SCOR, 41st Sess., 2764th mtg., at 8, U.N. Doc. S/PV.2764 (remarks by Manley (South Africa)) (Nov. 23, 1987).

[767] *Id.* at 9.

[768] U.N. SCOR, 41st Sess., 2766th mtg., at 13, U.N. Doc. S/PV.2766 (remarks by von Wartenburg (West Germany)) (Nov. 24, 1987).

rica.[769] The U.S. representative condoned "cross-border violence or South African military raids into neighboring countries."[770] Despite the American support for the subsequent resolution, the U.S. delegate regretted that Security Council resolution 602 (1987) failed to address all causes of the conflict surrounding Angola, Namibia, and South Africa, particularly the ongoing civil war in Angola, involving at least two major factions and foreign powers.[771] The United Kingdom, besides condemning South Africa, condoned all "cross-border fighting".[772] All of these comments do not reveal much about the states' views on self-defense vis-à-vis non-state actors. The non-state actors, foremost the SWAPO, but also UNITA and MPLA, do not play a decisive role in many comments as South Africa was denied to exercise any rights on behalf of Namibia, notwithstanding the opponent. Further legal reasoning, such as South Africa's frequent references to non-state actors as actual target of its operations, was apparently not considered necessary.

In 1988 Angola, Cuba, and South Africa reached an agreement according to which both Cuban and South African forces would be withdrawn from Angolan territory. The United Nations Security Council approved of such an agreement and issued resolution 626 (1988), establishing the United Nations Angola Verification Mission (UNAVEM).[773] The withdrawal commenced in 1989, and by 1990 the majority of Cubans had left.[774] The inner Angolan conflict between MLPA and UNITA continues until today.

South Africa's actions were condemned at all times as aggressions, as well as for other reasons. Their opponent being a non-state actor, incapable of triggering an armed attack as such, was never among them. However, of all conflicts, this is the one in which it is hardest to draw any conclusions in support of this work's assumption. This is mainly the case for two reasons: (1) South Africa disregarded several other conditions of self-defense, most often the requirement of an imminent armed attack to which it may have arguably been entitled to respond. On the occasions it did refer to prior terror attacks by anti-Apartheid movements those can arguably never be deemed to have amounted to the necessary degree of an armed attack; (2) the consistent general rejection of South Africa's Apartheid regime led to minimal, usually vague legal evaluations by third states which always culminated in condemnation. Individual legal aspects re-

---

[769] *Id.* at 48-51 (remarks by Ghebo (Ghana)).

[770] U.N. SCOR, 41st Sess., 2767th mtg., at 22, U.N. Doc. S/PV.2767 (remarks by Walters (United States)) (Nov. 25, 1987).

[771] *Id.* at 34-36.

[772] *Id.* at 32 (remarks by Birch (United Kingdom)).

[773] S.C. Res. 626 (Dec. 20, 1988), 1988 U.N.Y.B. 160.

[774] 1990 U.N.Y.B. 155.

main largely unidentified. Additionally, not only Apartheid as such but also Cold War lines along which the conflicts ran contributed to general condemnations instead of more careful legal analysis.

3. Foreign Interventions in Northern Iraq to Fight Kurdish Groups

The Kurdish people are deprived of their own national state while facing several others opposing their interests. More than once, the Kurds were subject to considerable persecution in almost any country in which they lived.[775] Genocide at best, Iraq's "Anfal" campaign became infamous in the late 1980s in which somewhere between 50,000 and 200,000 civilians were killed.[776]

a) Kurds in Turkey

Among the states opposing the Kurds and their desire for independence was first and foremost Turkey.[777] In return, Kurdish resistance movements formed, making Turkey their primary opponent. Since the beginning of the secular Turkish Republic in the 1920s, Turkey rendered the Kurds subject to their "Turkification" process and was often in violation of international human rights in doing so:[778] the Kurdish language was banned; Kurds disappeared after having been detained by security forces; and Kurdish parties were disallowed among numerous other prohibitions.[779]

The most famous among the Kurdish resistance groups against Turkish oppression was the Kurdish Worker's Party (Partiya Karkaren Kurdistan, PKK), known as People's Congress of Kurdistan or Kongra-Gel (KGK). The PKK's origins were closely linked with its former leader and current Turkish prison in-

---

775 For an overview of Kurdish history *see* Olivia Q. Goldman, *The Need for an Independent International Mechanism to Protect Group Rights: A Case Study of the Kurds*, 2 TULSA J. COMP. & INT'L L. 45 (1994).

776 For an overview of the Iraqi cruelties during the Anfal campaign *see* Catherine S. Knowles, *Life and Human Dignity, the Birthright of all human beings: An Analysis of the Iraqi Genocide of the Kurds and Effective Enforcement of Human Rights*, 46 NAVAL L. REV. 152, 157-69 (1998); in August 2006, Saddam Hussein and other individuals were charged with genocide for the crimes that occurred during the Anfal campaign; *see* Sudarsan Raghavan, For Kurds, a Long Wait for Justice, WASH. POST, Aug. 21, 2006, at A01.

777 Goldman, *supra* note 775 at 70-75.

778 Lucien J. Dhooge, *We arm the World: The Implications of American Participation in the Global Armaments Trade,* 16 ARIZ. J. INT'L & COMP. L. 577, 644-49 (1999); Goldman, *supra* note 775 at 70; *see also* Carole A. O'Leary, Karna A.J. Eklund, *Pluralism vs. Modern Iraqi Nationalism: Root Causes of State-Sponsored Violence Against Iraq's Kurdish Community and the Search for Post-Conflict Justice*, 13 MICH. ST. J. INT'L L. 91, 94 (2005) (noting that, despite opposing popular perceptions, many Kurds in Turkey are far more worried by Turkification than by Americanization).

779 See, e.g., *On Trial: Turkey's Kurdish Policy,* N.Y. TIMES, Dec. 15, 1994, at A28.

mate Abdullah Öcalan who founded the group in the late 1970s. After the Turkish military coup d'état and rising human rights violations against the Kurdish minority, the PKK began to engage in an armed battle against any kind of Turkish targets.[780] Since 1984 the conflict between the PKK and the Republic of Turkey has claimed over 30,000 lives.[781] Under the leadership of Abdullah Öcalan, the PKK has chosen terror as its primary response to Turkish cruelties. One commentator deemed its campaign "ruthless, . . . even by terrorist standards."[782] It should be noted that the PKK is likely to be a direct result of the systematic and reckless Turkish campaign against Kurds, their culture, and their living space, aggravating the Kurdish plight. However, the methods chosen in response cannot be labeled as anything other than terrorist in nature: they abducted people,[783] killed school teachers to compromise the Turkish school system,[784] and repeatedly attacked military forces as well as villages in South-East Turkey, rarely ever distinguishing between non-combatants and soldiers.[785] They also extended their actions against Turkish targets outside of Turkey, raiding Turkish embassies, consulates, and private businesses throughout Europe,[786] abducted children of Kurdish-Turkish refugees to 'recruit' them for PKK actions,[787] and even threatened to kill German politicians, who they considered to be pro-Turkish.[788] Germany responded with rigid countermeasures after PKK supporters engaged in heavy street fights with German police forces in March 1996. Afterwards, PKK leader Öcalan openly threatened to kill German tourists in

---

780 Hanz Chiapetta, *Rome 11/15/98: Extradition or Political Asylum for the Kurdistan Workers Party's Leader Abdullah Ocalan?*, 13 PACE INT'L L. REV. 117, 122 (2001).

781 Central Intelligence Agency, *Turkey*, THE WORD FACTBOOK, *available at* https://www.cia.gov/cia/publications/factbook/geos/tu.html (last visited Oct. 27, 2006).

782 Chiapetta, *supra* note 780, at 120.

783 Goldman, *supra* note 775, at 74; Jim Bodgener, *Violence Marks Kurdish Rebel Anniversary*, FIN. TIMES (London), Aug. 16, 1989, at 2.

784 Chiapetta, *supra* note 780, at 133.

785 *E.g. Guerillakrieg der militanten PKK eskaliert*, SÜDDEUTSCHE ZEITUNG, October 27, 1993, at Politik (reporting about a massacre in Yavi where PKK members killed 32 occupants of a local teahouse, because some of the Kurdish residents of Yavi had associated themselves with Turkey); David Barchard, *Turk Soldiers Killed By Kurds*, FIN. TIMES (London), May 1, 1987, at 2.

786 Tamara Jones, Hugh Pope, *Kurds Raid Turk Offices in Europe*, L.A. TIMES, June 6, 1993, at A1; Dieter Fabritius, *Mit Molotowcocktails gegen Reisebüros*, SÜDDEUTSCHE ZEITUNG, March 2, 1995, at München.

787 Global March Against Child Labor, *Report on Convention 182 Ratification Status, Country Report Sweden* (2000), available at http://www.globalmarch.org/resourcecentre/world/sweden.pdf (last visited Apr. 13, 2006).

788 *Morddrohungen der PKK gegen Kohl und Kinkel*, SÜDDEUTSCHE ZEITUNG, Apr. 2, 1996, at Politik.

Turkey and announced in an interview that the PKK would start to fight its enemies with suicide bombers, "turning every Kurd into a living bomb."[789]

The PKK was deemed a foreign terrorist organization by the U.S. State Department under Secretary of State Albright in 1997.[790] Öcalan was arrested in Kenya and brought to Turkey under unclear, but after all not illegitimate circumstances.[791] The PKK has remained on the State Department's list until today under its new name Kongra-Gel.[792] In 2004 the US government noted – according to Turkish and NGO sources – that the PKK/Kongra-Gel maintained 500 armed members in Turkey, and another approximately 3,500 in northern Iraq.[793] It had signed a cease-fire with the Turkish authorities but announced in June 2004 not to be bound by it any longer, resulting in new clashes between Turkish and terrorist forces.[794]

b) Kurds in Iraq and Iran

Iraq, together with Iran, the other major national state with significant Kurdish population, is involved in a conflict with Kurds for no fewer than four reasons: (1) between 1984 and prior to the Iraq invasion into Kuwait 1990-91, the Turkish government maintained good connections to the Iraqi regime which consented to repeated cross-border attacks by Turkish forces to hit Kurdish guerilla bases within a six mile buffer zone on Iraqi territory;[795] (2) Iraq continuously oppressed Kurdish Iraqis, culminating in the 1988 Halabja attacks during which the Iraqi army gassed about 5,000 civilians by means of chemical

---

789 Thomas Avenarius, *SZ-Gespräch mit Abdullah Öcalan: Jeder Kurde wird zu einer lebenden Bombe*, SÜDDEUTSCHE ZEITUNG, March 29, 1996, at Politik.

790 U.S. St. Dep't, *Public Notice 2612*, 62 Fed. Reg. 52650-01 (Oct. 8, 1997).

791 Öcalan v. Turkey, 37 Eur. Ct. H. R. 10, 242.

792 U.S. St. Dep't, *Fact Sheet* (Oct. 11, 2005), *available at* http://www.state.gov/s/ct/rls/fs/37191.htm (last visited Nov. 23, 2005).

793 U.S. St. Dep't, *Country Reports on Terrorism 2004, Chapter 5 – Country Report Turkey*, Apr. 2005, *available at* http://www.state.gov/documents/organization/45313.pdf (last visited Nov. 23, 2005).

794 Amnesty Int'l, *Amnesty International Report 2005 (Turkey)*, *available at* http://web.amnesty.org/report2005/tur-summary-eng (last visited Nov. 24, 2005); *see also, e.g., Krieg mit alten Mitteln; Die PKK bombt wieder und benutzt den Nordirak als Rückzugsort - die USA lässt das kalt,* SÜDDEUTSCHE ZEITUNG, June 9, 2005, at 8; Benjamin Harvey, *Three Killed In Explosion In Turkish Resort Town,* WASH. POST, Aug. 29, 2006, at A12 (stating that in the course of bombing attacks in Turkey "[t]he Kurdistan Freedom Falcons, a small militant group believed to be an offshoot of the Kurdistan Workers' Party, or PKK, asserted responsibility for the earlier attacks, including one Sunday in Istanbul that injured six people").

795 Goldman, *supra* note 775, at 72.

weaponry;[796] (3) because Iraq has, on the other hand, supported Kurdish factions during internal struggles;[797] and (4) because Iraq's northern territories served as bases for Kurdish terrorists since the early 1990s.[798] The fourth category is crucial here.

As the first Gulf War between Iraq and the American-led forces came to a halt by a ceasefire established through U.N. Security Council resolution 687 (1991), Iraq withdrew its troops from Kuwait and had to abide by the numerous terms the international community stipulated.[799] Eventually, France, the United Kingdom, and the United States insisted on the establishment of "no-fly zones" in northern Iraq in 1991 and in southern Iraq in 1992.[800] The former covered almost all of which is the predominately Kurdish part of Iraq and was turned into a 'safe haven' for the Kurds.[801] In the previous years the Iraqi government had unleashed a heinous campaign against the Kurdish fighters, the Peshmerga, and then gone on to murder as many Kurds as they could obtain.[802] The legal basis for the "no-fly-zones" remained vague.[803] In any event, the Kurds were sought to be protected from the Iraqi dictatorship's violence and humanitarian assistance without Iraqi interference was assured,[804] as northern Iraq became a protected area. According to claims of neighboring states, however, those areas served as bases for Kurdish incursions into Iran[805] and Turkey.[806] The Turkish government therefore continued to fight Kurdish groups in northern Iraq increasingly throughout the 1990s.[807]

Turkish forces repeatedly clashed with PKK fighters in close vicinity to the Iraq and Iran border.[808] The Turkish Kurds withdrew to the rocky border re-

---

[796] Natasha Carver, *Is Iraq/Kurdistan a State such as it Can Be Said to Operate State Systems and Thereby Offer Protection to its 'Citizens'?*, 14 INT'L J. REFUGEE L. 57, 61 (2002); Knowles, *supra* note 776 at 161.
[797] Carver, *supra* note 796, at 68.
[798] *Id.*
[799] S.C. Res. 687, U.N. Doc. S/RES/687 (Apr. 3, 1991).
[800] Alfred B. Prados, *The Kurds in Iraq: Status, Protection, and Prospects* Summary, Cong. Rep. Service 4-7 (May 12, 1994); for Iraq's view *see, e.g.*, U.N. Doc. A/51/328 (Sept. 5, 1996).
[801] GRAY, *supra* note 36, at 115, 116.
[802] Knowles, *supra* note 776, at 154-69.
[803] Sean D. Murphy, *Assessing the Legality of Invading Iraq*, 92 GEO. L.J. 173, 205 (2004).
[804] *Id.* at 204.
[805] U.N. Doc. S/25843 (May 26, 1993).
[806] U.N. Doc. S/1995/605 (July 24, 1995).
[807] Andreas Laursen, *The Use of Force and (the State of) Necessity*, 37 VAND. J. TRANSNAT'L L. 485, 514 (2004).
[808] *See, e.g.*, John Murray Brown, *Turkey gives military carte blanche against Kurds*, FIN. TIMES (London), Oct. 2, 1992, at 2; Carlyle Murphy, *Turkish Army Presses Offensive in Iraq;*

gions of northern Iraq and Iran. As Turkey started to pursue them, internal Kurdish arguments erupted over whether the PKK's actions were more harmful than useful to the Kurdish cause. Eventually, the Iraqi Kurds, also using military force,[809] urged the PKK to halt their cross-border attacks and to cease using Iraq as their bases, by which they had exposed all Iraqi Kurds to Turkish retaliation.[810] The conflict between the PKK and Turkey continued nevertheless with unabated brutality.

The most prominent Turkish retaliation raid was Operation Steel which commenced on March 20, 1995. Some 35,000 soldiers attacked PKK targets in Northern Iraq *inter alia* in response to a March 18 attack on Turkish troops in South Eastern Turkey.[811] Such raids continued in the coming years. Despite criticism from many states, Turkey did not refrain from applying force against Kurdish militant groups.[812] Finally, their successful scorched earth policy, coupled with the arrest of PKK leader Abdullah Öcalan in February 1999 in Nairobi, Kenya,[813] constituted major victories for the Turkish anti-terror policy. The PKK lost its force, perhaps in huge parts because their leader – fearing for his life in a Turkish prison – was now calling upon them to lay down their weapons instead of leading them to further terrorist acts.[814]

The situation slowly abated. In 2003 and the Turkish parliament enacted an amnesty for PKK fighters upon which attempts began to collect the rebel group's weapons.[815] Although Turkey loosened some of the restrictions on the Kurdish minority, it did not provide a proper solution that would respect the right of the Turkish Kurds to the extent that it could have satisfied the terror groups to resort to more peaceful countermeasures. In 2005 the truce was abandoned and Kurdish terror factions again began killing Turkish security personnel. Turkey responded by force and eventually requested U.S. assistance to fight

---

Troops Escalate Fight Against Kurdish Rebels; Iraqi Kurds Help Reluctantly, WASH. POST, Oct. 25, 1992, at A29.

809 *Kurds versus Kurds*, N.Y. TIMES, Nov. 30, 1992, at A14.

810 Chris Hedges, *An Odd Alliance Subdues Turkey's Kurdish Rebels*, N.Y. TIMES, Nov. 24, 1992, at A1.

811 Laursen, *supra* note 807, at 515.

812 *See, e.g., Turkish Forces Cross Border Into Iraq to Attack Kurdish Guerillas*, N.Y. TIMES, May 15, 1997, at A4.

813 Amberin Zaman, *Turkey Celebrates Capture of Ocalan*, WASH. POST, Feb. 18, 1999, at A17.

814 Amberin Zaman, *Rebel Kurd Urges End To Revolt*, WASH. POST, Aug. 4, 1999, at A15.

815 *Türkei gliedert PKK Kämpfer* ein, SÜDDEUTSCHE ZEITUNG, Aug. 6, 2003, at 7.

the Kurdish bases in northern Iraq and Iran.[816] The U.S. expressed understanding for Turkey's request for assistance but repeatedly pointed to lacking additional resources for military expeditions to the – relatively calm – northern Iraq.[817]

Not only Turkey, but also the government of Iran regarded itself forced to respond to "trans-border military attacks against and sabotage in Iranian border provinces" exercised by "bands of armed and organized terrorists" with headquarters in Iraq.[818]

Previously, Iran and Iraq both had supported rivaling Kurdish factions: the Kurdistan Democratic Party (Partiya Demokrat a Kurdistanê, KDP) is said to have received support from Hussein's regime, while the Patriotic Union of Kurdistan (PUK) was linked with Iran.[819] The PUK's founder, Jalal Talabani, was elected President of Iraq on April 7, 2005.[820] Apparently, Kurdish factions engaged in opposing sides during the Iran-Iraq war from 1980 to 1988.[821] On numerous occasions Iraq protested against Iranian military actions,[822] as they had done previously against Turkish attacks.

c) Singular Incidents and States' Responses

Turkey did not at all times expressly invoke self-defense against the PKK in Iraq, and neither did other states always explicitly deny them the right to do so. The very first military actions by Turkey were allegedly all covered by Iraqi consent. Sometimes, Iraq appears to have allowed the Turkish troops to enter in each individual case,[823] while on other occasions a 1984 agreement regulating

---

[816] Christiane Schlötzer, *Krieg mit alten Mitteln*, SÜDDEUTSCHE ZEITUNG, June 9, 2005, at 8 (referring to requests by the Turkish Prime Minister Tayyip Erdogan and the Foreign Minister Abdullah Gül for assistance by American forces stationed in Iraq).

[817] *See, e.g.*, Susan Sachs, *U.S. Tells Turks It Won't Fight Kurds*, N.Y. TIMES, Jan. 12, 2005, at 10 (referring to remarks by Gen. John P. Abizaid, head of the Army's Central Command, who expressed after a meeting with Turkish officials that the United States considered the main Kurdish separatist group, the PKK, a terrorist organization, but added "we also understand - all of us understand - that our troops have a lot of work to do there along with the Iraqi security forces, and we agree that, over time, we must deal with the P.K.K.").

[818] U.N. Doc. S/25843 (May 26, 1993).

[819] Carver, *supra* note 796 at 68.

[820] Ellen Knickmeyer, Carlyle Murphy, *Iraqis Pick Kurd As New President; Shiite Set to Be Named Prime Minister,* WASH. POST, Apr. 7, 2005, at A01.

[821] Knowles, *supra* note 776 at 157.

[822] U.N. Doc. S/25689 (Apr. 29, 1993); U.N. Doc. S/25772 (May 13, 1993).

[823] *Turkish Troops Reported to Battle Iraqi Kurds*, N.Y. TIMES, May 31, 1983, at A5 (referring to statements by Iraq's ambassador to Turkey); Loren Jenkins, *Turkish Kurds Fight Unheralded; Ankara Soft-Pedals War but Recent Clashes Hint at Wider Scope,* WASH. POST, Oct. 12, 1986, at A22 (referring to "Turkish officials" confirming that the military actions were undertaken with "approval of the Iraqi government").

the "hot pursuit" by Turkish troops into Iraq is cited.[824] Internally, the Turkish government released decrees allowing for cross-border use of force, given the "neighboring country's consent".[825] That situation changed upon the Turkish involvement in the First Gulf War. Iraq no longer consented to cross-border attacks and protested against Turkish incursions[826] and complained repeatedly about them to the United Nations.[827] In response Turkey complained heavily about the exodus of approximately 220,000 Kurdish-Iraqi refugees who attempted to flee Iraqi cruelties,[828] shortly before the United Nations Security Council issued resolution 688 (1991) to protect the Iraqi Kurds.[829] Iraq responded by noting that it was "extremely paradoxical" for the Security Council to act upon letters by Turkey, and Iran, as the "world knows full well that these states do not by any means recognize any of the rights of the Kurds . . . ."[830] The Turkish-Iraqi relations over the Kurdish issues kept deteriorating over several Turkish military operations into Iraq,[831] and reached a negative climax during the major operation Turkey launched on March 20, 1995, Operation Steel.[832]

Three days later, on March 23, 1995, the permanent representative of Iraq to the U.N. reported all incursions into Iraqi airspace since March 11, 1995. However, for March 20, 1995, the report merely stated "33 sorties, flown . . . at medium altitudes, centred over Nasiriyah, Samawah, Salman, Qurnah, Jalibah and Artawi" as well as "a United States TR-1 reconnaissance aircraft", allegedly violating Iraqi airspace.[833] Approximately two weeks later Iraq finally informed the United Nations specifically about the Turkish actions in the course of Operation Steel,[834] which turned out to be largest military operation Turkey had ever

---

[824] *Turkey Says its Planes Raided Kurdish Guerilla Bases in Iraq*, N.Y. TIMES, March 5, 1987, at A9 (referring to an according 1984 agreement between Turkey and Iraq).
[825] *Turkish Planes Bomb Kurdish Rebels in Iraq*, N.Y. TIMES, Aug. 16, 1986, at 4 (citing to remarks by Turkey's Prime Minster Turgot Özal who said "Iraq was told beforehand" and to a governmental decree, which allowed for pursuing "rebels into neighboring countries with the neighboring country's consent").
[826] Goldman, *supra* note 775, at 72.
[827] *See, e.g.*, U.N. Doc. S/1995/272 (Apr. 7, 1995); U.N. Doc. S/1997/318 (Apr. 15, 1997); U.N. Doc. S/1997/354 (May 6, 1997); 1998 U.N.Y.B. 287; 2000 U.N.Y.B. 314.
[828] U.N. Doc. S/22435 (Apr. 3, 1991).
[829] S.C. Res. 688, U.N. Doc. S/RES/688 (Apr. 5, 1991).
[830] U.N. Doc. S/22460 (Apr. 8, 1991) at 1, 2.
[831] *See, e.g.*, KEESING'S REC. OF WORLD EVENTS 38403 (August 1991); *id.* at 38547 (October 1991); *id.* at 38833 (March 1992).
[832] *Turks Attack Kurds In Iraq for a 2d Day; 200 Reported Killed*, N.Y. TIMES, March 22, 1995, at A7.
[833] U.N. Doc. S/1995/238 (March 29, 1995) at 4.
[834] *See* U.N. Doc. S/1995/272 (Apr. 7, 1995).

launched against Kurdish guerilla units. On March 31, 1995 Iraq listed all alleged violations of Iraq territory, including 56 violations since 1991 through Turkey including "the most recent violations of Iraq's sovereignty [which] is still under way".[835] On April 7 Iraq finally complained about over 100 sorties into Iraqi airspace between March 20 and 31, 1995.[836] Later, Iraq sent a memorandum to the UN Secretary General approximately 60 days after the beginning of the Turkish invasion, complaining that no counteractions had been undertaken despite international condemnation. Iraq blamed the United Nations' measures as double standards and called the member states "hypocrites".[837]

Turkey remained unimpressed by the hostile Iraqi attitude. In the beginning of the Turkish counter attacks into Iraqi territory, Turkey announced that it was exercising a right of self-defense against the "terrorist PKK".[838] During the course of the 1995 campaigns Turkey maintained this view but did not always rely on self-defense explicitly.[839] Prime Minister Tansu Çiller deemed Operation Steel as "one of the most important operations in our history, and this is a right of our self-defence" but she did not specifically mention Article 51 of the Charter.[840] Later Turkey announced that it resorted to "legitimate measures which are imperative to its own security" and which are "of limited time and scope".[841] Additionally, Turkey emphasized that it "cannot ask the Government of Iraq to fulfill its obligation under international law to prevent the use of its territory for the staging of terrorist acts against Turkey."[842] The Turkish ambassador to Washington stated that the Turkish actions were aiming at "eliminating a terrorist menace".[843] Iraq continued to complain about Turkish incursions.[844]

In 1996, Turkey continued its cross-border raids in response to PKK terror and, for the purposes of a legal justification, mentioned "the principle of self-preservation and necessities" along with Turkey's need "to take necessary and appropriate measures to eliminate the existing terrorist threat from the area".[845]

---

835 U.N. Doc. S/1995/254 (March 31, 1995) at 2.
836 U.N. Doc. S/1995/272 (Apr. 7, 1995).
837 *See* U.N. Doc. S/1995/379 (May 9, 1995) at 2.
838 *Kurd Raids Won't Stop*, THE HERALD SUN, Aug. 9, 1991 (quoting Turkey's Cabinet spokeswoman and State Minister Imren Aykut).
839 GRAY, *supra* note 36 at 116.
840 Televised address by Turkish Prime Minister Tansu Çiller, *Call to Nation*, March 25, 1995 (on file with author).
841 U.N. Doc. S/1995/605 (July 24, 1995) at 1.
842 *Id.*
843 Ambassador of Turkey Nuzhet Kandemir, *Turkey Moved on Iraq to Combat Terrorism*, N.Y. TIMES, March 30, 1995, at A22.
844 *See, e.g.*, U.N. Doc. S/1996/401 (May 31, 1996).
845 U.N. Doc. S/1996/479 (July 2, 1996).

The Iraqi side, somewhat interestingly, appears to have read these remarks as an invocation of self-defense, which Iraq rejected.[846]

In the course of a meeting of the General Assembly in October 1997, the Turkish U.N. delegate Çelem stated that "the Iraqi Foreign Minister contended in his statement that Turkey, through measures of self-defence, has been interfering in the internal affairs of Iraq . . . " and assured that indeed the Turkish Government will not hesitate to take all appropriate and necessary measures to remove this threat, directed from northern Iraq at the lives and property of its people."[847] Even though those remarks sound distinctly similar to self-defense against a non-state actor caused by the inability (here: caused by third party restraints) of the actually obligated state actor, Iraq, Turkey did not expressly rely on Article 51 of the Charter on this occasion. Before the United Nations, Turkey referred to its duty to defend its borders and people against the PKK.[848]

The United States, frequently Turkey's sole and though often critical ally during their grim anti-PKK policy, regarded the Turkish Operation Steel as exercise of self-defense,[849] but called for a quick withdrawal nonetheless.[850] The longer the Turkish military actions, that reached their peak with Operation Steel, lasted, the more difficult the situation became for the Clinton administration. Eventually, despite having acknowledged the action's initial legitimacy, voices rose that expressed uncertainty if the scope of Turkey's actions could still be covered by self-defense and about the length of the operation and the large numbers of Turkish soldiers remaining in Iraq.[851] Generally, the U.S. attitude towards Turkey did nonetheless remain quite stable. Also later military opera-

---

[846] U.N. Doc. S/1996/561 (July 17, 1996).

[847] U.N. GAOR, 52nd Sess., 22nd mtg., U.N. Doc. A/52/PV.22 (Oct. 2, 1997) (remarks by Celem (Turkey)).

[848] U.N. Doc. S/1997/7 (Jan. 3, 1997); U.N. Doc. S/1997/552 (July 16,1997).

[849] U.N. Doc. S/1995/566 (July 12, 1995) (quoting a spokesman for the United States Department of State who said on July 7, 1995, "that the use of United States aircraft and other military equipment by Turkey was justified, and that the United States took the view that the Ankara Government was simply exercising its right to self-defence").

[850] Alan Makovsky, *Turkey Merits US Backing As It Hunts Terrorists Christian Science Monitor*, CHRISTIAN SCI. MONITOR, Apr. 18, 1995, at 19 (quoting U.S. Secretary of State Warren Christopher who deemed the Turkish military campaign "an act of self-defense" but called for a "prompt withdrawal").

[851] Sid Balman Jr., *U.S. warns Turkey on Iraq operation*, WASH. POST, March 23, 1995, at Washington News (quoting State Department spokeswoman Christine Shelly as expressing uncertainty over the operation being a "self-defense issue"; U.S Secretary of State Warren Christopher "sent a message to both the prime minister and foreign minister telling them we are concerned about the passage of time and concerned about reports we've had of human rights violations").

tions were 'understood' by the U.S. State Department,[852] and deemed as "self-defense".[853] It seemed likely that not only Turkey's role as a close ally and long-standing U.S. partner played a role here. Perhaps an additional factor was that the U.S. government must have known the consequences for Turkey if the PKK is left without confinements in the Kurdish "safe haven". Burdening Turkey with an unleashed PKK probably promoted a U.S. view which otherwise may have been less supportive. However, to assume that the U.S. offered even "more consistent legal arguments"[854] than Turkey only because they particularly named the concept of self-defense rather than pointing at the preservation of "territorial integrity"[855] is not compelling but merely a fight of words. Whether or not self-defense according to Article 51 of the Charter can be relied upon does, after all, merely depend on whether its conditions are met, not how they are verbalized.[856] Here, the U.S. seems to have been of the opinion that those conditions were met on several occasions. At least, the fact that the PKK was a not state did not interfere with the American view of Turkey's right to self-defense.

The reaction from Europe was less supportive; in fact, it constitutes a harsh rejection of Turkey's view: The E.U. Parliament condemned the Turkish actions,[857] as did the Council of Europe through its Parliamentary Assembly.[858] It noted, however, that Turkey has the right to "fight - within the limits of international law and in particular the European Convention on Human Rights - against terrorism".[859] Those limits were regarded to have been violated by Turkey and their actions consequently deemed "as contrary to international law".[860] It did not find that Turkey was *a priori* forbidden to fight a terrorist group unless the host state consented. Equally, Turkey was not asked to limit itself to policing actions rather than military force. Initially, i.e. during the first Turkish military actions against targets in the Kurdish "safe haven" in Northern Iraq in 1991,[861]

---

[852] *U.S. Backs Turkish Troop Move*, N.Y. TIMES, Sep. 8, 1996, at 14 (quoting U.S. Secretary of State Warren Christopher).

[853] *Turkish Forces Cross Border Into Iraq to Attack Kurdish Guerillas*, N.Y. TIMES, May 15, 1997, at A4 (referring to an American acting Assistant Secretary of State, David Welch, who said the United States "understood Turkey's right of self-defense").

[854] Laursen, *supra* note 807 at 516.

[855] U.N. Doc. S/1995/605 (July 24, 1995) at 1.

[856] As to the notification requirement to the United Nations Security Council *see infra* 213 to 214.

[857] *See* ALEXANDROV, *supra* note 36 at 181.

[858] Eur. Parl. Ass., Resolution 1266, 49th Sess., Doc. No. REC 1266 (1995).

[859] *Id.* at no. 2.

[860] *Id.* at no. 4.

[861] *See* U.N. Doc. S/23141 (Oct. 14, 1991); U.N. Doc. S/23152 (Oct. 17, 1991); U.N. Doc. S/25153 (Oct. 20, 1991) (referring to three raids between October 10 and 12, 1991).

Western diplomats had then expressed a certain degree of comprehension given the Kurdish terror campaign and hoping that Turkey had exercised "a legitimate right of self-defence" exercised carefully.[862] In 1997 the Presidency of the European Union expressed "understanding of the Turkish wish to end terrorist actions" but considered military actions an improper means.[863] The Arab League of Nations considered Turkey's military actions since early May 1997 "a serious aggression".[864]

The European reaction allows to infer that it was not regarded to be illegal *per se* for a state to fight terrorism directly i.e. to use armed force to defend itself against whomever is responsible – no distinction was drawn on the grounds of whether or not the opponent was a state or perhaps merely a non-state actor – but meanwhile consider international law as valid boundary. With regard to self-defense, the relevant limits would be the elements of "necessity" and "proportionality" as identified above.[865] Whether those have been met goes beyond the scope of this work. The same goes for the question of whatever it was in particular that triggered the Turkish counteractions could possibly have amounted to a sufficiently grave armed attack. It can be doubted that the officially announced incident, the killing of 18 Turkish soldiers, was by itself sincere enough to constitute an armed attack as required by Article 51 of the Charter.[866] Even though one would probably be able to argue that an accumulation of a series of minor attacks must be recognized as an equal cause for self-defense, it shall be held that none of the cited reactions doubts that the PKK as such would have been unable to launch armed attacks merely because it is not a state actor.

The United Nations Security Council did not react, most likely due to a foreseeable U.S. veto.[867] Interestingly, the United Nations General Assembly also did not vote on the matter. The Arab League of Nations condemned the "continuing incursions into Iraq's territory by the Turkish armed forces."[868]

Germany had become involved in the Turko-Kurdish conflict on the one hand through arms deliveries to the Turkish government, and on the other hand through a large number of both Turks and Kurds living in Germany. Upon loud inner-German criticism shortly after Turkey had launched Operation Steel in

---

[862] *See* Jonathan Rugman, *Kurds bombed by Turkey in 'safe haven'*, THE GUARDIAN (London), Oct. 12, 1991 (quoting "senior Western diplomatic sources").
[863] U.N. Doc. A/52/157 (May, 16, 1997).
[864] U.N. Doc. S/1997/416 (June 4, 1997).
[865] *See supra* at p. 28.
[866] Michael Bothe, Torsten Lohmann, *Der türkische Einmarsch im Nordirak*, 5 SCHWEIZERISCHE ZEITSCHRIFT FÜR INTERNATIONALES UND EUROPÄISCHES RECHT 441, 445 (1995).
[867] GRAY, *supra* note 36 at 117.
[868] U.N. Doc. S/1997/461 (June 16, 1997).

1995, Foreign Minister Kinkel halted all financial and military support for Turkey.[869] Initially, along with the United Kingdom, Germany had urged the Turkish government to "practice restraint".[870] It must also be noted here that the – sometimes harsh – German criticism focused on the proportionality of the Turkish counter actions[871] and did at no point deny Turkey the right to fight the PKK because it did not constitute or represent a state.

France was among those who specifically condemned the Turkish military actions,[872] indicating, however, that they felt the operation was too "massive", as the French Foreign Minister Alain Juppé announced in the name of the E.U.[873]

Also in the following years Turkey launched military actions into Iraq,[874] about which Iraq complained to the United Nations repeatedly.[875] However, neither of these complaints were debated before the United Nations Security Coun-

---

[869] *Wegen der andauernden Offensive gegen Kurden im Nordirak: Bonn stoppt alle Rüstungslieferungen an die Türkei Güter für 150 Millionen Mark werden zurückgehalten*, SÜDDEUTSCHE ZEITUNG, March 30, 1995, at Politik.

[870] Chris Hedges, *Turks Reported Likely to Keep Troops in Iraq for Weeks*, N.Y. TIMES, March 23, 1995, at A3.

[871] *See, e.g., Völkerrechtler zögern mit der Verdammung. Türkisches Militär soll bei Operationen im Nordirak jedoch Verhältnismäßigkeit wahren,* SÜDDEUTSCHE ZEITUNG, March 23, 1995, at Politik (referring to the German government's opinion that Turkey might not be in violation of international law if it withdrew quickly, respected proportionality, and protected civilians).

[872] *Turk Attacks Kurds in Iraq for 2n Day; 200 Reported Killed*, N.Y. TIMES, March 22, 1995, at A7.

[873] *See, e.g., EU-Aussenminister-Troika spricht in Ankara über Einmarsch in den Nordirak Ciller sagt schnellstmöglichen Rückzug zu,* SÜDDEUTSCHE ZEITUNG, March 24, 1995, at Politik (quoting French Foreign Minister Alain Juppé who regarded the invasion in excess of what had been agreed upon between Turkey and Iraq in their border conflict against Kurds and complained about the intervention's "massive character").

[874] *See, e.g.,* Christopher S. Wren, *Iraq: Turkish Attack is Denounced*, N.Y. TIMES, Nov. 10, 1998, at A6; *Kurds Claim Fatal Downing of Turk Copter*, N.Y. TIMES, Nov. 29, 1998, at 110 (quoting a Kurdish news agency as saying that "that 15 [Turkish] soldiers had died and one was injured when the Sikorsky helicopter crashed on Friday near Cukurca close to the Iraqi border while returning from an operation against the rebels"); *Turks Press Attacks On Rebel Kurd Bases*, N.Y. TIMES, Feb 21, 1999, at 18; Terence Neilan, *Turkey: Move on Kurds Reported*, N.Y. TIMES, Apr. 8, 1999, at A6 (reporting that "[a]bout 15,000 Turkish troops have crossed into northern Iraq to hunt down Kurdish rebels, penetrating some nine miles . . . ."); Joseph R. Gregory, *Middle East – Turkey: Action in Iraq*, N.Y. TIMES, May 18, 1999, at A6.

[875] *See, e.g.,* U.N. Doc. S/1998/455 (June 2, 1998); U.N. Doc. S/1998/509 (June 15, 1998); U.N. Doc. S/1998/1049 (Nov. 9, 1998); U.N. Doc. S/1999/196 (Feb. 23, 1999); U.N. Doc. S/1999/560 (May 14, 1999); U.N. Doc. S/1999/610 (May 26, 1999); U.N. Doc. S/1999/778 (July 12, 1999); U.N. Doc. S/1999/1028 (Oct. 5, 1999); U.N. Doc. S/2000/353 (Apr. 28, 2000); U.N. Doc. S/2000/546 (June 7, 2000); U.N. Doc. S/2000/750 (July 31, 2000).

cil nor often times even responded to by Turkish officials. Accordingly, clear references to Turkish incursions specifically based upon Article 51 of the Charter were rare in these days. One on occasion, Turkish officials noted that a military action had been launched "in pursuit" of Kurdish fighters.[876] Also Iranian based Kurdish groups became a target of Turkish attacks but Iran denied that it harbored PKK forces.[877]

Iran, on the other hand, repeatedly invoked Article 51 of the Charter to defend itself against incursions by fighters apparently emanating from Iraqi territory, such as in 1993.[878] Iraq protested, complaining about its inability to launch defensive measures itself due to the foreign confinements imposed in Iraq.[879] Already prior to the air strikes Iran had admitted, Iraq had informed the United Nations Security Council about several minor incidents involving Iranian forces, presumably aiming at Kurdish targets in Iraq.[880]

On another occasion about one year later, the Iranian Foreign Ministry noted that an air-strike against Kurdish targets in Iraq "was within its rights to counter 'terrorism' by any necessary means."[881] Previously, Iran had – without specifically referring to Kurds – complained to the United Nations about "some anti-revolutionary elements who had crossed the border between the Islamic Republic of Iran and Iraq and penetrated into Iranian territory exploded [an] oil pipeline . . . ."[882]

In July 1996, Iranian troops once again penetrated Iraqi territory in order to take "immediate and proportional measures" necessary to curb and suppress aggression by "terrorist armed groups . . . in accordance with [the] inherent right to self-defense enshrined in Article 51 of the Charter . . . ."[883] Iraq protested.[884] A similar situation arose in September 1997 and again Iran explicitly invoked

---

876 Terence Neilan, *Turkey, Iraq: Troops Pursue Kurds*, N.Y. TIMES, Apr. 13, 1999, at A8 ("Thousands of Turkish troops pressed into Kurd-controlled territory in northern Iraq in pursuit of Turkish Kurd guerrillas, army officials said").

877 *See, e.g., Turkey Attacks in Iran*, N.Y. TIMES, July 19, 1999, at A2 ("Turkish warplanes attacked targets in northwestern Iran, killing 5 people and wounding 10, Iranian news media reported. . . . Turkey previously accused Iran of harboring Kurd guerrillas, which Iran denied").

878 U.N. Doc. S/25813 (May 21, 1993); U.N. Doc. S/25843 (May 26, 1993).

879 U.N. Doc. S/25864 (May 19, 1993).

880 U.N. Doc. S/25760 (May 12, 1993).

881 *Iranian Jets Bomb Kurdish Base in Iraq, Killing 1 and Hurting 3*, N.Y. TIMES, Nov. 10, 1994, at A12.

882 U.N. Doc. S/1994/1145 (Oct. 10, 1994) (the incident referred to had already occurred in August 1994).

883 U.N. Doc. S/1996/602 (July 29, 1996).

884 U.N. Doc. S/1996/617 (Aug. 1, 1996); U.N. Doc. S/1996/707 (Aug. 29, 1996).

self-defense based upon Article 51 of the Charter against "invading terrorist" and attacked their bases in Iraq.[885] As previously, the state of Iraq was largely left out of Iran's actions which focused merely on the terrorists elements it sought to pursue. The reference to Article 51 of the Charter is equally clear despite the absence of a state actor against which self-defense could have been exercised.

In June 1999, Iran fired several rockets on alleged terrorist facilities inside Iraq. Again, Iran's actions were based upon Article 51 of the Charter. Unlike on previous occasions, Iran this time openly blamed also the Iraqi government for violations of international obligations and direct support of terrorist groups. However, while holding Iraq "fully responsible", the "proportionate action was a necessary defensive measure against the perpetrators of the terrorist crimes that had already been carried out against Iran and its citizens."[886] In other words, while Iraq violated its obligation to prevent terrorism emanating from its territory it had nothing to do with the actual attacks and was hence not the primary of the attack by Iran. Further incidents with armed bands in which Iran referred to its right to self-defense specifically against non-state armed bands continued throughout 2000[887] and 2001.[888]

Summarizing the reactions by other states, the Turkish attacks, although consistently condemned and criticized, have at no times been regarded as unlawful due to the mere fact that the targets were terrorists or guerilla troops operating from a territory different from the victim state. The Turkish incursions were condemned for lack of other conditions necessary to successfully invoke self-defense, such as necessity or proportionality.

The Iranian incursions remained largely uncommented by the international community and were hence not criticized to a comparable degree, if at all. Iran clearly rested its frequent military incursions deep into Iraqi territory upon self-defense as permitted by the United Nations Charter.

4. U.S. Military Actions to Fight the Taliban and Al Qaeda

The fight against Al Qaeda's terrorist activities differs in some important issues from the above fact patterns, and is yet surprisingly similar in others. Most important, the decision to exercise self-defense against Al Qaeda and its host, the Taliban movement, was essentially triggered by a single event of un-

---

[885] U.N. Doc. S/1997/768 (Oct. 2, 1997).
[886] U.N. Doc. S/1999/781 (July 12, 1999).
[887] U.N. Doc. S/2000/127 (Feb. 17, 2000).
[888] U.N. Doc. S/2001/381 (Apr. 19, 2001); *see also Iraq: Iran Blamed for Missile Attack,* N.Y. Times, Apr. 19, 2001, at A8 (Iran launched a missile strike into Iraq "at camps inside Iraq belonging to an Iranian rebel group, the People's Mujahedeen Organization").

known gravity in conflicts between states and non-state actors. September 11, 2001 is said to have altered infinite aspects of world politics. Among those aspects is also the reception of the concept of self-defense. However, it must be noted that the United States acted in self-defense against Al Qaeda also prior to 2001.

a) History of the Conflict

The "Final Report of the National Commission on Terrorist Attacks Upon the United States" states that it took 102 minutes until the North Tower of the World Trade Center collapsed at 10:28 a.m. on September 11, 2001. Meanwhile, the South Tower had already collapsed,[889] the Pentagon had been hit by American Airlines Flight 77,[890] and United Airlines Flight 93 had crashed into a field in Pennsylvania. The latter's passengers had been able to prevent the hijackers from continuing their flight and crashing the airplane "into symbols of the American Republic, the Capitol or the White House."[891] In 102 minutes, 19 non-U.S. nationals had attacked the United States and caused more casualties on a single day than any event had since the days of the American Civil War.[892] In response, the United States and other members of the NATO[893] launched a military campaign against Al Qaeda and their Afghan hosts, the Taliban. Until today, U.S. and NATO soldiers are operating in Afghanistan to execute Operation Enduring Freedom, which began on October 7, 2001.[894]

The "War on Terrorism" is fought against an enemy that is like the PLO, Hezbollah, the ANC, SWAPO, and the PKK – irrespective of numerous dissimi-

---

889 National Commission on Terrorist Attacks upon the United States, *Final Report of the National Commission on Terrorist Attacks Upon the United States* 285 (2004) (hereinafter 9-11 Commission).

890 9-11 Commission at 10.

891 *Id.* at 14.

892 Sean D. Murphy, *Terrorist Attacks on World Trade Center and the Pentagon*, 96 AM. J. INT'L L. 237 (2002).

893 Alan Sipress, Vernon Loeb, *U.S. Welcoming Allies' Troops; Despite Pentagon's Concerns, Taliban War Is Multi-Country,* WASH. POST, Nov. 11, 2001, at A38 (stating that initially Australia, Canada, the Czech Republic, Germany, Italy, Japan, the Netherlands, New Zealand, and Turkey had agreed to supply troops to support U.S. and British forces operating in Afghanistan); including those NATO forces, 27 nations deployed military forces on Afghan territory; 90 nations were supportive of the Operation "Enduring Freedom"; the 'International Security Assistance Force' is meanwhile composed of 19 nations; for details *see* http://www.whitehouse.gov/infocus/defense/enduringfreedom.html (last visited March 6, 2006).

894 *See, e.g.,* Molly More, *Dutch Debate on Afghan Force Is Test for NATO,* WASH. POST, Feb. 2, 2006, at A17 (referring to "about 9,000 [NATO] troops in Afghanistan, operating as the International Security Assistance Force").

larities between the mentioned groups – a non-state actor that over time moved around between different host states and, by the time of the attacks on September 11, was operating from within a failing state under the control of a *de facto* regime of religious fanatics, the Taliban. This group had, as earlier other regimes had, allowed the Al Qaeda network to operate from within the territory under its control. Both non-state actors together were the objective of NATO's attacks and both are different from what had previously been the state of Afghanistan.

i) Al Qaeda

Al Qaeda ("The Base") was founded around 1989 by the Saudi millionaire Osama bin Laden.[895] It began in Afghanistan and Pakistan in an effort to fight the Soviet invasion but soon turned its attention to other struggles.[896] In 1989 bin Laden moved to Saudi Arabia and around 1991 to Sudan where he began to set up terrorist training facilities.[897] After having been forced to leave Sudan in May 1996,[898] Al Qaeda reorganized on the territory of Afghanistan. The terrorists utilized the liberty and support they received from the Taliban to unleash a series of deadly terrorist attacks against non-combatants and military targets.[899] Among them were, apart from September 11, the attacks on the American embassies in Kenya and Tanzania on August 7, 1998,[900] the attack on the U.S.S. Cole in Yemen in 2000,[901] the bombings of a synagogue in Tunisia in 2002,[902]

---

895 Peter L. Bergen, Holy War, Inc. – Inside the Secret World of Osama bin Laden 59 (2001).

896 *Id.* at 60, 61.

897 Kenneth Katzman, *Al Qaeda: Profile and Threat Assessment*, Cong. Rep. Service 3 (Aug. 17, 2005).

898 Ruth Wedgwood, *Al Qaeda, Military Commissions and Self-Defense*, 117 Pol. Sci. Q., 357, 359 (2002).

899 for an overview *see id.* at 357.

900 James C. McKinley Jr., *Bombings in East Africa: The Overview; Bombs Rip Apart 2 U.S. Embassies in Africa; Scores Killed; No Firm Motive Or Suspects,* N.Y. TIMES, Aug. 8, 1998, at A1; Michael Grunwald, *U.S. Complaint Links Bin Laden to Bombing,* WASH. POST, Aug. 29, 1998, at A01 ("Federal prosecutors yesterday accused Osama bin Laden's militant Islamic organization of bombing the U.S. Embassy in Kenya, offering the most detailed description to date of an alleged terrorist conspiracy to kill Americans in East Africa.").

901 Howard Schneider, Roberto Suro, *Death Toll Put at 17 In USS Cole Blast; Some Doubt Yemenis Will Aid in Probe,* WASH. POST, Oct. 14, 2000, at A01; John F. Burns, *F.B.I.'s Inquiry In Cole Attack Is Nearing Halt,* N.Y. TIMES, Aug. 21, 2001, at A1 ("After the Cole bombing on Oct. 12, F.B.I. investigators immediately suspected that Mr. bin Laden, from a sanctuary in Afghanistan, had inspired the attack, if not actively directed it . . . . In a videotape made by Mr. bin Laden that was posted on the Internet this summer, he appeared to claim

and a night club on Bali in 2002,[903] the attacks on an Israeli owned hotel and a failed attack on an Israeli civil airliner in Kenya in 2002,[904] the blasts before synagogues, the British consulate and a bank in Istanbul in 2003,[905] the bombings of the Madrid[906] and London[907] public transportation system in 2004 and

---

credit for the Cole bombing, saying that Allah 'made us victorious the day we destroyed the ship on the sea.'").

902 Peter Finn, *Al Qaeda-Linked Group Claims Blast; Deadly Explosion at Tunisian Synagogue Response to 'Israeli Crimes'*, WASH. POST, Apr. 17, 2002, at A09 ("A group linked to Osama bin Laden's al Qaeda network has claimed responsibility for an explosion at a historic synagogue in Tunisia last week that killed 16 people including 10 German tourists, according to two London-based Arabic newspapers.").

903 Ellen Nakashima, Alan Sipress, *Official Links Bali Bombing To Al Qaeda; Indonesian Says Group Worked Through Locals*, WASH. POST, Oct. 15, 2002, at A01 ("Osama bin Laden's al Qaeda network, working through a local group, played a role in the Saturday night bombing that killed more than 180 people in Bali, Indonesia's defense minister said today.").

904 David Johnson, *Threats And Responses: The Attacks; U.S. Says Evidence Possibly Ties Al Qaeda to the Attack in Kenya,* N.Y. TIMES, Dec. 3, 2002, at A1 ("Today the White House spokesman, Ari Fleischer, said there were "suspicions" that Al Qaeda was behind the Kenya attacks"); *see* also S.C. Res. 1450, U.N. Doc. S/RES/1450 (Dec. 13, 2002) (which condemned the Kenya attacks "in the strongest terms" and urged all states "to find and bring to justice the perpetrators, organizers and sponsors of these terrorist attacks" without mentioning Al Qaeda or any other specific group).

905 Sebnem Arsu, Dexter Filkins, *20 in Istanbul Die in Bombings At Synagogues,* N.Y. TIMES, Nov. 16, 2003, at A1; CRAIG S. SMITH, A Region Inflamed: Istanbul; *Blasts Hit 2 British Sites in Turkey as Bush Visits Blair,* N.Y. TIMES, Non. 21, 2003, at A1; Karl Vick, *Turks Assert Al Qaeda Link In Bomb Arrest; Man Is Seen as Contact With Cell,* WASH. POST, Dec. 20, 2003, at A14 ("Turkish and U.S. officials have said al Qaeda, Osama bin Laden's terrorist network, conducted the Istanbul bombings -- nearly simultaneous strikes on two synagogues Nov. 15 and five days later on the British Consulate and a British bank. The attacks killed 62 people, including four bombers.").

906 Keith B. Richburg, *Madrid Train Blasts Kill at Least 190; 10 Bombs Detonate Almost at Once; Nearly 1,500 Hurt,* WASH. POST, March 12, 2004, at A01; Glenn Frankel, Peter Finn, Keith B. Richburg, *Al Qaeda Implicated In Madrid Bombings,* WASH. POST, March 15, 2004, at A01 ("The officials said the preliminary investigation and interrogation of five arrested suspects . . . as well as other evidence indicated that the Thursday morning rush-hour bombings were carried out by the al Qaeda network, marking the first time the group has struck in Europe.").

907 Alan Cowell, *Subway and Bus Blasts in London Kill at Least 37,* N.Y. TIMES, July 8, 2005, at A1 ("A group describing itself as being affiliated with Al Qaeda took responsibility for the attacks on a Web site . . . ."); Glenn Frankel, *Londoners Warily Resume Their Lives; Toll in Bombings Rises to 49, With Bodies Yet Uncounted; Officials Urge Vigilance,* WASH. POST, July 9, 2005, at A01 ("Officials said it was likely the perpetrators were associated with the al Qaeda network.").

2005, the bombing of hotels in Jordan,[908] two attacks in Algiers in 2007,[909] and many more. Al Qaeda is frequently characterized as an association or network of Islamist terrorist cells that seems to exist in nearly 70 countries.[910]

ii) THE TALIBAN

The Afghan society is ethnically, religiously, and linguistically mixed. Somewhat similarly to the situation in Lebanon, there are competing ethnicities such as the Pushtuns, the Turkomans, the Uzbeks, as well as others. One also finds both Sunni, the majority of Afghans, and Shi'a Muslims.[911] And just as in Lebanon, Afghanistan was in a state of disintegration by the time the Taliban ("students of religion" or "seekers of knowledge") appeared on the scene around 1994: different warlords fought each other in varying coalitions and the government controlled little more than the capital Kabul.[912] The Taliban, with support from Pakistan and composed of students from Islamic religious schools – often non-Afghans – managed to prevail in this battle and slowly acquired almost complete control of what had constituted the state of Afghanistan as early as 1999.[913] They wanted to disarm all the competing factions and implement the *Sharia*, the Islamic law composed of the *Qur'an* and the *Sunna*, by standards unknown in their strictness, particularly with regard to women.[914] They eventually allowed Al Qaeda to operate in and from within the regions under their control and there grew strong and sometimes inseparable ties between both groups.[915] The Security Council demanded "that the Taliban stop providing sanctuary and training for international terrorists and their organizations, and that all Afghan factions cooperate with efforts to bring indicted terrorists to jus-

---

[908] Hassan M. Fattah, Michael Slackman, *3 Hotels Bombed in Jordan; At Least 57 Die*, N.Y. TIMES, Nov. 10, 2005, at A1; Hassan M. Fattah, *The Reach of War: Aftermath; Jordan Seized 12 Suspects in the Hotel Bombings*, N.Y TIMES, Nov. 12, 2006, at A8 ("An Internet posting by a group claiming to be Al Qaeda in Mesopotamia said Friday that four Iraqis, including a husband-and-wife-team, had carried out the suicide bombings [in Amman, Jordan]").

[909] Craig Whitlock, *Al-Qaeda Branch Claims Algeria Blasts,* WASH. POST, Apr. 12, 2007, at A01.

[910] Katzman, *supra* note 897 at 3, 4; BERGEN, *supra* note 895 at 195-220.

[911] PETER MARSDEN, THE TALIBAN: WAR, RELIGION AND THE NEW ORDER IN AFGHANISTAN 8-10 (1998).

[912] AHMED RASHID, TALIBAN 21 (2001).

[913] Christopher L. Gadoury, *Should the United States officially recognize the Taliban? The International Legal and Political Considerations*, 23 HOUS. J. INT'L L. 385, 390 (2001).

[914] Rüdiger Wolfrum, Christiane E. Philipp, *The Status of the Taliban: Their Obligations and Rights under International Law*, 6 MAX PLANCK Y.B.U.N.L. 559, 565 (2002).

[915] *See* RASHID, *supra* note 912 at 139 (stating that the ties between the Taliban and Al Qaeda grew consistently after the Taliban captured Kabul in 1996, despite prior rivalries between Bin Laden's predominantly non-Afghan fighters and the Afghan Taliban).

tice"[916] and furthermore "that the Taliban turn over Usama bin Laden without further delay to appropriate authorities in a country where he has been indicted".[917]

The Taliban sought to be regarded as the sole representatives of the state of Afghanistan. The United Nations Credentials Committee received two (identical) letters from the Taliban on October 10, 1996 in which "Haji Mula Mohammad Ghaus Akhund, Acting Minister of Foreign Affairs" claimed that "at the top of diplomatic mission of Afghanistan there are individuals and personnel who belong to the previous regime, who are not acceptable to the new ruling Government of Taliban".[918] Among the "individuals" to whom he referred was also acting President Rabbani, who was still internationally recognized as the sole representative of Afghanistan.[919] Subsequent Security Council resolutions mentioning the Taliban regard them merely as one of the factions in the ethnically diverse Afghan society.[920]

As of 2001 the Taliban had been recognized as legitimate government of Afghanistan only by Saudi Arabia, Pakistan, and the United Arab Emirates (U.A.E.).[921] After September 11, 2001, both Saudi Arabia and the U.A.E. quickly cut their ties with the Taliban,[922] leaving Pakistan the only country that maintained official diplomatic relations with the Taliban.

b) SINGULAR INCIDENTS AND STATES' RESPONSES

The first time that the United States invoked self-defense against Al Qaeda terror was in 1998. Al Qaeda training facilities in Afghanistan, as well as the El-Shifa pharmaceutical company in Sudan were destroyed by rockets launched from American navy vessels.[923] The United States responded through these attacks to previous Al Qaeda terror, particularly the embassy bombings in

---

916 S.C. Res. 1214, U.N. Doc. S/RES/1214 (Dec. 8, 1998) at 4.

917 S.C. Res. 1267, U.N. Doc. S/RES/1267 (Oct. 15, 1999) at 2.

918 Press Release, Credentials Committee, *Credentials Committee Defers Decision on Afghanistan*, U.N. Doc. GA/9127 (Oct. 11, 1996).

919 Wolfrum, Philipp, *supra* note 914 at 567.

920 S.C. Res. 1214, U.N. Doc. S/RES/1214 (Dec. 8, 1998) (calls on "the Taliban, as well as other Afghan factions"); S.C. Res. 1267, U.N. Doc. S/RES/1267 (Oct. 15, 1999) (speaking of "the Afghan faction known as the Taliban, which also calls itself the Islamic Emirate of Afghanistan").

921 George K. Walker, *The Lawfulness of Operation Enduring Freedom's Self-Defense Responses*, 37 VAL. U. L. REV. 489, 505 (2003); Wolfrum, Philipp, *supra* note 914 at n.75.

922 Jack M. Beard, *America's New War on Terror: The Case for Self-Defense under International Law*, 25 HARV. J. L. & PUB. POL'Y 559, 570-71.

923 James Bennet, *U.S. Fury On 2 Continents: The Overview; U.S. Cruise Missiles Strike Sudan and Afghan Targets Tied to Terrorist Network*, N.Y. TIMES, Aug. 21, 1998, at A1.

East Africa earlier in 1998. The U.S. government regarded the use of military force as justified under the concept of self-defense: "In accordance with Article 51 of the Charter of the United Nations, I wish, on behalf of my Government, to report that the United States of America has exercised its right of self-defence in responding to a series of armed attacks against United States embassies and United States nationals" as a U.S. representative announced.[924]

Sudan protested and complained about the violation of its territory and sovereignty.[925] Not surprisingly, the Security Council took no action.[926] The Taliban, not recognized by the United Nations as the legitimate government of Afghanistan,[927] called the attacks a "demonstration of enmity for the Afghan people."[928] Numerous countries expressed support or understanding for the American response, among them Australia, Japan, Spain, and the United Kingdom.[929] The German chancellor Helmut Kohl said that "every nation has the right to defend itself against such atrocities as happened at the American embassies in Africa."[930] France took "note of the decision of American authorities to carry out [the August 20th] bombings by invoking the right to legitimate defense recognized under international law," as the Foreign Ministry announced in a somewhat reserved statement.[931] Russian President Boris Yeltsin criticized that he had not been informed prior to the attacks, but Russia did not officially object to the invocation of self-defense.[932] The Arab League of Nations remained silent with regard to Afghanistan, but it condemned the attacks on Sudan,[933] and requested that the Security Council stayed concerned with the matter as well as a fact finding mission into Sudan.[934] The actions were not condemned by either the U.N. Security Council or the General Assembly. Some Muslim countries and

---

[924] UN Doc. S/1998/780 (Aug. 20, 1998) at 1.
[925] UN Doc. S/1998/786 (Aug. 21, 1998) at 2.
[926] *See* Jules Lobel, *The Use of Force to Respond to Terror Attacks: the Bombing of Sudan and Afghanistan*, 24 YALE J. OF INT'L L. 537, 537-38 (1999).
[927] *See supra* note 920; *see also* Sean D. Murphy, *Contemporary Practice of the United States Relating to International Law*, 93 AM. J. INT'L L. 161, 164 (1999).
[928] Howard Schneider, Nora Boustany, *A Barrage Of Criticism In Mideast; U.S. Accused of 'State Terrorism'*, WASH. POST, Aug. 21, 1998, at A20.
[929] William Drozdiak, *European Allies Back U.S. Strikes; Japan Says It 'Understands'*, WASH. POST, Aug. 21, at A20.
[930] Sharon Lafraniere, *Yeltsin 'Outraged' by Attacks, Angry at Not Being Informed*, WASH. POST, Aug. 22, 1998, at A15.
[931] *Id.*
[932] *Id.*
[933] UN Doc. S/1998/789 (Aug. 21, 1998); U.N. Doc. S/1999/424 (Apr. 15, 1999); U.N. Doc. S/1999/997 (Sept. 23, 1999).
[934] UN Doc. S/1998/791 (Aug. 21, 1998).

entities condemned both attacks, among them Iran, Iraq, Libya, and the Palestinian Authority.[935] But as was shown on numerous prior occasions, the fact that the American invocation of self-defense followed on an attack by a non-state actor that was supported by host states that were either unwilling (Sudan) or unable (Afghanistan) to prevent terrorist activities emanating from their territory, remained unchallenged.

Eventually, the United States asserted that at least the plant may not have been involved in the production of chemical weapons.[936] The El-Shifa Company and its owner brought a claim against the United States seeking compensation for their destroyed property. Their claim was rejected, partly because the designation of the plant as enemy property was considered a non-justiciable political question which was decided by President Clinton in good faith.[937]

While it seemed as if large parts of the international community either supported or at least not objected to the U.S. self-defense to prior attacks by the non-state actor Al Qaeda, the international reaction to the military actions in the aftermath of September 11 is even more unisonous in its findings: on September 12, 2001, the U.N. Security Council adopted resolution 1368 (2001) unanimously.[938] It recognized "the inherent right of individual or collective self-defence in accordance with the Charter" and allowed for taking "all necessary steps to respond to the terrorist attacks of 11 September 2001, and to combat all forms of terrorism, in accordance with its responsibilities under the Charter of the United Nations."[939] Roughly two weeks later, the United Nations Security Council, through resolution 1373 (2001) reaffirmed "the inherent right of individual or collective self-defence as recognized by the Charter of the United Nations as reiterated in resolution 1368 (2001)" and established a number of non-forcible reactions to be undertaken by the international community in order to fight terrorism effectively.[940] The resolution does not explicitly authorize the use of force; its operative part rather mandates economic sanctions.

The United Nations Security Council seems not to have intended to replace self-defense by the United States through according U.N. measures.[941]

---

[935] *See* Schneider, Boustany, *supra* note 928.

[936] Vernon Loeb, *U.S. Considers Array of Actions Against Bin Laden*, WASH. POST, Dec. 3, 2000, at A3 (stating that U.S. officials had "backed away from claims that its owner is linked to Bin Laden" and conceded "that the plant produced medicines and may not have been involved in making chemical weapons . . .").

[937] El-Shifa Pharmaceuticals Indus. v. U.S., 378 F.3d 1346 (Fed. Cir. 2004).

[938] U.N. SCOR, 56th Sess., 4730th mtg., at 8, U.N. Doc. S/PV.4730 (Sept.12, 2001).

[939] S.C. Res. 1368, U.N. Doc. S/RES/1368 (Sept. 12, 2001).

[940] S.C. Res. 1373, U.N. Doc. S/RES/1373 (Sept. 28, 2001).

[941] O'Connell, *supra* note 278 at 892-93.

Rather, it is likely to have followed the United States' preferences to respond militarily based upon U.S. and NATO self-defense, rather than on a Chapter VII authorization to use military force. As a former President of the ICJ later stated: "But whilst the United Nations was prepared to authorize military action by the United States and its allies in Afghanistan, the United States was not looking for such authorization. It was seeking to act freely by invoking its inherent right of self-defence pursuant to Article 51 of the Charter."[942] The U.S. confirmed this view when Operation Enduring Freedom was launched one month later. John Negroponte, US ambassador to the United Nations, announced on October 7, 2001, that the United States would use forcible measures in exercise of their right to self-defense pursuant to Article 51 of the UN Charter.[943] The United Kingdom supported the American findings and announced their military support immediately, based upon collective self-defense.[944]

NATO confirmed attacks "from abroad" through the events on September, 11.[945] It regarded Article 5 (1) of the Washington Treaty as triggered, allowing for self-defense in the event of an armed attack.[946] The Organization of American States (OAS) confirmed that the U.S. was facing an "armed attack". Consequently, Article 3 (1) of the Inter-American Treaty of Reciprocal Assistance,[947] a similar provision to Article 5 of the Washington Treaty, was regarded

---

[942] Gilbert Guillaume, *Terrorism and International Law*, 53 INT'L & COMP. L. Q. 537, 546 (2004).

[943] U.N. Doc S/2001/946 (Oct. 7, 2001) ("In accordance with Article 51 of the Charter of the United Nations, I wish, on behalf of my Government, to report that the United States of America, together with other States, has initiated actions in the exercise of its inherent right of individual and collective self-defence following the armed attacks that were carried out against the United States on 11 September 2001.").

[944] U.N. Doc S/2001/947 (Oct. 7, 2001) ("These forces have now been employed in exercise of the inherent right of individual and collective self-defence, recognized in Article 51, following the terrorist outrage of 11 September, to avert the continuing threat of attacks from the same source").

[945] Statement by the North Atlantic Council, Sep. 12, 2001; *available at* http://www.nato.int/docu/pr/2001/p01-124e.htm (last visited March 6, 2006).

[946] North Atlantic Treaty, art. 5 (1), Apr. 4, 1949, 34 U.N.T.S. 243; Article 5 (1) provides: "The Parties agree that an armed attack against one or more of them in Europe or North America shall be considered an attack against them all and consequently they agree that, if such an armed attack occurs, each of them, in exercise of the right of individual or collective self-defence recognized by Article 51 of the Charter of the United Nations, will assist the Party or Parties so attacked by taking forthwith, individually and in concert with the other Parties, such action as it deems necessary, including the use of armed force, to restore and maintain the security of the North Atlantic area".

[947] Inter-American Treaty of Reciprocal Assistance, art. 3 (1), Sept. 2, 1947, O.A.S.T.S. No. 8; Article 3 (1) provides: "The High Contracting parties agree that an armed attack by any

as applicable.[948] The Organization of the Islamic Conference, in representation of 56 nations, did not condemn or challenge the actions against Afghanistan.[949]

Germany participated with a large military contingent in the military actions. As far as the legal grounds for these extra-territorial activities are concerned, the German government's request for approval by the Bundestag for German armed forces to participate in the Operation Enduring Freedom merely mentions that UN Security Council resolution 1368 (2001) "underlined" the right of self-defense according to Article 51 of the UN Charter. It does, just like resolution 1368 (2001), not clearly state that Germany regarded September 11 as an "armed attack" triggering Article 51 of the U.N. Charter. The German participation was nevertheless considered as legally justified given the stipulations of Article 5 of the Washington Treaty, referring to collective self-defense as implemented into German law by virtue of Article 24 (2) of the German Basic Law.[950]

None of the official reactions by international organizations, particularly the Security Council, or by individual states mentions a requirement such as the statehood of the origin of the terrorist attacks. As Al Qaeda's responsibility may not have been entirely clear immediately after September 11, on October 7, 2001, neither the U.S. nor the U.K. left any doubt about whom they regarded responsible:

> The attacks on 11 September 2001 and the ongoing threat to the United States and its nationals posed by the Al-Qaeda organization have been made possible by the decision of the Taliban regime to allow the parts of Afghanistan that it controls to be used by this organization as a base of operation.[951]

---

state against an American State shall be considered as an armed attack against all American States and, consequently, each one of the said Contracting Parties undertakes to assist in meeting the attack in the exercise of the inherent right of individual or collective self-defense recognized by Article 51 of the Charter of the United Nations".

[948] Terrorist Threat to the Americas, Res. 1, Twenty-Fourth Meeting of Consultation of Ministers of Foreign Affairs Acting as Organ of Consultation In Application of the Inter-American Treaty of Reciprocal Assistance, OEA/Ser.F/II.24, RC.24/RES.1/01 (Sept. 21, 2001).

[949] Murphy, *supra* note 43 at 48.

[950] Antrag der Bundesregierung an den Deutschen Bundestag (Nov. 16, 2001), *available at* http://www.einsatz.bundeswehr.de/C1256F20002371 3E/vwContentByKey/W265YF37347IN FODE/$File/oef_bt147296.pdf (last visited Apr. 9, 2006).

[951] U.N. Doc S/2001/946 (Oct. 7, 2001), at 1; the letter by the United Kingdom contained a similar formulation, as it states the operation's targets: "This military action has been carefully planned, and is directed against Usama Bin Laden's Al-Qaeda terrorist organization and the Taliban regime that is supporting it", U.N. Doc S/2001/947 (Oct. 7, 2001).

Consequently, the world's reaction was unprecedented with regard to its degree of unanimity: the United States was under attack on September 11 and had the right to respond forcefully by virtue of self-defense. None of the states or international organizations seemed to have had further interest in specifying if it was actually Afghanistan who launched the attack. The combination of Al Qaeda and the supportive Taliban was sufficient.

The scholarly debate in the aftermath focused on this and other issues: it was argued that either Al Qaeda's actions by themselves were sufficient to give rise to self-defense as the U.N. Charter does simply not require states to be the origin of armed attacks.[952] September 11 was in addition thereof considered imputable to the *de facto* Taliban government of Afghanistan which in return was a legitimate target of self-defense.[953] Or, the Taliban themselves were regarded as – the only available and legitimate – target to which Al Qaeda's actions were attributed.[954] Some argued that Afghanistan could not have been a legitimate target because neither the Taliban's failure to extradite Al Qaeda operatives in the aftermath of September 11, nor the allowance to operate from Afghan territory under Taliban control, suffices to constitute the necessary "armed attack" by a state.[955]

On the other hand it was argued that at least in cases in which a state is indeed incapable of controlling a non-state actor – such as the failed state of Afghanistan – self-defense is available to victim states of the non-state actor's attacks. The same rule shall not apply if a state is merely reluctant to constrain a non-state actor.[956] Another issue meeting criticism was an alleged lack of immediacy and proportionality in the U.S. actions as of October 7, 2001.[957]

The international reaction to September 11 is clear: the United States was under attack and it acted in self-defense when it applied force against Al Qaeda

---

[952] DINSTEIN, *supra* note 72 at 207, 208.

[953] *See* M. Cherif Bassiouni, *Legal Control of International Terrorism: A Policy Oriented Assessment*, 43 HARV. INT'L L.J. 83, 100 (2002); Breard, *supra* note 922 at 589-90; Jost Delbrück, *The Fight Against Global Terrorism: Self-Defense or Collective Security as International Police Action? Some Comments on the International Legal Implications of the 'War Against Terrorism'*, 44 GERMAN Y.B. INT'L L. 9, 15 (2001); DINSTEIN, *supra* note 72 at 237; Murphy, *supra* note 98 at 50, 51; O'CONNELL, *supra* note 278 at 901; Walker, *supra* note 921 at 534.

[954] Rüdiger Wolfrum, *The Attack of September 11, 2001, the Wars Against the Taliban and Iraq: Is there a Need to Reconsider International Law on the Recourse to Force and the Rules in Armed Conflict?*, 7 MAX PLANCK Y.B.U.N.L. 1, 36 (2003).

[955] John Quigley, *The Afghanistan War and Self-defense*, 37 VAL. U. L. REV. 541, 545-46, 562 (2003); KNUT IPSEN, VÖLKERRECHT 1087-88 (5th ed. 2004); Stahn, *supra* note 245 at 50.

[956] Randelzhofer, *supra* note 6 at 802.

[957] CASSESE, *supra* note 178 at 476.

and the Taliban, both of which were present Afghanistan territory. Largely, this was regarded as legal. For the first time, the number of supporters clearly outweighed the critics of self-defense against a non-state actor. It may not be entirely clear which legal concept is applied to reach that result: was it actually an attack by Afghanistan to which Al Qaeda's conduct was attributed (through the de facto government of the Taliban)? Or were Al Qaeda's actions *per se* sufficient to trigger such an attack and is it consequently of no further interest in how far the state of Afghanistan actually effectively controlled Al Qaeda's "success"? It seemed as if the question whether it is required under Article 51 of the Charter to find a state actor to which one can successfully attribute a non-state actor's conduct was merely academic in nature. The reality was different: none of the states or international organizations that expressed initial support for the U.S. and NATO military actions seemed to have considered it to be a major problem that the attacks were likely to have been executed by a terrorist group that may or may not have been controlled by the Taliban, much less Afghanistan. In fact, that Afghanistan would be the destination for U.S. and NATO actions was not doubtlessly clear until Operation Enduring Freedom actually began in October. However, almost all states called immediately after September 11 for an appropriate reaction and the Security Council embodied such calls in resolution 1368 (2001) on September 12.

The scale of the armed attack – not the legal nature of the responsible entity – was crucial here. The international community bridged the "legal gap"[958] as it is upheld by the ICJ out of the necessity to fight an armed attack as such an attack's scale is by no means less dangerous than one by regular armed forces.

5. Further Conflicts

Undoubtedly, there are more conflicts that potentially meet the criteria outlined above.[959] In the following these conflicts shall be introduced briefly in chronological order. They have not been included in the same extensive manner as the four major situations above due to several reasons. Some of the following conflicts only have a comparably insignificant magnitude or unclear factual basis. In most cases it is doubtful if therefore essential conditions for the exercise of self-defense, primarily an armed attack of sufficient gravity, could have been met regardless of legal issues concerning the involved non-state actors. Also, and perhaps most importantly for the purpose of a legal distinction, in the following cases the states acting in self-defense often directed their military responses primarily against the host states, emphasizing that they were to blame for its contributions by virtue of active support or omissions towards non-state

---

[958] *See supra* pp. 20 et seq.
[959] *See supra* pp. 67 et seq.

actors. These states were mostly quite capable, albeit often not interested, in confining non-state actors in their cross-border attacks against victim states.

A majority of the evaluated conflicts has their roots in the Middle East conflict since 1948. Not all, but most of them involve the State of Israel. While this might speak against the possibility to draw conclusions for an international rather than merely a regional state practice and custom, it also reflects the extremely high degree of scrutiny that this conflict was under ever since it erupted. The availability of open source information, the participation of other states offering their legal views, and distinct governmental legal comments are without precedent. Additionally, the Middle East conflict is relatively over-represented as many of the states involved decided to pursue the same tactics in their fight against Israel. Egypt, Iran, Jordan, and others more and more refrained from using regular armies and preferred to continue the battle with rather subversive measures. There is no other conflict involving such a high number of states which deliberately abstain from taking advantage of their state prerogative to use armed forces against an enemy.

Many of the conflicts on the African continent, on the other hand, also received much attention but the factual circumstances are not nearly as undisputed as they are in the Middle East. Other conflicts simply hardly received any international recognition, such as for instance those in Eastern Asia. In both of the latter cases, the availability of undisputed open source information is limited.

a) ISRAEL'S MILITARY ACTIONS AGAINST FEDAYEEN IN EGYPT

Following the Israeli war of independence in 1948-49, in which Egypt hat occupied the Gaza strip, tensions between Israel and Egypt remained severe due to mutual violations of the General Armistice Agreement. Israel complained about both regular and irregular Egyptian troops operating from within Gaza;[960] Egypt complained about Israeli counter-force.[961]

On October 29, 1956, Israel attacked targets on the Sinai Peninsula in responses to continuous attacks by Palestinian terrorist groups operating from Egyptian territory.[962] Israel announced that it had acted in self-defense specifically against the armed bands referring to themselves as Fedayeen ("those who

---

[960] *See, e.g., Egyptians Paying the Price,* THE TIMES (London), Apr. 10, 1956, at 10 ("Bands of Egyptian irregulars, who have been raiding the southern Israel countryside since nightfall on Saturday, are being made to pay the price of their daring. Nine were killed to-day in a clash with Israel security patrols.").

[961] *See, e.g.,* 1955 U.N.Y.B. 31-35.

[962] *Israel Attack on Egypt*, THE TIMES (London), Oct. 30, 1956, at 8.

sacrifice their lives").[963] These bands, according to Israel, were "a product of [Egyptian president Gamal Abdel] Nasser's mind"[964] and attacked Israel only between April and October 1956 on forty different occasions.[965] Accordingly, in the course of the coming battles, the Israeli army would face regular Egyptian troops rather than irregular, non-state actor sent troops.[966] Egypt also referred to its right so self-defense, but against the Israeli "aggression".[967] The Security Council convened to debate a crisis that had begun with Egypt's unilateral nationalization of the Suez Canal Company on July 26, 1956,[968] and would eventually evolve into the 1956 war between Egypt on one side, and France, Israel, and the United Kingdom on the other side.

The Egyptian delegate chose "not even [to] answer" Israel's complaints as to Fedayeen actions but referred to Israel's military actions as an "armed aggression".[969]

The American representative urged the Council to respond to Israel's behavior due to a breach of the peace by Israel.[970] The United States was joined by Peru[971] and others: Yugoslavia[972] and Iran[973] considered Israel's military actions to constitute an aggression. The Soviet Union complained that even the American draft proposal failed to condemn Israel "for its act of aggression."[974] Australia regarded Israel to be in violation of prior armistice agreements and its reprisals not justified by "the particular events that have led up to them."[975]

---

963 U.N. SCOR, 11th Sess., 749th mtg., at 8, U.N. Doc. S/PV.749 (remarks by Eban (Israel)) (Oct. 30, 1956).
964 *Id.* at 9.
965 *Id.* at 12-14.
966 *See, e.g., The Battle of Sinai,* THE TIMES (London), Nov. 3, 1956, at 7 (quoting "Israeli Army authorities" as saying that "Egypt had roughly one half of her total military force committed in Sinai . . . and that frightful damage has been done to Colonel Nasser's Sinai army . . . .").
967 U.N. Doc. S/3712 (Oct. 30, 1956).
968 1956 U.N.Y.B. 19.
969 U.N. SCOR, 11th Sess., 749th mtg., at 18, U.N. Doc. S/PV.749 (remarks by Loutfi (Egypt)) (Oct. 30, 1956).
970 U.N. SCOR, 11th Sess., 748th mtg., at 2, U.N. Doc. S/PV.748 (remarks by Lodge (United States)) (Oct. 30, 1956).
971 *Id.* at 8,9 (remarks by Belaunde (Peru)).
972 *Id.* at 4 (remarks by Brilej (Yugoslavia)).
973 *Id.* at 5 (remarks by Entezam (Iran)).
974 U.N. SCOR, 11th Sess., 749th mtg., at 8 U.N. Doc. S/PV.749 (remarks by Sobolev (Soviet Union)) (Oct. 30, 1956).
975 U.N. SCOR, 11th Sess., 748th mtg., at 6, U.N. Doc. S/PV.748 (remarks by Walker (Australia)) (Oct. 30, 1956).

China, while expressing "a certain measure of sympathy with [Israel's] dilemma", considered the Israeli actions as disproportionate.[976]

The United Kingdom[977] and France[978] emphasized the importance of the Suez Canal as well as their desire to end the fighting and considered the Security Council as unable to contribute constructively to either objective. France added that Israel responded by a "pursuit" after government controlled Fedayeen fighters and that Egypt's sole aim had been to annihilate the State of Israel.[979] Both states vetoed two draft resolutions that would have called for an immediate Israeli withdrawal.[980] The General Assembly also did not condemn Israel for its use of forceful countermeasures.[981]

This conflict was not sparked solely by Israel's security concerns – some states even shared those. The question at stake was clearly the security of the Suez Canal and the United Kingdom's and France's aim to prevent Egypt from exercising control over it. Furthermore, the Fedayeen bands sent by Egypt were hardly operating beyond Egyptian control and also the main conflict inside Egypt was also fought between two states, rather than between Israel and a non-state actor. However, one can hold that the legal nature of the attacker as argued by Israel was not by itself subject of criticism with regard to self-defense. On the other hand, hardly any state ever commented on Israel's invocation of self-defense, most likely due to the openly recognizable two-sidedness of this conflict whose focus was on other issues, namely the Canal.

b) LEBANON'S AND JORDAN'S COMPLAINTS AGAINST UNITED ARAB REPUBLIC

In 1958, following a military *coup d'état* toppling the Hashemite government of the Arab Federation of Iraq and Jordan, replacing it with an Iraqi pro-Soviet government,[982] Lebanon and Jordan complained to the United Nations Security Council about the supply of arms to and training of "subversive elements" by the United Arab Republic (i.e. the union of Syria and Egypt between 1958 and 1961) and subsequent incursions into and terror attacks on the territory of Lebanon[983] and later also Jordan.[984] Both countries invoked Article 51 of the

---

[976] U.N. SCOR, 11th Sess., 749th mtg., at 22, U.N. Doc. S/PV.749 (remarks by Tsiang (China)) (Oct. 30, 1956).
[977] *Id.* at 4, 5 (remarks by Dixon (United Kingdom)).
[978] *Id.* at 29 (remarks by Cornut-Gentille (France)).
[979] *Id.*
[980] U.N. SCOR, 11th Sess., 749th mtg., at 31, U.N. Doc. S/PV.749 (Oct. 30, 1956); U.N. SCOR, 11th Sess., 750th mtg., at 5, U.N. Doc. S/PV.750 (Oct. 30, 1956).
[981] *Cf.* FRANCK, *supra* note 12 at 56.
[982] *See, e.g., Rebels Fighting at Iraq Palace*, THE TIMES (LONDON), July 15, 1958, at 8.
[983] U.N. SCOR, 11th Sess., 827th mtg., at 13, 14, U.N. Doc. S/PV.827 (remarks by Azkoul (Lebanon)) (July 15, 1958).

Charter and called for American and British help in exercise of collective self-defense.[985]

The United Arab Republic denied any involvement and consequently saw no room for the application of Article 51 of the Charter in the absence of an armed attack.[986] The Soviet Union[987] and Sweden[988] rejected the invocation of Article 51 of the Charter in absence of an armed attack. Both representatives added that the present conflict was not of the required international nature.[989]

The United States and the United Kingdom dispatched troops to Lebanon. They followed a Lebanese and Jordanian call for help in exercise of their right to collective self-defense based upon Article 51 of the Charter. The American representative referred insofar to a request by the Lebanese President and government for help.[990] Also the United Kingdom considered the appeal for help as "entirely justified"[991] and emphasized that "[t]he method of indirect aggression – the method of subversion . . . – can be just as dangerous as the open variety. We all abhor the latter; we should equally abhor the former."[992]

France,[993] Canada,[994] China,[995] and Japan,[996] explicitly endorsed the American and British view on self-defense. China added that it explicitly rejected the Swedish position as to the absence of an armed attack and hence Arti-

---

[984] 1958 U.N.Y.B. 36, 41.

[985] U.N. SCOR, 11th Sess., 827th mtg., at 16, U.N. Doc. S/PV.827 (remarks by Azkoul (Lebanon)) (July 15, 1958); U.N. SCOR, 11th Sess., 831st mtg., at 5, U.N. Doc. S/PV.831 (remarks by Toukan (Jordan)) (July 17, 1958).

[986] U.N. SCOR, 11th Sess., 828th mtg., at 6,7, U.N. Doc. S/PV.828 (remarks by Loutfi (United Arab Republic)) (July 15, 1958); U.N. SCOR, 11th Sess., 831st mtg., at 21, U.N. Doc. S/PV.831 (remarks by Loutfi (United Arab Republic)) (July 17, 1958).

[987] U.N. SCOR, 11th Sess., 827th mtg., at 20, U.N. Doc. S/PV.827 (remarks by Sobolev (Soviet Union)) (July 15, 1958).

[988] U.N. SCOR, 11th Sess., 830th mtg., at 8,9, U.N. Doc. S/PV.830 (remarks by Jarring (Sweden)) (July 16, 1958).

[989] *Id.* at 9; U.N. SCOR, 11th Sess., 834th mtg., at 16, U.N. Doc. S/PV.834 (remarks by Sobolev (Soviet Union)) (July 18, 1958).

[990] U.N. SCOR, 11th Sess., 827th mtg., at 6, U.N. Doc. S/PV.827 (remarks by Lodge (United States)) (July 15, 1958).

[991] U.N. SCOR, 11th Sess., 831st mtg., at 6, U.N. Doc. S/PV.831 (remarks by Dixon (United Kingdom)) (July 17, 1958).

[992] *Id.* at 7.

[993] U.N. SCOR, 11th Sess., 828th mtg., at 2, U.N. Doc. S/PV.828 (remarks by de Vaucelles (France)) (July 15, 1958).

[994] *Id.* at 3,4 (remarks by Holmes (Canada)).

[995] *Id.* at 5 (remarks by Kiang (China)).

[996] U.N. SCOR, 11th Sess., 829th mtg., at 14, U.N. Doc. S/PV.829 (remarks by Matsudaira (Japan)) (July 16, 1958).

cle 51 of the Charter as a justification for the American and British dispatch of troops. Rather, "indirect aggression is as dangerous as direct aggression" and inasmuch sufficient to trigger Article 51.[997]

Eventually, friendly relations between the United Arab Republic and its neighbors were restored and the foreign troops left.[998]

Despite the fact that Lebanon and Jordan referred to the right to self-defense, this conflict does not quite meet the criteria of a violent non-state actor committing cross-border violence from a weak host state. It does seem that the United Arab Republic directly supported irregular forces to exercise influence in bordering countries. If that behavior could theoretically have met the "effective control" threshold (of 1986) is unclear. It is furthermore unclear if there actually have been singular events amounting to armed attacks or if perhaps the alleged aggressive actions against Lebanon and Jordan may have been falling short of this requirement.

c) Military Actions of France Against Algerian Groups in Tunisia

In the course of the Franco-Algerian war of independence between 1954 and 1962, the French army engaged in fierce battles with the primary Algerian resistance group, the National Liberation Front (Front de Libération Nationale, FLN). France complained in February 1958 that Tunisia was supporting "rebels enabling them to conduct operations from Tunisian territory directed against [France]"[999] and in June 1958 that Tunisia allowed training and supply bases for Algerian rebels on its territory.[1000] France had attacked targets in Tunisia upon which the latter had turned to the United Nations Security Council invoking its right to self-defense against the French actions.[1001] The French representative asserted that the recent military actions inside Tunisia were the results of many Tunisian provocations by aiding and abetting the Algerian groups.[1002] After a similar incident later that year, France and Tunisia agreed that all French troops stationed in Tunisia were to be evacuated within four months.[1003]

In this case, the alleged host state invoked self-defense. France, the potential victim state, had not specified the grounds upon which it acted but complained about the violation of a *modus vivendi* of French troops operating in Tu-

---

[997] U.N. SCOR, 11th Sess., 831st mtg., at 19, U.N. Doc. S/PV.831 (remarks by Tsiang (China)) (July 17, 1958).
[998] 1958 U.N.Y.B. 48-49.
[999] *Id.* at 77.
[1000] U.N. SCOR, 11th Sess., 819th mtg., at 13, U.N. Doc. S/PV.819 (remarks by Georges-Picot (France)) (June 2, 1958).
[1001] 1958 U.N.Y.B. 77; *see also* U.N. Doc. S/3951 (Feb. 13, 1958).
[1002] 1958 U.N.Y.B. 77.
[1003] U.N. SCOR, 11th Sess., 826th mtg., U.N. Doc. S/PV.826 (June 18, 1958).

nisia as agreed by the Tunisian government in early 1958.[1004] With regard to Algeria, France insisted that the United Nations had no jurisdiction over any such matter since it regarded the conflict as an essentially domestic matter and hence any international involvement as violation of Article 2 (7) of the Charter.[1005] That view was supported by some, but rejected by most other states, perhaps because of the involvement of Tunisia, as the Tunisian representative argued.[1006]

For the purpose of this work, this is one of the cases in which a host state allegedly supported a non-state actor in return for which the victim state responded with military force against the host state directly – in order to confine a non-state actor, but while blaming the potent host state. It is not clear what legal view the international community would have taken regarding military self-defense against the non-state actor directly, partly also due to the relatively speedy solution of the crisis.

d) Israel's Military Actions Against Jordan

In the aftermath of the 1967 war, Israeli-Jordanian relations remained tense. Israel repeatedly complained about terrorist incursions emanating from Jordanian territory[1007] and turned to the United Nations Security Council.[1008] Also Jordan repeatedly complained about Israeli military incursions.[1009]

Israel blamed Jordan for violating the 1967 cease-fire agreement by not preventing and also actively supporting terror attacks emanating from Jordanian territory.[1010] Consequently, Israel would destroy any such terror-related facilities on Jordanian territory in exercise of its right to self-defense.[1011] Israel regarded

---

[1004] *See, e.g.,* U.N. SCOR, 11th Sess., 820th mtg., at 7, U.N. Doc. S/PV.820 (remarks by Georges-Picot (France)) (June 2, 1958).

[1005] *See, e.g.,* 1958 U.N.Y.B. 79.

[1006] *Id.*

[1007] *See, e.g.,* U.N. SCOR, 23rd Sess., 1401st mtg., at 5,6, U.N. Doc. S/PV.1401 (remarks by Tekoah (Israel)) (March 21, 1968); U.N. SCOR, 23rd Sess., 1434th mtg., at 6,7, U.N. Doc. S/PV.1434 (remarks by Tekoah (Israel)) (Aug. 5, 1968); despite continuous denials by Jordan that Fatah or any terrorist group operated from or even existed on Jordanian territory, King Hussein decided in 1970 to expel the Fatah and its leader Yasser Arafat forcefully in what became known as the PLO's "Black September", *see supra* p. 75.

[1008] *See, e.g.,* 1968 U.N.Y.B. 191; For an overview over Israel's and Jordan's submissions in 1968 in this regard *see* 1968 U.N.Y.B. 234.

[1009] *See, e.g.,* 1967 U.N.Y.B. 235, 236; 1968 U.N.Y.B. 191, 199, 203, 204, 214, 215; 1970 U.N.Y.B. 223.

[1010] *See, e.g.,* U.N. SCOR, 23rd Sess., 1404th mtg., at 6,7, U.N. Doc. S/PV.1404 (remarks by Tekoah (Israel)) (March 22, 1968; U.N. SCOR, 23rd Sess., 1434th mtg., at 6,7, U.N. Doc. S/PV.1434 (remarks by Tekoah (Israel)) (Aug. 5, 1968).

[1011] *See, e.g.,* U.N. SCOR, 23rd Sess., 1401st mtg., at 7, U.N. Doc. S/PV.1401 (remarks by Tekoah (Israel)) (March 21, 1968); U.N. SCOR, 23rd Sess., 1407th mtg., at 12, U.N. Doc.

Jordan as well as allied Arab states to act in continuation of prior hostilities, only this time with unofficial means. In fact, Israel blamed Jordan not only of having tolerated the establishment of terrorist training camps and recruiting centers in Amman, but also saw itself exposed to regular Jordanian military attacks and active Jordanian assistance and coordination with irregular forces.[1012] Members of the Iraqi and Egyptian military were also caught by Israel while executing raids from inside Jordan into the West Bank.[1013]

Jordan, in return, considered resistance to aggression in occupied territories as natural and denied responsibility or even the existence of terrorist bases on its territory.[1014] The Jordanian representative admitted, however, that

> [Palestinians] do go back [to the West Bank] – we have no control over them – to get killed, maybe, in their own homeland. They do go there, I admit, but we have no control over their movements. . . As long as [Israel is] there [in the West Bank] there is only one single answer to occupation: resistance.[1015]

On other occasions, Jordan merely referred to attacks on civilians by Israel, not mentioning any relation to armed bands.[1016]

The United States opposed any military or terrorist actions in violation of the cease-fire[1017] and considered an Israeli action in March 1968 as disproportionate.[1018] The United Kingdom, like Canada[1019] and Denmark,[1020] repeatedly

---

S/PV.1407 (remarks by Tekoah (Israel)) (March 24, 1968); U.N. SCOR, 23rd Sess., 1434th mtg., at 6,7, U.N. Doc. S/PV.1434 (remarks by Tekoah (Israel)) (Aug. 5, 1968); 1968 U.N.Y.B. 211, 213, 214, 215; 1970 U.N.Y.B. 224.

[1012] 1968 U.N.Y.B. 205, 210-11.

[1013] U.N. SCOR, 23rd Sess., 1436th mtg., at 4,5, U.N. Doc. S/PV.1436 (remarks by Tekoah (Israel)) (Aug. 7, 1968).

[1014] *See, e.g.,* U.N. SCOR, 23rd Sess., 1405th mtg., at 2, U.N. Doc. S/PV.1405 (remarks by El-Farra (Jordan)) (March 23, 1968); U.N. SCOR, 23rd Sess., 1436th mtg., at 2, U.N. Doc. S/PV.1436 (remarks by El-Farra (Jordan)) (Aug. 7, 1968); 1968 U.N.Y.B. 210, 211.

[1015] U.N. SCOR, 23rd Sess., 1434th mtg., at 16, U.N. Doc. S/PV.1434 (remarks by El-Farra (Jordan)) (Aug. 5, 1968).

[1016] *Id.* at 3-5 (remarks by El-Farra (Jordan)).

[1017] 1968 U.N.Y.B. 193, 200, 206, 212.

[1018] U.N. SCOR, 23rd Sess., 1402nd mtg., at 1, U.N. Doc. S/PV.1402 (remarks by Goldberg (United States)) (March 21, 1968); U.N. SCOR, 23rd Sess., 1407th mtg., at 2, U.N. Doc. S/PV.1407 (remarks by Goldberg (United States)) (March 24, 1968).

[1019] U.N. SCOR, 23rd Sess., 1403rd mtg., at 4, U.N. Doc. S/PV.1403 (remarks by Ignatieff (Canada)) (March 21, 22, 1968).

[1020] *Id.* at 4 (remarks by Borch (Denmark)).

deplored all violence[1021] but added that Israel's responses, constituted illegal reprisals.[1022] China denied Israel the right to retaliatory acts even following extreme provocations.[1023] France considered Israel's responses as illegitimate reprisal and also as disproportionate.[1024] India saw no justification at all for Israel's actions and a cease-fire violation.[1025] Most other states regarded Israel's military responses as "aggression".[1026] Some speakers chose an utterly hateful language, blaming Israel, among other things, for a continuous exploitation of the "conscience of the German Christian democracy in order to receive compensation for the Jewish victims in the form of armaments and money".[1027]

Largely the same responses were articulated in August 1968, after an Israeli air raid near the city of Salt: most states considered Israel's actions to constitute aggressions,[1028] or illegitimate reprisals.[1029] The United States did "not

---

1021 1968 U.N.Y.B. 194, 200, 207.

1022 U.N. SCOR, 23rd Sess., 1403rd mtg., at 2, U.N. Doc. S/PV.1403 (remarks by Caradon (United Kingdom)) (March 21, 22, 1968).

1023 *Id.* at 6 (remarks by Liu (China)); 1968 U.N.Y.B. 209.

1024 U.N. SCOR, 23rd Sess., 1402nd mtg., at 5, U.N. Doc. S/PV.1402 (remarks by Berard (France)) (March 21, 1968); 1968 U.N.Y.B. 208.

1025 *Id.* at 7 (remarks by Parthasarathi (India)).

1026 U.S.S.R: U.N. SCOR, 23rd Sess., 1402nd mtg., at 5, U.N. Doc. S/PV.1402 (remarks by Malik (Soviet Union)) (March 21, 1968); U.N. SCOR, 23rd Sess., 1405th mtg., at 2, U.N. Doc. S/PV.1405 (remarks by Malik (Soviet Union)) (March 22, 1968); U.N. SCOR, 23rd Sess., 1407th mtg., at 3, U.N. Doc. S/PV.1407 (remarks by Malik (Soviet Union)) (March 24, 1968); Algeria: U.N. SCOR, 23rd Sess., 1402nd mtg., at 2, U.N. Doc. S/PV.1402 (remarks by Bouattoura (Algeria)) (March 21, 1968); U.N. SCOR, 23rd Sess., 1407th mtg., at 7, U.N. Doc. S/PV.1407 (remarks by Bouattoura (Algeria)) (March 24, 1968); Hungary: U.N. SCOR, 23rd Sess., 1402nd mtg., at 14, U.N. Doc. S/PV.1402 (remarks by Csatorady (Hungary)) (March 21, 1968); U.N. SCOR, 23rd Sess., 1407th mtg., at 8, U.N. Doc. S/PV.1407 (remarks by Csatorady (Hungary)) (March 24, 1968); Iraq: U.N. SCOR, 23rd Sess., 1402nd mtg., at 10, U.N. Doc. S/PV.1402 (remarks by Pachachi (Iraq)) (March 21, 1968); U.N. SCOR, 23rd Sess., 1407th mtg., at 9, U.N. Doc. S/PV.1407 (remarks by Pachachi (Iraq)) (March 24, 1968); Morocco: U.N. SCOR, 23rd Sess., 1402nd mtg., at 13, U.N. Doc. S/PV.1402 (remarks by Benhima (Morocco)) (March 21, 1968); U.N. SCOR, 23rd Sess., 1407th mtg., at 10, U.N. Doc. S/PV.1407 (remarks by Benhima (Morocco)) (March 24, 1968); Pakistan: U.N. SCOR, 23rd Sess., 1402nd mtg., at 4, U.N. Doc. S/PV.1402 (remarks by Shahi (Pakistan)) (March 21, 1968), 1968 U.N.Y.B. 208; Saudi-Arabia 1968 U.N.Y.B. 202; Syria: U.N. SCOR, 23rd Sess., 1404th mtg., at 3, U.N. Doc. S/PV.1404 (remarks by Tomeh (Syria)) (March 22, 1968), 1968 U.N.Y.B. 201; United Arab Republic: U.N. SCOR, 23rd Sess., 1403rd mtg., at 2, U.N. Doc. S/PV.1403 (remarks by El Kony (United Arab Republic)) (March 21, 22, 1968).

1027 U.N. SCOR, 23rd Sess., 1402nd mtg., at 11, U.N. Doc. S/PV.1402 (remarks by Benhima (Morocco)) (March 21, 1968).

1028 Algeria: U.N. SCOR, 23rd Sess., 1434th mtg., at 11, U.N. Doc. S/PV.1434 (remarks by Bouattoura (Algeria)) (Aug. 5, 1968); Pakistan: U.N. SCOR, 23rd Sess., 1435th mtg., at 7,

condone" Israel's military actions but emphasized that "acts of terrorism . . . that have been launched with increasing frequency from Jordan . . . should not be judged as isolated events; . . . they are incidents in a concerted effort that cannot help but have a cumulative effect."[1030] The United Kingdom spoke out against all violence and deplored Israel's "deliberate new attack."[1031] Canada deplored all violence and urged all parties to the conflict to respect the cease-fire,[1032] and so did Brazil,[1033] Denmark,[1034] and Paraguay.[1035] India joined them but emphasized that Israel needed to be condemned individually.[1036] China reiterated its prior point of view that even extreme terrorist provocations should not trigger military responses such as the Israeli one due to risks to the civilian population. The Chinese delegate also seemed to be critical of the scale of the applied counter-measures when he says that "the action involving the deployment of heavy artillery and aircraft has assumed a magnitude uncalled for by the nature of the provocation."[1037] Twice in 1968 he Security Council condemned the Israeli military action in violation of the United Nations Charter and the cease-fire resolutions but also deplored all other violent incidents.[1038]

U.N. Doc. S/PV.1435 (remarks by Shahi (Pakistan)) (Aug. 6, 1968); Soviet Union: U.N. SCOR, 23rd Sess., 1434th mtg., at 12, U.N. Doc. S/PV.1434 (remarks by Malik (Soviet Union)) (Aug. 5, 1968); Syria: U.N. SCOR, 23rd Sess., 1436th mtg., at 7, U.N. Doc. S/PV.1436 (remarks by Tomeh (Syria)) (Aug. 7, 1968).

[1029] Ethiopia: U.N. SCOR, 23rd Sess., 1439th mtg., at 2, U.N. Doc. S/PV.1439 (remarks by Makonnen (Ethiopia)) (Aug. 15, 1968); France: U.N. SCOR, 23rd Sess., 1435th mtg., at 4, U.N. Doc. S/PV.1435 (remarks by Chayet (France)) (Aug. 6, 1968); Iraq: U.N. SCOR, 23rd Sess., 1434th mtg., at 10, U.N. Doc. S/PV.1434 (remarks by Pachachi (Iraq)) (Aug. 5, 1968); United Arab Republic: U.N. SCOR, 23rd Sess., 1435th mtg., at 3, U.N. Doc. S/PV.1435 (remarks by Hilmy (United Arab Republic)) (Aug. 6, 1968).

[1030] U.N. SCOR, 23rd Sess., 1434th mtg., at 14, U.N. Doc. S/PV.1434 (remarks by Ball (United States)) (Aug. 5, 1968).

[1031] *Id.* at 15 (remarks by Hildyard (United Kingdom)).

[1032] U.N. SCOR, 23rd Sess., 1435th mtg., at 4, U.N. Doc. S/PV.1435 (remarks by Beaulieu (Canada)) (Aug. 6, 1968).

[1033] U.N. SCOR, 23rd Sess., 1437th mtg., at 4, U.N. Doc. S/PV.1437 (remarks by De Araujo Castro (Brazil)) (Aug. 9, 1968).

[1034] U.N. SCOR, 23rd Sess., 1436th mtg., at 10, U.N. Doc. S/PV.1436 (remarks by Mellbin (Denmark)) (Aug. 7, 1968).

[1035] U.N. SCOR, 23rd Sess., 1437th mtg., at 2, U.N. Doc. S/PV.1437 (remarks by Solano Lopez (Paraguay)) (Aug. 9, 1968).

[1036] *Id.* at 3, 4 (remarks by Mishra (India)).

[1037] *Id.* at 3 (remarks by Liu (China)).

[1038] S.C. Res. 248 (March 24, 1968), 1968 U.N.Y.B. 234; S.C. Res. 256 (Aug. 16, 1968), 1968 U.N.Y.B. 212.

Only few of the states' representatives referred in greater detail to the right of self-defense as invoked by Israel: Hungary announced that self-defense as a justification was unavailable as the "so-called terror raids" constituted resistance to Israeli occupation and did not entitle Israel to use force against its neighbors. On the other hand, "the indigenous population" itself was subject to the actual aggression, which was why in return Israel could not be exposed to an aggression as well.[1039] The statement appears to imply that self-defense is not available against forceful resistance because the resistance itself is legitimate and hence no illegitimate application of force. If that is the case one could ask if illegitimate resistance would allow for self-defense, regardless of the legal nature of the resistance group. On the other hand, the Hungarian representative seems to support Jordan's denial of any responsibility for the, nonetheless legitimate, resistance. Accordingly, Israel had no right to use force against its neighbor, the Hashemite Kingdom of Jordan. Either way, the statement does not imply that Israel was barred from self-defense because the alleged aggressor was not a state.

Senegal listed the conditions of self-defense, namely that "[t]he victim of aggression may, in order to protect and defend himself, respond immediately, without delay and at the actual site of the aggression, to the aggressor's attack by means proportionate to those used by the aggressor."[1040] Jordan, in the view of Senegal's representative, was not the aggressor but was rather attacked by Israel.[1041] By inference one can hold that the cross-border raids from Jordan were regarded either as 1) non-existent – a fact that even the United Nations' resolutions accepted repeatedly by denouncing all forms of violence – 2) mere responses to prior Israeli violence, or 3) unable to be linked to the state of Jordan. The inability to exercise self-defense against a non-state actor is not expressed explicitly by this view and statehood of the aggressor is not named among the conditions of self-defense, according to Senegal. However, between the lines it does seem as if Senegal was of the opinion that self-defense could not be invoked due to the fact that the state of Jordan did not act towards Israel.

The Brazilian representative, commenting on the Karameh incident, explicitly referred to "a series of armed attacks launched from Jordanian territory", deploring it along with all use of force in the aftermath of the 1967 cease-fire.[1042] This statement, which he repeated in Brazil's explanation of its vote,[1043]

1039 U.N. SCOR, 23rd Sess., 1436th mtg., at 12, U.N. Doc. S/PV.1436 (remarks by Tardos (Hungary)) (Aug. 7, 1968).

1040 *Id.* at 13 (remarks by Boye (Senegal)).

1041 *Id.*

1042 U.N. SCOR, 23rd Sess., 1403rd mtg., at 5, U.N. Doc. S/PV.1403 (remarks by De Carvalho Silos (Brazil)) (March 21, 22, 1968).

seems to indicate that the violence to which Israel responded and which was "deplore[d]" by the Security Council resolutions is generally capable of triggering Article 51 of the Charter – which requires an "armed attack". The nature of the attacker, subject to dispute in the debates, was apparently of little importance.

As was seen before, only few statements allow one to infer that Israel may have a right to respond militarily to force by non-state terrorists. Mostly, however, self-defense was not an issue here, despite the Israeli invocation thereof. Slightly more detailed notions – apart from general rejections such as "Israeli aggression" – considered the Israeli actions as forceful responses to prior illegal actions that were apparently not regarded to amount to an "armed attack". Israeli counteractions would thus have been needed to be confined to a reprisal, which does not necessarily allow for the use of force.[1044] Israel's complaint that the attacks emanated from terrorist bases in Jordan and not necessarily from the regular Jordan army was not discussed. A possible non-state actor's responsibility as an essential obstacle for the invocation of the right to self-defense was not mentioned either. Partly, that is due to the fact that Israel often blamed Jordan for its inactivity or even support and thus attributed terrorist activity to the state of Jordan.

e) SOUTHERN RHODESIA'S MILITARY CAMPAIGNS

With varying intensity, Rhodesia's white minority regime under Prime Minister Ian Smith fought foreign incursions from various opponents that sought to overthrow and replace the government. Particularly shortly prior to the 1980 elections that eventually replaced Rhodesia with Zimbabwe as well as Ian Smith with Robert Mugabe,[1045] Rhodesia repeatedly invoked its right to exercise self-defense against non-state guerilla groups, predominantly the Zimbabwe African National Union (Zanu) operating from Mozambique, the Zimbabwe African People's Union (Zapu) launching their operations from inside Zambia and Botswana,[1046] and the Zimbabwe African National Liberation Army (Zanla) operating from Mozambique under Robert Mugabe.[1047]

1043 U.N. SCOR, 23rd Sess., 1407th mtg., at 5, U.N. Doc. S/PV.1407 (remarks by De Carvalho Silos (Brazil)) (March 24, 1968).

1044 *See, e.g.*, CASSESE, *supra* note 178 at 371-73.

1045 Nicholas Ashford, *Mr Mugabe planning broadly based government of national unity*, THE TIMES (London), March 5, 1980, at 1.

1046 *See, e.g.*, Michael Knipe, *Guerilla invasion timed for Geneva conference*, THE TIMES (London), Nov. 13, 1976, at 4.

1047 *See, e.g.* Frederick Cleary, *Rhodesians cross into Mozambique to hit bases*, THE TIMES (London), July 31, 1978, at 1

Shortly after the "Central African Federation" dissolved, Northern Rhodesia and Nyasaland became the independent "Republic of Zambia" and the "Republic of Malawi" in October 1964,[1048] the remainders, Southern Rhodesia, came under pressure from abroad. A unilateral declaration of independence leading to a racially discriminating state was rejected by the former colonial power, the United Kingdom.[1049] The United Nations "condemned" Southern Rhodesia's independence[1050] and eventually inflicted an economic embargo on Rhodesia in response to the ongoing internal repressions by the Smith-regime.[1051]

The relations between Southern Rhodesia and Zambia also deteriorated as Southern Rhodesia saw itself exposed to rising infiltrations by guerilla groups harbored by Zambia.[1052] A number of small-scale incursions were reported by Southern Rhodesia through 1973, all emanating from armed groups operating from training facilities in bordering states.[1053] Zambia denied the existence of guerilla camps on its territory, while Southern Rhodesia and also South Africa alleged the contrary and continued to launch counter-operations.[1054] Tanzania apparently did not conceal the fact that it allowed black Rhodesian guerilla groups to run training facilities on its territory.[1055]

Initially, Southern Rhodesia just like South Africa[1056] and Turkey,[1057] referred to its right to a "hot pursuit" to hunt down armed bands that allegedly infiltrated from abroad, for instance from Mozambique[1058] and Zambia.[1059]

[1048] *"Republic of Zambia" on October 24*, THE TIMES (London), May 20, 1964 at 9; WOLFRUM, *supra* note 643 at 311-12.
[1049] WOLFRUM, *supra* note 643 at 311-12.
[1050] S.C. Res. 216 (Nov. 12, 1965), 1965 U.N.Y.B. 132; S.C. Res. 217 (Nov. 20, 1965), 1965 U.N.Y.B. 133.
[1051] S.C. Res. 232 (Dec. 16, 1966), 1966 U.N.Y.B. 116-17; S.C. Res. 253 (May 29, 1968), 1968 U.N.Y.B, 152-54.
[1052] *Rhodesia warning to Zambia – 'Assisting terrorist raids'*, THE TIMES (London), Aug. 26, 1967, at 4 (quoting a warning to Zambia not to shelter terrorists, issued by the Rhodesian government and Deputy Prime Minster and Minister of Finance, John Wrathall).
[1053] *Rhodesia security alert after terrorists attack farm*, THE TIMES (London), Dec. 22, 1972, at 1; Ian Smith, *Rhodesia closes Zambia border after attacks by guerilla gangs*, THE TIMES (London), Jan. 10, 1973, at 1.
[1054] *See, e.g., Dr. Kaunda accuses Rhodesia of plotting with S Africa to attack Zambia towns,* THE TIMES (London), March 16, 1973, at 1; *see* also 1973 U.N.Y.B. 109.
[1055] *Rhodesian guerillas training in Tanzania*, THE TIMES (London), July 11, 1975, at 6 (reporting about an ANC mission to Tanzania in the course of which the training camps were inspected).
[1056] *See supra* notes 670, 672.
[1057] *See supra* note 824.

In 1977, the United Nations Security Council was concerned with an allegedly unprovoked attack by Southern Rhodesia against Botswana in December 1976.[1060] Southern Rhodesia rejected these allegations and blamed Botswana for harboring "black nationalist guerillas", but was not permitted to participate in the Security Council deliberations.[1061] The debate shows little if any understanding for Southern Rhodesia's actions. Not surprisingly, and much like on many other occasions, no state represented at the Council showed any sympathy for Rhodesia's racist regime and considered Southern Rhodesia's cross-border raids to constitute an illegal acts of "aggression" or "aggressive acts" and equally rejected Ian Smith's Rhodesian minority regime.[1062] Some states, such as Pakistan,

---

[1058] Nicholas Ashford, *Rhodesian forces cross into Mozambique*, THE TIMES (London), Feb. 26, 1976, at 1 (quoting "Rhodesian security forces" of having conducted a "follow-up hot pursuit operation"); *see also* U.N. Doc. S/12005 (March 8, 1976); the action was condemned by the United Nations Security Council as "provocative and aggressive acts", *see* S.C. Res. 386 (March 17, 1976), 1976 U.N.Y.B. 195.

[1059] Michael Knipe, *Rhodesia warning on 'hot pursuit' after border firing*, THE TIMES (London), June 18, 1976, at 6 (quoting Rhodesian Prime Minister Ian Smith).

[1060] Michael Knipe, *Rhodesia accused of attack in Botswana*, THE TIMES (London), Dec. 21, 1976, at 6; U.N. Doc. S/12262 (Dec. 22, 1976); U.N. SCOR, 32nd Sess., 1983rd-85th mtgs., U.N. Docs. S/PV 1983-85 (Jan. 12-14, 1977).

[1061] Michael Knipe, *UN to ignore plea by Rhodesia over Botswana complaint*, THE TIMES (London), Jan. 14, 1977, at 10.

[1062] Benin: U.N. SCOR, 32nd Sess., 1983rd mtg., at 9 U.N. Docs. S/PV 1983 (remarks by Boya (Benin)) (Jan. 12, 1977); Canada: U.N. SCOR, 32nd Sess., 1984th mtg., at 9 U.N. Docs. S/PV 1984 (remarks by Barton (Canada)) (Jan. 13, 1977); China: *id.* at 6 (remarks by Lay Ya-Li (China)); Cuba: U.N. SCOR, 32nd Sess., 1985th mtg., at 13 U.N. Docs. S/PV 1985 (remarks by Alarcon (Cuba)) (Jan. 14, 1977); Equatorial Guinea: *id.* at 15 (remarks by Ecua Miko (Equatorial Guinea)); German Democratic Republic: *id.* at 11 (remarks by Neugebauer (German Democratic Republic)); India: U.N. SCOR, 32nd Sess., 1984th mtg., at 12 U.N. Docs. S/PV 1984 (remarks by Jaipal (India)) (Jan. 13, 1977); Kenya: *id.* at 15 (remarks by Kasina (Kenya)); Lesotho: *id.* at 6 (remarks by Mathaba (Lesotho)); Libya: U.N. SCOR, 32nd Sess., 1983rd mtg., at 10 U.N. Docs. S/PV 1983 (remarks by Kikhia (Libya)) (Jan. 12, 1977); Mali: U.N. SCOR, 32nd Sess., 1985th mtg., at 16 U.N. Docs. S/PV 1985 (remarks by Kante (Mali)) (Jan. 14, 1977); Mauritius: U.N. SCOR, 32nd Sess., 1983rd mtg., at 6 U.N. Docs. S/PV 1983 (remarks by Ramphul (Mauritius)) (Jan. 12, 1977); Morocco: *id.* at 7 (remarks by Zaimi (Morocco)); Mozambique: U.N. SCOR, 32nd Sess., 1985th mtg., at 1 U.N. Docs. S/PV 1985 (remarks by Lobo (Mozambique)) (Jan. 14, 1977); Nigeria: *id.* at 8 (remarks by Harriman (Nigeria)); Panama: U.N. SCOR, 32nd Sess., 1984th mtg., at 5 U.N. Docs. S/PV 1984 (remarks by Illueca (Panama)) (Jan. 13, 1977); Romanis: *id.* at 7 (remarks by Datcu (Romania)); Sierra Leone: *id.* at 14 (remarks by Gbujama (Sierra Leone)); Somalia: U.N. SCOR, 32nd Sess., 1985th mtg., at 6 U.N. Docs. S/PV 1985 (remarks by Hussein (Somalia)) (Jan. 14, 1977); Soviet Union: *id.* at 17 (remarks by Troyanoysky (Soviet Union)); Tanzania: U.N. SCOR, 32nd Sess., 1984th mtg., at 10 U.N. Docs. S/PV 1984 (remarks by Sepetu (Tanzania)) (Jan. 13,

even praised Botswana for harboring opponents of Rhodesia.[1063] The Federal Republic of Germany,[1064] France,[1065] and the United Kingdom,[1066] affirmed a violation of Botswana's sovereignty and rejected Southern Rhodesia's regime, but avoided terms such as "aggression". The United States also regarded Southern Rhodesia's regime as illegal[1067] and more broadly rejected "all illegal use of force".[1068] Both the United States and the United Kingdom abstained in the subsequent vote on a resolution condemning Southern Rhodesia[1069] and referred to their central roles in ongoing negotiations to reach a majority regime in Southern Rhodesia.[1070]

Along with a united rejection of Southern Rhodesia as a whole, foreign incursions continued.[1071] Southern Rhodesia responded with "defensive" cross-border raids aiming to destroy guerilla facilities abroad,[1072] which in return were severely criticized by the United States and the United Kingdom.[1073]

In mid-1977, the Southern Rhodesian government explicitly referred to its "inherent right to defend itself" vis-à-vis military actions emanating from Mozambique,[1074] an apparent reference to the wording of Article 51 of the Charter. Subsequent deliberations of the United Nations Security Council upon a request by Mozambique[1075] proved, again, little understanding for Southern

---

1977); Yugoslavia: *id.* at 13 (remarks by Petrić (Yugoslavia)); Zambia: *id.* at 1 (remarks by Mwale (Zambia)).

1063 U.N. SCOR, 32nd Sess., 1985th mtg., at 14 U.N. Docs. S/PV 1985 (remarks by Mirza (Pakistan)) (Jan. 14, 1977).

1064 *Id.* at 4,5 (remarks by von Wechmar (Federal Republic of Germany)).

1065 *Id.* at 7 (remarks by Leprette (France)).

1066 *Id.* at 19 (remarks by Murray (United Kingdom)).

1067 U.N. SCOR, 32nd Sess., 1984th mtg., at 16 U.N. Docs. S/PV 1984 (remarks by Scranton (United States)) (Jan. 13, 1977).

1068 U.N. SCOR, 32nd Sess., 1985th mtg., at 20 U.N. Docs. S/PV 1985 (remarks by Sherer (United States)) (Jan. 14, 1977).

1069 S.C. Res. 403 (Jan. 14, 1977), 1977 U.N.Y.B. 223.

1070 U.N. SCOR, 32nd Sess., 1985th mtg., at 20 U.N. Docs. S/PV 1985 (Jan. 14, 1977).

1071 *See, e.g.*, Frederick Cleary, *Guerillas kidnap 400 pupils from school in Rhodesia*, THE TIMES (London), Feb. 1, 1977, at 1.

1072 *See, e.g.*, Michael Knipe, *Rhodesians destroy Mozambique camps*, THE TIMES (London), May 31, 1977, at 1; David Spanier, *Rhodesia replies to criticism over raid*, THE TIMES (London), June 2, 1977, at 1 (quoting the Southern Rhodesian Foreign Minister that the recent raid into Mozambique "was a defensive operation to halt terrorist incursions into [Southern Rhodesia]").

1073 *Dr Owen condemns Rhodesian raid into Mozambique*, THE TIMES (London), June 1, 1977, at 1 (referring to the British Foreign Secretary and the U.S. State Department).

1074 *Rhodesians 'fighting in Mozambique now'*, THE TIMES (London), June 20, 1977, at 1 (referring to the Southern Rhodesian Minister of Combined Operations).

by Mozambique[1075] proved, again, little understanding for Southern Rhodesia and sometimes even according legal arguments: Mozambique saw itself exposed to yet another aggression by Rhodesia[1076] and was joined by all African states present in the meeting.[1077] Egypt also complained about Rhodesian "international terrorism",[1078] while Zambia accused Southern Rhodesia of genocide.[1079] Angola denounced Southern Rhodesia's reference to "defensive exercises" as "euphemisms", but did not offer a more detailed legal analysis.[1080] Nigeria did not take further reference to alleged self-defense by Southern Rhodesia, but asserted that if the latter could rely on the right to a "hot pursuit", such a right would exist for others as well.[1081] China considered the invocation of self-defense by Southern Rhodesia as "sheer gangster's logic".[1082]

The representative of Lesotho, on the other hand, took some time to explore the unavailability of the "so-called principle of preemptive self-defense", assuming "for the sake of the argument . . . that Rhodesia is a State according to international law." In his view, there had been no prior armed attack "within the confines of classical international law" by Mozambique, which would have been

---

[1075] U.N. Doc. S/12350 (June 22, 1977); U.N. SCOR, 32nd Sess., 2014th mtg., at 2 U.N. Docs. S/PV 2014 (remarks by dos Santos (Mozambique)) (June 28, 1977).

[1076] U.N. SCOR, 32nd Sess., 2014th mtg., at 2 U.N. Docs. S/PV 2014 (remarks by dos Santos (Mozambique)) (June 28, 1977).

[1077] U.N. SCOR, 32nd Sess., 2014th mtg., at 7 U.N. Docs. S/PV 2014 (remarks by Mkapa (Tanzania)) (June 28, 1977); *id.* at 9 (remarks by dos Santos (Angola)); *id.* at 11 (remarks by Djigo (Senegal)); U.N. SCOR, 32nd Sess., 2015th mtg., at 2 U.N. Docs. S/PV 2015 (remarks by Garba (Nigeria)) (June 28, 1977); *id.* at 4 (remarks by C.D. Molapo (Lesotho)); *id.* at 6 (remarks by Houngavou (Benin)); U.N. SCOR, 32nd Sess., 2016th mtg., at 2 U.N. Docs. S/PV 2016 (remarks by Rawiri (Gabon)) (June 29, 1977); *id.* at 3 (remarks by Rahal (Algeria)); *id.* at 4 (remarks by Al Gayed (Libyan Arab Jamahiriya)); U.N. SCOR, 32nd Sess., 2017th mtg., at 3 U.N. Docs. S/PV 2017 (remarks by Medani (Sudan)) (June 29, 1977); *id.* at 7 (remarks by Ramphul (Mauritius)); U.N. SCOR, 32nd Sess., 2018th mtg., at 2 U.N. Docs. S/PV 2018 (remarks by Kwelagobe (Botswana)) (June 30, 1977); U.N. SCOR, 32nd Sess., 2019th mtg., at 1 U.N. Docs. S/PV 2019 (remarks by Malinga (Swaziland)) (June 30, 1977).

[1078] U.N. SCOR, 32nd Sess., 2015th mtg., at 7 U.N. Docs. S/PV 2015 (remarks by Adbel Meguid (Egypt)) (June 28, 1977).

[1079] U.N. SCOR, 32nd Sess., 2014th mtg., at 5 U.N. Docs. S/PV 2014 (remarks by Mwale (Zambia)) (June 28, 1977).

[1080] *Id.* at 9 (remarks by dos Santos (Angola)).

[1081] U.N. SCOR, 32nd Sess., 2015th mtg., at 2 U.N. Docs. S/PV 2015 (remarks by Garba (Nigeria)) (June 28, 1977).

[1082] U.N. SCOR, 32nd Sess., 2018th mtg., at 11 U.N. Docs. S/PV 2018 (remarks by Chen Chu (China)) (June 30, 1977).

necessary to invoke Article 51 of the Charter.[1083] The allegations of Southern Rhodesia as to forceful cross-border raids were apparently not considered as either sufficient or even existing. However, Lesotho's representative had previously acknowledged that there was "an armed struggle of . . . freedom fighters"[1084] against Southern Rhodesia. One the other hand, he did not attribute their actions to Mozambique as he left not doubt that "[n]o one – not even Smith himself – can say that Mozambique has attacked or attempted to attack Rhodesia."[1085] That view can only be explained if guerilla groups (self-proclaimed freedom fighters i.e. non-state actors are *per se*) regarded as incapable of launching an armed attack and thus triggering Article 51 of the Charter. Another possible explanation would be if their actions were simply not considered as amounting to the gravity as required for an "armed attack". If the former interpretation is accurate, it would be one of the few situations in which non-state actors are exempt from the possible actors within the framework of Article 51 of the Charter.

Also the Indian representative spent some time on legal thoughts as to Article 51 of the Charter – albeit from a different angle:

> It must be remembered that we are not dealing with a case of ordinary aggression which, by legal definition, is the use of armed force by one State against another State. We are instead dealing with an armed group, which is regarded as illegal by the international community. It is legitimate for those States threatened by that illegal group . . . and the international community as a whole, to co-operate in order to liquidate that group . . ., if necessary, militarily, and thus liberate the people of Southern Rhodesia . . . .[1086]

It is not entirely clear if by "liquidate" militarily the Indian representative referred to self-defense as a legal foundation, but it appears likely. No other legal justifications for the use of force seem to be available as the Security Council resolutions condemning Rhodesia did not authorize the use of armed force. If, therefore, the Indian representative is of the opinion that individual or collective self-defense is to be applied against "an armed group" that is not an ordinary state – regardless of the accuracy of such assumptions – then the formal nature

[1083] U.N. SCOR, 32nd Sess., 2015th mtg., at 5 U.N. Docs. S/PV 2015 (remarks by C.D. Molapo (Lesotho)) (June 28, 1977).
[1084] *Id.* at 4.
[1085] *Id.* at 5.
[1086] U.N. SCOR, 32nd Sess., 2018th mtg., at 8 U.N. Docs. S/PV 2018 (remarks by Jaipal (India)) (June 30, 1977).

of the attacker is regarded as irrelevant for the exercise of Article 51 of the Charter.

The Federal Republic of Germany,[1087] France,[1088] and the United Kingdom[1089] noted a Rhodesian aggression. The United States "deplored" the Rhodesian attacks.[1090] Accordingly, also the subsequent resolution condemned Rhodesia's aggression and rejected any Southern Rhodesian claims of self-defense.[1091]

The cross-border raids and subsequent Rhodesian operations continued, however, all through 1977.[1092] Especially in 1978, Southern Rhodesia again pointed at its right to self-defense against armed bands, and only those, operating from Zambia[1093] and Mozambique.[1094]

Just like South Africa, the Southern Rhodesian racist regime was under constant pressure, its actions were justified at no times. On the other hand, one argument that was made only implicitly – and that only once – was the general unavailability of self-defense against foreign-based guerilla groups. One speaker even explicitly expressed his support for a right to self-defense against non-state armed bands, even though he was pointing at Mozambique *et al.* in their fight against Southern Rhodesia which was not welcomed into the international community of states. As was noted previously, constant references to an "aggression" by a state do allow to infer that no justification, hence also no self-defense, was regarded as applicable. However, this does not mean that self-defense as a legal concept was excluded only because of the legal nature of the attacker.

f) Portugal's Military Campaigns in Africa

Beginning in the early 1960s inside Portugal's African colonies, several conflicts developed which eventually involved non-state guerillas forces operat-

---

1087 U.N. SCOR, 32nd Sess., 2019th mtg., at 3 U.N. Docs. S/PV 2019 (remarks by von Hassel (Federal Republic of Germany)) (June 30, 1977).

1088 *Id.* at 3 (remarks by Leprette (France)).

1089 *Id.* at 5 (remarks by Richard (United Kingdom)).

1090 *Id.* at 7 (remarks by Young (United States)).

1091 S.C. Res. 411 (June 30, 1977) 1977 U.N.Y.B. 243-44.

1092 *See, e.g.*, Nicholas Ashford, *Rhodesian raid across border lasts six days*, THE TIMES (London), Nov. 28, 1977, at 1.

1093 Nicholas Ashford, Lawrence Pintak, *Rhodesian jets and army strike at base in Zambia*, THE TIMES (London), March 8, 1978, at 1 (quoting a communiqué by Rhodesian officials as describing the raids as "self-defence operation").

1094 Frederick Cleary, *Rhodesians cross into Mozambique to hit bases*, THE TIMES (London), July 31, 1978, at 1 (referring to military command headquarters which described the raids as "self-defensive" action against selected bases); *Rhodesian troops hit Mozambique bases*, THE TIMES (London), Sep. 21, 1978, at 1 (Quoting an official Rhodesian communiqué: "Rhodesian security forces are presently engaged in self-defence operations against Zanla terrorist bases in Mozambique. These operations are not aimed at Mozambique troops or civilians").

ing from host states against targets in victim states, namely the Portuguese colonies Angola, Guinea-Bissau, and Mozambique. In the course of these conflicts, Portugal only occasionally, but explicitly, invoked self-defense according to Article 51 of the Charter.[1095]

On other occasions, Portugal merely denied the accusations and did not refer to specific legal grounds on which it may have acted.[1096] Many states continuously considered the Portuguese recourse to force on the territory of either of the accused state supporters of guerilla action to constitute aggressions.[1097]

One of these conflicts concerned Portugal and its colony in Portuguese-Guinea (Guinea-Bissau) internally,[1098] but eventually Senegal (as of 1961)[1099]

[1095] 1969 U.N.Y.B. 138; 1969 U.N.Y.B. 142; 1971 U.N.Y.B. 117.

[1096] *See, e.g.*, 1963 U.N.Y.B. 24, 25 (Portugal admitted "manoeuvres", but no bombings or overflights concerning Senegal); 1966 U.N.Y.B. 121 (Portugal denied accusations by Congo (Brazzaville) concerning air space violations); 1966 U.N.Y.B. 122 (Portugal denied accusations by Tanzania and Zambia concerning military operations); 1970 U.N.Y.B. 187 (Portugal denied charges regarding Guinea's accusations of prior attacks against targets in Conacry, Guinea); 1970 U.N.Y.B. 191-92 (Portugal denied accusations concerning cross-border attacks into Senegal and accused in return Senegalese bands from attacking targets inside Guinea-Bissau); 1971 U.N.Y.B. 116, 120 (Portugal denied accusations by Senegal and Guinea concerning acts of aggression).

[1097] *See, e.g.*, Algeria 1969 U.N.Y.B. 139, 1969 U.N.Y.B. 142, 1970 U.N.Y.B. 189; Democratic Republic of Congo 1969 U.N.Y.B. 136; Cuba 1970 U.N.Y.B. 189; Ethiopia 1970 U.N.Y.B. 189; Finland 1970 U.N.Y.B. 189; Gabon 1969 U.N.Y.B. 136; Haiti 1970 U.N.Y.B. 189; Hungary 1969 U.N.Y.B. 139, 1969 U.N.Y.B. 142; India 1970 U.N.Y.B. 189; Kenya 1969 U.N.Y.B. 136; Liberia 1969 U.N.Y.B. 136, 1969 U.N.Y.B. 139, 1970 U.N.Y.B. 189; Madagascar 1969 U.N.Y.B. 136; Mali 1970 U.N.Y.B. 189; Nepal 1969 U.N.Y.B. 136, 1969 U.N.Y.B. 142; Pakistan 1969 U.N.Y.B. 136, 1969 U.N.Y.B. 142; Poland 1970 U.N.Y.B. 189, 1971 U.N.Y.B. 118, 1971 U.N.Y.B. 120-21; Sierra Leone 1969 U.N.Y.B. 139, 1970 U.N.Y.B. 189, 1971 U.N.Y.B. 118; Somalia 1969 U.N.Y.B. 136, 1971 U.N.Y.B. 118, 1971 U.N.Y.B. 119; Syria 1970 U.N.Y.B. 189, 1971 U.N.Y.B. 118, 1971 U.N.Y.B. 119; Uganda 1970 U.N.Y.B. 189; United Arab Republic 1969 U.N.Y.B. 136, 1969 U.N.Y.B. 139; United Republic of Tanzania 1969 U.N.Y.B. 136; USSR 1969 U.N.Y.B. 139, 1969 U.N.Y.B. 142, 1971 U.N.Y.B. 118, 1971 U.N.Y.B. 119, 1971 U.N.Y.B. 120-21, 1972 U.N.Y.B. 137; western states did also refuse to show sympathy for Portugal and rejected violations of the integrity of foreign states; *see, e.g.*, France 1969 U.N.Y.B. 139, 1972 U.N.Y.B. 137; Spain 1969 U.N.Y.B. 139.

[1098] *See, e.g.*, *Tension in Portugal's Oversea Territories*, THE TIMES (London), March 16, 1960, at 10 (reporting that, while clashes at other Portuguese colonies remain unclear, from "Portuguese Guinea it was unofficially reported that in August, 1959, 50 persons were killed in a clash between African strikers and police at Bissau").

[1099] *See, e.g.*, 1963 U.N.Y.B. 24-26 (also referencing to incidents as early as 1961); 1967 U.N.Y.B. 131; 1969 U.N.Y.B. 137-40;); 1970 U.N.Y.B. 191-92; U.N. SCOR, 26th Sess., 1569th mtg., at 2-6, U.N. Doc. S/PV.1569 (remarks by Gaye (Senegal)) (July 12, 1971); 1972

and Guinea as well.[1100] Portugal complained about armed bands, mainly the African Party for the Independence of Guinea and Cape Verde (Partido Africano da Independência de Guiné e Cabo Verde, PAIGC). PAIGC operated from and was supported by the neighboring countries, attacking Portuguese forces in Guinea-Bissau to reach the colony's independence.[1101] PAIGC's headquarters were located in Conacry, the capital of the neighboring Republic of Guinea.[1102] Portugal fought PAIGC militarily in Guinea-Bissau as well as inside all neighboring countries which it blamed for supporting PAIGC.[1103] In 1973,

U.N.Y.B. 136; *see also, e.g., Senegal warning to Portugal*, THE TIMES (London), Dec. 31, 1969, at 5 (quoting Senegalese President Senghor as having said that "Senegal would reply to any shelling of its villages by the Portuguese from neighbouring Guinea . . . .").

1100 *See, e.g.*, 1967 U.N.Y.B. 131; 1969 U.N.Y.B. 140-43; 1970 U.N.Y.B. 187-91; 1971 U.N.Y.B. 119-21; *see also, e.g., Guinea seeks planes to fight raiders*, THE TIMES (London), Nov. 26, 1970, at 6 (stating that Guinean President Touré appealed "to all 'friendly countries' to supply him with bomber and fighter aircraft to fight to fight a new series of 'enemy incursions'" by Portugal); Michael Leapman, *UN Team back Guinea charges against Portugal on invasion*, THE TIMES (London), Dec. 3, 1970, at 6; on one occasion, Guinea also complained about Senegal's support to "elements preparing aggression against Guinea" but then withdrew its complaint, *see* 1973 U.N.Y.B. 149.

1101 1969 U.N.Y.B. 136; *see also, e.g., Portuguese Guinea Entered*, THE TIMES (London), July 26, 1961, at 10 (stating that, according to a Portuguese Ministry, approx. 200 intruders "entered Portuguese Guinea from Senegal . . . cut telephone wires and damaged some villas. . . ." Previously, on July 21, "50 Senegalese had attacked a Portuguese military barracks [sic] on the Senegal-Guinea frontier"); *Part of Portuguese Guinea in Rebel Hands*, THE TIMES (London), July 18, 1963, at 10 (stating that Portugal's Defense Minister, Gomes de Araujo, complained that "in the north of [Guinea-Bissau] terrorist groups, mostly from Senegal, had made incursions into the territory . . . .").

1102 *Guinea's vital self-reliance*, THE TIMES (London), Nov. 24, 1970, at 12.

1103 *See, e.g.*, 1966 U.N.Y.B. 122; 1967 U.N.Y.B. 131; 1969 U.N.Y.B. 136; *see also, e.g., Portuguese Denial on Insurgents*, THE TIMES (London), Apr. 12, 1965, at 9 (stating that the Secretary-General of PAIGC, Cabral, claimed that Portugal only exercised full control over the capital, Bissau. Portugal denied such claims); *Portugal's Black Africa*, THE TIMES (London), Apr. 7, 1967, at 13 (stating that "[t]he nationalists have the advantage that they can operate from the African states which border on Portuguese frontiers . . . ."); Basil Davidson, *Unknown war in Portuguese West Africa*, THE TIMES (London), Nov. 10, 1967, at 9 (reporting that "[r]ear support from the neighbouring republics of Guinea and Senegal helps to explain some of [PAIGC's] success. Thanks to it, P.A.I.G.C. commanders can move their military and civilian supplies across the frontier with not difficulty . . . .); another Portuguese denial of an alleged raid into Conacry, Guinea, occurred in November 1970, 1970 U.N.Y.B. 187.

PAIGC declared Guinea-Bissau's independence from Portugal.[1104] Portugal finally recognized this independence in 1974.[1105]

The Security Council repeatedly criticized or condemned Portugal for its recourse to force against Senegal and Guinea.[1106]

The factual situation was, however, unclear due to a lack of impartial reports confirming some of the allegations – which sometimes occurred even among the states Portugal accused of sheltering guerillas –[1107] particularly with regard to the actual degree of state involvement on either side. Spain, the United Kingdom, and the United States at some point even regarded themselves as unable to support further United Nations Security Council actions,[1108] such as, for instance, sanctions against Portugal. One of the unclear circumstances was in how far PAIGC actions were in fact exercised by regular Senegalese troops.[1109] Accordingly, Portugal seems to have directed its foreign incursions directly against the state of Senegal, rather than against guerillas operating from Senegalese soil,[1110] but later apologized for this attack and the death of regular Senegalese troops.[1111] This could not prevent the majority of states from considering also this Portuguese intervention into Senegal an aggression.[1112] The Security Council condemned Portugal once again.[1113]

[1104] 1973 U.N.Y.B. 143-47; *See also Recognition of 'Guinea-Bissau state' spreads,* THE TIMES (London), Sept. 28, 1973, at 7.

[1105] *Lisbon hands over Guinea-Bissau,* THE TIMES (London), Aug. 27, 1974, at 1.

[1106] *See, e.g.,* S.C. Res. 178 (Apr. 24, 1963) 1963 U.N.Y.B. 26; S.C. Res. 204 (May 19, 1965), 1965 U.N.Y.B. 136; S.C. Res. 273 (Dec. 9, 1969), 1969 U.N.Y.B. 144; S.C. Res. 275 (Dec. 22, 1969), 1969 U.N.Y.B. 145; S.C. Res. 289 (Nov. 22, 1970), 1970 U.N.Y.B. 192; S.C. Res. 290 (Dec. 8, 1970), 1970 U.N.Y.B. 193; S.C. Res. 294 (July 15, 1971), 1971 U.N.Y.B. 121-22; S.C. Res. 302 (Nov. 24, 1971), 1971 U.N.Y.B. 122; S.C. Res. 321 (Oct. 23, 1972), 1972 U.N.Y.B. 138; also the United Nations General Assembly condemned Portugal; *see, e.g.,* G.A. Res. 3061 (XXVIII) (Nov. 2, 1973), 1973 U.N.Y.B. 146-47.

[1107] *See, e.g.,* allegations of Guinea that Senegal – not Portugal – was supporting "elements" planning aggression against Guinea. The complaint was ultimately withdrawn, 1973 U.N.Y.B. 149.

[1108] 1969 U.N.Y.B. 137; *see also id.* at 143.

[1109] *Id.* at 138-39.

[1110] Such as an attack on a regular Senegalese army post at Nianao by Portuguese army, 1972 U.N.Y.B. 136-38.

[1111] U.N. Doc. S/10810 (Oct. 18, 1972).

[1112] Algeria: U.N. SCOR, 27th Sess., 1667th mtg., at 7, U.N. Doc. S/PV.1667 (remarks by Rahal (Algeria)) (Oct. 19, 1972); China: U.N. SCOR, 27th Sess., 1668th mtg., at 3, U.N. Doc. S/PV.1668 (remarks by Chen (China)) (Oct. 20, 1972); Guinea: U.N. SCOR, 27th Sess., 1667th mtg., at 6, U.N. Doc. S/PV.1667 (remarks by Cisse (Guinea)) (Oct. 19, 1972); Mali: U.N. SCOR, 27th Sess., 1668th mtg., at 3, U.N. Doc. S/PV.1668 (remarks by Traore (Mali)) (Oct. 20, 1972); Mauritania: U.N. SCOR, 27th Sess., 1667th mtg., at 5, U.N. Doc. S/PV.1667

The second, quite similar, conflict erupted between Portugal and forces attempting to establish autonomous regimes for the Portuguese colonies in Angola and Mozambique. This conflict also concerned neighboring states which harbored the anti-Portuguese guerillas. Beginning in the early 1960s, local Angolan groups such as MPLA, FNLA, and UNITA[1114] began to rise against the Portuguese rulers,[1115] as did the Liberation Front of Mozambique (Frente de Libertação de Moçambique, FRELIMO).[1116]

Among the states that were suspected by Portugal of sheltering anti-Portuguese militias supporting the uprising in Angola and Mozambique was the DRC.[1117] Here, again, it was not always clear who it actually was that infiltrated Angola from the DRC. Sometimes the suspected guerillas wore Congolese military uniforms.[1118] And while the DRC complained repeatedly about Portuguese military incursions,[1119] it also blamed Portugal for supporting "mercenaries" using Angola as a base for launching armed attacks against the DRC,[1120] allegedly because the DRC had accepted Angola's exiled revolutionary government.[1121] The Security Council repeatedly condemned Portugal, mostly for the use of

---

(remarks by El Hassen (Mauritania)) (Oct. 19, 1972); Panama: U.N. SCOR, 27th Sess., 1668th mtg., at 7, U.N. Doc. S/PV.1668 (remarks by Boyd (Panama)) (Oct. 20, 1972); Somalia: *id.* at 1 (remarks by Nur Elmi (Somalia)); Soviet Union: U.N. SCOR, 27th Sess., 1667th mtg., at 12, U.N. Doc. S/PV.1667 (remarks by Malik (Soviet Union)) (Oct. 19, 1972); Sudan: *id.* at 8, (remarks by Abdulla (Sudan)); Yugoslavia: *id.* at 10 (remarks by Mojsov (Yugoslavia)).

1113 S.C. Res. 321 (Oct. 23, 1972), 1972 U.N.Y.B. 138-39.

1114 *See supra* note 662.

1115 *See, e.g., Tension in Portugal's Oversea Territories*, THE TIMES (London), March 16, 1960, at 10.

1116 Mocimbo da Praia, *Holding the guerillas in Mozambique*, THE TIMES (London), Nov. 21, 1966, at 7 (referring to FRELIMO's leader Eduardo Mondlane, stating that "the guerillas have killed 3,000 Portuguese and wounded 4,000 . . . ." since 1964); *Portuguese take rebel bases*, THE TIMES (London), July 29, 1970, at 5 (referring to a Portuguese military communiqué which stated that "scores of Frelimo . . . bases had fallen to the Portuguese forces" operating in northern Mozambique); Dan van der Vat, *Mozambique guerilla loses*, THE TIMES (London) , Dec. 23, 1970, at 8 (referring to Portuguese military officials as estimating that FRELIMO had "between 5,000 and 6,000 armed men operating in [Mozambique's] Cabo Delgado district . . . .").

1117 *See, e.g., Terrorists from Tanganyika,* THE TIMES (London), Oct. 12, 1964, at 11.

1118 *Many killed in Angola wave of attacks*, THE TIMES (London), Apr. 15, 1961, at 8 (quoting Portuguese newspapers as reporting that "[h]undreds of terrorists came over the [Congolese] border into the Cabinda enclave [, a disputed Angolan province] . . . . Many of them wore Congolese uniforms . . . .").

1119 *See, e.g.,*1967 U.N.Y.B. 123-30; 1968 U.N.Y.B. 159; 1974 U.N.Y.B. 172.

1120 1966 U.N.Y.B. 117-21; 1967 U.N.Y.B. 123-31.

1121 1966 U.N.Y.B. 118.

armed force,[1122] but also for the "recruitment and training, as well as transport and supply of arms . . . ." to armed bands operating from Angola, attacking targets in the DRC.[1123]

However, self-defense against a non-state actor was not an issue here. The DRC did not refer to either Article 51 of the Charter or customary justifications for a possible recourse to force. Had it done so, it would have been against the state of Portugal acting through mercenaries. The latter's existence and support through Portugal was at stake, not the general possibility to attribute such a force's action to their master. Portugal on the other hand seemed, as in the case of Senegal, rather to be attributing full responsibility to the government of the DRC for its support of guerillas.

Another state that repeatedly complained about Portuguese incursions was the Republic of Zambia.[1124] One of the events Zambia complained about before the Security Council was an attack near the village of Lote in June 1969.[1125] As previously,[1126] Portugal did not merely complain about "hostile elements" harbored by Zambia, but suspected also Zambian armed forces to participate in armed attacks against Portuguese colonies. Otherwise, Portugal announced that Zambia was violating its international obligations by not confining attacks on Portuguese forces emanating from Zambian territory against which Portugal could rely on Article 51 of the Charter.[1127]

Most states, on the other hand, considered Portugal's action an aggression.[1128] The United Kingdom deplored all loss of life and the "continuation of

---

1122 *See, e.g.*, S.C. Res. 226 (Oct. 14, 1966), 1966 U.N.Y.B. 121; S.C. Res. 239 (July 10, 1967), 1967 U.N.Y.B. 130; S.C. Res. 241 (Nov. 15, 1967), 1967 U.N.Y.B. 130-31.

1123 S.C. Res. 241 (Nov. 15, 1967), 1967 U.N.Y.B. 131.

1124 *See, e.g.*, 1966 U.N.Y.B. 122; 1968 U.N.Y.B. 159-60; U.N. SCOR, 24th Sess., 1486th mtg., at 2-5, U.N. Doc. S/PV.1486 (remarks by Mwaanga (Zambia)) (July 18, 1969).

1125 1969 U.N.Y.B. 135-37.

1126 *Zambia accuses Portugal of border explosions*, THE TIMES (London), July 22, 1966, at 8.

1127 U.N. SCOR, 24th Sess., 1486th mtg., at 8, U.N. Doc. S/PV.1486 (remarks by Miranda (Portugal)) (July 18, 1969).

1128 Algeria: U.N. SCOR, 24th Sess., 1486th mtg., at 11, U.N. Doc. S/PV.1486 (remarks by Azzout (Algeria)) (July 18, 1969); Democratic Republic of Congo: U.N. SCOR, 24th Sess., 1490th mtg., at 2, U.N. Doc. S/PV.1490 (remarks by Nguza (Democratic Republic of Congo)) (July 25, 1969); Gabon: U.N. SCOR, 24th Sess., 1489th mtg., at 2, U.N. Doc. S/PV.1489 (remarks by Davin (Gabon)) (July 24, 1969); Hungary: U.N. SCOR, 24th Sess., 1487th mtg., at 3, U.N. Doc. S/PV.1487 (remarks by Csatorday (Hungary)) (July 22, 1969); Kenya: U.N. SCOR, 24th Sess., 1488th mtg., at 6, U.N. Doc. S/PV.1488 (remarks by Osanya-Nyyneque (Kenya)) (July 23, 1969); Liberia: U.N. SCOR, 24th Sess., 1489th mtg., at 5, U.N. Doc. S/PV.1489 (remarks by Diggs (Liberia)) (July 24, 1969); Sierra Leone: *id.* at 7, (remarks by Savage (Sierra Leone)); Somalia: U.N. SCOR, 24th Sess., 1487th mtg., at 5, U.N. Doc. S/PV.1487 (remarks by Farah (Somalia)) (July 22, 1969); Soviet Union: U.N. SCOR, 24th

these incidents".[1129] Spain noted that both Zambia and Portugal had submitted accusations, leaving an unclear picture.[1130] The Security Council condemned Portugal.[1131]

Also Tanzania was accused of allowing guerillas, namely FRELIMO, to use its territory before crossing the border into northern Mozambique and attack Portuguese targets. Portugal's counter-measure seem, however, to have concentrated on preventing FRELIMO to cross the border rather than attacking targets in Tanzania.[1132]

Generally, Portugal was rather directing its armed force at the regimes that it blamed for supporting PAIGC in Guinea-Bissau and groups operating against Portuguese targets in Angola and Mozambique. Again, that would point to the direction of attribution issues rather than shedding more light on the problem of recourse to force against non-state actors. In either case, the argument that PAIGC or others were "immune" to Portuguese self-defense due to their plain legal nature as non-state actor was not made explicitly.

g) ISRAEL'S AIR RAID AGAINST THE PLO IN TUNIS

One example of a rather small-scale attempt to exercise self-defense against a non-state actor, despite the latter's well known position, were the 1985 Israeli attacks on the PLO headquarters in Tunisia,[1133] which were largely re-

---

Sess., 1488th mtg., at 3, U.N. Doc. S/PV.1488 (remarks by Zakharov (Soviet Union)) (July 23, 1969); Tanzania: U.N. SCOR, 24th Sess., 1487th mtg., at 5, U.N. Doc. S/PV.1487 (remarks by Foum (Tanzania)) (July 22, 1969); United Arab Republic: U.N. SCOR, 24th Sess., 1488th mtg., at 10, U.N. Doc. S/PV.1488 (remarks by El-Erian (United Arab Republic)) (July 23, 1969).

[1129] U.N. SCOR, 24th Sess., 1491st mtg., at 2, U.N. Doc. S/PV.1491 (remarks by Hildyard (United Kingdom)) (July 28, 1969).

[1130] U.N. SCOR, 24th Sess., 1491st mtg., at 2, U.N. Doc. S/PV.1491 (remarks by Cañadas (Spain)) (July 28, 1969).

[1131] S.C. Res. 268 (July 28, 1969), 1969 U.N.Y.B. 143-44.

[1132] *Tanzan troops on Mozambique border*, THE TIMES (London), Oct. 20, 1964, at 9 (referring to Portuguese reports "that guerilla fighters had entered Mozambique from Tanganyika, and accused the United Republic [of Tanzania, composed of Tanganyika and Zanzibar, established in 1964] of being a base for subversion"); *Portugal tries to seal border in Mozambique*, THE TIMES (London), Dec. 4, 1970, at 8 (referring to a Portuguese military communiqué and stating that "Portuguese troops were . . . trying to seal the northern Mozambique border with Tanzania to halt infiltration by African nationalists").

[1133] Ian Murray, Robert Fist, *Israel bombs PLO headquarters in Tunis revenge raid*, THE TIMES (London), Oct. 2, 1985, at 1.

garded as disproportionate,[1134] and condemned by the Security Council as an "armed aggression".[1135]

Israel had announced that its actions against the PLO were a "legitimate response to acts of terrorism" in exercise of self-defense. Israel referred not only two the killing of three Israelis immediately prior to the Tunis raid but also to "more than 600 attacks" in the past twelve months.[1136] As to the host state, the Israeli representative accused Tunisia that it – unlike the incapable Lebanese government – "knowingly harboured the PLO and allowed it complete freedom of action in planning, training, organizing and launching murderous attacks from its soil." Since Tunisia was thus regarded to have been in violation of its duty not to allow its soil to be used as springboard for armed groups against other states "it risks taking upon itself all the consequences of such dereliction of duty." As no other remedies were available to Israel, it saw itself legally justified to invoke Article 51 of the Charter in the present case.[1137]

From these words it is not entirely clear if Israel perhaps sought to attribute PLO terror to Tunisia – rather than defending itself directly against the PLO directly – by virtue of Tunisia's failure to confine the non-state actor on its territory. On the other hand, Israel's spokesman made clear that the ". . . limited [and] surgical strike [was] aimed at the culprits, *and at the culprits alone*. . . the target was the headquarters of the PLO, the nerve centre of its world-wide operations. . . ."[1138] Tunisia, by inference, had to endure the violation of its sovereignty i.e. the destruction of buildings situated in Tunis, because it failed to control the buildings' occupant PLO. It appears likely that Israel invoked self-defense against the PLO, not Tunisia. Consequently, it seems more plausible to assume that Tunisia's omissions were not regarded as reasons to attribute a non-state actor's actions to a state, but rather that only PLO committed the alleged armed attack and thus triggered Israel's invocation of Article 51 of the Charter.

Tunisia regarded itself as a victim of "a blatant act of aggression against the territorial integrity, sovereignty and independence of Tunisia and a flagrant violation of the rules and norms of international law. . . ."[1139]

1134 *See, e.g.*, Erich H. Singer, *Terrorist Attacks on Nationals: The Lawful Use of Force Against Terrorist Bases on Foreign Soil*, 1 TERRORISM AND POL. VIOLENCE 435, 442-45 (1989).

1135 S.C. Res. 573 (Oct. 4, 1985) 1985 U.N.Y.B. 287.

1136 U.N. SCOR, 40th Sess., 2611th mtg., at 5 U.N. Docs. S/PV 2611 (remarks by Netanyahu (Israel)) (Oct. 2, 1985).

1137 *Id.* at 6.

1138 *Id.* at 5 (emphasis added).

1139 U.N. SCOR, 40th Sess., 2610th mtg., at 2 U.N. Docs. S/PV 2610 (remarks by Essebsi (Tunisia)) (Oct. 2, 1985).

Initial responses by U.S. officials were not entirely consistent: President Reagan announced that Israel was entitled to retaliate against prior PLO terror attacks, while Secretary of State Shultz expressed its administration's depreciation. Then again, the White House considered Israel's raid as an "understandable" expression of self-defense.[1140] In the course of the Security Council deliberations, the American representative explained the U.S. abstention in the Security Council's vote on October 4, 1985 was based upon the disproportionate allocation of blame for the – deplorable – acts of violence in Tunis on Israel "while not also holding at fault those responsible for the terrorist acts which provoked it." And, "a State subjected to continuing terrorist attacks may respond with appropriate use of force to defend itself against further attacks. This is an aspect of the inherent right of self-defence recognized in the Charter of the United Nations. We support this principle regardless of attacker, and regardless of victim."[1141] Accordingly, the U.S. representative was mostly concerned about the manner in which Israel had exercised its otherwise clearly existing right to defend itself against a series – not just one – of terrorist attacks by a non-state actor.

France regarded Israel "in violation of the rules of international law" and its actions as inexcusable.[1142] France's reaction does not quite allow one to infer why precisely international law did not provide an excuse. Denmark was of the opinion that condemnable terrorist attacks on Israel could not justify such a reaction and thus equally condemned it.[1143] That could mean that the Danish representative regarded the PLO's actions *per se* not capable of triggering the right to self-defense, as one possible justification for such a military response. However, other reasons are also conceivable, for instance a lack of gravity in the PLO's immediately prior attacks on Cyprus. Algeria,[1144] China,[1145] Greece,[1146] Peru,[1147] and the Soviet Union[1148] and others chose not to elaborate on such causes, but

1140 Mohsin Ali, *Washington denies Israel raid on PLO was described as terrorist act*, THE TIMES (London), Oct. 24, 1985, at 7.
1141 U.N. SCOR, 40th Sess., 2615th mtg., at 22 U.N. Docs. S/PV 2615 (remarks by de Walters (United States)) (Oct. 4, 1985).
1142 U.N. SCOR, 40th Sess., 2611th mtg., at 2 U.N. Docs. S/PV 2611 (remarks by de Kémoularia (France)) (Oct. 2, 1985).
1143 *Id.* at 2 (remarks by Bierring (Denmark)).
1144 *Id.* at 7 (remarks by Taleb Ibrahimi (Algeria)).
1145 *Id.* at 3 (remarks by Huang Jiahua (China)).
1146 U.N. SCOR, 40th Sess., 2613th mtg., at 10 U.N. Docs. S/PV 2613 (remarks by Dountas (Greece)) (Oct. 3, 1985).
1147 U.N. SCOR, 40th Sess., 2611th mtg., at 3 U.N. Docs. S/PV 2611 (remarks by Alzamora (Peru)) (Oct. 2, 1985).
1148 *Id.* at 8 (remarks by Troyanovsky (Soviet Union)).

simply condemned Israel's aggression. The representative of Madagascar rejected Israel's reference to self-defense, rather considering its actions as preemptive attacks and reprisals.[1149] Turkey joined those condemning the raid as an aggression but elaborated in greater detail on why it did so: armed force could be justified as a reprisal;[1150] Israel had not engaged in prior peaceful deliberations; the attack was executed indiscriminately, and the actual perpetrators had already been arrested.[1151] The Thai representative focused on the fact that Israel's illegal retaliation was in disregard of the principle of proportionality.[1152] Australia saw Israel in breach of international law due to the use of violence and also saw "the question of the strength of the response to the alleged actions that were used to justify Israel's reaction."[1153] With the latter, the Australian representative seems to refer to proportionality issues.

The United Kingdom also criticized Israel primarily stating that "[a]rbitrary and disproportionate violence of this sort, even in retaliation, is in clear breach of [Article 2 of the Charter]." The British representative continued that "even if there had been demonstrable responsibility by the PLO [for the murder of three Israelis in Cyprus], this would not have justified the retaliation taken against Tunisia. . . ."[1154] Again, these remarks are not completely clear with regard to the question if the legal nature of the PLO as a non-state actor makes self-defense unavailable for Israel. Military retaliation – self-defense is not mentioned by the British representative – appears generally justifiable, but only within the limits of proportionality. The second statement also appears to point to this direction, but it could also mean that since it would have been the PLO's responsibility – and hence not for instance Tunisia's – retaliatory counter-force had to be illegitimate.

Egypt could not "understand the position of some that see Israel's right to revenge for its citizens when it undertakes actions that kill innocent people or when it threatens the sovereignty and territorial integrity of other States" but rather considered Israel's actions as an aggression as well.[1155] By this, it appears as if the Egyptian representative seeks to deny any right to military counter-

---

[1149] U.N. SCOR, 40th Sess., 2613th mtg., at 3 U.N. Docs. S/PV 2613 (remarks by Rabetafika (Madagascar)) (Oct. 3, 1985).
[1150] U.N. SCOR, 40th Sess., 2611th mtg., at 3 U.N. Docs. S/PV 2611 (remarks by Halefoğlu (Turkey)) (Oct. 2, 1985).
[1151] *Id.* at 4 (remarks by Halefoğlu (Turkey)).
[1152] *Id.* at 4 (remarks by Kasemsarn (Thailand)).
[1153] *Id.* at 5 (remarks by Woolcott (Australia)).
[1154] *Id.* at 9 (remarks by Sir Thomson (United Kingdom)).
[1155] U.N. SCOR, 40th Sess., 2610th mtg., at 7 U.N. Docs. S/PV 2610 (remarks by Khalil (Egypt)) (Oct. 2, 1985).

measures in cases of attacks against a state's civilians – disregarding both the magnitude and the origin of such attacks.

Coming to a conclusion, Israel was once again at the center of criticism. Most states did not follow the arguments Israel had put forward as to the exercise of self-defense against the PLO. Some states focused on a lack of proportionality in Israel's actions, hinting that perhaps self-defense as a concept might have been available and hence not illegitimate *per se*. The United States clearly supported self-defense irrespective of the nature of the attacker but also deplored the use of violence in general, but particularly by Israel. No state expressly denied Israel's self-defense based upon the attacker being a non-state actor.

h) TAJIKISTAN'S MILITARY RESPONSES AGAINST AFGHANISTAN

Shortly after the outbreak of a civil war in 1992, the newly independent country of Tajikistan faced incursions from armed Afghan bands that crossed the Tajik-Afghan border in order to support local rebel groups engaged in the civil uprising.[1156] Together, they managed to gain control over entire cities and villages. Combined Tajik and Russian forces struggled to regain control over the former Soviet Republic for several years. Tajikistan did not explicitly refer to self-defense to fight such incursions but at all times reserved the right to military counter-force on its own territory.

All through 1993, Tajikistan fought armed bands which attacked Tajik installations.[1157] In mid-1993 Tajikistan complained to the Security Council about an incursion of 200 Afghan "mujahidin". Tajikistan announced that it would repel "any aggressive action . . . with all available means."[1158] Accordingly, Tajik and Russian forces attacked rebel targets inside Afghanistan.[1159] The Security Council eventually issued a statement in which it "stressed the urgent need for the cessation of all hostile actions on the Tajik-Afghan border."[1160] In September 1993, Kazakhstan, Kyrgyzstan, the Russian Federation, Tajikistan, and Uzbeki-

---

[1156] For an overview over the history of the conflict *see* Serge Schmemann, *War Bleeds Ex-Soviet Land at Central Asia's Heart*, N.Y. TIMES, Feb. 21, 1993, at 11.

[1157] *See, e.g., Tajik Forces Report Retaking Bases From Islamic Militants,* N.Y. TIMES, Feb. 22, 1993, at A6; *45 Reported Killed in a Clash in Tajikistan,* N.Y. TIMES, July 19, 1993, at A2; *Schwere Gefechte in Tadschikistan*, FRANKFURTER ALLGEMEINE ZEITUNG, Feb. 25, 1993, at 1 ("In Tadschikistan haben muslimische Kämpfer nach Angaben der Regierung in einem Hinterhalt 118 Soldaten getötet"); *Clash at Tajik-Afghan Border*, N.Y. TIMES, Oct. 8, 1993, at A8.

[1158] U.N. Doc. S/26091 (July 16, 1993) at 2.

[1159] *Angriff auf Tadschiken in Afghanistan,* FRANKFURTER ALLGEMEINE ZEITUNG, July 23, 1993, at 5 ("Russische Artillerie hat am Donnerstag nach offiziellen Angaben Stellungen tadschikischer Rebellen in Afghanistan beschossen").

[1160] U.N. Doc. S/26341 (Aug. 23, 1993).

stan agreed to form a peace-keeping force,[1161] which, according to Tajikistan, significantly helped to decrease the conflict which, however, still continued due to "foreign instructors [in the adjacent territory of Afghanistan that] are training armed bands, which carry out regular armed incursions into Tajikistan." Tajikistan nonetheless also "welcome[d] efforts of the Afghan authorities to improve the situation on the border with Tajikistan. . . ."[1162] According to a subsequent report of the Secretary General, however, "[c]ross-border infiltration by armed opposition groups from the territory of Afghanistan and fighting between them and government and CIS forces occur on a daily basis."[1163]

Early in 1994, Tajikistan again emphasized its "right to take firm and decisive measures to halt such provocations," by which it referred to "[a]rmed groups of members of the anti-Government opposition who have found refuge in the territory of the Islamic State of Afghanistan are continuing to violate the [Tajik-Afghan] frontier . . . ."[1164]

The cross-border incursions by Muslim extremists based in Afghanistan[1165] and counter-raids by Tajik and Russian forces continued nonetheless.[1166] A cease-fire negotiated under auspices of the United Nations also eventually failed and the fighting continued through 1996.[1167] The civil war and with it for-

---

[1161] For the according agreement *see* U.N. Doc. S/26610 (Oct. 21, 1993).

[1162] U.N. Doc. S/26659 (Oct. 27, 1993) at 1, 2.

[1163] U.N. Dos. S/26743 (Nov. 14, 1993) at 2.

[1164] U.N. Doc. S/1994/235 (March 1, 1994) at 2, 3.

[1165] *See, e.g., Angriff auf russische Soldaten in Tadschikistan*, FRANKFURTER ALLGEMEINE ZEITUNG, Aug. 24, 1994, at 2 ("Am vergangenen Freitag waren bei einem Vorstoß der Rebellen aus ihren Stützpunkten im benachbarten Afghanistan sieben russische Soldaten und 50 Angreifer ums Leben gekommen"); *Kämpfe in Tadschikistan*, FRANKFURTER ALLGEMEINE ZEITUNG, Apr. 10, 1995, at 5 ("Seit Freitag toben heftige Kämpfe zwischen der tadschikischen Opposition, die von Afghanistan aus operiert, und den Grenztruppen, die im Rahmen von GUS-Beschlüssen stationiert wurden"); *Tote bei Kämpfen in Tadschikistan*, FRANKFURTER ALLGEMEINE ZEITUNG, May 16, 1995, at 2 ("Wie die Nachrichtenagentur Itar-Tass am Montag unter Berufung auf das Hauptquartier der russischen Genzwachen in Tadschikistan meldete, wurden bei dem Angriff der Rebellen auf einen Grenzposten ferner fünf tadschikische Soldaten verletzt").

[1166] *Islamic Rebels Flee Afghan Border*, N.Y. TIMES, Aug. 20, 1994, at 16; *Russische Bombenangriffe auf Ziele in Afghanistan*, FRANKFURTER ALLGEMEINE ZEITUNG, Jan. 06, 1995, at 1; *Russischer Generalstab dementiert Luftangriff in Afghanistan,* FRANKFURTER ALLGEMEINE ZEITUNG, Apr. 15, 1995, at 5 ("Die russische Armee geht seit mehreren Tagen auch in Afghanistan gegen islamische Rebellen vor, die die Regierung im benachbarten Tadschikistan mit Waffengewalt bekämpfen").

[1167] *Nach Waffenstillstand wieder Kämpfe in Tadschikistan,* FRANKFURTER ALLGEMEINE ZEITUNG, July 24, 1996, at 1; *Russische Truppen in Tadschikistan töten 14 Rebellen,* FRANKFURTER ALLGEMEINE ZEITUNG, Aug. 5, 1996, at 6; *Russische Truppen an der tadschikisch-*

eign incursions only ceased in mid-1997 by virtue of a December 1996 peace agreement.[1168]

As on many prior occasions, legal statements were rare in the course of this conflict that was fuelled by several controversial interests, among them Russia's claim for continuing dominance in one of its former satellite republics and the latter's doubtful new regime. None of the involved powers clearly invoked Article 51 of the Charter, but Russia and Tajikistan used according rhetoric to justify their cross-border military actions into Afghanistan. No state seems to have protested against these based upon the legal nature of the armed bands operating from within Afghanistan.

i) Israel's Military Responses Against Targets in Syria

In 2003, Israel complained to the Security Council and invoked self-defense against Syrian-based terror groups in response to a suicide bombing in Haifa killing 19 Israeli civilians. Almost no state shared Israel's interpretation of the concept of self-defense and hence its applicability *in casu.* Only the United States expressed understanding. On the other hand, no state explicitly rejected self-defense based upon the legal nature of the entity, the Islamic Jihad, which had previously attacked Israel and was in return fought by Israel inside Syria.

Before the Security Council, Syria condemned Israel's air raid as "aggression"[1169] and was joined by Algeria,[1170] the Arab League of States,[1171] Bahrain,[1172] Egypt,[1173] Iran,[1174] Kuwait,[1175] Lebanon,[1176] Saudi Arabia,[1177] Tunisia,[1178] and others. Later, in the course of one of the frequent General Assembly sessions condemning the Israeli occupation of the West Bank, Gaza, and East

---

afghanischen Grenze, FRANKFURTER ALLGEMEINE ZEITUNG, Oct. 7, 1996, at 7; *Heftige Kämpfe in Tadschikistan*, FRANKFURTER ALLGEMEINE ZEITUNG, Dec. 2, 1996, at 8 ("Nach einem Überraschungsangriff muslimischer Rebellen im Osten Tadschikistans hat sich die Lage in der mittelasiatischen Republik zugespitzt . . . . Die Truppen der Opposition operieren teilweise von Afghanistan aus und kontrollieren große Gebiete im Osten des Landes").

1168 *Tajik Adversaries Sign a Cease-Fire*, N.Y. TIMES, Dec. 24, 1996, at 6; *Hopes for Peace Pact Gain in Tajikistan*, N.Y. TIMES, May 19, 1997, at A4.

1169 U.N. SCOR, 58th Sess., 4836th mtg., at 3, U.N. Doc. S/PV.4836 (remarks by Mekdad (Syria)) (Oct. 5, 2003).

1170 *Id.* at 16 (remarks by Baali (Algeria)).

1171 *Id.* at 14 (remarks by Mahmassani (Arab League of States)).

1172 *Id.* at 22 (remarks by Almansoor (Bahrain)).

1173 *Id.* at 18 (remarks by Aboul-Gheit (Egypt)).

1174 *Id.* at 21 (remarks by Zarif (Iran)).

1175 *Id.* at 20 (remarks by Al-Otaibi (Kuwait)).

1176 *Id.* at 15 (remarks by Kronfol (Lebanon)).

1177 *Id.* at 20 (remarks by Shobokshi (Saudi Arabia)).

1178 *Id.* at 19 (remarks by Hachani (Tunisia)).

Jerusalem, the Syrian representative confirmed that the bombing of targets in Syria constituted an "absolutely unjustified aggression"[1179] In addition, Syria announced that the camps bombed by the Israeli Air Force outside Damascus had long been abandoned by the previous military occupant, "Palestinians groups."[1180] If Israel had resumed its attacks, Syria, in return, would have exercised its right to self-defense.[1181]

Israel justified its actions with self-defense. The Israeli representative at the United Nations stated that "[s]afe harbour and training facilities are provided throughout Syria for terrorist organizations such as Islamic Jihad, Hamas and Hizbollah, both in separate facilities and in Syrian army bases. The [base targeted today] is just one of those facilities sponsored by Syria and Iran." The attack in Haifa had been committed by one of the groups harbored by Syria: "Islamic Jihad, a terrorist organization that . . . has headquarters in Damascus, Syria, proudly claimed responsibility for this massacre."[1182] Therefore, "Israel's measured defensive response to the horrific suicide bombings against a terrorist training facility in Syria is a clear act of self-defence in accordance with Article 51 of the Charter."[1183]

Pakistan, regarding self-defense as justification for the use of armed force and without further explanation, announced that "[t]he attack perpetrated by Israel . . . did not meet these strict requirements set out in the Charter with regard to the use of force."[1184] Spain, seemed to imply that Israel's use of force was out of proportion as its representative announced that one could not "overlook or minimize the extreme gravity of the attack perpetrated against Syria today. That attack is clearly a patent violation of international law."[1185] China simply condemned Israel's forceful response,[1186] while Russia "urge[d] all parties to the

---

[1179] U.N. GAOR, 58th Sess., 21st mtg, at 9, U.N. Doc. A/ES-10/PV.21 (remarks by Mekdad (Syrian Arab Republic)) (Oct. 20, 2003).

[1180] Neil MacFarquhar, *Syrian Official Says Relations With U.S. Plunge to New Low*, N.Y. TIMES, Oct. 12, 2003, at 8 (quoting Bushra Kanafani, a spokeswoman of the Syrian Foreign Ministry).

[1181] Neil MacFarquhar, *New Rules for Israel and Syria*, N.Y. TIMES, Oct. 13, 2003, at A5 (again quoting Bushra Kanafani, a Syrian Foreign Ministry spokeswoman).

[1182] U.N. SCOR, 58th Sess., 4836th mtg., at 5, U.N. Doc. S/PV.4836 (remarks by Gillerman (Israel)) (Oct. 5, 2003).

[1183] *Id.* at 7; *see* also U.N. Doc. S/2003/972 (Oct. 9, 2003) at 2 (stating that: "Israel, like any sovereign state, possesses the inherent right and shoulders the fundamental obligation to defend its citizens against such attacks, no matter where they originate").

[1184] U.N. SCOR, 58th Sess., 4836th mtg., at 8, U.N. Doc. S/PV.4836 (remarks by Akram (Pakistan)) (Oct. 5, 2003).

[1185] *Id.* at 9 (remarks by Arias (Spain)).

[1186] *Id.* at 9 (remarks by Wang Guangya (China)).

conflict to show maximum restraint and to act in a balanced and responsible way so as to avert any further escalation . . . ."[1187] The latter also appeared to refer to Israel's misapplication of proportionality principles.

The United Kingdom, in somewhat milder terms, considered Israel's action as "unacceptable" but noted that "we have to recognize that terrorists are continuing to attack Israel and that they are being permitted to do so."[1188] Bulgaria[1189] and Chile[1190] also considered Israel's responses "unacceptable". Germany merely announced that it "feels that a violation of the sovereignty of a neighbouring State does not facilitate peace and stability in the region . . . ."[1191] France, albeit in a different tone, said roughly the same as its representative announced that "[t]he Israeli operation today . . . is . . . an unacceptable violation of international law and the rules of sovereignty."[1192] Mexico[1193] and Guinea saw illegitimate "reprisals" in Israel's application of force, while the latter added that the reprisal was also "disproportionate".[1194]

Morocco explicitly denied Israel's claim of self-defense announcing that "[i]f words still have meaning and if international law still exists, the concept of legitimate self-defence has nothing to do with the deliberate attack against Syrian territory."[1195] One could argue that this statement means that prior terror attacks by groups operating from within Syria did not suffice, according to Morocco, to trigger Article 51 of the Charter. If that is due to the legal nature of the non-state attacker or the gravity of the attack cannot be resolved.

Jordan spent more time on explaining why Israel could not rely on Article 51 of the Charter: "[T]he use of force is used under Article 51 of the Charter, which reflects the principle of self-defence. However, the exercise of that right on the part of any State is conditioned on a prior armed attack against it."[1196] Such an armed attack was, according to Jordan, missing. By inference, this remark could also mean that a non-state actor is *per se* incapable of launching an armed attack as required by Article 51 of the Charter – however, if that is what the Jordanian representative sought to express he failed to do so *expressis verbis*.

[1187] *Id.* at 10 (remarks by Gatilov (Russian Federation)).
[1188] *Id.* at 9, (remarks by Sir Emyr Jones Parry (United Kingdom)).
[1189] *Id.* at 11, (remarks by Tafrov (Bulgaria)).
[1190] *Id.* at 11, (remarks by Muñoz (Chile)).
[1191] *Id.* at 10, (remarks by Pleuger (Germany)).
[1192] *Id.* at 10, (remarks by De La Sablière (France)).
[1193] *Id.* at 11, (remarks by Aguilar Zinser (Mexico)).
[1194] *Id.* at 13, (remarks by Sow (Guinea)).
[1195] *Id.* at 17, (remarks by Bennouna (Morroco)).
[1196] *Id.* at 18, (remarks by Al Hussein (Jordan)).

The United States approved of the Israeli air raids.[1197] Before the Security Council, however, the American representative added, without justifying or even mentioning Israel's claim to self-defense, that "[t]he United States and . . . Israel agreed that it is important to avoid actions that could lead to a further heightening of tension in the Middle East."[1198]

The reaction Israel is confronted with is largely the same as on prior occasions. Israel's claim for self-defense against non-state actors harbored in neighboring countries is supported by few, if any countries. If Article 51 requires a state actor as attacker is, once more, not an issue brought forward by those denying Israel a right to self-defense. The possibility that also non-state actors are capable of triggering self-defense measures under Article 5 of the Charter is never denied explicitly.

j) Military Responses Against Hamas by Israel

Particularly in recent times, Israel repeatedly responded militarily against the Hamas terror organization. An insofar typical event was a military response by the Israeli Air Force in the aftermath of a suicide bombing in the Israeli city of Ashdod in March 2004. As on other occasions, Israel did not clearly refer to its right to self-defense. A spokesperson of Prime Minister Ariel Sharon merely announced that Israel would "put these terrorist groups under continuous pressure."[1199]

Sometimes, however, Israel explicitly invoked self-defense against terror attacks by Hamas. In October 2004, a series of Qassam rockets was fired into Israel from within the Gaza strip by Hamas. Previously, Israel had been accusing Syria of supporting and sheltering Hamas terrorists.[1200] This time, the relevant

---

[1197] *See, e.g.*, Glenn Kessler, *Bush: Israel Must Defend Itself; President Ties Attack on Syria to a Need to Protect 'Homeland'*, WASH. POST, Oct. 7, 2003, at A19 (referring to U.S. President Bush who supported Israel's invocation of self-defense: "Israel's got a right to defend herself").

[1198] U.N. SCOR, 58th Sess., 4836th mtg., at 14, U.N. Doc. S/PV.4836 (remarks by Negroponte (United States)) (Oct. 5, 2003).

[1199] Greg Myre, *Israel Kills 2 Islamic Militants As It Steps Up Raids in Gaza*, N.Y. TIMES, March 17, 2004, at A4 (referring to Raanan Gissin); in the course of this campaign, Israel eventually killed the founder and "spiritual leader" of Hamas, Ahmed Yassin; *see* James Bennet, *Leader of Hamas Killed by Missile in Israeli Strike*, N.Y. TIMES, March 22, 2004, at A1.

[1200] *See supra* p. 192; Hamas' political leader Khaled Meshal has been residing in Damascus, Syria; *see, e.g.*, Greg Myre, *Hamas Is Silent on Leaders As the Power Tilts to Gaza*, N.Y. TIMES, Feb. 3, 2006, at A10 ("The other top [Hamas] figures include Khaled Meshal, the group's overall leader, who is in exile and has spent most of the past few years in Damascus, Syria."); Israel unsuccessfully attempted to assassinate him in Jordan in 1997, *see* Serge Schmemann, *Release of a Hamas Leader: A Tangle of Mideast Intrigue*, N.Y TIMES, Oct. 2, 1997, at A1 ("But Channel 2 television in Israel broadcast what it described as an authorita-

territory from which Hamas was operating was not Syria but rather the areas under Palestinian sovereignty which do not yet constitute a state.[1201] On several prior occasions, Israel had already referred to its right to self-defense in the course of military actions against Palestinian groups operating from territory under Palestinian control but without clearly mentioning Article 51 of the Charter.[1202] On other occasions, Israel simply emphasized that its actions against Hamas operatives were meant to "protect" Israeli citizens.[1203] In recent years, different representatives of the United Nations occasionally confirmed Israel's right to defend itself against ongoing terror from within the Palestinian areas.[1204]

Much like during its military responses against the PLO and Hezbollah in the paralyzed Lebanese south, Israel complained in October 2004 about the inability or unwillingness of the Palestinian Authority to confine non-state terrorist groups. Israel claimed that terrorist groups such as Hamas were

---

tive account of a bizarre story that began last Thursday with the attempted poisoning of the political leader of Hamas, Khaled Meshal, on an Amman street").

1201 *See, e.g., Advisory Opinion*, at paras. 70-79 (describing the ICJ's evaluation of the legal status of the Palestinian territory and coming to the conclusion that "[a]ll these territories (including East Jerusalem) remain occupied territories and Israel has continued to have the status of occupying Power").

1202 *See, e.g.*, U.N. SCOR, 59th Sess., 4929th mtg., at 6, U.N. Doc. S/PV.4929 (remarks by Gillerman (Israel)) (March 23, 2004) (stating that "[b]y any reasonable standard of international law, Israel has a legitimate right, in fact a duty, to defend itself against . . . illegal combatants and their commanders . . . ."); U.N. SCOR, 59th Sess., 4972nd mtg., at 10, U.N. Doc. S/PV.4972 (remarks by Gillerman (Israel)) (May 19, 2004) (stating that Israel, "[f]aced with the failure of the Palestinian leadership to comply with its obligations to fight terrorism, . . . remains obligated to act in self-defence against a threat that poses a clear and present danger to innocent lives, while upholding its obligations under international law"); U.N. Doc. S/2005/609 (Sept. 28, 2005) at 1.

1203 *See, e.g.*, U.N. SCOR, 57th Sess., 4588th mtg., at 6, U.N. Doc. S/PV.4588 (remarks by Jacob (Israel)) (July 24, 2002).

1204 *See, e.g.*, U.N. SCOR, 58th Sess., 4757th mtg., at 3, U.N. Doc. S/PV.4757 (remarks by Roed-Larsen (Special Coordinator for the Middle East Peace Process and Personal Representative of the Secretary-General)) (May 19, 2003) (emphasizing that the United Nations "do not question Israel's right to self-defence in the face of repeated terrorist attacks. The United Nations must, however, repeat the call on the Israeli authorities to abandon the use of excessive force. . . .); U.N. SCOR, 58th Sess., 4773th mtg., at 3, U.N. Doc. S/PV.4773 (remarks by Pendergast (Under-Secretary-General for Political Affairs)) (June 13, 2003) (affirming that "Israel has a right to self-defence in the face of repeated terrorist attacks"); U.N. SCOR, 59th Sess., 5077th mtg., at 8, U.N. Doc. S/PV.5077 (remarks by Roed-Larsen (Special Coordinator for the Middle East Peace Process and Personal Representative of the Secretary-General)) (Nov. 15, 2004) (confirming that "[t]he basic principles that underlay the Oslo process remain valid and alive today. They are: . . . Israel's legitimate right to self-defence and to exist in security").

> operating with complete freedom and immunity from Palestinian Authority territory . . . . Despite the fact that the Palestinian Authority has thousands of police and security personnel in the northern Gaza Strip, they are doing nothing, and have done nothing for years, to halt the firing of Qassam rockets on Israeli communities.[1205]

Accordingly, "Israel is compelled to act in accordance with its recognized right and duty of self-defence in an effort to halt the firing of these rockets and the murder of its citizens."[1206]

Spain, with regard to self-defense, announced in response:

> Clearly, we recognize Israel's right to protect itself and to protect its citizens when confronted with acts of terrorism, but . . . any State's right to self-defence must be exercised within respect for international norms, in particular the norms of humanitarian law. We understand Israel's security concerns, but we cannot but condemn the methods it is using, with acts of force that have excessive and indiscriminate effects.[1207]

With this, as on countless prior occasions, Israel was primarily criticized for its application of force, rather than for issues regarding the *ius ad bellum*. Germany stated largely the same as its representative announced:

> No doubt, the State of Israel has the right to self-defence, in particular to protect its citizens against militant attacks. At the same time, we believe that that right should be exerted in accordance with the rule of law and within the framework of international law. We believe that it is clearly in Israel's interest to respect the principle of proportional reaction and to take into consideration the medium-term consequences of its actions.[1208]

Russia "[l]ike many who spoke before . . . confirm[ed] Israel's right to self-defence — to protect itself fully against terrorist raids . . . . but urge[ed] Israel to demonstrate restraint . . . ."[1209] Benin stated that "self-defence cannot justify the massacre of innocent civilians. . . " and thus "condemn[s] in the strongest terms the disproportionate use of force. . . ." Nonetheless, also Benin "recognize[d] Israel's right to protect its territory and its people against terrorist at-

---

1205 U.N. SCOR, 59th Sess., 5049th mtg., at 5, U.N. Doc. S/PV.5049 (remarks by Gillerman (Israel)) (Oct. 4, 2004).
1206 *Id.* at 6.
1207 *Id.* at 9 (remarks by Yáñez-Barnuevo (Spain)).
1208 *Id.* at 12 (remarks by Pleuger (Germany)).
1209 *Id.* at 12 (remarks by Denisov (Russian Federation)).

tacks."[1210] The Pakistani representative stated "the rationale of the right to self-defence can not be invoked for attacks that cause mainly civilian casualties. " Israel as "an occupying power, . . . is bound by the Geneva Conventions, especially by the Fourth Geneva Convention"[1211] The United Kingdom "recognize[d] Israel's right to defend itself against terrorism, but that response must be proportionate and within international law."[1212] Additionally, the Dutch representative, speaking for the European Union, recognized that "Israel has the right to protect its citizens from terrorist attacks, [but] the exercise of that right should take place within the boundaries of international law."[1213] Turkey aligned itself with the European statement and added that "Israel's disproportionate and indiscriminate use of force does not strengthen the security it seeks."[1214]

A draft resolution was vetoed by the United States since it was considered as "lopsided and unbalanced" and because it failed to mention "the legitimate need for Israel to defend itself."[1215] France, which supported the draft resolution, nonetheless emphasized once again that Israel has a right "to defend itself against the heinous terrorist acts perpetrated against its people."[1216] Other states, which had also voted in favor of the resolution or abstained, while explaining their vote once again clearly expressed their support for Israel's right to defend itself against terror.[1217]

The emphasis most states expressed in the course of these debates was clearly on proportionality issues. Israel's right to defend itself, despite the lack of a state opponent, was expressed repeatedly and unconditionally.

As the rocket attacks by Hamas continued, Israel declared again in October 2006 that it would "be forced to exercise its right to self-defence" unless the attacks from inside Palestinian territory stopped.[1218] In early November, Israel began a military operation into northern Gaza to stop the rockets from being

---

[1210] *Id.* at 13 (remarks by Adechi (Benin)).
[1211] *Id.* at 14 (remarks by Akram (Pakistan)).
[1212] *Id.* at 16 (remarks by Sir Emyr Jones Parry (United Kingdom)).
[1213] *Id.* at 19 (remarks by van den Berg (The Netherlands)).
[1214] *Id.* at 26 (remarks by Cengizer (Turkey)).
[1215] U.N. SCOR, 59th Sess., 5051st mtg., at 1, U.N. Doc. S/PV.5051 (remarks by Danforth (United States)) (Oct. 5, 2004).
[1216] *Id.* at 4 (remarks by De la Sablière (France)).
[1217] Chile: U.N. SCOR, 59th Sess., 5051st mtg., at 5, U.N. Doc. S/PV.5051 (remarks by Maquieira (Chile)) (Oct. 5, 2004); Romania: *id.* at 5 (remarks by Motoc (Romania)); United Kingdom: *id.* at 6 (remarks by Sir Emyr Jones Parry (United Kingdom)).
[1218] U.N. Doc. S/2006/798 (Oct. 10, 2006).

fired[1219] and produced[1220] and to destroy tunnels dug by militants to smuggle weapons into Gaza.[1221] The Palestinian Authority considered Israel's military actions an aggression.[1222] The United States supported Israel's claim to self-defense, emphasizing that Israel was merely reacting to prior attacks "from Palestinian Authority areas."[1223]

United Nations Secretary-General Kofi Annan urged "Israel to exercise maximum restraint, do their utmost to protect civilians and to refrain from further escalating an already grave situation."[1224] Annan did not comment on Israel's right to self-defense and focused on *ius in bello* issues instead. Neither did he reject Israel's legal reasoning expressly.

After the official end of the military campaign and withdrawal of most Israeli forces from Gaza,[1225] Israeli artillery accidentally destroyed a civil home, killing 17 civilians in Beit Hanoun inside the Gaza strip.[1226] Before the United Nations Security Council Israel apologized and expressed its "deep sorrow and regret over the deaths of innocent civilians" but emphasized that "if the terrorist attacks from Gaza stop, Israel will have no need for self-defence." [1227]

A number of states considered Israel's entire military campaign an aggression.[1228] Most states, while criticizing Israel for the violation of *ius in bello*

[1219] Greg Myre, *Israel Vows to Attack Gaza Until Rockets Subside*, N.Y. TIMES ONLINE, Nov. 6, 2006, *available at* http://www.nytimes.com (last visited Nov. 6, 2006) (referring to statements by Israel's Prime Minister Ehud Olmert).

[1220] Steven Erlanger, *Israel Presses Attacks in Gaza, Killing a Rocket Maker*, N.Y TIMES ONLINE, Nov. 5, 2006, *available at* http://www.nytimes.com (last visited Nov. 6, 2006).

[1221] Scott Wilson, *In Wake of War, Israel Steps Up Effort Against Gaza Tunnels*, WASHINGTON POST, Nov. 4, 2006, at A16.

[1222] U.N. Doc. S/2006/858 (Nov. 1, 2006).

[1223] *See* Erlanger, *supra* note 1220 (quoting U.S. State Department spokesman Sean McCormack).

[1224] Press Release, Secretary-General, Secretary-General Deeply Concerned By Escalating Violence, Rising Death Toll Caused By Israeli Military Operation in Northern Gaza, U.N. Doc. SG/SM/10713 (Nov. 3, 2006).

[1225] Scott Wilson, *Israel Withdraws Most Forces From Gaza Strip,* WASH. POST, Nov. 8, 2006, at A03.

[1226] Scott Wilson, *'Shells Kept Falling' On Gaza Apartment, Killing 17 in Family,* WASH. POST, Nov. 9, 2006, at A03.

[1227] U.N. SCOR, 61st Sess., 5564th mtg., at 6, 7, U.N. Doc. S/PV.5564 (remarks by Carmon (Israel)) (Nov. 9, 2006).

[1228] Egypt: U.N. SCOR, 61st Sess., 5564th mtg., at 23, 24, U.N. Doc. S/PV.5564 (remarks by Abdelaziz (Egypt)) (Nov. 9, 2006); Lebanon: *id.* at 26 (remarks by Ziade (Lebanon)); Malaysia: *id.* at 27 (remarks by Hamidon (Malaysia)); Qatar (speaking also on behalf of the League of Arab States): *id.* at 8 (remarks by Al-Bader (Qatar)); Saudi-Arabia: *id.* at 25 (remarks by Shobokshi (Saudi Arabia)); Tanzania: *id.* at 13 (remarks by Taj (Tanzania)).

rules particularly with regard to Beit Hanoun, confirmed Israel's right to exercise proportionate self-defense against terror attacks from inside Gaza.[1229] China,[1230] Japan,[1231] and Russia[1232] heavily criticized Israel and called upon all sides to stop the violence, not indicating their legal views as to self-defense. Cuba and with it the Movement of Non-Aligned States also considered Israel of having committed an aggression.[1233]

The conflict between Israel and the Palestinian terror groups is, in many regards, exceptional. For the purposes of this work it can be held that there is no typical host state involved. Egypt occupied the Gaza strip in 1948, then belonging to the Palestine Mandate. Israel replaced Egypt as belligerent occupier in 1967.[1234] Neither has ever claimed title to the Gaza area.[1235] Transjordan occupied the West Bank in 1948, annexed it in 1950, and the Kingdom of Jordan eventually ceded its assumed sovereignty over the area to the PLO in 1988.[1236] While the Palestinian Authority – an institution that emerged in the course of the 1994 Oslo accords and was initially largely identical with the PLO leadership –[1237] enjoys several rights and duties, the areas under Palestinian Authority have never constituted a state.[1238] Accordingly, in absence of a state party, the Israeli government has not been of the opinion that the relevant legal regime covering

---

[1229] Argentina: *id.* at 18 (remarks by Mayoral (Argentina)); Congo: *id.* at 14 (remarks by Gayama (Congo)); Denmark: *id.* at 15 (remarks by Løj (Denmark)); Finland (speaking also on behalf of the European Union): *id.* at 22 (remarks by Lintonen (Finland)); France: *id.* at 11 (remarks by De la Sablière (France)); Greece: *id.* at 15 (remarks by Vassilakis (Greece)); Peru: *id.* at 20 (remarks by Voto-Bernales (Peru)); Slovakia: *id.* at 12 (remarks by Matulay (Slovakia)); United Kingdom: *Id.* at 16 (remarks by Pierce (United Kingdom)).

[1230] *Id.* at 18 (remarks by Liu Zhemin (China)).

[1231] *Id.* at 19 (remarks by Shinyo (Japan)).

[1232] *Id.* at 17 (remarks by Churkin (Russia)).

[1233] *Id.* at 21 (remarks by Malmierca Díaz (Cuba)).

[1234] Yehuda Blum, *The Missing Reversioner: Reflections on the Status of Judea and Samaria*, 3 ISR. L. REV. 279, 294 (1968) (coming to the conclusion that "[t]he legal standing of Israel in the territories in question is . . . that of a State which is lawfully in control of territory in respect of which no other States can show a better title. [At least the legal standing of Israel is] that of a belligerent occupant of territory in respect of which Jordan is *not* entitled to the reversionary rights of a legitimate sovereign.").

[1235] Peter Malanczuk, *Israel: Status, Territory And Occupied Territories, in* 2 ENCYCLOPEDIA OF PUBLIC INTERNATIONAL LAW 1468, 1489 (Rudolf Bernhardt ed., 1995).

[1236] Malanczuk, *supra* note 1234 at 1490-91.

[1237] STEPHAN SINA, *Der völkerrechtliche Status des Westjordanlandes und des Gaza-Streifens nach den Osloer Verträgen* 29 (2004).

[1238] SINA, *supra* note 1237 at 306; Malanczuk, *supra* note 1234 at 1492-93; *see also supra* note 1201.

the conflict is the Fourth Geneva Convention.[1239] The United Nations Security Council,[1240] the General Assembly,[1241] the ICJ,[1242] and also the Israeli Supreme Court[1243] disagreed.

While the rules of international humanitarian law seem therefore to apply, the question remains if a state is permitted to continue referring to the international self-defense regime while occupying a certain territory (here: that is considered not a state itself).

The international self-defense regime can be applied exclusively to repel an attack[1244] – an occupation of foreign territory is only possible if such conduct

---

1239 *Advisory Opinion*, para 90; for an overview over Israeli legal contentions *see* Adam Roberts, *Prolonged Military Occupation: The Israeli-Occupied Territories Since 1967*, 84 AM. J. INT'L L. 44, 62-66 (1990).

1240 S.C. Res. 237 (June 14, 1967) 1967 U.N.Y.B. 190-91; S.C. Res. 271 (Sept. 15, 1969) 1969 U.N.Y.B. 221; S.C. Res. 446 (March 22, 1979) 1979 U.N.Y.B. 400; S.C. Res. 681, U.N. Doc. S/RES/681 (Dec. 20, 1990); S.C Res. 799, U.N. Doc. S/RES/799 (Dec. 18, 1992); S.C. Res. 904, U.N. Doc. S/RES/904 (March 18, 1994).

1241 *See, e.g.*, G.A. Res. 36/15, U.N. Doc. A/RES/36/15 (Nov. 3, 1981); G.A. Res. 37/123, U.N. Doc. A/RES/37/123 (Dec. 16, 1982); G.A. Res. 39/101, U.N. Doc. A/RES/39/101 (Dec. 14, 1984); G.A. Res. 40/161, U.N. Doc. A/RES/40/161 (Dec. 16, 1985); G.A. Res. 41/162, U.N. Doc. A/RES/41/162 (Dec. 5, 1986) ; G.A. Res. 43/21, U.N. Doc. A/RES/43/21 (Nov. 3, 1988); G.A. Res. 44/2, U.N. Doc. A/RES/44/2 (Oct. 6, 1989); G.A. Res. 45/83, U.N. Doc. A/RES/45/83 (Dec. 13, 1990); G.A. Res. 46/46, U.N. Doc. A/RES/46/46 (Dec. 9, 1991); G.A. Res. 47/69, U.N. Doc. A/RES/47/69 (Dec. 14, 1992); G.A. Res. 48/59, U.N. Doc. A/RES/48/59 (Dec. 14, 1993); G.A. Res. 49/36, U.N. Doc. A/RES/49/36 (Dec. 9, 1994); G.A. Res. 50/22, U.N. Doc. A/RES/50/22 (Dec. 4, 1995); G.A. Res. 51/128, U.N. Doc. A/RES/51/128 (Dec. 13, 1996); G.A. Res. 51/223, U.N. Doc. A/RES/51/223 (March 13, 1997); G.A. Res. 52/65, U.N. Doc. A/RES/52/65 (Feb. 20, 1998); G.A. Res. 53/54, U.N. Doc. A/RES/53/54 (Feb. 10, 1999); G.A. Res. 54/77, U.N. Doc. A/RES/54/77 (Feb. 22, 2000); G.A. Res. 55/131, U.N. Doc. A/RES/55/131 (Feb. 28, 2001); G.A. Res. 56/56, U.N. Doc. A/RES/56/56 (Feb. 14, 2002); G.A. Res. 57/188, U.N. Doc. A/RES/57/188 (Feb. 6, 2003); G.A. Res. 58/99, U.N. Doc. A/RES/58/99 (Dec. 17, 2003) ; G.A. Res. 59/251, U.N. Doc. A/RES/59/251 (Dec. 22, 2004); G.A. Res. 60/183, U.N. Doc. A/RES/60/183 (Dec. 22, 2005)

1242 *Advisory Opinion*, para 101.

1243 *See, e.g.*, HCJ 4764/04 (High Ct. Justice, May 30, 2004) Physicians for Hum. Rts. v. Commander of the IDF Forces in the Gaza Strip at para. 19, *available at* http://elyon1.court.gov.il/eng/home/index.html (last visited Oct. 20, 2006) (stating that Israel's military operations "in Rafah, to the extent they affect civilians, are governed by Hague Convention IV Respecting the Laws and Customs of War on Land 1907 . . . and the Geneva Convention Relative to the Protection of Civilian Persons in Time of War 1949"); *cf.* Hamdan v. Rumsfeld, *supra* note 179 (which also held that the Geneva Conventions and its Common Article 3 is to be applied in armed conflicts of international nature, even when the opponent did not – and could not – sign on to the Conventions).

1244 *Nicaragua* case, at para. 176; *see* also *infra* p. 216 et seq.

constitutes the only and necessary means to prevent the aggressor from continuing its armed attack.[1245] There is no rule among the norms constituting the legal regime of forceful occupation that explicitly entitles or prohibits the occupying power to continue acting in self-defense based upon Article 51 of the Charter or the customary law of self-defense. The relevant norms as to the rights of the occupying power vis-à-vis forceful resistance are Articles 5, 49 and 68 of the Fourth Geneva Convention.[1246] Article 7 of the 1974 United Nations Definition of Aggression,[1247] and the 1970 Friendly Relations Declaration[1248] preserve the rights of occupied peoples to self-determination towards the occupier. And while these peoples retain such rights under occupation, which by itself is governed by special rules protecting the individuals in the occupied territories, self-defense as a means of protection for the occupier vis-à-vis organized military resistance different from the civilian population remains an applicable legal justification for the recourse to force.

Particularly in recent years, many states do not seem to doubt that self-defense – without clarifying on what legal grounds – has been an available op-

---

[1245] *See, e.g.*, CASSESE, *supra* note 178 at 355.

[1246] Article 5 of the Fourth Geneva Convention provides in part "(1) Where in the territory of a Party to the conflict, the latter is satisfied that an individual protected person is definitely suspected of or engaged in activities hostile to the security of the State, such individual person shall not be entitled to claim such rights and privileges under the present Convention as would, if exercised in the favour of such individual person, be prejudicial to the security of such State.";
Article 49 provides in part: "(2) . . . the Occupying Power may undertake total or partial evacuation of a given area if the security of the population or imperative military reasons so demand. . . . (5) The Occupying Power shall not detain protected persons in an area particularly exposed to the dangers of war unless the security of the population or imperative military reasons so demand.";
Article 68 provides in part "Protected persons who commit an offence which is solely intended to harm the Occupying Power, but which does not constitute an attempt on the life or limb of members of the occupying forces or administration, nor a grave collective danger, nor seriously damage the property of the occupying forces or administration or the installations used by them, shall be liable to [proportionate] internment or simple imprisonment, ... Furthermore, internment or imprisonment shall, for such offences, be the only measure adopted for depriving protected persons of liberty. . . .".

[1247] Definition of Aggression, Article 7, G.A. Res. 3314 (XXIX), U.N. Doc. A/RES/3314 (Dec. 14, 1974); it suggests in part that "[n]othing in this Definition . . . could in any way prejudice the right to self-determination . . . of peoples forcibly deprived of that right . . ., particularly peoples under . . . alien domination; nor the right of these peoples to struggle to that end . . . .".

[1248] Friendly Relations Declaration, *supra* note 73; it provides in part that "[e]very State has the duty to refrain from any forcible action which deprives peoples . . . of their right to self-determination . . . ."

tion for Israel as it repels Hamas' rocket barrages. Proportionality and the *ius in bello*, not the defensive action *per se* i.e. the *ius ad bellum*, were at stake as it has been on countless prior occasions.

6. Conflicts Without Clear Self-Defense Against Non-State Actor

On certain other occasions, non-state actors played an important role in the military struggle between two or more states. However, the victim states either did not respond at all militarily or directed their counter-measures explicitly against the host or third states which they considered as the true motor behind the events.

a) Senegal's Military Incursions Into Guinea-Bissau

Senegal fought a war against rebel forces which withdrew to bordering countries. Ever since the early 1980s the Mouvement des Forces Démocratiques du le Casamance (Movement of Democratic Forces in the Casamance, MFDC) fought for the independence of the southern Senegalese province of Casamance.[1249] The situation calmed down with a peace accord in 2004,[1250] which appears to be lasting until today.[1251]

On several occasions, Senegal extended its military campaign against the rebel forces beyond its borders and attacked the MFDC inside Guinea-Bissau, the country neighboring Senegal to the south.[1252] A clear reference to self-defense against the non-state actor MFDC is not available. Evidently, no U.N. body condemned Senegal for the – timely, and with regard to its magnitude, limited – military responses.[1253]

[1249] *See, e.g., 19 Are Dead in Senegal In Clashes With Police,* N.Y. TIMES, Dec. 19, 1983, at A9 ("According to an official communique [sic], 15 members of the Movement of Casamance Democratic Forces were killed [by Senegalese security forces] . . . .).

[1250] *World Briefing Africa: Senegal: Peace Pact Signed,* N.Y. TIMES, Dec. 31, 2004, at A6.

[1251] Amnesty Int'l *2006 Report (Senegal)*, summary *available at* http://web.amnesty.org/report2006/sen-summary-eng (last visited Jan. 10, 2007) ("Following the December 2004 peace agreement, which ended two decades of conflict in Casamance, reconstruction work and demining began in the region").

[1252] *See, e.g.,* KEESING'S REC. OF WORLD EVENTS 39228 (1992) ("Senegalese infantry forces bombed alleged Casamance rebel bases in . . . Guinea-Bissau on Dec. 12 . . . . The attack followed an ambush by [MFDC] members . . . in which two Senegalese soldiers were killed.); *id.* at 40396 (1995) ("On. Feb. 10, [Senegalese] government aircraft bombed a village within Guinea-Bissau . . . . [T]he bombing appeared to be directed at the [MFDC] and followed rebel attacks in January."); *Army pushes rebels back across border*, ST. LOUIS POST DISPATCH, Apr. 1, 2000, at A12 ("The [Senegalese] army forces back secessionist rebels attempting to cross into southern Senegal from Guinea-Bissau, the military said late Tuesday. At Least 18 people were killed in the fighting").

[1253] FRANCK, *supra* note 12 at 66.

b) BURMA'S MILITARY ACTIONS AGAINST FORCES RETREATED TO THAILAND

Burma, referred to by the local regime as Union of Myanmar, forced rebels opposing the Burmese junta to withdraw into areas right across the border with Thailand.[1254] Consequently, the Burmese military also attacked the guerilla troops on Thai soil in 1995. There is no official reference to Article 51 of the Charter with regard to these military raids.

The government in Bangkok announced that it "will no longer tolerate any such acts of infringement and will take appropriate retaliatory action in the strongest form to safeguard Thailand's sovereignty and territorial integrity . . . ."[1255] However, even as the cross-border raids continued, the Thai government refrained from military actions against the Burmese forces, perhaps due to the inexperience and expected weakness of its own troops.[1256] Eventually, the Burmese refugees as a whole were forced to return to Burma[1257] and rivaling groups began to fight each other.[1258]

c) DISPUTE BETWEEN ETHIOPIA, ERITREA, SUDAN, AND UGANDA

A complex situation developed between several Eastern African states throughout the 1980s and reached its peak in the early 1990s. Many states, particularly Uganda and Sudan, hosted and supported non-state actors to destabilize its neighbors and to exercise foreign policy by unofficial means. In return, the affected states would respond by counter-force, albeit only rarely, with clear references to Article 51 of the Charter.

In June 1995, Ethiopia and Egypt accused Sudan of sheltering Islamist terrorists who had sought to assassinate Egyptian President Mubarak while visiting Ethiopia.[1259] Sudan, since 1993 considered by the U.S. Department of State a state sponsor of terrorism, in return accused its neighbors of supporting Christian and other militias operating in Sudan's south[1260] and rejected the Organiza-

---

1254 *Burmese Forces Press Insurgents*, N.Y. TIMES, Jan. 29, 1995, at 8; *Burmese Increasing Attacks on Rebels*, N.Y. TIMES, Feb. 12, 1995, at 3.

1255 *Thailand Warns Burmese on Raids On Refugee Camps*, N.Y. TIMES, Apr. 30, 1995, at 12 (quoting from a letter from Thailand sent to the military Government of Myanmar).

1256 *Burmese Raid Border Camps In Thailand*, N.Y. TIMES, May 14, 1995, at 9 (quoting a "Western diplomat in Bangkok").

1257 Erhard Haubold, *Schwere Schläge für eine der ältesten Guerrillagruppen Asiens,* FRANKFURTER ALLGEMEINE ZEITUNG, March 3, 1997, at 8.

1258 *Karen-Flüchtlingslager in Thailand überfallen*, FRANKFURTER ALLGEMEINE ZEITUNG, March 28, 1998, at 7 (stating that an offshoot of the Karen National Union, supported by Burma, attacked their fellow Karens", an ethnic minority).

1259 U.N. Doc. S/1995/867 (Oct. 3, 1995) at 1.

1260 *See* Douglas Jehl, *Sudan Pays High Price for Ties to Islamic Militants*, N.Y. TIMES, Feb. 13, 1996, at 3; *see* also, *e.g.*, allegations against guerilla support by Eritrea: U.N. Doc.

tion of African Unity's requests to comply with its obligations under an extradition treaty. The United Nations Security Council eventually called upon Sudan to comply and to "desist from engaging in activities of assisting, supporting and facilitating terrorist activities and from giving shelter . . . to terrorist elements . . . ."[1261] Sudan, on the other hand, "consistently stated that [it] will not allow its territory, nationals or institutions to be used in any manner whatsoever for direct or indirect terrorist activities."[1262] A subsequent report by the Secretary General showed that Ethiopia,[1263] Eritrea,[1264] Uganda,[1265] Egypt,[1266] and also Tunisia[1267] complained about Sudanese involvement in terrorist activities emanating from its territory.[1268] One of the groups that the United States also considered to be supported by Sudan was the Christian fundamentalist group "Lord's Resistance Army", operating in Uganda.[1269] Sudan kept rejecting such allegations.[1270] The

---

S/1996/358 (May 13, 1996); U.N. Doc. S/1996/1007 (Dec. 4, 1996); U.N. Doc. S/1997/2 (Jan. 2, 1997); U.N. Doc. S/1997/11 (Jan. 6, 1997); U.N. Doc. S/1997/271 (Apr. 3, 1997); U.N. Doc. S/1997/342 (Apr. 29, 1997); U.N. Doc. S/1997/395 (May 27, 1997); by Uganda: U.N. Doc. S/1996/359 (May 20, 1996).

[1261] S.C. Res. 1044, U.N. Doc. S/RES/1044 (Jan. 31, 1996).

[1262] U.N. SCOR, 51st Sess., 3627th mtg., at 4 U.N. Docs. S/PV 3627 (remarks by Yassin (Sudan)) (Jan. 31, 1996).

[1263] U.N. Doc. S/1996/179 (March 11, 1996) at 3 (referring to remarks by the Ethiopian authorities expressing their conviction that an "[e]xtradition of the suspects would also send a message to other neighbours of the Sudan that the Sudan had broken with the terrorist elements on its territory and stopped its support for their activities").

[1264] U.N. Doc. S/1996/179 (March 11, 1996) at 3 (stating that: "[Eritrea's] President Afwerki pointed out that Eritrea had been the target of subversion and destabilizing acts supported by the Sudan for several years").

[1265] U.N. Doc. S/1996/179 (March 11, 1996) at 4 (stating that "[Ugandan Prime Minister Kintu Musoke] said that the Sudan was supporting two Ugandan rebel movements with a view to destabilizing the Government by arming and training them as well as by providing bases for their activities").

[1266] *Id.* (referring to Egyptian Minister of Foreign Affairs, Amre Moussa, as having said that "the regime in Khartoum was engaged in activities of promoting and supporting terrorism in neighbouring countries, posing a threat to the stability of the neighbours").

[1267] *Id.* at 5 (referring to the Tunisian Minister for Foreign Affair, Habib Ben Yahia, and the Minister of the Interior, Mohamed Jeghan, revealing that "Tunisia had also detailed evidence . . . of training camps for terrorists in the Sudan").

[1268] *See* also *supra* pp. 157 et seq.

[1269] *See, e.g.*, James C. McKinley Jr., *Albright, in Uganda, Steps Up Attack on Sudan's War of Terror*, N.Y. TIMES, Dec. 11, 1997, at A7.

[1270] U.N. Doc. S/1996/179 (March 11, 1996) at 6 (referring to Sudanese authorities that "maintained to [the Secretary General's] Special Envoy that the allegations regarding the Sudan's support for terrorist activities in the neighbouring countries were unfair and unfounded"); U.N. Doc. S/1996/201 (March 15, 1996).

United Nations Security Council repeated its request that Sudan must extradite the suspects, refrain from supporting terrorists, and comply with the previous resolution.[1271]

In the following years, most of the reported incidents directly affected two or more states such as Eritrea, Sudan, and Uganda which all referred to self-defense.[1272] Sometimes, however, non-state groups sponsored by either party to the conflict were in the center of the exchange of violence. In August 1998 Eritrea once again emphasized the active role that Islamic militants played in the ongoing hostilities and that it would defend itself against Sudan if the latter does not begin to confine terrorist activities emanating from its territory.[1273] However, rather than invoking self-defense against the "Islamic Jihad", the group referred to in this situation, Eritrea regarded such groups as closely intertwined with Sudan and attributed their activities at all times to the regime in Khartoum.

In 2002, Sudan emphasized its "natural and legal right to defend its territory, its citizens and its installations, in accordance with . . . Article 51 of the Charter . . . ."[1274] The country had been struggling with the Sudan People's Liberation Army ever since 1983,[1275] which at this time, was also admitting its responsibility for an attack. Sudan, however, blamed its neighbor Eritrea of having not only directly supported the rebel group but that it even provided for "the core of the attacking force".[1276] Hence, Sudan's self-defense was directed primarily against Eritrea, rather than against a non-state actor. As had happened on prior occasions, the states involved abused militant groups to conduct foreign policy and to destabilize opponents.

[1271] S.C. Res. 1054, U.N. Doc. S/RES/1054 (Apr. 26, 1996); S.C. Res. 1070, U.N. Doc. S/RES/1070 (Aug. 16, 1996).

[1272] *See, e.g.,* Eritrea's complaints about Sudan U.N. Doc. S/1998/127 (Feb. 13, 1998); U.N. Doc. S/1998/180 (March 2, 1998); U.N. Doc. S/1998/1153 (Dec. 10, 1998); *see also* Sudan's complaints about Eritrea U.N. Doc. S/1998/258 (March 19, 1998); U.N. Doc. S/1998/708 (Aug. 3, 1998) and about Uganda and Eritrea U.N. Doc. S/1998/922 (Oct. 7, 1998).

[1273] U.N. Doc. S/1998/733 (Aug. 7, 1998) (stating that the "Government of the Sudan has created and continued to arm and infiltrate into Eritrea an assortment of terrorist elements – members of the so-called Islamic jihad. Eritrea stands ready to defend its sovereignty from these or any future Sudanese attacks . . . .).

[1274] U.N. Doc. S/2002/1117 (Oct. 8, 2002) at 4, 5.

[1275] For a brief overview over the conflict *see* Bill Berkeley, *The Longest War in the World*, N.Y. TIMES, March 3, 1996, at 59.

[1276] U.N. Doc. S/2002/1117 (Oct. 8, 2002) at 2.

d) Tensions Between Burundi and Tanzania

Due to a fierce civil war since 1993 between the Tutsi minority and the Burundian Hutus, several thousand Hutu refugees escaped to Tanzania.[1277] In 1997, Burundi accused armed bands among the refugees of instigating raids into Burundi from inside the refugee camps located right across the Tanzanian border[1278] and also accused Tanzania of directly attacking Burundi.[1279] Tanzania, in return, invoked Article 51 of the Charter and replied that it had come under an attack by Burundian forces.[1280] Burundi reiterated its allegations that "refugee camps which have been transformed into training camps for armed groups" were tolerated by Tanzania in close vicinity to the Burundian border.[1281] Burundi, despite the fact that it had come under an attack by militant non-state actors, did not invoke self-defense against such groups.

e) Guinea's Complaint About Foreign Incursions

Another conflict, in which neighboring African countries supported rebel groups to weaken other states was between Sierra Leone, Liberia, and Guinea.[1282]

Two fierce civil wars in Guinea's neighbor countries, Sierra Leone and Liberia, brought thousands of refugees into the small Western African nation Guinea during a period of more than ten years, namely between 1991 and 2003.[1283] Eventually, the regime in Sierra Leone accused Guinea of not preventing cross-border raids emanating from inside the refugee camps located in Guinea[1284] – and Great Britain for supporting the Anti-Liberian rebels.[1285] In re-

---

1277 For an overview over the conflict *see, e.g.*, James C. McKinley Jr., *In the Wars of Central Africa, an Ethnic Hot Zone*, N.Y. TIMES, Aug. 10, 1997, at 13; James C. McKinley Jr., *Hutu Families Pay Price in Burundi's Crackdown Against Guerrillas*, N.Y TIMES, Aug. 12, 1997, at A10.

1278 U.N. Doc. S/1997/764 (Oct. 2, 1997); *see also, e.g., Burundi Army Admits It Killed 126 Hutu Refugees*, N.Y. TIMES, Jan. 12, 1997, at 15; *Tansania verstärkt Druck auf Burundi*, FRANKFURTER ALLGEMEINE ZEITUNG, Sept. 30, 1997, at 7 ("Burundi wirft Tansania vor, unter den 300000 Hutu-Flüchtlingen in Lagern in Nordwesttansania Rebellen Unterschlupf zu gewähren").

1279 U.N. Doc. S/1997/822 (Oct. 28, 1997) at 2.

1280 U.N. Doc. S/1997/850 (Nov. 5, 1997) at 2.

1281 U.N. Doc. S/1997/956 (Dec. 5, 1997) at 2.

1282 *See, e.g.*, Norimitsu Onishi, *Sierra Leone Endures In the Grip of Civil War*, N.Y. TIMES, Nov. 19, 2000, at 18; *West Africa's Widening Conflict*, N.Y. TIMES, Dec. 6, 2000, at A32.

1283 Norimitsu Onishi, *Guinea in Crisis as Area's Refugees Pour In*, N.Y. TIMES, Feb. 24, 2001, at A1.

1284 *Liberian Troops Fight Rebels*, N.Y. TIMES, Feb. 11, 2002, A4 ("The [Liberian] government accuses neighboring Guinea of supporting the rebels and says its own response to the

turn, armed bands from Sierra Leone attacked targets in Guinea. In September 2000, the cross-border incursions erupted and dozens of civilians and soldiers were killed by armed groups operating from inside Sierra Leone.[1286] As the situation worsened, the Security Council issued a statement in which it condemned the "recent incursions into Guinea by rebel groups coming from Liberia and Sierra Leone . . . ." While in the statement the Council "reaffirme[d] its commitment to the sovereignty, political independence and territorial integrity of Guinea" and "expresse[d] its serious concern . . . over reports that external military support is being provided to these rebel groups . . . ." it did not address the right of Guinea to resort to forcible counter-measures.[1287] Neither does it appear as if Guinea had invoked its right to self-defense.

7. Conclusion

Looking back at the legal framework as the ICJ shaped it and the strict adherence to the concept of attribution by virtue of "effective control", one is tempted to hold that state practice did not adopt such an approach. Indeed, states rarely openly accepted non-state actors as equal in their capability of triggering an armed attack as required by Article 51 of the Charter. All states that acted under a different assumption were subject to criticism. But it must be held that the international community's decline of self-defense against non-state actors never rested upon the *de facto* lack of statehood of the attacker.[1288] Rather, other legal arguments were put forward, mostly a lack of proportionality by the states' responses or the absence of an armed attack due to an insignificant application of force through the non-state actor. Often states either did not want to elaborate legal reasons to a more detailed degree – perhaps in order to be able to argue

---

attacks is hamstrung by a United Nations arms embargo. Guinea denies supporting the rebels.")

[1285] *Liberian Accuses Britain of Stirring Regional War*, N.Y. TIMES, May 30, 2001, at A6.

[1286] *See, e.g., Border Raids Terrifying Guinea Town*, N.Y. TIMES, Sept. 17, 2000, at 112 (referring to local authorities and an army colonel which stated that "[t]errified villagers in southwest Guinea are calling for army reinforcements to protect them from gunmen suspected of being rebels from neighboring Sierra Leone"); *Guinean Rebels Kill Scores*, N.Y TIMES, Oct. 2, 2000, at A8 (referring to "officials" as saying that "[v]iolent clashes between Guinean soldiers and armed groups operating from across the country's southern borders left 77 people dead in the last three days . . . .".

[1287] The President of the Security Council, *Statement on behalf of the Council*, at 1, U.N. Doc. S/PRST/2000/41 (Dec. 21, 2000).

[1288] *See also* SCHOLZ, *supra* note 34 at 171-72 ("Mit ungewohnter Eindeutigkeit bezeichnet die überwältigende Mehrheit der Staaten in ihrer Konfliktpraxis terroristische Gewalttaten durchweg als bewaffnete Angriffe und dem gesteht dem angegriffenen Staat ein auf Art. 51 SVN gestütztes Selbstverteidigungsrecht grundsätzlich zu.").

from a broad legal basis –[1289] or they simply did not regard the legal nature of the attacker as crucial to deny the invocation of Article 51 of the Charter.

The events of September 11, 2001, and the subsequent conflicts between a state and a non-state actor indicate a change with regard to self-defense against non-state actors, if not already the manifestation of a broader regime. States have not suddenly agreed that self-defense may be applied vis-à-vis non-state actors – to reiterate this clearly: nobody had ever denied it *expressis verbis* – but post-September 11 states openly announced their support for an according interpretation of Article 51 of the Charter. Most importantly, states that are otherwise criticized more or less automatically, such as Israel in first place, have also enjoyed such a right: the raid against terrorist bases in Syria in 2003 was already accepted as self-defense by some, the military actions against Hezbollah in 2006 by almost all states as well as by the United Nations, the Council of the European Union, and the G 8. Immediately following – and sometimes hastily – criticism as to proportionality issues cannot negate this general stance towards a broad self-defense regime.

This analysis does not comport with the relevance of statehood as it was implied recently in the *Advisory Opinion*[1290] and *Congo*[1291]. In the view of the ICJ, the statehood of the aggressor is one of two crucial thresholds. It will disallow evaluating a state's recourse to force by means of proportionality or necessity if it is applied as categorically as the ICJ seems to intend for it to. Such a legal understanding can be quite hazardous for a state if it strictly abides by this concept. Non-state actors have long evolved beyond a group of American patriots shipping supplies on the *Caroline* to a group of desperate Canadian insurgents. They grew into globally or regionally outstandingly powerful entities that influence world politics on a daily basis. They have no respect for basic rules of warfare. In fact, indiscriminate mass murder of non-combatants is one of their crucial and most effective means of warfare. Non-state actor structures reach from loose, although effective, networks (Al Qaeda) to almost regular standing armed forces (Hezbollah). And irrespective of their organizational structures, their capabilities extend beyond those of many states. Not only the events of September 11 and Hezbollah's rockets barrages in July and August 2006 prove that non-state actors are indeed very well capable of launching armed attacks. The devastation they cause in relation to the size of a country such as Israel has

[1289] The term used most frequently without further recourse to a legal explanation thereof in the respective situation is the term "aggression".
[1290] *See supra* note 20.
[1291] *See supra* note 140.

always been significant,[1292] and does not seem to be declining. The events of September 11 brought this to the attention of all states, and not merely those which have traditionally suffered from terrorism. Hezbollah's conflict with Israel confirmed that armed conflicts between politically diverse factions are nowadays fought by non-state actors, heavily supported by state sponsors – which have, however, no difficulties in denying their involvement. It is therefore a necessity to apply the same rules to non-state actors as are applied to states. The formal legal nature of an aggressor must not determine if a state may defend itself or must witness its own destabilization or even destruction.[1293] If host states are willing and capable to fight non-state actors operating from within their territory, they must have a prerogative to stop the non-state entity. Otherwise, the victim state must be allowed to become fully active.[1294] States cannot be allowed to hide behind non-state actors which they may not be controlling as effectively as the ICJ imagines they should. Allowing states to respond to armed attacks by non-state actors by invoking Article 51 of the Charter is one means to face such hidden warfare by some states.

The only alternative for victim states to an effective self-defense regime would be turning to the United Nations Security Council in order to obtain permission for recourse to force based upon Chapter VII of the Charter. This attempt will in most cases be rather futile. Many states, Israel being the prime example,[1295] have few if any serious chances at ever being granted an according resolution.

[1292] Note for instance the remarks by Israel's representative to the United Nations: "In comparative terms, the number of innocents deliberately murdered by Palestinian terrorists as of March 2004 is equivalent to 22,499 Russian citizens; 43,136 citizens of the United States, or 58,936 citizens of the European Union", U.N. SCOR, 59th Sess., 4929th mtg., at 6, U.N. Doc. S/PV.4929 (remarks by Gillerman (Israel)) (March 23, 2004)).

[1293] *Cf.* Norman G. Printer, *The Use of Force Against Non-State Actors Under International Law: An Analysis of the U.S. Predator Strike in Yemen,* 8 UCLA J. INT'L L. & FOREIGN AFF. 331, 346 (2003).

[1294] *Cf.* DINSTEIN, *supra* note 72 at 204.

[1295] Beside the usual difficulties for any state to convince all permanent Security Council members, the United Nations have a long history of open bias towards Israel which should render a permission to use force nearly unimaginable. The most infamous example was G.A. Res. 3379 (XXX) (Nov. 10, 1975), 1975 U.N.Y.B. 599-600 that determined Zionism to be "a form of racism and racial discrimination"; this determination was finally revoked 1991 by virtue of G.A. Res. 46/86, U.N. Doc. A/RES/46/86 (Dec. 16, 1991); the newly founded United Nations Human Rights Council, succeeding the helplessly one-sided U.N. Commission for Human Rights, immediately following its first gathering in July 2006 held two special sessions each of which culminated with a resolution concerning Israel exclusively, *see* U.N. Doc. A/HRC/S-1/L.1 (July 6, 2006), U.N. Doc. A/HRC/S-2/L.1 (Aug. 11, 2006); *see also Reform Run Amok - The U.N.'s new Human Rights Council makes the old one look good,*

PART 3 – LEGAL CONSEQUENCES OF AN EXTENSIVE RIGHT TO SELF-DEFENSE

Recourse to force against non-state actors directly based upon Article 51 of the Charter has to be limited by all safeguards which are traditionally incorporated into this article: states can only apply counter-force if they face a sufficiently grave armed attack that already occurred or is imminent. They must not react beyond what is necessary and proportionate.

In the following it will be outlined briefly if and to what extent these rules are subject to adaptation due to non-state actor involvement.

I. ARMED ATTACK

The main condition for the exercise of the right to self-defense is the use of force amounting to an armed attack.[1296] The burden of proof as to the origin and extent of an attack is on the defending state.[1297] State practice as outlined above shows some examples in which this threshold was arguably considered to be met by a majority of states despite the fact that the attacker was not a state actor, but a non-state terrorist group.[1298] In chronological order these were:

- Al Qaeda's bombing of U.S. embassies in Eastern Africa in 1998
- Destruction of the World Trade Center, the attack on the Pentagon along with the destruction of four civil airliners by Al Qaeda on September 11, 2001
- Rocket barrages fired into Israel from Gaza by Hamas in 2004

WASH. POST, Oct. 12, 2006, at A26 ("[T]he council has treated itself to report after report on the alleged crimes of the Jewish state; in all, there were six official 'rapporteurs' on that subject in the latest session alone."); for further examples of Israel's unbalanced treatment by the United Nations *see* Robert A. Caplen, *Mending the "fence": How treatment of the Israeli-Palestinian conflict by the International Court of Justice at the Hague has redefined the doctrine of self-defense*, 57 FLA. L. REV. 717, 739-44 (2005); Yehuda Blum, *Israel and the United Nations: A Retrospective Overview*, *supra* note 641 at 69, 75-77; *but see* Bowett, *supra* note 37 at 22, 23 (suggesting that the U.N. Security Council "objectively to be right" with regard to incidents involving Israel between 1948 and 1972).

1296 *See supra* p. 64; but *see* DEREK W. BOWETT, SELF-DEFENCE IN INTERNATIONAL LAW 270 (1958) (expanding the right to self-defense since "it is neither a necessary nor an accurate conclusion that the right to self-defence applies only to measures involving the use of force").

1297 *Oil Platforms* case, at para. 57.

1298 See *Cf.* Baker, *supra* note 37 at 42, 47-49 (demanding such an approach already in 1987, but concluding that Article 51 of the Charter was not yet interpreted accordingly); Murphy, *supra* note 43 at 51 (concluding post September, 11, that Article 51 of the Charter was in 1945 "closely associated with the idea or armies crossing border . . . . Today, our appreciation of these non-traditional means of engaging in an armed attack must also comprehend the pernicious methods of terrorist organizations")

- Rockets barrages launched from Lebanon and the killing and abduction of Israeli military personnel by Hezbollah between 2000 and 2006, culminating in the attacks in the summer of 2006

All other examples of the use of force followed by the invocation of self-defense in responses to an attack by non-state actors were criticized by most or at least by a majority of states and international organizations.

1. Methods and Impact

The attacks on U.S. installations in 1998 and 2001 represent singular and massive attacks and were considered more or less exceptionally as armed attacks. The methods employed by the responsible individuals were "terrorist" in nature as opposed to "military". Al Qaeda chose a type of warfare that attempted to achieve a maximum degree of efficiency considering the methods used and the harm caused. They relied on captured airplanes and trucks full with explosives, not on artillery, tanks, and rockets.

On the other hand, the latest extensions of the conflicts involving Israel received less, but still strong support as to the existence of an armed attack. The fact that Israel was involved may have been one reason for the limited degree of acceptance. More importantly, however, the attacks against Israel consist of a rather small-scale, but clearly military-type application of force, albeit over long periods of time. Ordinary terrorist attacks, e.g. suicide or car bombings, even on a reoccurring basis, seem not to have been awarded the status of armed attacks at least with regard to Israel. Once the non-state actor employed military-like measures, such as continuous rocket barrages, this changed (e.g. those by Hamas in 2003-04 and Hezbollah in July and August 2006). Armed attacks and the right to respond with self-defense based upon Article 51 of the Charter were accepted by a great number of states and international organizations, regardless of the unaltered legal nature of the attacker, namely Hamas and Hezbollah.

While in the case of Al Qaeda mainly the impact and gravity of the attacks was relevant, Hamas and Hezbollah found recognition only once they resorted to army-like behavior. Previous and numerous suicide bombings and other rather classic terrorist warfare were not accepted by the international community as armed attacks. In either case the formal nature of the attacker was irrelevant, or at least not a determinative factor for the application of defensive force.

Except perhaps for the situation between Hamas, Hezbollah, and Israel, there seems to be hardly any example in which the accumulation of smaller attacks was accepted as an armed attack which confirms traditional interpretations of Article 51 of the Charter.[1299] It remains to be seen if a "Nadelstichtaktik"[1300] – continuous attacks, "needle pricks", which not by themselves, but perhaps collectively amount to an armed attack – will on future occasions be considered to amount to an equal alternative to a singular armed attack of sufficient gravity. In *Nicaragua*, the ICJ noted that "certain transborder incursions" from abroad could not be considered "as amounting, singly or collectively, to an 'armed attack'" due to a lack of information "as to the circumstances of these incursions or their possible motivations".[1301] Provided such a lack of information could be overcome, it inferentially appears as if this phrase does allow for the possibility of "collective" armed attacks as opposed to reducing armed attacks to one-time events in disregard of cumulative gravity. Such an approach, while not yet accepted by state practice,[1302] seems one way to respond to the abnormalities of terrorist warfare.

2. Notification Requirement

In addition to the armed attack requirement, Article 51 of the Charter stipulates that the defending state is obliged to report to the Security Council. The legal nature of this condition is disputed.

The ICJ considered this requirement not to be part at least of the customary right to self-defense, but stated that "the absence of a report may be one of the factors indicating whether the State in question was itself convinced that it was acting in self-defence."[1303] Between the lines this remark hints to a more substantive, albeit implicit understanding of the notification requirement. In *Congo*, the ICJ referred briefly to the failure of Uganda to report to the Security Council but did not explore the nature of this requirement in greater depth.[1304]

On the other hand, it does seem hardly plausible that the international community or even the Security Council would reject a claim for self-defense plainly because the recourse to force was not formally submitted to the Council. The impact of an armed attack appears likely to outweigh such a formal flaw.[1305] Moreover, the notification through the directly affected victim state is likely to

---

1299 *See, e.g.*, Bowett, *supra* note 37 at 6, 7 (coming to the conclusion that the Security Council was largely ignorant to an "accumulation of events" caused by non-state entities until the early 1970s); Baker, *supra* note 37 at 49 (calling for an acceptance of continuous intrusions as an armed attack in 1987).

1300 Baker, *supra* note 37 at 42.

1301 *Nicaragua* case, at para. 231.

1302 *But see* Erickson, *supra* note 36 at 143 (considering the theory of accumulated attacks as accepted Untied States practice).

1303 *Nicaragua* case, at para. 200.

1304 *Congo* case, at para. 145.

1305 *Cf.* Dinstein, *supra* note 72 at 217.

be one, but not the exclusive, ground upon which the Security Council will decide to act.[1306] Article 51 of the Charter confirms the provisional nature of the Charter's self-defense regime as it lays out that self-defense may only be applied until the Council "has taken the measures necessary to maintain international peace and security" – until then, the flow of information can and should continue in order for the Council to rest any further decision on solid grounds. The Security Council must have access to all relevant information to maintain its supremacy over war and peace. Where this information comes from is of secondary importance provided its reliability. A supply of sound information is even more important in the light of unclear factual situations and alliances as they keep occurring in cases of international non-state actions. A victim state's obligation to submit a note to the Council also has in this regard rather formal reasons, but to formulate yet another substantive condition precedent to the exercise of self-defense.

Sometimes, the material irrelevance of a notification is considered to stem from practical reasons: as it is very likely that covert armed attacks occur, also covert self-defense without notifying anyone must be permissible.[1307]

The notification requirement can therefore be considered not as a substantive condition of Article 51 of the Charter.[1308] The meaning of an immediate report is thus likely to be of mere procedural nature and will not be crucial for the application of a self-defense regime vis-à-vis non-state actors.

3. Immediacy of an Armed Attack

Issues of anticipatory or pre-emptive self-defense and hence immediacy of an armed attack are not more or less of a concern in cases of non-state attackers than they are ordinarily and will therefore not be addressed specifically here. In summary, some consider self-defense as potentially available in anticipation of the armed attack;[1309] others call for a narrower interpretation of Article 51 of the

---

[1306] Bowett, *supra* note 1296 at 198.

[1307] Dinstein, *supra* note 72 at 217.

[1308] *Nicaragua* case, at 374-76 (dissenting opinion of Judge Schwebel).

[1309] *See, e.g.*, Bowett, *supra* note 1296 at 191; Jean-Gabriel Castel, *The Legality and Legitimacy of Unilateral Armed Intervention in an Age of Terror, Neo-Imperialism, and Massive Violations of Human Rights: Is International Law Evolving in the Right Direction*, 42 Can. Y.B. Int'l L. 3, 12 (2004); Franck, *supra* note 12 at 98; Rainer Hofmann, *International Law and the Use of Military Force Against Iraq*, 45 German Y.B. Int'l L. 9, 31 (2002); Jennings, Watts, *supra* note 64 at 421; Peter Malanczuk, *Countermeasures and Self-Defence as Circumstances Precluding Wrongfulness in the International Law Commission's Draft Articles on State Responsibility*, 43 Zeitschrift für ausländisches öffentliches Recht und Völkerrecht 705, 764 (1983); *id. supra* note 266 at 314; *Nicaragua case* (dissenting opinion of

Charter which does not allow for anticipatory, much less "pre-emptive" self-defense even prior to an anticipation of a particular attack.[1310]

Of specific concern with regard to immediacy of an armed attack by non-state actors is the question as to whether victim states are given more time than ordinarily in order to investigate the attack and to gather information about its precise origin and the true perpetrator. While a traditional armed attack undertaken by a state's regular armed forces is comparably easy to prove, reliably tracing non-state actors is unequally harder. States must be given reasonable time to gather sound information about the perpetrator and its whereabouts without violating the immediacy requirement embedded in Article 51 of the Charter.[1311] This does not violate the idea behind Article 51 of being a narrow exception to Article 2 (4) but it rather preserves the idea of an effective, yet limited safeguard to prevent and deter aggression as opposed to indiscriminate recourse to armed force whenever a state feels attacked.

II. Necessity and Proportionality

Necessity to resort to and the proportionate application of counter-force is a major issue in most of the cases outlined above and therefore plays an important role in armed conflicts between states and non-state actors as well.

As far as necessity of the applied defensive force is concerned, it is on the defending state to explore and exhaust peaceful alternatives to the application of force before responding militarily.[1312] This does not mean that the attacked state would have to wait for a full-scale invasion to occur while it is standing idly by, still attempting to negotiate a peaceful settlement of the dispute.[1313]

Such an understanding of "necessity" is independent of the legal nature of the aggressor. Each victim state will first have to resort to less harmful alternatives to military self-defense against a non-state actor. Negotiating or policing efforts will have to include the alleged host and supportive third states as they may vitally contribute to a less harmfully resolved dispute. Such an approach does exclude immediate recourse to force if peaceful or at least less destructive means prove futile from the very beginning on. If, for instance, the host state can no longer act effectively and has reached the status of a failed state, bare of or-

---

Judge Schwebel), at 347-48; OSCAR SCHACHTER, INTERNATIONAL LAW IN THEORY AND PRACTICE 151-51 (1991).

[1310] *See, e.g.*, IAN BROWNLIE, INTERNATIONAL LAW AND THE USE OF FORCE BY STATES 264 et seq. (1963); *id. supra* note 267 at 702; CASSESE, *supra* note 178 at 358-59; Kammerhofer, *supra* note 4 at 168; HANS KELSEN, THE LAW OF THE UNITED NATIONS 797-98 (1950); Randelzhofer, *supra* note 6 at 803.

[1311] *See* Krajewski, *supra* note 12 at 201.

[1312] DINSTEIN, *supra* note 72 at 237.

[1313] Schachter, *supra* note 44 at 1635.

gans that can neither engage in nor act consequent to negotiating efforts, subsidiary peaceful measures are unlikely to remain a necessary condition prior to the use of force.[1314]

While the above is largely independent of the legal nature of the party responsible for an armed attack, the requirements for a proportionate recourse to force raise some questions. It has become a seemingly automatic response by countless states to complain about the disproportionate use of counter-force whenever states relied upon self-defense against non-state actors. Mostly, these remarks rather appear to concern issues of international humanitarian law and thus the *ius in bello*; a distinction between "proportionality" as incorporated in Article 51 of the Charter as one of primary norms of the *ius ad bellum* is, however, rarely ever made. Rather, such remarks are often used to show how the lack of proportionate use of force ridicules any reference to self-defense at all. The context of such criticism thus allows one to infer that frequently proportionality issues are already used as an argument to rule out the application of counter-force *per se*, rather than merely the particular mode of such use.

One explanation for this phenomenon is merely of a political nature: questioning the proportionate application of force leaves ample argumentative space to maneuver for both the supporters and the opponents of the victim state. Actual, rather unconditional support or rejection of one state can be disguised more convincingly by resorting to broader proportionality issues. Such expression of political alliances and dependencies are hardly to be regulated or altered by different legal interpretations of international norms. However, there are also legal issues concerning proportionality that deserve a reevaluation in the face of non-state actors as aggressors. In the following, the traditional proportionality regime will be outlined, followed by suggestions for an adapted application thereof in cases of non-state actor involvement.

1. Proportionality and States

The traditional self-defense regime envisions states as more or less equal opponents in an armed struggle executed by regular armed forces. Any recourse to force in self-defense must not only be necessary but also proportionate by virtue of a "rule well established in customary international law", as the ICJ stated repeatedly.[1315] And both necessity and proportionality apply not only to customary law but "equally to Article 51 of the Charter".[1316] As to the precise content of both requirements, beginning with the stipulations as formulated in the course

---

[1314] *Cf.* Scholz, *supra* note 34 at 123.

[1315] *Nicaragua* case, at para. 176; *Oil Platforms* case, at para. 76.

[1316] Legality of the Threat or Use of Nuclear Weapons, Advisory Opinion (Int'l Ct. Justice July 8, 1996), 1996 I.C.J. 226, 245 (hereinafter *Nuclear Weapons* Advisory Opinion).

of the *Caroline* incident,[1317] it is established that proportionality of self-defense is measured by a comparison of defensive use of force and the severity of the initial armed attack.[1318] Insofar, the ICJ does not only take a singular military response into consideration, but as in *Oil Platforms*, "the whole operation" into which each act of recourse to defensive force was embedded.[1319] For instance, in *Congo* the court hinted that "taking of airports and towns many hundreds of kilometres from [the defending state's] border would not seem proportionate to the series of transborder attacks it claimed had given rise to the right of self-defence, nor to be necessary to that end."[1320] Accordingly, counter-force as applied in its entirety may not be without a due relation to the armed attack. The amount of force applied must not be more than what is required to repel the attack and may not exceed the amount of force used by the aggressor.[1321] Partly, this reflects once again the provisional nature of the traditional self-defense regime.

The proportionate use of defensive force is considered to permit only the restoration of the *status quo ante*.[1322] History shows that states which engaged in full-scale wars based upon self-defense interpreted this limit extensively, aiming at nothing less than the complete destruction of the military capabilities of their opponents in order to end the current and prevent further armed attacks.[1323] And while a military response in the form of a full-scale war is probably one of the highest degrees of counter-force imaginable, it does not constitute an absolute limit to the traditional self-defense regime and particularly not with regard to the measures applied. If only the degree of danger for the existence of a state is grave enough, even the use of nuclear weapons is not prohibited.[1324] It is important to note that such a grave danger can already occur in response to an attack short of the use of nuclear weapons. Accordingly, even conventional weapons

---

[1317] "instant, overwhelming and leaving no choice of means, and no moment of deliberation" and "limited by that necessity . . . .", *see supra* note 48.

[1318] Jost Delbrück, *Proportionality,* in 3 ENCYCLOPEDIA OF PUBLIC INTERNATIONAL LAW 1140, 1141 (Rudolf Bernhardt ed., 1997); MICHAEL KRUGMANN, DER GRUNDSATZ DER VERHÄLTNISMÄßIGKEIT IM VÖLKERRECHT 20 (2004).

[1319] *Oil Platforms* case, at para 77.

[1320] *Congo* case, at para. 147.

[1321] *Nicaragua* case, at para. 237; CASSESE, supra note 178 at 355; Randelzhofer, *supra* note 6 at 805.

[1322] Delbrück, *supra* note 1318 at 1142.

[1323] *Cf.* DINSTEIN, *supra* note 72 at 241 (referring to World War II).

[1324] *Nuclear Weapons* Advisory Opinion, at 266 ("There is neither in customary nor conventional international law any comprehensive and universal prohibition of the threat or use of nuclear-weapons as such" provided there is an "extreme circumstance of self-defence, in which the very survival of a State would be at stake").

can pose a threat serious enough so that a nuclear defense is legitimate despite a perhaps significant difference between the (conventional) threat and the (nuclear) response. The principle of proportionality as such does insofar not provide with an absolute limit for an effective self-defense, even with nuclear weapons.[1325] More importantly, the due relation required to meet proportionality standards is here not between the degree of use of force applied by the attacker and the defender, but between the seriousness of the – immediate – threat and the means of responsive self-defense.

2. Proportionality and Non-State Actors

The idea of substantial threats endangering a state most seriously, thus creating a need to neutralize them in excess of the means employed to launch the initial armed attack is an approach particularly important regarding armed conflicts between states and non-states.

Proportionality of military self-defense was meant to regulate classic armed struggles between two states so that recourse to force would not automatically end in devastating wars. However, a traditional military goal such as, for instance, the defeat of an opposing army or prevalence in a particular battle, is not what non-state actors strive for. An open military conflict is in fact what the non-state actor hopes to avoid. For terrorist groups or guerillas it constitutes a success when the military superiority of the defending nations becomes irrelevant. By and large, terrorist non-state actors achieve that goal by removing their struggle from the ordinary battlefield. Terrorist non-state actors do not primarily aim to destroy larger enemy forces, despite the fact that they do not distinguish between military and civilian targets. Usually, terrorist non-state actors do not possess the equipment to face the opposing armed forces in the open, neither are they capable of assembling necessary manpower. Their primary goal is a long-term destabilization of states. For that purpose, they attack – either exclusively or predominantly – civilian targets or abuse civilian installations to shield them from military responses. A non-state actor's means of warfare can – but must not – be utterly limited or even primitive, such as Al Qaeda's box cutters of September 11. Removing these means from a terrorist or prosecuting the individually responsible perpetrator is often not an effective countermeasure against the non-state actor as a whole. Replacing both the weapons and the personnel is hardly ever problematic for the non-state actor.[1326]

[1325] *Nuclear Weapons* Advisory Opinion, at 245.

[1326] Accordingly, the United States and NATO attempted to destroy the operative backbone of their most prominent non-state opponent, Al Qaeda, in accordance with S.C. Res. 1368, U.N. Doc. S/RES/1368 (Sept. 12, 2001).

Aside from a necessary degree of efficiency embedded in any proportionality regime, all rules governing armed conflicts have one additional primary goal: to shorten the military dispute, limit the harm to the inevitably necessary extent, and enable the opponents to enter peaceful negotiations quickly.[1327] An unbalanced application of either rule covering a conflict could lead to the precise opposite as disfavoring one or the other side is likely to provoke further violence or at least not contribute to a quick cessation of armed hostilities.

Proportionality is the primary safeguard seeking to prevent excessive use of force and limit harm to the extent absolutely unavoidable. It is not meant to confine the defender's effective protection along the lines of the limited capabilities of the attacker. If it is interpreted to protect the attacker and unreasonably confine the defender, it might encourage further aggressors and lead to an extension of conflicts. With regard to non-state actors this means that if the only measures available to the non-state are continuous acts of murder of individual civilians – provided that they reach the degree of an armed attack – the state cannot in return be confined to respond by counter-force of an equally limited degree as the impact of the terrorist attacks exceeds the plain figures of dead and wounded victims. No strictly limited response would ever prevent further attacks of a similar kind. A prolonged conflict between a non-state actor and a state can amount to, and should be treated as, a regular international armed conflict. It is therefore submitted that once the state is forced to respond continuously, and not merely to isolated small-scale attacks, it can be proportionate to neutralize the origin of the threat from wherever it may emanate.[1328] As one Special Rapporteur to the ILC once noted with regard to ongoing international armed conflicts:

> In the case of self-defence, it was essential to avoid the error of thinking that there should be some proportionality between the action of the aggressor and the action of the State defending itself. Proportionality could be judged only in terms of the objective of the action, which was to repel an attack and prevent it from succeeding. No limitations that might prejudice the success of a response to attack could be placed on the State suffering the attack. The concept of reasonable action must of course enter into the matter . . . .[1329]

[1327] *See, e.g.*, GREEN *supra* note 222 at 15.
[1328] *Cf.* Schachter, *supra* note 44 at 1638.
[1329] Robert Ago, *Eight Report on State Responsibility*, 1980/I Y.B. INT'L L. COMMISSION 188.

Such an approach is limited to defensive 'wars' and does not necessarily apply to individual responses undertaken in self-defense.[1330] However, most of the conflicts outlined above fall into this category: the PLO, Hezbollah, SWAPO, the PKK, Al Qaeda, Fedayeen fighters and others have been fighting against states for years, sometimes decades. Their actions cannot be treated as isolated events, but rather as ongoing campaigns. With few exceptions, such as for instance the South African movements, these campaigns aimed at killing as many civilians as possible to weaken and frustrate their opponents and to destabilize the state. These conflicts, which – as can be seen best in the Middle East – have the potential to spill over into other regions and continue for years. Their political, economic, and social impacts are lasting and severe. A proportionate self-defense regime must be capable to evaluate due responses not limited to isolated attacks that ought to be repelled but to accept ongoing terror campaigns, its perpetrators, and the backbone structures as legitimate targets in response to an armed attack. Proportionate self-defense against non-state actors must not be limited to win a battle, but allow to win the war.

3. Proportionality and Violations of the Host State's Rights

Another feature of a proportionality regime and the permissible extent of the application of force against a non-state actor are the sovereign rights of the host state. If non-state actors are targeted in self-defense on the territory of host states, the sovereign rights of the latter will be violated automatically.[1331] Among these rights are the right to territorial integrity[1332] along with a state's right to political independence as mentioned in Article 2 (4) of the Charter; the right to protection of its nationals;[1333] and the state's economic interests.[1334] While the host state may not even be in control of the area from which the non-state actors operate, recourse to force by the victim state will nonetheless infringe these rights conferred exclusively upon any state as long as the host state's consent cannot be obtained to operate on its territory. Moreover, since the non-state actor will also inevitably make use of the state's infrastructure – roads, electricity and water supply, harbors, ports, etc. – the defending state may even consider it necessary to destroy such installations as well as those in other areas which are primarily inhabited or controlled by the non-state actor.

[1330] Dinstein, *supra* note 72 at 221, 240 (distinguishing self-defense "short of war" from "war" as most serious, but permissible act of self-defense).

[1331] *See* Krajewski *supra* note 12 at 202-03.

[1332] *See, e.g., Corfu Channel* case, at p. 35; Article 2 (4) of the Charter.

[1333] Bowett, *supra* note 1296 at 87.

[1334] *Id.* at 106-14.

Ordinarily a defending state is justified to violate the above rights in light of a prior armed attack by the state. This is not the case if the aggressor is not the host state, but rather the non-state actor. However, the host state may be acting contrary to international law in this situation even if it has no immediate responsibility for the armed attack emanating from its territory. The applicable standard in order to determine a state's responsibility in such a case is due diligence, as explained by the ICJ in *Corfu Channel*.[1335] It requires both the host state's knowledge and opportunity.[1336] This means that by already knowingly tolerating non-state actor activity within their borders, host states will be violating their obligation not to acquiesce in terrorist activity emanating from their territory – provided the state has the general capability to respond.[1337] In most cases, host states will even go beyond merely acquiescing to non-state actor violence by providing some form of active support. And sometimes, while still being short of effective control, host states might do much more than just this to ensure a non-state actor's success.

It is therefore reasonable that the extent to which victim states may apply defensive force against the host state depends on the level of support provided by the latter to the non-state actor.[1338] This is, after all, merely an adapted application of proportionality principles.

For the purpose of categorization, different levels of support have been suggested, namely toleration, sponsorship, support, and the inability to act.[1339] Except for the last category all of these trigger a state's responsibility and thus the breach of international obligations – albeit short of an armed attack by the host state – assuming that either of the above requires at least partial knowledge of the non-state actor's operations. Still, the host state's degree of responsibility and accordingly a proportionate extent of defensive force against the non-state actor to be endured by the host state vary.

[1335] *Corfu Channel* case, at p. 18 ("The State may . . . be bound to supply particulars of the use made by it of the means of information and inquiry at its disposal. But it cannot be concluded from the mere fact of the control exercised by a state over its territory . . . that that state necessarily knew, or ought to have known, of any unlawful act perpetrated therein . . . ."); *see also Lotus* case, at 88 (dissenting opinion of Judge Moore) (stating that "[i]t is well settled that a State is bound to use due diligence to prevent the commission within its dominions of criminal acts against another nation or its people").

[1336] ERICKSON, *supra* note 36 at 101.

[1337] *See also supra* pp. 33 to 34.

[1338] Bruha, *supra* note 12 at 406; Travalio, Altenburg, *supra* note 86 at 112-13.

[1339] *See* ERICKSON, *supra* note 36 at 98-102.

a) TOLERATION

The weakest form of acquiescence is toleration. The host knows about the non-state actor and may or may not share its goals but decides not to confine or support it specifically. The state as such is not involved by any of its agents or institutions and cannot be subject to self-defense. Any measures the victim state undertakes must not endanger any of the host state's military and governmental installations, public roads, buildings, etc. All installations on the other hand used by the terrorists without any interference by the host state become targets. That includes training and residential facilities, vehicles, weapons, etc.

Such an understanding of proportionality flows from the international *ius in bello* as embedded in the Hague Convention (V), regulating the relation between belligerent and neutral states.[1340] It basically sets out the idea that, as long as the neutral power does not interfere with the belligerents, it has the right to have their territory unaffected because of the conflict.[1341] As the ICJ noted in *Nuclear Weapons*, the principle of neutrality applies universally "to all international armed conflict, whatever type of weapon might be used."[1342] However, "neutral States are not unaffected by the existence of a state of war" as the ILC carefully notes in addition to article 21[1343] of the Articles on State Responsibility.[1344] In other words, they may have to live even with collateral damage despite their neutrality.[1345] Once they endanger their neutral status, such as by allowing one belligerent party to use their territory other than stipulated in the Hague Convention (V),[1346] their protection cannot remain inviolable. Consequently, one of the basic rules applicable in such an international armed conflict includes a neutral state that allows for belligerent states to use their territory for military purposes or recruiting combatants violates its neutral position and must bear the consequences.[1347] Following this *telos* of the rules governing the role of neutral states, host states just as neutral third states would have to accept the use of de-

[1340] Hague Convention (V) Respecting the Rights and Duties of Neutral Powers and Persons in Case of War on Land arts. 2, 4, 5, 11, 205 C.T.S. 299 (Oct. 18, 1907) (hereinafter Hague Convention (V)).

[1341] *See, e.g.*, GREEN, *supra* note 222 at 268.

[1342] *Nuclear Weapons* Advisory Opinion, at 261.

[1343] Article 21 provides: "The wrongfulness of an act of a State is precluded if the act constitutes a lawful measure of self-defence taken in conformity with the Charter of the United Nations."

[1344] *Articles on State Responsibility,* at 180.

[1345] SCHOLZ, *supra* note 34 at 118.

[1346] *E.g.*, the neutral power may grant refuge to belligerent troops, but is obliged to intern them and prevent their return to the battlefield, *cf.* Hague Convention (V), Article 11.

[1347] Travalio, Altenburg, *supra* note 86 at 111.

fensive force against all areas belonging to its territory that are directly used by the non-state actors.[1348]

Beside the neutrality argument, the concept underlying Article 51 of the Charter also supports such an approach: proportionality is one means to limit the use of force applied in response to an armed attack. Meanwhile, the mere existence of such a doctrine evidences the acceptance of rights' violations that may not be immediately warranted by prior wrongdoing of the entity eventually affected by a recourse of defensive force.[1349] Proportionality as a concept seeks to limit such harm to the extent unavoidable. This notion is supported by suggestions submitted by the ILC Articles on State Responsibility which propose in the commentary to Article 22[1350] that

> [as] a response to internationally wrongful conduct of another State countermeasures may be justified only in relation to that State. . . . On the other hand, indirect or consequential effects of countermeasures on third parties, which do not involve an independent breach of any obligation to those third parties, will not take a countermeasure outside the scope of article 22.[1351]

This is even more true once an entity does not meet all requirements in order to respond by self-defense (i.e. the host state does not commit an armed attack), but neither meets its obligations under international law vis-à-vis the confinement of non-state actor activity from within its territory. This is the case once a state decides to actively support or sponsor a hostile non-state actor.

b) SPONSORSHIP, SUPPORT

If a state decides to actively support the non-state actor regardless of the extent that such support might reach the host state also becomes a legitimate target. The extent to which it can be held accountable depends again on the degree of the host state involvement.[1352] The highest degree of host state involvement

---

[1348] *Cf.* Krajewski, *supra* note 12 at 203.

[1349] *Cf.* SCHOLZ, *supra* note 34 at 113 ("Die Existenz des Verhältnismäßigkeitsgrundsatzes . . . [wäre] nicht erklärbar, schlösse Art. 51 SVN von vorneherein die Beeinträchtigung Unbeteiligter aus.").

[1350] Article 22 provides: "The wrongfulness of an act of a State not in conformity with an international obligation towards another State is precluded if and to the extent that the act constitutes a countermeasure taken against the latter State in accordance with chapter II of Part Three."

[1351] *Articles on State Responsibility,* at 181.

[1352] Although some prefer to distinguish between sponsorship/direction and support, *see supra* note 40.

would be just short of an armed attack by the host state itself. Above that level the supportive state becomes an attacker and hence an immediate target for self-defense itself. Usually, however, assistance provided for by host states will comprise of financial and logistic support. Some suggest that at least those state agents and facilities directly involved in rendering such support are legitimate targets of the victim state's counter force.[1353] Indeed, it appears reasonable to limit a host state's responsibility accordingly in order to maintain a due relation between involvement and consequent harm. Otherwise any recourse to force would be allowed against a state that is not responsible for an armed attack. Consequently, victim states must be very precise in their choice of targets different from those belonging to the actual attacker, i.e. the non-state actor. If a host state does only provide monetary assistance to a non-state actor besides offering shelter, the victim state must, for example, not attack the host state's military as it has no connection to the non-state actor. In fact, financial assistance might only give rise to according counter-measures, such as freezing of foreign assets, for which self-defense must not even constitute a prerequisite as such measures do not involve the use of force. Logistic support, on the other hand, will establish a direct connection between tangible institutions of the host state and the non-state actor. The responsible agents and organizations will be legitimate targets.

In the course of a military campaign it will be of utmost difficulty to identify all necessary details to abide by such a legal regime. However, uncertainties may not be blamed on the host state. If the victim state cannot soundly establish the degree and at least some details of a host state's involvement, it cannot assume state responsibility and extend it to all agents that normally would carry out the suspected supportive work. Here, again, the burden of proof is that of the defending state.[1354]

Proportionate self-defense cannot be extended beyond any other entity but the host state. Third states do not possess the necessary proximity between the actual use of armed force through the non-state actor and the origin of their actions, namely the territory of the host state. Unlike the host state, a third state does not violate its duty to stop violent activity originating from within its territory.

[1353] Travalio, Altenburg, *supra* note 86 at 112.

[1354] *Cf. Oil Platforms* case, at para. 57 ("[T]he Court has . . . to determine whether the United States has demonstrated that it was the victim of an "armed attack" by Iran such as to justify it using armed force in self-defence; and the burden of proof of the facts showing the existence of such an attack rests on the United States").

c) INABILITY TO ACT

That leaves the question as to how to deal with failed, failing, or temporarily incapacitated state actors. Regularly, such states will not have any opportunity to act as they lack the required organs or at least any control over them.[1355] According to the due diligence standard – requiring both knowledge and opportunity[1356] –, state responsibility can therefore not be assumed. While the state may not have satisfied its duty to prevent attacks emanating from within its territory,[1357] even the continued existence of such a duty does after all not lead to an extended state responsibility absent of the capability to act accordingly. Accordingly, while the self-defense regime as suggested presently allows for defensive force against the non-state actor directly, a lack of state responsibility prohibits extending such actions to any agents or installations of a failed state. And since the absence of governmental authority is the main indication for a failed state will render any authorization to apply force against such an non-existent authority futile, consent by a crippled or exiled government is also not available.

[1355] *See supra* note 3.
[1356] *See supra* notes 1335, 1336.
[1357] ERICKSON, *supra* note 36 at 201.

Part 4 – Summary

This part briefly summarizes the content of this work (Part 4.I.) and then provides an overview of the United Nations Security Council's responses to alleged acts of self-defense against non-state actions (Part 4.II).

I. Summary of the Content

This work has sought to interpret Article 51 of the Charter in light of more than 50 years of state practice. It has been submitted that actual conflicts between state and non-states indicate that self-defense in response to an armed attack by a non-state actor is fully legitimate. The formal nature of the attacking entity is of little relevance in order to invoke Article 51 of the Charter. The degree of control exercised by a state over a violent non-state entity becomes irrelevant for a military response directed immediately against the non-state actor.

Part 1 introduced a legal obscurity in the international law of armed self-defense: the magnitude of an armed attack is of no relevance once the attacker does not meet all criteria of statehood. The traditional legal regime surrounding Article 51 of the Charter as developed and shaped mainly by the ICJ, was laid out above to show that states cannot act legally in self-defense unless it is another state which exercises "effective control" over a non-state actor. Only this state can in return be responded to by counter-force. This understanding of the international customary law of state responsibility as developed in *Nicaragua* and then manifested in Article 8 of the Articles on State Responsibility was upheld by the ICJ particularly in the recent *Advisory Opinion,* as well as a number of other contentious decisions, most recently in *Congo* and *Bosnia.*

Part 1 concluded with an attempt to define the term "non-state actor" for the purpose of Article 51 of the Charter: of all traditional entities recognized by international law only "liberation movements" appear to have had the capacity of triggering armed responses based upon Article 51 of the Charter. It was submitted that a broader definition of groups to be considered as potentially able to launch an "armed attack" is required. The rising importance of powerful non-state entities created a need for states not to be limited to prosecutorial countermeasures but also to be able to employ military force. This work came to the conclusion that, based upon the requirements of the United Nations Charter and the jurisprudence of the ICJ, all groups that act internationally and are capable of committing an "armed attack" intense enough to meet the traditional gravity requirements of Article 51 of the Charter, can be responded to by defensive military force. A particular organizational structure of the attacker is of no relevance.

Part 2 evaluated four primary and ten secondary conflicts between states and non-state actors in which the state relied upon self-defense vis-à-vis the non-state entity. Another five conflicts were briefly introduced which were related to the issue and involved states and non-states, but could not, for different reasons, provide precise results as to the interpretation of Article 51 of the Charter as introduced in Part 1.

In the course of all reviewed conflicts, different legal arguments were put forward as to why self-defense was or was not available against the non-state actors. The cases in which recourse to self-defense was denied illustrate several reoccurring legal convictions. Most frequently, criticism focused on a lack of proportionality during the exercise of self-defense. It can be inferred that criticism as to the degree of a particular defensive action implicitly excludes the general rejection of self-defense as a valid concept in the fight against non-state actors. Another important, yet unspecified ground for the denial of Article 51 of the Charter was to deem the actions in question as mere "aggressions", which is likely to indicate the general absence of a prior situation that would have entitled a state to invoke Article 51 of the Charter as one of two legitimate exceptions to Article 2 (4) of the Charter. Frequently, states criticized allegedly defensive actions, *inter alia*, as illegitimate "reprisal", "terror", "breach of the peace", "hostilities", "escalation", or "premeditated". On a few more recent occasions, self-defense against non-state actors was explicitly accepted. Most of these rare explicit references to legitimate self-defense occurred since 1998.

More important, it was submitted that never, at least not since the mid-1950s, did a state announce explicitly that a defending state would be barred from an invocation of Article 51 of the Charter based upon the lack of statehood of the aggressor.

Part 3 drew the conclusions from the state practice. A self-defense regime, in which the right to use force directly against non-state actors is legitimate, was suggested. The conditions for this legitimate exercise of the right to self-defense within the framework of Article 51 of the Charter were laid out in the following: (1) the primary condition for the exercise of self-defense is a prior "armed attack". Such an attack can be executed by non-state actors, provided that it reaches a sufficient degree of magnitude. An accumulation of a series of smaller attacks instead of one "armed attack" is not yet accepted by state practice; (2) as long as the Security Council has sufficient access to all information necessary to evaluate the danger and seriousness of a factual situation, the notification requirement of Article 51 of the Charter has no substantive meaning; (3) an armed attack must be responded to immediately, although states are likely to be awarded a slightly extended time frame to gather all information necessary to respond properly to an "armed attack". Additionally, all responsive force applied must be (4) necessary and proportionate, irrespective of the legal nature of the attacker. While the conditions under which self-defense can be deemed necessary do not differ from the traditional approach, a slightly adapted proportionality regime was suggested: (a) vis-à-vis states, all force applied in self-defense may not be without a due relation to the attack. Relevant are a relation between the defensive measures and the entirety of the offensive operation underway. Usually, the defending state may not use more force than the attacker, unless the former is endangered in its existence. Then, nuclear weapons may also be employed. Hence, proportionality does not provide an absolute limit of the available force; (b) vis-à-vis non-states, a state is entitled to self-defense limited by the same safeguards as the proportionality regime provides vis-à-vis regular states. It is in conformity with the rationale of the proportionality requirement – i.e. to shorten the conflict and limit the number of victims to the absolutely inevitably – if states do not merely respond to a single attack at a time, but also destroy the root cause of such an attack. This is only possible if the state has been previously facing continuous attacks rather than merely isolated threats; (c) vis-à-vis host states, a gradual proportionality regime was suggested: (aa) if a host-state merely tolerates a non-state actor on its territory, no installations of the host state may be targeted – unless the host state violates its neutrality and thus its international obligations also towards the defending state; (bb) if the host-state supports the non-state actor, all direct means of support may be targeted provided that the defending state can soundly establish the host state's involvement; (cc) given the absence of any opportunity to confine a non-state actor active on the territory of a failed state by the crippled authorities of the latter, the failed state and its remaining institutions may not be targeted.

II. The United Nations Security Council's Responses

The following chart lists events involving the use of armed force as discussed above. Incidents were included only if the victim state explicitly or implicitly referred to self-defense against a non-state actor. Some of the conflicts discussed in this work were thus not mentioned since defensive action was rather employed against host states than against the groups to which the latter had been giving support. Mostly, victim states would also invoke arguments referring to a need to protect its borders and citizens. The latter was only included in absence of clear references to self-defense as primary motivation.

The chart lists "aggression" as an international reaction only if that was expressed by at least one other source but the host state, preferably before the United Nations. Frequent comments such as "breach of the peace" or "violation of international law" were omitted. The reactions are limited to those available and are by no means exhaustive.

With regard to United Nations Security Council resolutions, the first figure in parenthesis indicates the number of votes in favor, the second the votes against, and the third the abstentions. If a resolution was vetoed by one of the permanent members of the Security Council the name of the veto power is indicated in further parenthesis.

1. Israeli Actions on Lebanese Territory to Fight the PLO and Hezbollah

Incident	Nature	Justification	Int'l Reactions	Security Council
Attack on Beirut airport, December 1968	Air strikes	Self-defense after attacks on Israeli civil aviation by PLO	Aggression Reprisal Disproportionate No Lebanese responsibility for prior attacks on Israeli airplane	Unanimous condemnation, S.C. Res. 268
Attack on targets in vicinity to the border, August 1969	Air strikes	Self-defense against armed irregulars (Fatah, PLO)	Aggression Reprisal No armed attack "Excessive" response No Lebanese responsibility for prior attacks on Israel	Unanimous condemnation, S.C. Res. 270
Destruction of terrorist camps in Lebanon, May 1970	Air and ground strikes	Self-defense against Lebanon for terrorist cross-border raids	Aggression Reprisal Disproportionate	Condemnation (11-0-4), S.C. Res. 280
Shelling of Lebanese villages, May 1970	Artillery strikes	Self-defense against terrorist ambush on school bus	--	No action
Attacks in the area of Kfar Chouba, Lebanon, September 1970	Air and ground strikes	Self-defense to continuous armed raids from Lebanon	Aggression Violation of Art. 2 (4) of the Charter	Condemnation (14-0-1), S.C. Res. 285
Attack on terrorists near the	Helicopter-borne units	Reaction to government sup-	--	No action

village of Sarafand, January 1971		ported sabotage raids		
Shelling of border region with Lebanon, summer 1971	Ground forces	Defense against continuous armed attacks emanating from Lebanon to protect citizens	--	No action
Destruction of buildings, January 1972	Ground forces	Self-defense against armed aggressions for which Lebanon is held responsible	--	No action
Destruction of terrorist camps, February 1972	Air and ground strikes	Self-defense against bases supporting terrorists that had been caught inside Israel; Lebanon cannot complain as it is unwilling or unable to prevent such attacks	Aggression Lebanon cannot be held accountable Disproportionate	Unanimous Condemnation, S.C. Res. 313
Destruction of terrorist facilities; clash with Syrian forces in convoy in Lebanon, June 1972	Air and ground strikes	Self-defense after PLO attack on Israeli public bus and soldiers	Aggression Reprisal Inappropriate and ineffective Beyond self-defense	Condemnation (13-0-2), S.C. Res. 316
Air raid of Lebanese and Syrian targets, September 1972	Air force strikes	Response to terrorist attacks in Munich against states harboring terrorists	Aggression Violation of international law	Resolution vetoed (13-1-1) (United States)
Bombing of targets in Lebanon, September 1972	Air and ground strikes	Defense against terror organizations operating from Lebanon	--	No action

Raid of Fatah installations in Beirut, April 1973	Plain clothes operatives	Protection of citizens against terror attacks emanating from Lebanon with governmental consent	Aggression 'Counter-terrorism'	Condemnation (11-0-4), S.C. Res. 332
Destruction of houses in Lebanon, April 1974	Ground forces	Responses to killing of 19 civilians in Kiryat Shmona by terrorists from Lebanon	Aggression Retaliation Reprisal	Condemnation (13-0-0) (China and Iraq did not participate in the vote), S.C. Res. 347
Violation of Lebanese air space and waters, abduction of individuals, May 1975	Air and ground forces	Defensive measures against 30 act of aggression in five weeks emanating from Lebanon while the government refuses to enforce its sovereignty	--	No action
Overflights by aircrafts, gunfights in village Aita Ech Chaab, May 1975	Air and ground forces	Obligation to protect Israeli citizens against rockets and other PLO attacks from inside Lebanon	--	No action
Attacks at Palestinian camps, December 1975	Air strikes	--	Aggression	Resolution vetoed (13-1-1) (United States)
Naval and air attacks at several targets along the Lebanese border, Operation	Naval, ground, and air attacks	Self-defense against terror attack by PLO inside Israel, killing 37 and wounding 76	Aggression Punitive action	Condemnation (12-0-2) (China did not participate in the vote), S.C. Res. 425; Deployment of UNI-

Litani, March 1978		civilians		FIL (12-0-2) (China did not participate in the vote), S.C. Res. 426
Clashes inside Lebanon between Israeli Defense Forces and PLO forces, January 1979	Air and ground forces	Self-defense against threats against Israeli and Lebanese civilians by PLO	Aggression	Extension of UNIFIL mandate (12-0-2) (China did not participate in the vote), S.C. Res. 444
Artillery and mortar fire in the Tyre area, May 1979	Ground forces	Self-defense against PLO	--	No action
Army excursion into UNIFIL's area of operation, April 1980; Southern Lebanese army attacked UNIFIL	Ground forces	Self-defense against PLO attack on Kibbutz Misgav Am emanating from UNIFIL-controlled area	Aggression Attack on Misgav Am no justification for invasion	Condemnation of Israel's invasion and the use of force (12-0-3), S.C. Res. 467
Attack on targets in Beirut, July 1981 (in the course of the "July-Mini-War")	Air and ground forces	Response to past PLO terror and current weapons buildup	Preemptive actions not covered by Article 51 of the Charter Aggression Disproportionate	Resolution calling to cease all armed attacks adopted unanimously, S.C. Res. 490
Air raids into southern Lebanon, April, May 1982	Air strikes	Duty to protect its citizens by all necessary means from cross-border PLO raids and failure of Lebanon to meet its obligations to prevent terrorist	--	No action

		groups from operating from inside Lebanon		
Invasion of southern Lebanon incl. Beirut, Operation Peace for Galilee, June-September 1982	Air, ground, and naval forces	Self-defense against cross-border PLO attacks and against worldwide attacks against Israeli and Jewish targets (including a immediately preceding attempted assassination of an Israeli ambassador)	Aggression Disproportionate (with regard to the assassination attempt as cause for self-defense)	Resolutions calling to cease all armed attacks adopted unanimously, S.C. Res. 508, 509, 512, 516, 518; Resolutions condemning Israel for failure to comply with the above resolutions vetoed (14-1-0) (United States); Resolution placing Beirut under U.N. supervision and ordering regular Lebanese and U.N. forces between Israel and PLO combatants vetoed (14-1-0) (United States); Resolution calling to respect civilian populations adopted unanimously, S.C. Res. 513; Resolution calling to lift the Israeli blockade of Beirut adopted (14-0-0) (the United States did not participate in the vote), S.C. Res. 515; Resolution censor-

				ing Israel for failure to comply with previous resolutions adopted (14-0-1), S.C. Res. 517; Resolution condemning Israel for cease-fire violations adopted unanimously, S.C. Res. 520; Resolution condemning the massacre in Sabra and Shatila adopted unanimously, S.C. Res. 521
Air raids on targets in Lebanon, January 1984	Air strikes	Self-defense against terrorist bases in Lebanon, abusing civilian installations to shield	--	No action
Seizure of passenger boat en route from Cyprus to Lebanon; detention of two passengers, July 1984	Naval forces	Self-defense as the there were strong indications that the boat carried individuals closely related to an imminent threat to Israel	--	No action

Armed attacks on four villages in southern Lebanon; arrest of 20 individuals, December 1984	Air and ground forces	Prevention of attacks expected to emanate from terrorist bases	--	No action
Pursuance of suspected terrorists after ambush on Southern Lebanese Army and Israeli forces, January 1986	Ground forces	Necessity to protect citizens from terror attacks emanating from bases in Lebanon	Aggression	Resolution vetoed (11-1-3) (United States)
Several Israeli and Southern Lebanese Army raids at Kabrikha, Khirbet-Salum, Yatar, Kafra, Sidon, Nabatiye, Soultaniyé, Yanta and other places all through 1987	Air, ground, and naval forces	Self-defense against terrorist attacks launched from Lebanese territory by remaining PLO and also Hezbollah units	Continuous Israeli rejection to implement resolution 425 (1978)	No action
Bombing of facilities near Sidon killing 26, January 1988	Air strikes	Ongoing self-defense absent effective Lebanese countermeasures against PLO terror	Aggression Illegal measures against civilians	Resolution vetoed (13-1-1) (United States)

Invasion as far as north of Lebbaya (beyond the "security zone), May 1988	Air and ground forces	Prevention of rebuilding of terrorist infrastructure to protect Israeli civilians	Aggression	Resolution vetoed (14-1-0) (United States)
Bombardment of PFLP targets north of Beirut, December 1988	Air and naval forces	Ensuring Israel's safety following prior PFLP attacks (using e.g. hang-gliders) emanating from the targeted areas	Aggression	Resolution vetoed (14-1-0) (United States)
Exchanges of hostilities between Israeli and "Southern Lebanese Army" (SLA) forces with other Lebanese groups, all through 1989-91	Air and ground forces	Responses to attacks or anticipated attacks on IDF or SLA forces in the "security-zone"	--	No action
Actions against Hezbollah and other forces, January 1992	Air and ground forces	Escalation of terror attacks by Hezbollah and others and failure of Lebanon to confine their attacks	Lebanon's sovereignty, independence, and borders must be respected and any state must refrain from violence	Statement by the President of the Security Council on behalf its member states
Actions against Hezbollah forces, May 1992	--	Self-defense	--	No action
Military campaign against Hezbollah tar-	Air and ground forces	Self-defense	--	No action

gets, July 1993				
Bombing of targets near Baalbek, June 1994	Air strikes	Self-defense and prevention of further Hezbollah attacks	--	No action
Actions against Hezbollah, early 1995	--	Self-defense and prevention of further Hezbollah attacks	--	No action
Large-scale attacks on Hezbollah targets, April 1996 (Operation Grapes of Wrath)	Air, naval, and ground forces	Self-defense to continuous rocket barrages killing eight and wounding 29 civilians since Feb. 1, 1996	Self-defense understandable, but disproportionate Aggression Disproportionate	Resolution calling to cease all hostilities adopted unanimously, S.C. Res. 1052
Raids against Hezbollah targets, February 1997	Air and ground forces	Self-defense	--	No action
Raids against Hezbollah targets, January 1998	Air and ground forces	Self-defense	--	No action
Military actions against Hezbollah, November 1999	Air and ground forces	Self-defense	--	No action
Raid against Hezbollah forces (and Syrian radar installations), April 2001	Air forces	Self-defense against prior Hezbollah attacks on IDF personnel	--	No action
Air and artillery strikes against Hezbollah in the	Air and ground forces	Self-defense against rocket attacks by Hezbollah	--	No action

Shab'a area, April 2002				
Repeated actions against Hezbollah, 2004 (e.g. destruction of road side bombs near the village of Marwahin; air raids near Beirut airport)	Air and ground forces	Self-defense against prior rocket and other attacks by Hezbollah (and the PFLP)	--	No action
Repeated actions against Hezbollah, 2005 (e.g. bombing of targets near Shab'a)	Air and ground forces	Self-defense against rocket and mortar shells into northern Israel	--	No action
Invasion into southern Lebanon, July 2006	Air, ground, and naval forces	Self-defense	Self-defense justified, but disproportionate Aggression Reprisal	Resolution calling to cease all hostilities adopted unanimously, S.C. Res. 1701

2. South Africa's Military Actions In Neighboring Countries

Incident	Nature	Justification	Int'l Reactions	Security Council
Attack on Senegalese Port, October 1972	Ground forces		Aggression	Condemnation (11-0-3), S.C. Res. 321
Bombardment of Namibian camp in Angola, May 1978	Air and ground strikes	Response to border violations by SWAPO units in protection of South-West Africa (Namibia)	Aggression	Unanimous condemnation, S.C. Res. 428
Intrusions into Zambian air	Air and waterborne troops	Responses to presence of	Aggression	No action

and land space, March 1979		SWAPO in border area and responsibility to protect South West African civilians		
Military excursions into Zambia, April 1980	Air and ground forces	Protective action against aggressions committed from Zambian soil into South West Africa (Namibia) for which South Africa was responsible	Aggression	Unanimous Condemnation, S.C. Res. 466
Invasion by South African forces into Angola, May and June 1980	Air and ground forces	Responses to SWAPO attacks, explicitly not directed against Angola	Aggression	Condemnation (12-0-3), S.C. Res. 475
Raids into Angola following SWAPO raids and abductions, September 1980	Air and ground forces	Self-defense against SWAPO operations in South West Africa/ Namibia	Aggression No danger for South African territory	Resolution vetoed (13-1-1) (United States)
Attack on apartment buildings in Maseru, Lesotho, December 1982	Ground forces	Preemptive strikes against ANC facilities to prevent further attacks on South African installations Lesotho harbored terrorists	Aggression	Unanimous condemnation, S.C. Res. 527
Armed incursions into Angola, December 1983	Air and ground forces	Protection of Namibia against SWAPO attacks	Aggression Illegal occupation	Condemnation (14-0-1), S.C. Res. 545

Armed incursions into Angola, January 1984	Air and ground forces	Protection of Namibia against SWAPO attacks	Aggression Illegal occupation	Condemnation (13-0-2), S.C. Res. 546
Planned commando raid on oil installations in Angola; foiled by Angolan security forces, May 1985	Ground forces	Self-defense against continuous ANC attacks on South Africa emanating from bases in Angola	Aggression	Unanimous condemnation, S.C. Res. 567
Attacks on installations in Botswana's capital Gaborone, June 1985	Ground forces	Prevention of further ANC attacks on South Africa emanating from bases in Botswana which the government did not curtail, leaving South Africa with no alternative	Aggression	Unanimous condemnation, S.C. Res. 568
Attacks on installation in Lesotho's capital Maseru, December 1985	Ground forces	Prevention of further ANC attacks in South Africa emanating from bases in Lesotho in absence of any governmental action against them	Aggression 'State-terrorism' 'Hot pursuit' has no legal basis	Unanimous condemnation, S.C. Res. 580
Attacks on targets in Botswana, June 1985	Air and Ground forces	Prevention of further ANC attacks in South Africa; necessity to act due to Botswana's inactivity	Aggression No prior armed attack	Resolution vetoed (12-2-1) (United Kingdom; United States)

Invasion-type military incursions into Angola, October, November 1987	Air and Ground forces	Protection of Namibian citizens against SWAPO intrusions; defense of Angolan UNITA militia	Aggression Interference with domestic Angolan matters No mandate to protect Namibians Abuse of UNITA as South African agents	Unanimous condemnation, S.C. Res. 602
Attacks on ANC members in Botswana, June 1988	Commando unit	Compelled to curtail ANC activities emanating from Botswana as the group receives logistic and other support from there	Aggression	Statement by the President of the Security Council on behalf its member states confirming South Africa's disregard of Security Council resolutions, in particular S.C. Res. 568

3. Foreign Interventions in Northern Iraq to Fight Kurdish Groups

Incident	Nature	Justification	Int'l Reactions	Security Council
Turkish raids against several Kurdish villages in Iraq, October 1991	Air and ground strikes	Self-defense	Self-defense justified	No action
Iranian raids into Iraq, May 1993	Air strikes	Self-defense	--	No action
Iranian air strikes into northern Iraq, November 1994	Air strikes	Self-defense	--	No action
Turkish raids into northern Iraq, as of March 1995	Air and ground strikes	Self-defense	Self-defense justified Aggression Disproportionate	No action

(Operation Steel)			in light of less harmful alterna-tives available	
Iranian strikes against bases of armed groups located in Iraq, July 1996	Ground forces	Self-defense	--	No action
Iranian air strikes against two terrorist bases in Iraq, September 1997	Air strikes	Self-defense	--	No action
Repeated Turkish attacks against Kurd-ish factions in northern Iraq; January, May and December 1997	Air and ground strikes	Self-defense	Understandable to fight terror, but military means inappro-priate Aggression	No action
Iranian rocket attack on ter-rorist bases in Iraq, June 1999	Rocket strikes	Self-defense	--	No action
Incursion by armed bands from Iraq into Iran, February 2000	--	Iran reserved its right to exercise self-defense against such groups	--	--
Iranian mili-tary actions against targets in Iraq, April 2001	Rocket strikes	Self-defense against "People's Mujahedeen Organization"	--	No action

4. U.S. MILITARY ACTIONS TO FIGHT THE TALIBAN AND AL QAEDA

Incident	Nature	Justification	Int'l Reactions	Security Council
Air strikes on Al Qaeda targets in Sudan and Afghanistan, August 1998	Naval forces	Self-defense in response to AL Qaeda attacks on American embassies	Violation of territorial integrity (of Sudan) Self-defense appropriate	No action
Attacks on Taliban and Al Qaeda in Afghanistan, October 2001	Air, ground, and naval forces	Self-defense in response to Al Qaeda attacks on September 11	Self-defense justified	Resolution acknowledging the Unite States' right to defend itself adopted unanimously, S.C. Res. 1368

5. ISRAEL'S MILITARY ACTIONS AGAINST FEDAYEEN IN EGYPT

Incident	Nature	Justification	Int'l Reactions	Security Council
Attacks on Fedayeen bases in Sinai Peninsula, October 1956	Ground and air forces	Self-defense against several attacks on Israel by Egyptian Fedayeen since 1955	Aggression Reprisal Disproportionate Violation of armistice agreement Pursuit	Two resolutions vetoed (7-2-2) (France, United Kingdom)

6. LEBANON'S AND JORDAN'S COMPLAINTS AGAINST UNITED ARAB REPUBLIC

Incident	Nature	Justification	Int'l Reactions	Security Council
Dispatch of British and American forces to Jordan and Lebanon in response to subversive actions on behalf of the United Arab Republic, July 1958	--	Intrusions by armed bands from the United Arab Republic into Jordan and Lebanon need to be repelled in collective self-defense based upon Art. 51 of the Charter	Self-defense Aggression (mainly: in absence of any armed attack) Disproportionate Purely domestic matter	Five resolutions vetoed (1-8-2) (Canada, China, Colombia, France, Iraq, Panama, United Kingdom, United States); (10-1-0) (USSR); (2-9-0) (Canada, China, Colombia, France, Iraq, Japan, Panama,

				United Kingdom, United States); (1-8-2) (Canada, China, Colombia, France, Iraq, Panama, United Kingdom, United States); (10-1-0) (USSR); Resolution calling for emergency special session of General Assembly adopted unanimously (S.C. Res. 129)

7. MILITARY ACTIONS OF FRANCE AGAINST ALGERIAN GROUPS IN TUNISIA

Incident	Nature	Justification	Int'l Reactions	Security Council
Military action against Algerian camps inside Tunisia, February 1958	Air strikes	Response to Algerian attacks against French targets inside Algeria	No internal French affair Violation of Tunisian sovereignty	No action
Military action against Algerian camps inside Tunisia, June 1959	Air strikes	Response to Algerian attacks against French targets inside Algeria	No internal French affair Violation of Tunisian sovereignty	No action

8. Israel's Military Actions Against Jordan

Incident	Nature	Justification	Int'l Reactions	Security Council
Military actions against terrorist targets in the Karameh refugee camp, March 1968	Air and ground forces	Self-defense against cross-border raids and prevention of further attacks	Aggression Violation of armistice agreement Areas "defended" not under Israel's jurisdiction Illegitimate reprisal	Unanimous condemnation, S.C. Res. 248
Air strikes against targets near Salt, August 1968	Air force	Self-defense against numerous cross-border raids by armed bands	Aggression Illegitimate reprisal Disproportionate Violation of cease-fire	Unanimous condemnation, S.C. Res. 256

9. Southern Rhodesia's Military Campaigns

Incident	Nature	Justification	Int'l Reactions	Security Council
Raid against facilities in Mozambique, August 1976	Air and ground forces	Protection against armed bands operating in Mozambique	--	No action
Military actions against camps in Botswana, December 1976	Air and ground strikes	Response to armed bands operating from Botswana; "hot pursuit"	Aggression	Condemnation (13-0-2), S.C. Res. 403
Raid against camps in Botswana, May 1977	Air and ground forces	Response to military activities by armed band located in the camps	Aggression	Unanimous condemnation, S.C. Res. 406

Military action against armed bands operating from Mozambique, June 1977	Ground forces	Self-defense against military actions emanating from Mozambique	Aggression Genocide "Hot pursuit" No prior armed attack	Unanimous condemnation, S.C. Res. 411
Attack against base in Zambia, March 1978	Air and ground forces	Self-defense to foil invasion by armed bands	Aggression	Condemnation (10-0-5), S.C. Res. 423
Raid against camps in Mozambique, July 1978	Air and ground forces	Self-defense against externally based groups	--	No action
Attacks against camps in Mozambique, September 1978	Air and ground forces	Self-defense against armed bands, not Mozambique's government	--	No action

10 PORTUGAL'S MILITARY CAMPAIGNS IN AFRICA

Incident	**Nature**	**Justification**	**Int'l Reactions**	**Security Council**
Attack on Targets in Senegal, September 1967	Ground forces	Response to attacks from "elements" that crossed the border in Guinea-Bissau from Senegal; pursuit, but no cross-border attack	--	No action
Attacks on targets near Lote (Zambia), June 1969	Air strikes	Self-defense against armed bands operating under Zambian protection as well as regular Zambian troops	Illegitimate "hot pursuit" Aggression	Condemnation (11-0-4) S.C. Res. 268,

Attacks on targets near Samine in Senegal, November 1969	Ground strikes	Self-defense against anti-Portuguese organizations	Aggression	Condemnation (13-0-2), S.C. Res. 273
Shelling of targets inside Guinea, December 1969	Ground strikes	Self-defense against armed bands from Guinea attacking targets inside Guinea-Bissau	Aggression Not enough information to judge situation	Condemnation (9-0-6), S.C. Res. 275
Raid into Senegal, November 1971	Air and ground strikes	Self-defense	Aggression	Condemnation (14-0-1), S.C. Res. 302
Attack on Senegalese port killing Senegalese army personnel, October 1972	Ground forces	Response against bands operative from Senegal into Guinea-Bissau; Portugal apologized for attacking Senegalese troops and offered compensation	Aggression Retaliation Unprovoked attack	Condemnation (12-0-3), S.C. Res. 321

11. Israel's Air Raid Against the PLO in Tunis

Incident	Nature	Justification	Int'l Reactions	Security Council
Air strikes against PLO targets near Tunis, October 1985	Air strikes	Self-defense on the occasion of a terrorist attack against Israelis in Cyprus and in response to several PLO attacks against Israeli and Jewish targets	Aggression Self-defense understandable Disproportionate Unprovoked attack	Condemnation (14-0-1), S.C. Res. 573

12. Tajikistan's Military Responses Against Afghanistan

Incident	Nature	Justification	Int'l Reactions	Security Council
Military action against armed band crossing into Tajikistan from Afghanistan, July 1993	Air and ground forces	Repulsion of attack by "mujahidin"	--	Issuance of statement urging all parties to cease hostilities
Attack of Afghan groups inside Afghanistan and Tajikistan by various states, mainly Russia and Tajikistan, July 1993 until May 1997	Air and ground forces	Response to cross-border raids by "mujahidin"	--	No action

13. Dispute Between Ethiopia, Eritrea, Sudan, and Uganda

Incident	Nature	Justification	Int'l Reactions	Security Council
Sudan, October 2002	--	Announcement by Sudan that it would respond to armed bands operating from Eritrea in exercise of Article 51 of the Charter	--	--

14. Israel's Military Responses Against Targets in Syria

Incident	Nature	Justification	Int'l Reactions	Security Council
Air raid against camps near Damascus, October 2003	Air strikes	Self-defense after suicide bombing in Haifa executed by the Islamic Jihad, operating from bases in Syria	Aggression Self-defense understandable Disproportionate Illegitimate Reprisal No prior armed attack	No action

15. Military Responses Against Hamas by Israel

Incident	Nature	Justification	Int'l Reactions	Security Council
Attack on targets near Rafah, March 2004	Air strikes	Military response to terror attacks in Ashdod	--	No action
Attack on targets in the Rafah area, May 2004	Air and ground forces	Self-defense; destruction of support routes for Hamas	Self-defense justified Disproportionate Violation of humanitarian provisions Aggression	Condemnation (14-0-1), S.C. Res. 1544
Raid into Gaza, October 2004	Air and ground forces	Self-defense against rocket attacks on Israel by Hamas	Self-defense justified Disproportionate Violation of humanitarian provisions Aggression	Resolution vetoed (11-1-3) (United States)
Military operation targeting Hamas infrastructure in Gaza, October-November 2006	Air and ground forces	Self-defense against Hamas' rockets	Self-defense justified Disproportionate Violation of humanitarian provisions Aggression	Resolution vetoed (10-1-4) (United States)

BIBLIOGRAPHY

Ago, Robert; Eight Report on State Responsibility, 1980/I Y.B. Int'l L. Commission 184-88.

Akehurst, Michael; The Hierarchy of the Sources of International Law, 47 Brit. Y.B. Int'l L. 273 (1974-75).

Alexandrov, Stanimir A; Self-Defense Against the Use of Force in International Law, 1996.

Arts, Bas (ed.); Non-State Actors in International Relations, 2003.

— *Math Noortmann*, Non-State Actors in International law 59-76.

Baker, Mark B.; Terrorism And The Inherent Right Of Self-Defense (A Call To Amend Article 51 Of The United Nations Charter), 10 Hous. J. Int'l L. 25 (1987).

Bassiouni, Cherif M.; Legal Control of International Terrorism: A Policy Oriented Assessment, 43 Harv. Int'l L.J. 83 (2002).

Beck, Robert J.; "Don't Treat On Us": International Law and Forcible State Responses to Terrorism, 12 Wis. Int'l L.J. 153 (1994).

Beres, Louis Rene; Israel, Lebanon, and Hizbullah: A Jurisprudential Assessment, 14 Ariz. J. Int'l Comp. L. 141 (1997).

Bergen, Peter L.; Holy War, Inc. – Inside the Secret World of Osama bin Laden, 2001.

Bernhardt, Rudolf (ed.); Encyclopedia of Public International Law, Volumes II (1995), III (1997), IV (2000).

Blum, Yehuda; The Missing Reversioner: Reflections on the Status of Judea and Samaria, 3 Isr. L. Rev. 279 (1968).

Bothe, Michael; Lohmann, Torsten; Der türkische Einmarsch im Nordirak, 5 Schweizerische Zeitschrift für internationales und europäisches Recht 441 (1995).

Bowett, Derek W.; Self-Defence in International Law, 1958.

— Reprisals Involving Recourse to Armed Force, 66 Am. J. Int'l L. 1 (1972).

Brown, E.D.; The International Law of the Sea, Volume I, Introductory Manual, 1994.

Brownlie, Ian; International Law and the Use of Force by States, 1963.

— Principles of Public International Law, 6th ed., 2003.

Bruha, Thomas; Gewaltverbot und humanitäres Völkerrecht nach dem 11. September 2001, 40 Archiv des Völkerrechts 383 (2002).

Caplen, Robert A.; Mending the "fence": How treatment of the Israeli-Palestinian conflict by the International Court of Justice at the Hague has redefined the doctrine of self-defense, 57 Fla. L. Rev. 717 (2005).

Carlowitz, Leopold von; Interpreting Self-Defense Restrictively: The World Court in the Oil Platforms Case, 23 Sicherheit und Frieden 79 (2005).

Carpenter, G.; The South African Raid on Terrorist Bases in Lesotho, 8 S. Afr. Y.B. Int'l L. 154 (1982).

Carver, Natasha; Is Iraq/Kurdistan a State such as it Can Be Said to Operate State Systems and Thereby Offer Protection to its 'Citizens'?, 14 Int'l J. Refugee L. 57 (2002).

Cassese, Antonio; International Law, 2nd ed., 2005.

— Mercenaries: Lawful Combatants or War Criminals?, 40 Zeitschrift für ausländisches öffentliches Recht und Völkerrecht 1 (1986).

Castel, Jean-Gabriel; The Legality and Legitimacy of Unilateral Armed Intervention in an Age of Terror, Neo-Imperialism, and Massive Violations of Human Rights: Is International Law Evolving in the Right Direction, 42 Can. Y.B. Int'l L. 3 (2004).

Chiapetta, Hans; Rome 11/15/98: Extradition or Political Asylum for Kurdistan Workers Party's Leader Abdullah Ocalan?, 13 Pace Int'l L. Rev. 117 (2001).

Constantinou, Avra; The Right of Self-Defense Under Customary International Law and Article 51 of the U.N. Charter, 2000.

Crook, John R.; Contemporary Practice of the United States Relating to International Law, 100 Am. J. Int'l L. 455 (2006).

D'Amato, Anthony; The Concept of Custom in International Law, 1971.

Damrosch, Lori F. (ed.); The International Court of Justice At A Crossroads, 1987.

— *Eugene V. Rostov*; Disputes Involving the Inherent Right of Self-Defense, 264-287.

Delbrück, Jost; The Fight Against Global Terrorism: Self-Defense or Collective Security as International Police Action? Some Comments on the International Legal Implications of the 'War Against Terrorism', 44 German Y.B. Int'l L. 9 (2001).

Dhooge, Lucien J.; We arm the World: The Implications of American Participation in Global Armaments Trade, 16 Ariz. J. Int'l & Comp. L. 577 (1999).

Dinstein, Yoram; War, Aggression and Self-Defence, 4th ed., 2005.

Erickson, Richard J.; Legitimate Use of Military Force Against State-Sponsored International Terrorism, 1989.

Finch, George A.; Mexico and the United States, 11 Am. J. Int'l L. 399 (1917).

Franck, Thomas M.; Recourse to Force, 2002.

Friedman, Thomas L.; From Beirut to Jerusalem, 1990.

Frowein, Jochen Abr. (ed.); Verhandeln für den Frieden, Negotiating for Peace, 2003.

— *Rüdiger Wolfrum*, Fighting Terrorism at Sea: Options and Limitations under International Law, 649-668.

Gadoury, Christopher L.; Should the United States officially recognize the Taliban? The International Legal and Political Considerations, 23 Hous. J. Int'l L. 385 (2001).

Garcia-Mora, Manuel R.; International Responsibility for Hostile Acts of Private Persons Against Foreign States, 1962.

Gassama, Ibrahim J.; Reaffirming Faith in the Dignity of each Human Being: The United Nations, NGOs, and Apartheid, 19 Fordham Int'l L.J. 1464 (1996).

Gazit, Shlomo; Israel in Transition: Israel and the Palestinians: Fifty Years of Wars and Turning Points, 555 Annals Am. Acad. Pol. Soc. Sci. 82 (1998).

Geiss, Robin; Failed States – Legal Aspects and Security Implications, 47 Germ. Y.B. Int'l L. 457 (2004).

Gilboa, Amos; Die Bedrohung durch den PLO-Terrorismus, 1985.

Gray, Christine D.; International Law and the Use of Force, 2nd ed., 2004.

Green, Leslie C.; The Contemporary Law of Armed Conflict, 2nd ed., 2000.

Guillaume, Gilbert; Terrorism and International Law, 53 Int'l & Comp. L. Q. 537 (2004).

Halberstam, Malvina; Terrorism on the High Seas: Achille Lauro, Piracy and the IMO Convention on Maritime Safety, 82 Am. J. Int'l L. 269 (1988).

— The Evolution of the United Nations Position on Terrorism: From Exempting National Liberation Movements to Criminalizing Terrorism

Wherever and by Whomever Committed, 41 Colum. J. Transnat'l L. 573 (2003).

Harik, Judith P.; Hezbollah – The Changing Face of Terrorism, 2004.

Hofmann, Rainer; International Law and the Use of Military Force Against Iraq 45 German Y.B. Int'l L. 9 (2002).

Henckaerts, Jean-Marie; Doswald-Beck, Louise (eds.); International Committee of the Red Cross, Customary International Humanitarian Law, Vol. I, Rule, 2005.

*International Institute for Strategic Studies;*The Military Balance, 2006.

Ipsen, Knut; Völkerrecht, 5th ed., 2004.

Jennings, Robert (ed.); Oppenheim's International Law, Vol. I, 9th ed., 1992.

Kadelbach, Stefan; Zwingendes Völkerrecht, 1992.

Kammerhofer, Jörg; Uncertainties of the Law of Self-Defence in the United Nations Charter, 35 Neth. Y.B. Int'l L. 143 (2004).

Katzman, Kenneth; Al Qaeda: Profile and Threat Assessment, Cong. Rep. Service, RL33038 (Aug. 17, 2005).

Kearly, Timothey; Raising the Caroline, 17 Wis. Int'l L.J. 325 (1999).

Kellermann, Alfred E. (ed.); Israel Among the Nations, 1998.

— *Yehuda Blum*, Israel and the United Nations: A Retrospective Overview, 69-77.

— *Yoram Dinstein*, The International Legal Dimensions of the Arab-Israeli Conflict, 137-154.

Kelsen, Hans; The Law of the United Nations, 1950.

Knowles, Catherine S.; Life and Human Dignity, the Birthright of all human beings: An Analysis of the Iraqi Genocide of the Kurds and Effective Enforcement of Human Rights, 46 Naval L. Rev. 152 (1998).

Krajewski, Markus; Selbstverteidigung gegen bewaffnete Angriffe nichtstaatlicher Organisationen – Der 11. September 2001 und seine Folgen, 40 Archiv des Völkerrechts 183 (2002).

Krugmann, Michael; Der Grundsatz der Verhältnismäßigkeit im Völkerrecht, 2004.

Kwakwa, Edward; South Africa's May 1986 Military Incursions Into Neighboring African States, 12 Yale J. Int'l L. 421 (1987).

Laursen, Andreas; The Use of Force and (the State of Necessity), 37 Vand. J. Transnat'l L. 485 (2004).

League of Nations; Hunderste Tagung des Völkerbundrates, 18 Monatsberichte über die Tätigkeit des Völkerbundes 23 (1938).

Lobel, Jules; The Use of Force to Respond to Terrorist Attacks: the Bombing of Sudan and Afghanistan, 24 Yale J. Int'l L. 537 (1999).

MacBride, Seán; Israel in Lebanon – The Report of the International Commission, 1983.

MacCormack, Timothey; Self-Defense in International Law, 1996.

Malanczuk, Peter; Akehurts's Modern Introduction to International Law, 7th ed., 1997.

— Countermeasures and Self-Defence as Circumstances Precluding Wrongfulness in the International Law Commission's Draft Articles on State Responsibility, 43 Zeitschrift für ausländisches öffentliches Recht und Völkerrecht 705 (1983).

Marsden, Peter; The Taliban: War, religion and the new order in Afghanistan, 1998.

Murphy, Sean D.; Contemporary Practice of the United States Relating to International Law, 93 Am. J. Int'l L. 161 (1999).

— Terrorism and the concept of "Armed Attack" in Article 51 of the U.N. Charter, 43 Harv. Int'l L.J. 41 (2002).

— Assessing the Legality of Invading Iraq, 92 Geo. L.J. 173 (2004).

— Self-Defense and the Israeli Wall Advisory Opinion: An Ipse Dixit from the ICJ?, 99 Am. J. Int'l L. 62 (2005).

Nolte, Georg; Eingreifen auf Einladung, 1999.

O'Brien, William; Reprisals, Deterrence and Self-Defense in Counterterror Operations, 30 Va. J. Int'l. L. 421 (1990).

O'Connell, Mary-Ellen; Lawful Self-Defense to Terrorism, 63 U. Pitt. L. Rev. 889 (2002).

— Enhancing the Status of Non-State Actors Through a Global War on Terrorism?, 43 Colum. J. Transnat'l L. 435 (2005).

O'Leary, Carole A.; Eklund, Karna A.J.; Pluralism vs. Modern Iraqi Nationalism: Root Causes of State-Sponsored Violence Against Iraq's Kurdish Community and the Search for Post-Conflict Justice, 13 Mich. St. J. Int'l L. 91 (2005).

Occelli, Maria Benvenuta; "Sinking" the Caroline: Why the Caroline Doctrine's Restrictions on Self-Defense should not be regarded as Customary International Law, 4 San Diego Int'l L.J. 467 (2003).

Perry, Nicholas J.; The Numerous Federal Definitions of Terrorism: The Problem of Too Many Grails, 30 J. Legis. 249 (2004).

Peters, Butz; RAF, Terrorismus in Deutschland, 1993.

Pflieger, Klaus; Die Rote Armee Fraktion RAF, 2004.

Prados, Alfred B.; The Kurds in Iraq: Status, Protection, and Prospects, Cong. Rep. Service 94-423 F (May 12, 1994).

Printer, Norman G.; The Use of Force Against Non-State Actors under International Law: An Analysis of the U.S. Predator Strike in Yemen, 8 UCLA J. Int'l L. & Foreign Aff. 331 (2003).

Quigley, John; The Afghanistan War and Self-defense, 37 Val. U. L. Rev. 541 (2003).

Ranstorp, Magnus; Hizb'allah in Lebanon; The Politics of the Western Hostage Crisis, 1997.

Rashid, Ahmed; Taliban, 2001.

Roberts, Adam; Prolonged Military Occupation: The Israeli-Occupied Territories Since 1967, 84 Am. J. Int'l L. 44 (1990).

Ruys, Tom; Verhoeven, Sten; Attacks by Private Actors and the Right of Self-Defense, 10 J. Conflict & Security L. 289 (2005).

Sandoz, Yves; Swinarski, Christophe; Zimmermann, Bruno; Commentary on the Additional Protocols of 8 June 1977 to the Geneva Conventions of 12 August 1949, 1987.

Schachter, Oscar; The Right of States to use Armed Force, 82 Mich. L. Rev. 1620 (1984).

— International Law in Theory and Practice, 1991.

Schiff, Ze'ev; Ya'ari, Ehud; Israel's Lebanon War, Updated ed., 1986.

Scholz, Michael; Staatliches Selbstverteidigungsrecht gegen terroristische Gewalt, 2006.

Simma, Bruno (ed.); The Charter of the United Nations, A commentary, Vol. I, 2nd ed., 2002.

Sina, Stephan; Der völkerrechtliche Status des Westjordanlandes und des Gaza-Streifens nach den Osloer Verträgen, 2004.

Singer, Erich H.; Terrorist Attacks on Nationals: The Lawful Use of Force Against Terrorist Bases on Foreign Soil, 1 Terrorism and Pol. Violence 435 (1989).

Sofaer, Abraham D.; On the Necessity of Pre-emption, 15 Eur. J. Int'l L. 209 (2003).

Stahn, Carsten; Terrorist Acts as "Armed Attacks": The Right of Self-Defense, Article 51 (1/2) of the UN Charter, and International Terrorism, 27-Fall Fletcher F. World Aff. 35 (2003).

Travalio, Greg; Altenburg, John; Terrorism, State Responsibility, and the Use of Military Force, 4 Chi. J. Int'l L. 97 (2003).

Travalio, Gregory M.; Terrorism, International Law, and the Use of Military Force, 18 Wisconsin Int'l L.J. 145 (2000).

United States Department of State; Diplomatic and Official Papers of Daniel Webster While Secretary of State, 1848.

Walker, George K.; The Lawfulness of Operation Enduring Freedom's Self-Defense Responses, 37 Val. U. L. Rev. 489 (2003).

Walter, Christian (ed.); Terrorism as Challenge for National and International Law – Security versus Liberty?, 2004.

— *Carsten Stahn*; Nicaragua is dead, long live Nicaragua" – the Right to Self-defense Under Art. 51 UN Charter and International Terrorism, 827-877.

Wandscher, Christiane; Internationaler Terrorismus und Selbstverteidigungs-recht, 2006.

Wedgwood, Ruth; Al Qaeda, Military Commissions and Self-Defense, 117 Pol. Sci. Q. 359 (2002).

Wolfrum, Rüdiger; The Attack of September 11, 2001, the Wars Against the Taliban and Iraq: Is there a Need to Reconsider International Law on the Recourse to Force and the Rules in Armed Conflict?, 7 Max Planck Y.B.U.N.L. 1 (2003).

— United Nations: Law, Policies and Practice, Vol 1, 1995.

Wolfrum, Rüdiger; Philipp, Christiane E.; The Status of the Taliban: Their Obligations and Rights under International Law, 6 Max Planck Y.B.U.N.L. 559 (2002).

Yoo, John C.; Using Force, 71 U. Chi. L. Rev. 729 (2004).

INDEX

S

T

U

V

W

Z

Christian Wicker

The Concepts of Proportionality and State Crimes in International Law

An Analysis of the Scope of Proportionality in the Right of Self-Defence and in the Regime of International Countermeasures and an Evaluation of the Concept of State Crimes

Frankfurt am Main, Berlin, Bern, Bruxelles, New York, Oxford, Wien, 2006.
177 pp.
Schriften zum internationalen und zu öffentlichen Recht.
Herausgegeben von Gilbert Gornig. Bd. 69
ISBN 978-3-631-55884-3 · pb. € 39.–*

It is generally recognised in both literature and jurisprudence that the notion of proportionality constitutes a key requirement of self-defence and of countermeasures. The determination of the exact content of the proportionality principle is, however, very complex and controversial. In both areas questions such as 'proportionate to what?' or 'what role does the objective of the response play?' arise. Elucidation of the scope of proportionality in the two spheres in which it is most contentious is thus sought. Ever since the abandonment of former Draft Article 19 the term 'State crime' no longer exists. This study demonstrates that consequently a State can no longer commit an international crime. Yet it also shows that by applying more serious consequences to the commission of a serious breach of peremptory norms the idea behind the concept does add something valuable to the existing concepts of jus cogens and obligations erga omnes.

Contents: Proportionality in the right of self-defence · The relationship between jus ad bellum and jus in bello · Proportionate to what? · Proportionality in the law of international countermeasures · and many more